Free Trade Between the United States
and Canada

HARVARD ECONOMIC STUDIES
VOLUME CXXIX

The studies in this series are published by
the Department of Economics of Harvard
University. The department does not assume responsibility for the views expressed.

FREE TRADE
BETWEEN THE UNITED STATES
AND CANADA

The Potential Economic Effects

Ronald J. Wonnacott
and
Paul Wonnacott

HARVARD UNIVERSITY PRESS
Cambridge, Massachusetts

To Our Parents

PREFACE

Free trade between the United States and Canada has been a recurring issue for more than a hundred years. The topic has been of particular interest in Canada — naturally enough, since economic relations with her giant southern partner are of predominant importance to Canada. In spite of this recurring interest in "reciprocity," remarkably little systematic work has been done on its probable economic consequences. Rather, the discussion has been primarily in terms of political issues. Ringing down through Canadian history have come calls to the barricades in the struggle for economic independence. These have ranged from political appeals quite devoid of economic rationale ("No truck or trade with the Yanks") to appeals based on untested economic assumptions ("With free trade, Canadians would become hewers of wood and drawers of water"). The list is familiar to any Canadian schoolboy. It is the authors' hope that this economic treatise will help to redress the balance between the economic and political aspects of this continuing debate.

Because of the prominent role which reciprocity plays in Canadian history, it is not surprising that each author was led by his previous studies of Canadian-U.S. economic relations to consider, more or less independently, a major attack on the question of a bilateral free trade agreement. In mid-1963 forces were joined; the study began to take its final form, including an analysis of the most important and difficult problem encountered: general equilibrium pressures on the exchange rate and relative income levels.

Even as late as 1962 or 1963, there was little public interest in free trade evident in Canada. But in the intervening years there has been a considerable change in outlook caused in part by interesting developments in the automotive industry. Therefore, a caveat which seemed unnecessary when this study was initiated must now be made explicit. Although the object of this study is to find out what the economic effects of free trade would be, regardless whether good or bad, the results show the probable economic consequences to be so desirable, particularly for Canada, that this study may be considered an outright advocacy of a free trade arrangement. This is a reasonable conclusion only if economic considerations are taken to be controlling. Since no such dominant claim can be made for economics, the favorable economic results must be weighed in the balance with probable political and socio-logical consequences. But here problems arise. Although these issues have been discussed at great length in Canada, they have not been clarified with any degree of precision. Thus favorable — as well as unfavorable — political and social consequences have not been defined. Moreover, a fundamental proposition has been over-looked: various forms of economic integration have substantially different political implications. There are political issues south of the border as well: for example, historically the United States has considered most-favored-nation treatment to be an important trad-ing principle, both for economic and political reasons, and these considerations cannot be brushed aside. Our hope has been to shed light on one of the most important dimensions of the free trade question and thus provide background for a decision; we make no categorical claim to have demonstrated the overall advisability of free trade.

It is customary in a joint work to indicate the sections written by each author, but we make no attempt to do so. Although each of us has drafted the first version of parts of the study, we have worked so closely over such an extended period that it is impos-sible to attribute specific ideas to this one or that; the omelet cannot be unscrambled.

Because of the length of time during which this study has been in progress, much of the data is several years out of date. Our basic statistical material is drawn from the period 1958–1962, although in several instances more recent information has been used. Although details of the current situation differ from those which existed during 1958–1962, we believe that our analysis accurately reflects the current relative positions of the two economies.

During the course of this study, we have shamelessly imposed on our colleagues' time to test our ideas. The list of those who have given us advice on the manuscript has grown so long that it is not feasible to reproduce it in its entirety. Special thanks must, however, go to Richard Caves and Harry Johnson, whose perceptive interest and continuing encouragement have contributed greatly to the final product. We are indebted to Wassily Leontief and Harvey Perloff for numerous improvements in content and exposition. Valuable suggestions have been received from Bela Balassa, John Cumberland, Donald Daly, Ted English, Bill Hood, Larry Krause, V. J. Macklin, Grant Reuber, Rudolf Rhomberg, Jack Young, and many others, particularly in Ottawa, Washington, and London, Ontario. We have greatly benefited from the discussions at the Seignory Club Conference sponsored by the Economic Council of Canada in the fall of 1964, and at the Carleton University Conference sponsored by the Private Planning Association of Canada in the spring of 1965. A number of students assisted in programming, data collection, and analysis. We wish especially to thank Don Angevine, Bob Baguley, Ken Grant, Peter Gunther, John Hughes, Henning Rasmussen, Robin Richardson, and Lyle Sager.

For financial assistance, we wish to thank the Canada Council, the Ford Foundation, the General Research Board of the University of Maryland, and especially Resources for the Future, whose generosity made this study possible. In addition, many friends at RFF provided advice, interest, and encouragement. The above individuals and institutions are not, of course, to be implicated in the opinions expressed in this work.

The Canadian Journal of Economics and Political Science has kindly consented to the reproduction of our studies on the automotive industry, which are presented with minor changes as Appendices A and B. The Upper Midwest Economic Study has graciously agreed to the reproduction of several appendices which first appeared in Study Paper #9, *Manufacturing Costs and the Comparative Advantage of United States Regions.*

R. J. W.
P. W.

London, Ontario
College Park, Maryland
July 1966

CONTENTS

Part I

Absolute Advantage: The Location of Industry under Free Trade

Part II

Comparative Advantage: The International Adjustment Mechanism

80870

Part III

The Incidence of Tariffs:
Analysis of Present Prices, Costs and Money Incomes

Part IV

Policy Issues and Conclusions

Appendices

Contents

TABLES

FIGURES

Free Trade Between the United States and Canada

PART I

Absolute Advantage: The Location

of Industry under Free Trade

1

INTRODUCTION

Canada is the most important international market for United States products. The United States is not only the largest single purchaser of Canadian goods — it dominates the market for Canadian exports, absorbing over one half of the total.[1] At present, there is speculation that tariffs may be reduced between the two countries, either as a result of multilateral negotiations to lower tariffs across the board (the "Kennedy Round") or as a follow-up of the recent elimination of automotive tariffs between the two countries. These two approaches are not mutually exclusive. However, only the latter, involving a bilateral arrangement, will be given intensive consideration here.

The objective of this treatise is not to pass judgment on the political feasibility of free trade between Canada and the United States, nor to make any prediction of how likely it is that the two countries will move in this direction. Instead this study will be devoted exclusively to examining the likely economic effects of such

[1] In the past five years (1960–1964), the United States has absorbed between 53.4 percent (in 1964) and 59.0 percent (in 1962) of Canadian merchandise exports excluding gold. The United States has provided between 67.0 percent (in 1961) and 68.9 percent (in 1964) of total Canadian merchandise imports. Canada took between 18.6 percent (in 1963) and 19.3 percent (in 1960) of United States exports, and supplied between 19.7 percent (in 1960) and 22.5 percent (in 1964) of United States imports. Thus, approximately one fifth of all U.S. trade is with Canada, and roughly three fifths of Canadian trade is with the United States. Sources: United States Bureau of Commerce, *Survey of Current Business,* June 1965, pp. 16–17; Bank of Canada, *Statistical Summary, Supplement,* 1964, pp. 142–143.

a move. How would patterns of U.S. and Canadian production be altered if tariffs between the two countries were to be eliminated? Because of the recent momentum of policy, this question is presently of great significance, particularly for Canadians. Historically it has also been a policy issue of prime importance; one Canadian election has been fought explicitly on the question of reciprocal tariff reductions with the United States. It is hoped, therefore, that this study may serve a threefold purpose: to assist evaluation of current proposals; to provide guidelines for analyzing similar proposals as they recur in the future; and finally, to suggest techniques useful for other countries considering reciprocal tariff reductions.

The Necessary Reorganization of Industry

In the event of free trade, the pattern of industry in the two countries would be substantially altered; it is to be expected (and the evidence in later chapters supports this expectation) that a number of industries in both Canada and the United States would be reorganized to service a total market of over two hundred million population. U.S. industry, which now operates in a market embracing about ninety percent of this total, is already producing on a scale that would at least approximate the most efficient scale in these new circumstances. However, many of those Canadian industries that are presently servicing a domestic market of only twenty million would be likely to face a substantial reorganization in terms of scaling up to longer production runs. There are two reasons for this. Elimination of U.S. tariffs would open the rich markets in the United States to Canadian producers, and Canadian producers would be forced to reorganize to cut prices and costs of production because of the pressure from increased U.S. imports entering Canada duty free. Cost reductions through reorganization are feasible in Canada as production runs are increased. Moreover, survival under free trade competitive pressures would require that inefficiencies in Canada be eliminated. International competition would also tend to eliminate whatever high prices and profits may now exist in Canada because of oligopolistic marketing arrangements that are indirectly supported by the Canadian tariff.

North American protection results in higher Canadian prices and costs because of three organizational factors: the size of firm; the level of managerial efficiency necessary to survive; and oligopolistic opportunities offered by the protected market. It is by no means clear which of these three is the most important; indeed it is very difficult to isolate these three influences.[2] However, their total effect may be measured, and the implication of this study is that this total effect is substantial in almost all industries. A specific technique for measuring this is developed in Chapter 12; the sample industries examined in Chapters 13 and 14 all exhibit a sizable combined effect of these three influences.

To summarize: the rationalization problem for the United States is a relatively simple one. In those lines in which the United States continues to specialize, its output would be increased by ten percent or less, depending on its ability to invade the Canadian market. For this reason, present U.S. techniques of production, designed to satisfy a market of two hundred million, should be similar to the techniques that would be appropriate for servicing the whole North American market of two hundred and twenty million population. The rationalization of production in Canada would be more extensive and, as a result, much more costly in terms of the temporary dislocations involved. Since Canadian facilities would require gearing up to a market of more than two hundred million from one of only twenty million, the necessary scale increase in production in Canada is not limited to ten percent, nor even one hundred percent, but instead roughly one thousand percent — depending on the ability of a rationalized Canadian industry to invade the U.S. market.

The major burden of North American rationalization, therefore, would fall on Canada — or, more precisely, on the owners of the production facilities in Canada that would require reorganization. (These owners are, of course, both Canadians and Americans.) There is in addition a burden which may fall on the labor force in the interim period of adjustment. As the employment structure

[2] H. C. Eastman, "Some Aspects of Tariff Protection in Canada," *International Journal* (University of Toronto), 18: 353–360 (Summer 1960); H. Edward English, *Industrial Structure in Canada's International Competitive Position* (Montreal: Canadian Trade Committee, Private Planning Association of Canada, 1964).

changes, there may be temporary periods of unemployment, and in some cases an investment of time will be necessary to acquire new skills. It should be noted that adjustment costs are once-and-for-all, short-term costs. Once made, they are disposed of, and in this respect they are even less severe than those similar adjustment costs necessary to support growth in a dynamic economy, such as costs required by automation, the discovery of new techniques and products, and shifting patterns of demand. Moreover, the real cost of a reorganization of industry to service a larger market may well be less than its apparent money costs because, within the framework of such a reorganization, more efficient techniques may be introduced and productivity increased as a result. (This argument is analogous to the view that the real cost of replacing German industry was less than the apparent postwar reconstruction costs because this reconstruction left Germany with a more efficient industry than before.) In any event, since these are once-and-for-all adjustment costs, they are considered explicitly in the discussion of the international adjustment process in Part II. In passing it should be noted that the common market countries in Europe have found that rationalization costs have been less severe than expected because of the overall expansion of the total European market, induced at least partly by the reduction in trade barriers. This common market experience, however, should not necessarily be regarded as an appropriate precedent for Canada and the United States because these European countries are of relatively equal economic size. Consequently, rationalization effects have not been focused on any one country as they would be in the Canadian-U.S. case.

As a hypothetical illustration of the changed pattern of North American industry that free trade might bring, consider the iron and steel industry. One of the basic resources of this industry, iron ore, is likely to be increasingly drawn from eastern Canadian sources. Canadian steel production in the Hamilton area, which now produces a broad line of steel products for domestic consumption, would be subject to pressures to specialize in a smaller number of specific products for North American distribution. The U.S. steel industry might be expected to concentrate on other steel products, satisfying total North American demand by a modest increase in the scale of its present operations. In these circumstances the Canadian steel industry might lose some of its Canadian markets to U.S. steel producers, with these losses tending to be offset by expansion into U.S. markets in the limited lines of Canadian specialization.

Clearly this illustration is an oversimplification. Rationalization may not occur in this way *within* an industry. Instead it may occur *between* industries, with an entire industry in one country being displaced and employment shifted into another expanding sector. It is essential, therefore, to interpret the iron and steel case cited above as only a hypothetical example of the reorganization that *might* occur; the industries that would survive in Canada and the lines along which rationalization would take place cannot be specified without, first, comparing costs of production in each industry and in each region in Canada and the United States and, second, considering the effects on costs of the process of adjustment. These two tasks are undertaken in Parts I and II, respectively.

Comparative Costs in a Free Trade Area with Present Relative Wage and Price Levels in Canada and the United States

Great care must be taken if free trade is to be assumed and the resulting costs of production in Canada and the United States are to be compared. Specifically, an examination of present Canadian costs or domestic product prices will not disclose a true picture of Canadian prospects in the event of free trade, since present costs and prices in Canada are higher, at least to some degree, because of North American protection.[3] These higher costs and prices include the effects of small scale and inefficiency discussed above that would be eliminated by the rationalization of Canadian industry. In addition, prices under free trade would fall to whatever extent present higher Canadian prices can be explained by the greater exercise of oligopoly power in Canada than in the United States.[4] Also, certain higher Canadian costs would automatically

[3] The degree to which protection raises costs in selected Canadian industries is studied in Part III.

[4] Tariff reductions would have implications for Canadian antitrust policy; these are dealt with in Part III.

disappear, with or without rationalization. For example, material inputs for any industry are often priced higher in Canada because of the protection the Canadian tariff structure affords to supplying industries.[5] Because the effects of protection are so tightly bound into Canadian costs, it is not reasonable to analyze the reaction of Canadian secondary industry to free trade conditions by examining its present costs, the present price at which its product is sold, its present supply reactions, or any of the other present conditions that are at least in part a reflection of protection.

This basic fallacy — that Canadian firms could not compete in a free trade area because of their *present* higher costs — has too often been accepted in Canadian debate. To avoid this error, cost differences between the two countries must be carefully divided into two groups. The first are those inherent differences in cost that would remain, at least in the initial stages, regardless of the commercial policy of the two countries: these include differences in labor costs, transport costs, taxes, capital costs, and so on. The second group of cost differences are those that result from North American protection. If judgment is to be made as to what would happen in the event of free trade, it is necessary to consider only the first group of inherent cost differences, i.e., those that would persist into a period of free trade.

In effect the strategy amounts to this. Disregard the present structure of Canadian costs. Focus attention not on what costs *are* but on what they *would be*. Throw all Canadian and U.S. regions into a hypothetical free trade area and rephrase the problem as an interregional location study in which only inherent cost advantages of each North American region are considered and all cost differences resulting historically from protection are disregarded. The relevant question becomes: In these circumstances would Canadian regions be attractive areas for industrial growth? To answer this, Part I is devoted to an examination of these relevant interregional differences in labor, capital, transport costs, and so on. But it is not sufficient to examine only these explicit costs: the relative attractiveness of an area cannot be completely determined within the

---

[5] U.S. costs may also be high because of duties on inputs. However, because the U.S. economy is much larger, imported inputs are less important than in Canada, and the effect of tariffs in raising costs is much less marked.

compass of this kind of cost calculation. Accordingly, it has been necessary in Part I to rank all regions in the United States and Canada in terms of the other desirable location characteristics that cannot simply be costed out: proximity to markets and to manufactured supplies and possible external economies that present areas of industrial concentration may provide.

Since the problem is to define attractive growth areas in a free trade North American economy, it makes little sense to compare Canada as a whole with the continental United States. The regional dimensions of this problem cannot be overlooked because adjacent regions in the two countries are already more closely integrated than distant regions in the same country. For example, the economy of British Columbia is now more closely tied to the U.S. Pacific Northwest than to the Canadian Maritimes — and with free trade these ties would be almost certain to increase. A careful blending of two related economic fields — international trade theory and interregional theory — is required on both the theoretical and the empirical level. The authors have found this to be an interesting study, partly because of the necessary coordination of these two sets of theory. It will be evident that both international and interregional problems are considered together throughout; however, the major focus in Part I is on interregional problems, whereas the major focus in the balance of the study is on international trade problems. The five Canadian regions and thirteen U.S. regions used in this study are shown in Figure 1.[6]

[6] The Canadian regions in Figure 1 are composed of the following provinces: *Maritimes:* Newfoundland (including Labrador), Prince Edward Island, Nova Scotia, and New Brunswick; *Quebec; Ontario; Prairies:* Manitoba, Saskatchewan, and Alberta; *British Columbia.* The U.S. comparison areas have the following composition by state: *Upper Midwest:* Montana, North Dakota, South Dakota, and Minnesota; *West Lake:* Illinois, Indiana, and Wisconsin; *East Lake:* Michigan and Ohio; *Lower Midwest:* Iowa, Kansas, Missouri, and Nebraska; *Middle Atlantic:* Connecticut New Jersey, New York, and Pennsylvania; *New England:* Massachusetts, Maine, New Hampshire, Rhode Island, and Vermont; *South:* Mississippi, Alabama, Georgia, South Carolina, North Carolina, Virginia, West Virginia, Kentucky, and Tennessee; *Capital:* Delaware, District of Columbia, and Maryland; *Florida; Southwest:* Arizona, Arkansas, Louisiana, New Mexico, Oklahoma, and Texas; *Mountain:* Colorado, Idaho, Nevada, Utah, and Wyoming; *Pacific Southwest:* California; *Pacific Northwest:* Oregon and Washington.

Figure 1. Regional division of the United States and Canada.

The Process of International Adjustment

Throughout Part I it is assumed that relative wage levels in the two countries and the rate of exchange of the two currencies remain constant at their present levels — or, more precisely, at the levels prevailing in 1958, the base year of this study. In 1958 the Canadian dollar fluctuated slightly above par with the U.S. dollar. A parity rate ($1.00 U.S. = $1.00 Can.) is used in Part I and greatly simplifies computations of comparative costs. The subsequent depreciation of the Canadian dollar has provided Canada with a cost advantage, but account of this is deferred until Chapter 10.

Because Part I involves the assumption of constant relative wages and a parity exchange, it is concerned only with absolute advantage under these conditions. Comparative advantage and the long-run changes in relative wage and exchange levels resulting from a period of international adjustment are dealt with in Part II.

It is quite possible that the cost analysis of Part I (based on present wages levels and exchange parity) might indicate that most industries would find one country (e.g., Canada) the lower cost area, and more attractive for expansion, and the better location for servicing North American markets. However, there are obvious limitations — for example, on the available labor force in Canada — that prevent concurrent expansion to this degree in all or most Canadian industries. Specifically, the governing mechanism that would keep Canadian expansion more or less within the bounds defined by available resources and labor supply is the following process of international adjustment. If industry were to grow rapidly in Canada, partly to service U.S. markets, two pressures would build up: first, accumulation of foreign exchange reserves by Canada and a simultaneous unfavorable movement in the U.S. balance of payments as Canadian exports to the United States increase, and second, demand pressure on the Canadian labor force due to new job openings in these growing industries. Both pressures would tend to bring costs into line in the two countries: the first by upward pressure on the international value of the Canadian dollar and the second by upward pressure on the Canadian domestic wage level. In turn, these revisions in relative costs in the two countries would control the growth mechanism by making Canada an increasingly less attractive location and hence no longer favored as an area of expansion by such a large number of industries.

It is simply not possible a priori to specify that this growth process would be focused on Canada as a preferred site in this way. Initial expansion might occur in the United States because of cost advantages there; alternatively, the free trade cost structure may already be in line, a situation that would indicate no substantial relative cost adjustment of this kind. The first problem, obviously, is to estimate the necessity and direction of this adjustment process by evaluating how free trade costs would compare in the two countries — given present relative wage levels and a parity exchange. Therefore it is essential that precisely the sort of cost analysis undertaken in Part I be completed prior to the discussion in Part II of the equalization of international costs, for without this it is not possible to specify even the direction in which this adjustment of relative costs will operate. Moreover, the whole picture of all initial cost differences in the two countries must be examined because the equalization of total costs does not imply the equalization of all cost components. To take a hypothetical example: if free trade total costs are initially higher in Canada than in the United States, the process of total cost equalization may involve a *reduction* in the Canadian wage level relative to that of the United States, thus causing a consequent further divergence, rather than convergence, in this particular element of cost in the two countries.

A corollary proposition is that an industry which appears from the cost analysis shown in Part I to have an (absolute) advantage in Canada will not necessarily retain a (comparative) advantage after the process of international adjustment has taken place. If other manufacturing sectors have an even greater absolute advantage, then their expansion may be expected to cause adjustments in relative costs sufficient to eliminate the smaller absolute advantage that the first industry may initially have enjoyed.

In summary, Part II is concerned with this process of international adjustment. The direction of this adjustment is specified, along with tentative estimates of its extent and some indication of how its effect may be divided between domestic wage and price levels on the one hand, and the exchange rate on the other. This in turn provides a basis for certain conclusions on exchange rate and wage policies that might be appropriate in terms of easing the adjustment process. Part II also includes a rough specification of those industries and activities most likely to retain a comparative advantage in the two countries after this adjustment process has taken place; these sectors are likely to be those with the greatest absolute advantage at current wage and exchange rate levels. Part II also presents an analysis of changing foreign investment patterns in Canada; such resulting changes in the capital account in the balance of payments must be examined because the process of international adjustment depends on pressures in the capital, as well as the current, account.

The general strategy used in Parts I and II of this study is set out in Figure 2. It may be useful to think of this strategy as somewhat analagous to a manufacturing production line which involves

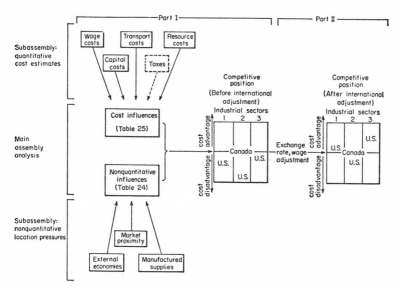

Figure 2. Illustration of locational forces and their general equilibrium effects.

a main assembly supported by numerous subassembly lines from which necessary components are drawn.

The model framework of this analysis, which runs horizontally through the center of Figure 2, represents the main assembly operation. It involves drawing together quantifiable cost estimates (such as labor, transport costs, etc., which are summed in Table 25,[7]) and the rankings of regions in each industry in terms of nonquantifiable location pressures (such as external economies).

In combination these two sets of data provide a rough estimate of the competitive position of various industries in the two countries at present relative wage levels and dollar parity. There is, of course, no way in general of summing the quantitative cost estimates with the nonquantitative location pressures. However, because of the rather fortunate configuration of the latter, an approximate summation is possible in a very rough-and-ready way

[7] Tax costs are dealt with separately because, as a policy variable, they may be adjusted with changes in commercial policy.

for this Canada-U.S. study. (For exposition purposes we reduce the comparison from the thirteen regions in sixteen industrial categories of this study to the simple Canadian-U.S. comparison in three industries shown in Figure 2.)

Suppose it turns out that Canada is advantageously situated in all industrial categories, as has been assumed in Figure 2. (The assumption that the United States was favorably situated overall would give rise to a contrary adjustment process; the assumption that the two countries were in initial competitive balance would require no adjustment of wages and prices.) The resulting appreciation of the Canadian dollar or wage level or both would improve the competitive cost position of U.S. producers. The new long-run equilibrium situation is shown hypothetically in the right-hand block of Figure 2. It implies Canadian specialization in industry 2, and U.S. specialization in industries 1 and 3.[8] Since this new situation involves long-run balance-of-payments equilibrium, it depends not only on the initial cost configuration but also on the relative productive capacity of the two countries and on the potential importance of each industrial output in international trade.

The Manufacturing, Resource, and Service Sectors

A basic difficulty in this analysis is that formally it is not possible to specify comparative advantage by an across-the-board examination of manufacturing activity alone; changing cost patterns in all economic activities should be examined, including the resource and service sectors. For a number of reasons the authors have not considered these sectors in detail but have concentrated on manufacturing. The greatest adjustment problems will be in the Canadian manufacturing sector; it is here also that the greatest potential gains lie.

We must deal directly with the common assumption in Canadian debate that an expansion of the Canadian resource industries and

---

[8] The reader will note that this method is similar to Edgeworth's logarithmic illustration of the adjustment of international costs. See Jacob Viner, *Studies in the Theory of International Trade* (New York: Harper, 1937), p. 459.

a contraction of Canadian manufacturing would be brought about by free trade. Canada already exports resources in large quantities to the United States, and there is no reason why this will not continue. The amount of increase in Canadian resource exports as U.S. tariffs are reduced is suggested in Chapter 11. A further critical consideration is that these Canadian resource sectors have not been protected by tariffs; as a consequence, Canadian tariff elimination would not increase competition from resource imports in the Canadian market. The same proposition does not hold for manufacturing, since tariff elimination would bring drastic changes in import competition. Consequently, manufacturing is a sector of greater potential vulnerability and more difficult to analyze. A critical question arises: Would expansion of resource extraction in Canada be sufficient under free trade to shift the Canadian-U.S. cost structure and thus make manufacturing in Canada less attractive than the analysis in Part I implies?

The answer to this is likely to be no for two reasons. U.S. tariffs on raw materials are relatively modest, and the resource sectors (except agriculture, discussed below) are not heavy employers of labor. Consequently, it is very doubtful that free trade would bring such an enormous expansion of exports and employment in this sector as to cause independently a revision in the cost structure in the two countries. The assumption is being made in this study that free trade expansion of the resource extraction activities in Canada would not in itself be sufficient to shift any Canadian manufacturing industry from an initial absolute advantage to an ultimate comparative disadvantage. (The same assumption is made about the service sector. This seems reasonable enough since most services are of necessity provided locally and are, as a consequence, not greatly influenced by commercial policy.) The possible exception is agriculture, which is an important source of employment in both countries. The importance of this sector should not be minimized — in terms of the difficulties it can raise both for negotiations and for economic analysis. Is it likely that Canadian agricultural employment or exports to the United States would increase sufficiently to cause the overall structure of costs in Canada to rise relative to the cost structure in the United States?

It is quite possible that changes in Canadian agricultural exports might affect the external value of the Canadian dollar. However, it is hard to conceive of a situation in which increased employment in Canadian agriculture would put great general upward pressures on the Canadian manufacturing wage level. The population trend is away from the farm; the rapid rise of output per farm worker means that sizable increases in agricultural production may occur without drawing a large number of workers back to the farm. Thus, it does not seem plausible to expect significant upward pressures on manufacturing wages even if there were a substantial increase in agricultural exports.

The agricultural problem is admittedly a very difficult one, and in Chapter 11 we will examine the extent to which free trade in this sector might modify the conclusions. In the interim it is assumed either that the overall effects on relative costs in the two countries are not affected by changing agricultural patterns — or, more simply, that agricultural goods are excluded from free trade arrangements. This latter assumption is probably the more realistic. Because of complicated subsidy programs, agriculture would be by far the most difficult sector in which to introduce free trade and, as a consequence, the most likely activity to be excluded from a free trade arrangement.

√ In summary, insofar as the impact of free trade on resource and service trade is limited and agricultural products are excluded, the critical sector to study is manufacturing. Because of the importance of economies of scale, manufacturing would undergo the most drastic transformation. And from the Canadian point of view, it is also the sector of greatest potential competitive weakness. For all these reasons, manufacturing is the focus of this study.

The Incidence of Protection

In Parts I and II of this study, the North American economy is examined, not in terms of its present structure, but in terms of *what it would be* in the event of free trade. Consequently no attempt is made in these sections to estimate the importance of those influences on prices and costs — the higher price of protected inputs, diseconomies of scale, inefficiency, or oligopolistic pricing —

that arise because of protection and would tend to be eliminated with it.

In Part III these questions are addressed directly. In examining the incidence or effects of Canadian and U.S. tariffs, the descriptive question of *what is* must be answered; specifically, How has Canadian industry been organized behind the Canadian tariff structure? And how has Canadian real income been affected as a result? Since in the context of this question the structure of Canadian industry as it presently exists is relevant, all costs must be studied. And these include not only the inherent Canadian costs detailed in Part I but also those influences arising from North American protection that raise Canadian costs or prices: higher input prices, diseconomies of scale, inefficiency, and oligopolistic pricing practices.

The combined effect of these latter influences is estimated for any industry as follows: first, the price of its output is expressed in U.S. dollars; then the amount by which this price is higher in Canada than in the United States is estimated. (This price difference is not necessarily exactly equal to the ad valorem Canadian tariff rate, since the Canadian price may be somewhat less than the maximum level allowed by the tariff. This lower price differential can be explained by domestic Canadian demand conditions or by the fact that Canadian firms may wish to divert consumption from imports to domestically produced goods.) To the price difference is added the wage advantage Canadian firms enjoy. Together these provide the range of advantages facing a Canadian firm. The question then becomes: How is this margin of advantages absorbed because of inherent disadvantages of producing in Canada or dissipated by costs directly attributable to North American protection? The inherent disadvantages, such as higher transport costs, are computed by a method roughly similar to the one used in Part I; one of the protection-generated costs — the higher price of protected inputs — may be estimated directly by examining the importance of each major input required, along with the appropriate Canadian tariff rate. When these computations are completed an unexplained residual remains and becomes the best estimate of the combined effects of those influences resulting from protection that cannot be independently measured: diseconomies of scale, inefficiency, or oligopolistic pricing.

The precise strategy employed in this analysis is discussed in detail in Chapter 12, the introduction to Part III. However, certain points should be noted at this stage. In contrast to Part I, the analysis in Part III concentrates on the effects of the present tariff structure on the two countries rather than on the regional location of industry in the event of free trade; it is thus not surprising that different techniques are used in the two parts. For example, the cost analysis in Part III involves only the comparison of present Canadian and U.S. sites of greatest concentration in each industry studied; interregional cost differences are not considered. The question of whether U.S. or Canadian technology and factor use should be used in computing differences in factor cost also presents problems. In line with the assumption that present U.S. techniques roughly approximate those that would be used by industry servicing a North American market of over two hundred million, U.S. techniques and factor combinations are used as the base for the free trade cost analysis of Parts I and II; however, in the descriptive analysis of present Canadian cost conditions in Part III, Canadian factor combinations are used.

The cost analysis of Part III, like that of Part I, yields an estimate of the absolute Canadian advantage (or disadvantage) in an industry, given present domestic wage and price levels and the present value of the exchange rate. However, a very high level of aggregation is required in Parts I and II, since comparative, as opposed to absolute, advantage for a single industry cannot be specified in isolation but requires an across-the-board scan of all industries; on the other hand the descriptive analysis in Part III is designed to analyze the reaction pattern of single industries to a given set of external conditions and can consequently be carried out in isolation. Industries studied in Part III can be defined at a more meaningful level of disaggregation. Any attempt to apply the techniques in Part III to the broad industry groupings used in Parts I and II would be neither desirable nor feasible for two reasons: the necessary computations are too complex, and the chance of obtaining reliable price information falls as the degree of aggregation rises. In summary, the analysis of Part III is based on a much finer, more detailed industry definition; it involves specifically analyzing (tariff-generated) cost elements that could be ignored in earlier sections. Precisely because of the additional difficulties encountered, the broad interregional and interindustry dimensions of the analysis have been restricted.

Chapters 13 and 14 illustrate how tariff effects in sample industries become embedded in the Canadian cost structure. Chapter 15 examines the other side of the coin: how protection influences Canadian real income. Potentially, there are two ways that North American tariffs may affect Canadian real income — by influencing money wages and other factor payments and by changing final Canadian prices. Each influence is evaluated by estimating the present Canadian money income (or price) level and comparing it with the estimated level under free trade conditions.

How Protection Affects Canadian Prices

The prices of many goods are higher in Canada than in the United States because of the protective Canadian tariff. Not all of the Canadian-U.S. price differential represents a cost to Canada. The extent to which *domestically produced* goods are sold in Canada at a higher price represents the upper limit of this cost.[9] The higher price on similar goods which are *imported* represents an income redistribution rather than a cost because this revenue accrues as customs receipts to the Canadian government and hence to the Canadian taxpayer. On the basis of this reasoning, an upper limit is set on the cost of the Canadian tariff by the average ad valorem tariff rate. If the Canadian tariff is ten percent across the board, then the cost in terms of GNP to Canada of this tariff cannot exceed ten percent[10] and in fact is certain to be substantially less for a number of reasons. A large proportion of Canadian consumption is in goods which are not internationally traded, that is, in domestically produced goods and services that are presently not

[9] The cost of the Canadian tariff will be lower than the upper limit to the extent that Canadian factors receive quasi-rents arising from the tariff.

[10] Even this statement must be qualified to the extent that Canadian consumer surplus is reduced by more than the quantity consumed times the tariff.

protected because they would not be imported in any event. Even considering only goods that are protected and imported, there is the benefit mentioned above that partially offsets the ten percent protection cost: tariffs collected on imports reduce the tax burden on the Canadian public.

It is important to note that with free trade the increased competition of duty free imports from the United States would reduce Canadian prices toward the U.S. level but would be unlikely to bring complete equality of prices because transportation and distribution costs to consumption points in Canada[11] are often higher than similar costs to consumption points in the United States.

The net cost of the Canadian tariff computed along these lines has been estimated in a recent Royal Commission study as three and one half to four and one half percent of Canadian gross private expenditure (net of direct taxes).[12]

How Protection Affects Canadian Factor Incomes

There are two effects of North American protection on money incomes of Canadian factors: the U.S. tariff tends to lower factor prices, while the Canadian tariff tends to raise them.

The major impact of the U.S. tariff on Canada is that it effectively surrounds the richest North American markets with a barrier. The result is to depress most Canadian factor payments, in particular, wages. In the simplest terms the effect of the U.S. tariff is equivalent to removing Canada in space from U.S. markets. Canadian producers attempting to exploit U.S. markets must overcome the U.S. tariff barrier and, in addition, any natural disadvantages (in terms of transport costs, climate, etc.) of the Canadian location. The result is that Canadian money wages are lower than those in the United States.

This separation of the two national markets may be illustrated in terms of both Canadian export industries and Canadian industries producing for the domestic Canadian market and protected

[11] From producing points either in Canada or the United States.
[12] John Young, *Canadian Commercial Policy* (Ottawa: Royal Commission on Canada's Economic Prospects, 1957), p. 73.

from U.S. competition by a Canadian tariff. The former case is the simpler one: a Canadian export industry suffers under one substantial disadvantage that its U.S. competitors need not face — it must leap the U.S. tariff. Hence it will have higher costs than its U.S. competitor to the extent that it must pay U.S. customs duties, plus or minus any location disadvantages. In the long run its higher costs will tend to be passed back, at least partly, onto labor in terms of lower wages.[13]

(Lower product prices in Canada may also result from the U.S. tariff; for example, by depressing Canadian wages it may result in a lower price for many Canadian services. However, it will be shown in Part III that whatever reductions in the Canadian price level (and cost of living) that result in this way from the U.S. tariff will not offset its depressing effect on Canadian money incomes; hence the net effect of the U.S. tariff is to reduce Canadian real income.)

The second illustration of the depressing effects of the U.S. tariff on Canadian money incomes relates to a firm that is unable to overcome the tariff barrier to the U.S. market. The Canadian firm producing for a domestic Canadian market generally, but not always, uses less efficient techniques. For example, there may be diseconomies of scale for firms confined to the Canadian market; wages are observably lower in such industries. Again the lower money income level in Canada is a reflection of both the U.S. pro-

---

[13] Although the overall effects of U.S. tariffs will be to lower Canadian money incomes, there may be exceptions to this general rule. Canadian producers using inputs whose prices have been depressed by exclusion from the U.S. market may have their money incomes raised, particularly if they are producing goods which would not be marketed in the United States even in the event of free trade.

An analysis of this exceptional case, where U.S. tariffs may raise the money incomes of Canadian factors, is complicated by a paradox in value theory. In a competitive situation, a fall in the cost of an input (e.g., labor) may, under certain circumstances, cause a fall rather than a rise in rents. For a discussion of these circumstances (with special reference to the California bracero question), see Paul A. Meyer, "A Paradox on Profits and Factor Prices," *American Economic Review,* forthcoming. See also R. R. Nelson, "Increased Rents from Increased Costs: A Paradox of Value Theory," *Journal of Political Economy,* 65: 387–393 (October 1957).

tective tariff [14] and the inherent Canadian location disadvantages. But in both this case and the preceding one, Canadian money wages are not as low as the U.S. tariff and natural location influences together imply because of an offsetting influence: the Canadian tariff tends to raise *money* incomes of Canadian factors.

By allowing firms to sell their product in Canada at a higher price, the Canadian tariff allows greater *money* wages than would otherwise occur. The fact that money wages in Canada are observably below those in the United States suggests that there are natural location disadvantages involved in producing in Canada or that the U.S. tariff lowers Canadian money wages more than the Canadian tariff raises them, or both. The net combined effect of the Canadian and U.S. tariffs on Canadian money wages is shown in Figure 3, an illustrative but purely hypothetical diagram. The extent to which wages in Canada may be lower than in the United States due to natural disadvantages (such as greater distance from markets, etc.) is shown as *AB*. *BD* represents the extent to which the existence of the U.S. tariff depresses Canadian money wages, whereas *DC* represents the extent to which money wages are higher in Canada due to the Canadian tariff. The observed lower Canadian wage level (*AC*) may be attributed to natural disadvantages (*AB*) and the net effect of the two tariffs (*BC*). Neither *BD* nor *DC* is estimated;[15] hence the position of *D* is not empirically defined. Although the effect of each tariff must as a consequence remain a mystery, the net effect of the two tariffs can never-

---

[14] It should be noted that the cost of U.S. protection includes not only the effects of the present U.S. tariff, but also the effects of potential revisions in the U.S. tariff. This is especially true for a firm which may be barred from setting up a rational operation to service the North American market, not because present cost considerations are a restraint, but because of potential increases in the U.S. tariff that may occur in the future. If the U.S. duty is viewed as a "protective" tariff, these potential effects may be as important as the actual effects of the present U.S. tariff. In this way, U.S. protection imposes a two dimensional effect on Canadian incomes involving both the effects of the tariff as it exists and as it might be increased.

The same general argument may be applied to the effects of Canadian tariffs on U.S. incomes. However, because of the great disparity of size of the two economies these effects are much smaller than the impact on Canadian income.

[15] However, a method of estimating a maximum bound for each effect is suggested in Part III.

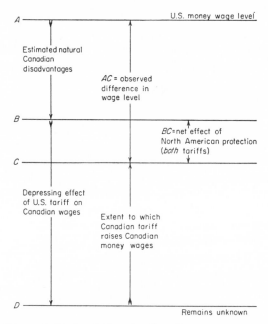

Figure 3. Factors influencing Canadian money wages.

theless be estimated by reducing the observed money wage difference (AC) by the amount attributable to other influences (AB).[16]

Up to this point factor payments and wages have been used almost synonymously. Would protection affect income payments to other factors in the same way? The answer depends largely on the international mobility of the factor. Land and resources are even less mobile internationally than labor, and a heavy incidence is almost certain to fall on Canadian rents; however, it cannot be measured because of the incomparability of resource and land units in the two countries. On the other hand, capital is more mobile; consequently, the possibilities of shifting any of the incidence of protection onto interest payments is limited. Any reduction in interest rates will tend to cut off the flow of capital into

[16] For purposes of illustration, AB and BC have been assumed to have unfavorable effects on Canadian money wages. This analysis is still applicable, however, if AB or BC is assumed to have a different sign.

Canada. For the same reason, profit returns in Canada are better insulated than wages from the incidence of protection.

It should be noted that this entire argument has been presented with no reference to the exchange rate. Given parity the argument obviously holds. Even without parity this analysis may be undertaken for any given exchange rate simply by expressing all prices, factor payments, etc., in terms of one currency (that is, in U.S. dollars). At the same time it should be recognized that a *change* in the level of the exchange rate will, like protection, have an effect on Canadian real income. For example, an appreciation of the Canadian dollar (resulting, for example, from a capital flow into Canada) would reduce the difference in money wages (expressed in U.S. dollars) in the two countries and partially offset the incidence of protection on Canadian real income.

To summarize: the U.S. tariff lowers both real and monetary incomes of Canadian factors of production. The Canadian tariff tends to raise money incomes in Canada and also the prices of final goods; however, as seen below in Chapter 15, its overall effect on Canadian real income is unfavorable.

The Empirical Approach

This study should be viewed on two levels: first, the model employed to examine the changing Canadian position under free trade, illustrated as the main assembly analysis in Figure 2; and second, the empirical cost components (shown as the subassembly processes in Figure 2).

It is on the main assembly process that the authors wish Parts I and II to be judged. The overview of how this type of problem should be handled is outlined there, and on this central argument this treatise must stand or fall.

However, the subassembly processes should be judged in somewhat different terms; although the overall picture shown is a relatively unambiguous one, the authors have no doubt that specific empirical estimates of each of the subcomponents could be improved. However, no theoretical difficulty would be involved in any such modifications; with one or two exceptions, each empirical subcomponent may be computed independently of feedback effects from the main assembly process.[17] Hence an improved set of estimates could easily be inserted into this analysis.

The two major reasons for the limited precision of the estimates in this study are: the figures from public documents that have been used throughout are themselves subject to some range of error; and simplifying assumptions have in many cases been necessary to reduce a large mass of data to a proportion that warrants sensible interpretation. Special attention has been devoted in the text to clarifying the nature of these assumptions.

Care must therefore be taken in translating the empirical results, and none of the individual estimates should be interpreted too precisely. However, overall cost patterns are sufficiently unambiguous to ensure that, although errors may reduce the accuracy of individual estimates, they should not affect the overall conclusion. This can be confidently stated for two reasons. First, in many cases the conclusions were tested for sensitivity to alternative assumptions; in no instance were conclusions retained if they were significantly modified by these alternative assumptions. Second, many of the estimates in this study are "bounding estimates" rather than "best estimates." In other words, maximum and minimum bounding values for a variable are frequently estimated, rather than its most likely value. Using this strategy, decisions can be easily made to throw all biases in the estimate in the appropriate direction. For example, when in doubt in estimating a maximum bound, the highest estimate generated at each stage is retained. The great advantage of this technique is that much more confidence may be attached to the conclusions. Its disadvantage is

[17] Wage costs become modified in the international adjustment transition from Part I to Part II, but no logical problem is involved here. The only possible major difficulty is that transport costs, market potential, and supply potential are estimated on the basis of the present spatial pattern of economic activity. Since this pattern may change substantially under free trade, there may be some feedback between the (main assembly) international adjustment process and the estimation of (subassembly) cost components. However, the reader will be able to verify later that the results of this study support the conclusion that this is only a very minor difficulty; hence no recourse need be made to either successive iterative approximations or a more general system in which the main assembly and the relevant subassembly components are tied together in a system of simultaneous relationships.

that conclusions are necessarily much less precise. For many problems this method is simply not precise enough to yield a conclusion of any kind. Fortunately, however, in this study, firm unambiguous conclusions have been reached even though this technique has been used at many junctures. In summary, the authors do not claim a high degree of precision for the individual estimates in this study; however, they are prepared to stand by the general conclusions.

It is necessary perhaps to modify such a confident statement just slightly. There are two provisos which must be accepted in interpreting this study; other countries do not concurrently enter this free trade area, and institutional influences on location are not significant. With reference to the former, limitations of time and resources have simply prevented a careful analysis of the noise that might be introduced into the results by inclusion of Europe and the rest of the world in a free trade scheme. If third countries are included, these effects may be expected to be substantial. Consequently, this study should be strictly interpreted as the economic effects of a free trade scheme involving only Canada and the United States. Potential secondary effects of the entry of other countries should be borne in mind; an attempt to analyze them is being made elsewhere.

The second proviso is that private institutional arrangements do not significantly affect the location decision. Government imposed institutions such as the tariff, potential common currency areas, etc., are of course very influential in determining growth patterns, and it is indeed the purpose of this study to analyze their impact in full. But what can be said about the institutional arrangements of private business — for example, the purchase by a parent of the entire output of a subsidiary? It is assumed implicitly in this study that this purchase occurs because the subsidiary is one of the least cost sources. But suppose it is not? It may still be sensible in this type of study to analyze least cost sources, as opposed to this current supplying pattern, because in these circumstances one would expect supplying patterns to change in the long run. But they may not, and this should be recognized. However, no attempt has been made to analyze private business arrangements of this kind because of their infinite complexity and variability. Hence this must be regarded as a study of long-run economic growth pressures under free trade conditions; it should be recognized that the patterns that would emerge in these circumstances are likely to be modified by institutional arrangements.

One final comment is in order before turning directly to the analysis. It has become evident that one simply cannot hope to answer the questions addressed in this study without approaching them concurrently on both a theoretical and empirical level. Theory alone is not enough. The factor price equalization theorem provides an example. Unless all costs are empirically examined, it is not clear that this equalization theorem will cause one factor cost (wages) to converge — or diverge. Another example is the proposition that free trade would bring expansion of resource extraction and contraction of manufacturing in Canada; this has probably been suggested by international trade theory in the absence of empirical investigation of Canadian manufacturing costs.

At the same time, an empirical study alone might fail to produce data relevant to the most important questions. The limitations of empirical studies unaccompanied by searching theoretical analysis may be illustrated by the common attempt to deduce free trade effects from an examination of present costs in the two countries — a procedure that overlooks the extremely simple but fundamental proposition that cost differences resulting from protection would tend to disappear with the introduction of free trade.

This study is developed as a mixture of theory and empirical evidence; it is hoped that theory will point up the right questions and that empirical evidence will throw light on the answers.

2

WAGE COSTS

Canadian wage rates, and consequently Canadian income levels, have historically followed the upward pattern of wage and income movements in the United States. However, Canadian wages have traditionally lagged behind U.S. wage levels; as a consequence, Canadian wages today are approximately one quarter below U.S. levels. Since wage payments are an important component of industrial costs, it is to be expected that in a free trade North American economy lower Canadian wages would be an influence tending to attract industry to Canada. It is the objective of this chapter to establish the extent of this advantage by analyzing how costs in various industries and regions of the United States and Canada vary because of differing wage levels.

Wage and labor costs only are considered in this chapter; the question of whether lower Canadian wages might be offset in a free trade situation by other disadvantages specific to Canadian locations will be dealt with later. However, it should be noted at this stage that even if wage advantages are not offset, there would be limits to the possible expansion of Canadian industry under the stimulus of lower wage rates. If industry expanded faster in Canada than in the United States, the Canadian wage rate would eventually tend to be bid up toward the U.S. level, and any wage advantages of Canadian locations would be reduced.

It cannot, however, be argued in the same breath that Canadian wages will jump to the U.S. level while industry is closing down in

Canada. The Canadian wage advantage will tend to disappear only if there is an expansion of Canadian industry[1] resulting in a more rapid growth in employment opportunities in this country than in the United States. There is, of course, no guarantee of this fortunate set of circumstances. But whatever wage equalization might occur would reflect two trends that Canadians should view as highly attractive: Canada would enjoy substantial industrial growth and Canadian incomes would rise.

To eliminate the confusion that often surrounds this discussion, it is essential to distinguish between the short and long run. In the short run, present wage levels may be considered as given; along with other location factors, these wage differences determine changing patterns of industry. In the long run, however, as the adjustment process of industry relocation works itself out, relative wage levels in the two countries are likely to change. The country with the initial advantage of lower wages or other costs will experience a more rapid rate of growth and employment, and demand pressure on its labor force will drive up its relative wage level.[2] The long-run process of wage, price, and exchange adjustment[3] are analyzed in detail in a following section; however, before any judgment is possible on the direction of this adjustment process, it is necessary to specify which regions have an initial advantage. This requires an examination of present wage levels and other costs (which are studied in later chapters).

[1] It has been suggested that with free trade, U.S. unions might move in and set Canadian wages at U.S. levels. This suggestion attributes a power to these unions that they do not enjoy. It is interesting to note that often there is a proposal, in the initial phases of Canadian bargaining, that the wage be raised to the U.S. equivalent, a proposal put forward with equal vigor by U.S. affiliated and domestic Canadian unions. However, the final bargain is determined on more realistic grounds of economic pressure, such as the demand for labor in Canada. Unions cannot reverse basic economic conditions, and there is no reason to argue that free trade would change this. The best evidence of this is the difference in wage levels that persists between regions within the United States.

[2] This adjustment in relative wage levels may not occur entirely via wage revisions; it may be effected in part through a revision in the exchange rate.

[3] Along with underlying labor supply factors such as mobility between regions, countries, and industries.

Wage Rates by Area and Industry

Average per hour earnings of production workers in manufacturing in each industry and in each area of Canada and the
United States are shown in Table 1; a detailed description of how
the figures were derived is provided in Appendix C. The average
wage rate for all industries in a region is shown in the last row of
this table. Similarly there are summary columns on the right-hand
side of this table; the average manufacturing sector wage rate in
all North American regions is shown in the right-hand column;
this rate is broken down into an average sector wage in the
United States and Canada, shown in the second and third last
columns on the right.[4] The last three figures in the bottom right-
hand corner of this table represent both industry and national
averages: the average Canadian wage rate of production workers
in all industries is $1.65, whereas the average U.S. wage rate in
all industries is $2.19, or roughly one third higher. The North
American average wage rate is approximately $2.14 per hour, a
figure quite similar to the U.S. wage because of the heavy weight
of U.S. employment.

It should be emphasized that this table is based on U.S. wages
expressed in terms of U.S. dollars and Canadian wages expressed
in terms of Canadian dollars. Comparisons are strictly appropriate,
therefore, only if the Canadian and U.S. dollars exchange at parity.
However, since the Canadian dollar is now at a discount, U.S.
wages exceed Canadian wages by an even greater degree than
this sort of comparison implies, assuming that the wage gap has
not been closed as the relative value of the Canadian dollar declined. This should be kept in mind throughout the discussion that
follows.

It is interesting to examine the figures along the last row in order
to compare average wage rates in various regions in North
America. First, consider wage rates in the five Canadian regions.

[4] The average wage of each Canadian industry shown in the third column
from the right-hand side of the table compares reasonably well with the
average figures given in Dominion Bureau of Statistics, *Review of Man-
hours and Hourly Earnings, 1945–1961,* and D.B.S., *Earnings and Hours
of Work in Manufacturing, 1958.* The correspondence here is not exact,
nor is it exact in the two D.B.S. publications.

TABLE 1. Average per Hour Earnings for Production Workers, by Area and Manufacturing Sector, Canada and United States, 1958 (in domestic dollars).

Manufacturing sector[a]	Maritimes	Quebec	Ontario	Prairies	British Columbia	Upper Midwest	West Lake	East Lake	Lower Midwest	Middle Atlantic	New England	South	Capital	Florida	Southwest	Mountains	Pacific Southwest	Pacific Northwest	Canadian Average	U.S. Average	Canadian-U.S. Average
Food	1.00	1.40	1.46	1.71	1.79	2.21	2.12	2.11	2.18	2.10	1.81	1.52	1.66	1.45	1.59	1.87	2.23	2.05	1.51	1.97	1.90
Tobacco	b	1.65	c	b	b		1.36	1.56	b	1.45	1.31	1.82	b	1.34	b	b	1.21	b	1.65	1.63	1.63
Textiles	1.45	1.07	1.29	1.66	c	1.65	1.74	1.84	1.39	1.75	1.49	1.44	1.60	1.36	1.23	1.32	1.81	1.79	1.28	1.54	1.52
Apparel	1.49	1.10	1.14	1.10	c	1.52	1.54	1.72	1.38	1.64	1.49	1.22	1.45	1.40	1.23	1.40	1.63	1.58	1.09	1.51	1.48
Wood products	1.00	1.87	1.34	1.68	1.91	2.03	1.84	2.07	1.75	1.90	1.61	1.23	1.60	1.40	1.33	2.16	2.31	2.42	1.48	1.74	1.71
Paper	2.00	1.94	1.90	c	2.39	2.18	2.18	2.31	1.94	1.90	2.05	2.14	2.02	2.27	2.29	1.96	2.35	2.56	1.94	2.18	2.15
Printing	1.43	1.66	2.02	1.66	c	2.59	2.72	2.64	2.35	2.70	2.35	2.20	2.55	2.51	2.26	2.56	2.96	2.97	1.98	2.60	2.55
Electrical equipment	b	b	1.76	1.58	c	2.15	2.24	2.42	2.01	2.22	1.95	1.94	2.46	1.92	2.26	1.94	2.33	2.49	1.73	2.21	2.18
Chemicals	1.48	1.71	1.89	1.71	c	2.19	2.40	2.60	2.41	2.44	2.33	2.38	2.24	1.97	2.81	2.56	2.51	3.17	1.81	2.47	2.42
Petroleum products	b	c	2.34d	2.21d	c	2.87	3.07	2.93	2.79	2.98	2.50	2.31	2.51	1.92	3.08	3.07	2.90	b	2.29	2.98	2.93
Rubber and plastics	b	1.40	1.83	1.60	c	2.02	2.24	2.64	1.99	2.14	1.99	2.22	1.99	1.53	2.12	b	2.36	b	1.69	2.27	2.23
Leather goods	1.46	1.06	1.24	1.58	2.01	b	1.76	1.76	1.47	1.59	1.67	1.39	1.68	1.45	1.33	b	1.79	b	1.15	1.60	1.56
Nonmetallic mineral products	1.47	1.92	1.74	1.64	c	2.14	2.29	2.34	2.21	2.28	2.20	1.88	2.15	1.68	1.89	2.24	2.45	2.56	1.77	2.19	2.16
Metallic products	1.89	1.77	1.96	1.72	2.20	2.32	2.59	2.72	2.35	2.56	2.24	2.35	2.65	1.88	2.25	2.68	2.60	2.76	1.91	2.55	2.51
Transportation equipment	1.67	1.78	1.99	1.74	2.26	2.43	2.64	2.80	2.49	2.65	2.59	2.39	2.69	2.08	2.65	2.25	2.68	2.46	1.91	2.65	2.59
Miscellaneous	1.46	1.50	1.74	1.71	2.02	2.11	2.11	2.19	2.11	2.19	1.78	1.67	2.05	2.17	1.77	2.69	2.72	2.24	1.65	2.17	2.15
Area average	1.41	1.49	1.73	1.67	2.03	2.32	2.59	2.57	2.35	2.56	1.91	1.67	2.21	1.76	2.05	2.08	2.48	2.45	1.65	2.19	2.14

Basic Source for wage rates: Dominion Bureau of Statistics, 72–202. Provincial employment weighting to compute each area average wage taken from Dominion Bureau of Statistics, 31–204 to 31–208 inclusive. For U.S. data, see Appendix C.

[a] The complete list of manufacturing sectors includes: Food and beverages; Tobacco and tobacco products; Textiles and knitting mills; Apparel and related products; Lumber and wood products; Pulp and paper products; Printing and publishing; Electrical machinery and apparatus; Chemicals and products; Petroleum and coal products; Rubber and plastic products; Leather and leather products; Nonmetallic mineral products; Metallic products and nonelectrical machinery; Transportation equipment; Miscellaneous manufacture.

[b] No employment reported by Dominion Bureau of Statistics or in U.S. Census of Manufactures.

[c] Data too fragmentary to include in this table; but wherever feasible they were used to fill out Table 2 and App. D.

[d] No wage information in original sources above, but information is available in Dominion Bureau of Statistics, 72–204, *Earnings and Hours of Work in Manufacturing, 1958,* p. 25. This source was not used for all data because it usually gives a less satisfactory interindustry breakdown of wages.

It will be noted that wages in the Maritimes are the lowest in Canada, with wages in Quebec somewhat higher. Moving up the scale, wages in the Prairies are approximately equal to the Canadian average, while wages in Ontario and British Columbia are higher.

Within the United States, wages on the Pacific Coast and in the Chicago-Cleveland area are the highest. (Michigan has the highest wage of any state.) Especially in the South, and to a lesser degree in New England, wages are substantially below the U.S. average. Other regions in the United States have wage levels that conform approximately to the national average.

It is of particular interest to compare the wage rate in Ontario (the Canadian region of heaviest industrial concentration) with wage rates in various U.S. regions that might be competing with Ontario as an industrial location in the event of free trade. With one apparent exception wages in all U.S. areas are higher than wages in Ontario and, in most cases, much higher. The U.S. region of highest wage rates is the East Lake region, the area adjacent to Ontario and having as a consequence similar location characteristics in other respects. The only U.S. region which seems to be an exception is the South, in which the average wage appears to be slightly less than in Ontario. However, it will be evident in the discussion below that this particular comparison is quite misleading; for almost all industries, Ontario is a lower wage region than the U.S. South.

An examination of the Canadian and U.S. wage differences among manufacturing sectors (shown in the second and third last columns of this table) indicates that there are wide differences in average wages between industries. Moreover, even though the overall Canadian wage level is lower than that of the United States, the interindustry pattern is similar in the two countries. Those industries with higher than average wages in the United States are also in general the industries with higher than average wages in Canada. The textile and apparel sectors, along with the closely associated leather industry, pay the lowest wages in both the United States and Canada. The highest U.S. wage sectors are petroleum and coal products, the primary metal industries, and transportation equipment. These are also among the highest wage sectors in Canada. The most important exception to this rule is the pulp and paper industry: in Canada this industry pays wages substantially above the national average, while its wage in the United States is slightly below the national average. The other industry that deserves special note is tobacco and tobacco products. The industry pays a wage in Canada similar to the national average, while in the United States the wage paid is substantially below average — indeed, so far below that this is the one industry in which the U.S. wage is lower than the Canadian.

The variations of wages by both area and manufacturing industry are shown in the main body of Table 1. The absence of symmetry indicates that wage patterns are complex and must be viewed in terms of this type of interindustry as well as interarea breakdown. For example, an examination of the Ontario column in this table indicates that wages in Ontario are higher than the Canadian average in all sectors except four — food and beverages, lumber and wood products, pulp and paper, and nonmetallic mineral products.[5] It is also interesting to compare in detail Ontario wages with those in the South, the U.S. area of most comparable wages. A comparison of elements in the Ontario and South columns suggests that, although the average wage in the South may be somewhat lower than in Ontario, in almost all sectors wages in the South *exceed* those in Ontario. (The three exceptions are lumber and wood products, petroleum and coal products, and miscellaneous manufacture, and even in these cases the Southern wage is almost as high as that in Ontario.) How is this paradox — one area having a higher average wage while the other area has higher wages in almost every industry — to be explained? An obvious possible explanation might be that employment in both regions is overwhelmingly concentrated in the three exceptional industries in which the South has lower wages. But this is not the case. The explanation is more subtle; employment is heavily concentrated in the South in industries which pay low wages anywhere (e.g., in textiles), while in Ontario employment is concentrated in high wage industries. In the section below that deals with the struc-

---

[5] In the case of lumber and wood products, and pulp and paper, the high Canadian average wage is largely a reflection of the high wages paid in British Columbia.

tural analysis of average wage rates, this effect of employment structure on wage averages will be analyzed, and in the process a quantitative method of comparing all areas in this regard will be developed.

Effects of Wage Differences on Total Costs

A substantial difference in wage rate paid will have considerable impact on the total cost of a labor-intensive industry; at the same time such a difference in wage rate will have little impact on total costs of an industry using very little labor. The real significance of wage rate differences in a specific industry is measured by this criterion: How do interregional wage differences affect total costs between areas? Before this question can be answered it is clear that information is required on the labor intensity of each industry under consideration.

Specifically the problem becomes one of deciding whether to use the labor intensity of a particular industry in the United States or in Canada. For the purposes of Part I the most appropriate labor intensity is that of the industry observed in the United States. The relevant employment of labor in an industry is the employment that would occur in a free trade area of two hundred and twenty million people. This cannot be predicted precisely; however, present employment in U.S. industry (serving a population of two hundred million) is almost certain to provide a closer approximation than present labor use in Canadian industry (which serves a population of roughly twenty million).[6]

[6] Specifically, it is assumed that there is an appropriate production function for each industry in a free trade North American economy, and that this is closely approximated by the U.S. production function which reflects production already rationalized for almost the total North American market.

This assumption seems reasonable enough: to this must be added the additional assumption that firms would operate in Canada and the United States at roughly the same point on this production function. This second assumption is necessary, along with the first, to justify labor intensity in the U.S. industry as appropriate for production that might take place under free trade in Canada. This second assumption may not be entirely justified to the extent that, operating on a similar production function, a producer in Canada may find it profitable to move along this production function by substituting (relatively) cheap Canadian labor for (relatively)

The effects of interregional wage differences on total costs are shown in Table 2. Each figure in this table was computed by applying the (U.S.) labor intensity of the industry to the percentage interarea wage difference shown in Appendix D. Ontario was used as a basis for all comparisons. Wherever wages and, consequently, costs are higher in the comparison area than in Ontario, the element in this table carries a positive sign, and wherever costs are lower in the comparison area, the element carries a negative sign. To illustrate: the appropriate figure in Appendix D indicates that in the apparel sector, the wage rate in the East Lake area is 50.9% higher than that in Ontario. The effect of this wage difference on total costs is computed by adjusting for the labor intensity of this industry. (Just over one fifth of the total costs of this industry goes to wage payments.) The resulting cost difference of 10.24% is shown in Table 2.

It is no surprise that the percentage impact on total cost is always considerably less than the percentage difference in wage rates; in some cases substantial wage differences are of almost no significance because of the low labor intensity of the industries involved. For example, this is true of Ontario's advantage in food processing and in chemicals. In both cases wages are about forty to forty-five percent higher in the adjacent U.S. East Lake area around Detroit and Cleveland. Yet this provides Ontario with only a three quarter percent edge in total costs. The importance of differing labor-intensities in various sectors is illustrated by a comparison of Ontario with the U.S. Pacific Southwest. In the textile industry the wage in this U.S. area exceeds that in Ontario by forty percent; this results in an eight percent higher level of costs. On the other hand, in the food and beverage industry, wages in the Pacific Southwest exceed those in Ontario by a substantially larger margin of over fifty percent; however, this results in a much smaller advantage in total costs of less than four percent.

To sum up: wage rates in most U.S. regions exceed those in Ontario by a substantial margin, running up to almost seventy percent. The impact of these differences on total costs, however, is

---

expensive capital; but insofar as such substitution may take place, the advantage of low-cost labor in Canada will be greater than the analysis of this study suggests.

TABLE 2. *Estimated Percentage that Total Costs in Comparison Areas Are Higher or Lower (−) than in Ontario because of Difference in Wage Rates, by Industry, 1958 ($1.00 U.S. = $1.00 Can.).*

Manufacturing sector[b]	Maritimes	Quebec	Ontario	Prairies	British Columbia	Upper Midwest	West Lake	East Lake	Lower Midwest	Middle Atlantic	New England	South	Capital	Florida	Southwest	Mountain	Pacific Southwest	Pacific Northwest
Food	−2.17	−0.28	0	1.18	1.55	3.53	3.11	3.06	3.39	3.01	1.65	0.28	0.94	−0.05	0.61	1.93	3.63	2.78
Tobacco	a	−0.47	0	a	a	a	−1.98	−0.94	1.54	−1.51	−2.24	0.42	4.77	−2.09	a	a	−2.77	a
Textiles	2.46	−0.31	0	5.69	11.23	5.54	6.92	8.46	4.24	7.08	5.54	2.31	5.47	3.88	0.77	0.46	8.00	7.69
Apparel	6.18	−1.24	0	−0.71	15.53	6.71	7.06	10.24	6.65	8.82	6.18	1.41	4.22	0.97	1.59	4.59	8.65	7.77
Wood products	−5.52	−3.89	0	5.52	9.25	11.19	8.11	11.84	0.30	9.09	4.38	−1.78	0.89	2.76	−0.16	13.30	15.74	17.52
Paper	0.75	−0.22	0	−1.43	3.65	2.09	2.09	3.06	3.37	1.57	1.12	1.79	5.41	5.00	2.91	0.45	3.36	4.92
Printing	−6.02	−0.82	0	−3.67	a	5.81	7.14	6.32	2.58	6.94	3.37	1.84	7.23	1.65	2.45	5.51	9.59	9.69
Electrical equipment	a	−1.03	0	−1.86	2.68	4.03	4.96	6.82	2.68	4.75	1.96	1.86	1.80	0.41	2.48	1.86	5.89	7.54
Chemicals	−2.11	−0.93	0	−0.93	a	1.55	2.63	3.66	0.90	2.83	2.27	2.52	0.34	0.84	4.74	4.12	3.19	6.59
Petroleum products[c]	a	−4.29	0	−0.26	a	1.06	1.46	1.18	1.59	1.28	0.32	−0.06	1.59	−2.99	1.48	1.12	1.12	1.04
Rubber and plastics	4.00	−3.27	0	−2.29	1.79	1.89	4.09	8.07	4.18	3.09	1.59	3.89	7.99	3.81	2.89	1.46	5.28	a
Leather goods			0	6.17	14.17		9.44	9.44		6.36	7.81	2.72			1.63	a	9.99	
Nonmetallic mineral products	−2.92	1.95	0	−1.09	3.04	4.34	5.97	6.52	5.10	5.86	5.00	1.52	4.45	−0.65	1.63	5.43	7.71	8.90
Metallic products	−0.66	−1.80	0	−2.27	2.27	3.41	5.96	7.19	3.69	5.68	2.65	3.69	6.53	−0.76	2.74	6.81	6.05	7.57
Transportation equipment	−2.63	−1.72	0	−2.05	2.22	3.61	5.34	6.65	4.11	5.42	4.93	3.29	5.75	0.74	5.42	2.14	5.67	3.86
Miscellaneous	−3.02	−2.58	0	−0.32	3.02	3.99	3.99	4.85	3.99	4.85	0.43	−0.75	3.34	4.63	0.32	10.23	10.56	5.39

a Wage data inadequate.
b See Table 1, note a.
c Estimates in this row are less reliable than in the balance of this table.

reduced to about ten percent or less. The one exception is the lumber and wood products industry in which there are substantial interarea differences in wages (running up to eighty percent) combined with the heaviest labor intensity of any sector. The result is that total costs in this industry vary between some regions in the United States and Ontario by nearly twenty percent; moreover, there are even greater differences in total costs if the U.S. Pacific Northwest is compared with the Canadian Maritimes or Quebec.

Differences in Labor Productivity and the Exchange Rate

There are two important reasons why wage rates in the two countries may not give an accurate description of differences in labor costs. The first is possible differences in labor productivity; the second is the exchange rate, which (unless the Canadian and U.S. dollars are trading at par) does not allow the equation of a dollar's worth of wage payment in Canada with a dollar's worth of wage payment in the United States.

Since it is the objective of this study to describe labor costs, differences in wage rates should be modified whenever there are regional differences in labor productivity. However, reliable information on this subject is difficult to establish. It is true that estimates of average output per man-hour can be computed in each industry in each area, but these figures take no account of differences in capital intensity and other factors used. If labor costs are to be compared, it is necessary to hold the employment of these other factors constant.[7] This *ceteris paribus* requirement

[7] In comparing labor costs between regions it is necessary to choose between two alternative techniques, neither of which is entirely satisfactory. Wage rates may be compared, on the assumption that labor quality is roughly equal in each region; alternatively, labor costs per unit of output may be computed and compared on the assumption that factor proportions and technology in an industrial sector are similar in each region. Although neither strategy is entirely satisfactory, it is probably reasonable to conclude that if the analysis is based on a disaggregated, well defined industry breakdown comparing regions within one country, the latter assumption might be preferred. However, if each sector is an aggregative mix of quite diverse industrial activities, then any assumption of fixed labor proportions becomes difficult to justify because of the possibility of factor substitution both within any industry and between subindustries in a sector. In this case the former assumption is likely to be more realistic.

restricts comparisons of labor efficiency to firms that are engaged in operations in several regions involving reasonably similar processes, organization, labor and capital mix, and technology. In comparing an industry as it exists in Canada and the United States, however, it is virtually impossible to impose the restriction that processes and organization will be similar because, except for export industries, the whole structure of Canadian production is designed to service a much smaller market and, as a consequence, involves a different organization of labor and capital facilities.

This fundamental difficulty becomes immediately evident in any comparison of labor productivity in Canada and the United States. Measuring labor productivity in terms of total output divided by man-hours employed, it is evident that the average worker is substantially less productive in Canada than in the United States. There are two possible explanations for this: the Canadian worker may be less able in terms of his inherent physical and mental equipment, or the Canadian working force may labor under some disadvantages specific to the Canadian situation.

In this study, it is maintained that the most important explanation lies along the second of these two lines; specifically, lower Canadian labor productivity is primarily the result of the present organization of Canadian industry aimed at a small domestic market. Many Canadian industries are not producing on a scale large enough to achieve the cost-cutting efficiencies of long production runs. Consequently, if Canadian industry is reorganized on a high volume, low cost basis to service both the Canadian and U.S. markets, average Canadian labor productivity (measured by output divided by employment) is likely to increase. No attempt is made here, at this stage, to judge the quantitative extent of this possible increase. However, this point is important: tariff protection in the North American economy that tends to corner Canadian producers in their domestic market results in lower Canadian labor productivity. With the free trade reorganization of Canadian industry, substantial changes in Canadian labor productivity may be expected. Consequently any measurement of present produc-

Hence in this highly aggregated sectoral study, the labor cost analysis was based on the former strategy. This strategy is also dictated by the international nature of this analysis. (See the discussion on the following pages.)

tivity differences between the two countries is of limited relevance in a study of labor costs in a free trade situation. The assumption on which our study is based — that the inherent "quality" of Canadian labor is similar to that of U.S. labor — is in line with the conclusions of three comparative surveys of labor productivity in the two countries, by John H. Young,[8] Mordechai E. Kreinin,[9] and the National Industrial Conference Board.[10]

It should be noted, however, that there is no universal agree-

[8] "Some Aspects of Canadian Economic Development" (unpub. diss., Cambridge University, 1955). Young addressed the question of whether lower observed average labor productivity in Canada reflected lower inherent efficiency of the labor force (Table 4, p. 63).

In an extensive survey, he received one hundred and forty-nine replies from American firms to the question (p. 70): "How does labor in your Canadian plant(s) compare with labor in your American plant(s) with respect to efficiency or effectiveness? (The question is concerned entirely with labor effort and ability, and you are asked as far as possible to eliminate any difference arising from different plant, equipment and management.)"

Twenty-six reported that Canadian labor was more efficient, eighty-five that there was no difference, and forty that U.S. labor was more efficient. In addition, twenty-seven replies were received from Canadian subsidiaries of U.S. firms: nine reported that Canadian labor was superior, thirteen found no difference, and five found U.S. workers more efficient. (Reasons given for preferring Canadian labor were a less pampered and more cooperative attitude and less difficulty with unions (pp. 72, 73); the reasons it was felt to be inferior were that it was more leisurely and less responsive to incentives (p. 71).

Young's conclusion from this and other evidence was that lower observed average productivity of labor in Canada was not because of a difference in inherent efficiency but was caused primarily by the size of the market and resulting lower volume output (p. 86). Other contributing factors cited were differences in equipment and production techniques (not associated directly with the size of the market but because of lower wages, for example) and a less alert and aggressive Canadian management (pp. 86–87).

[9] "Comparative Labor Effectiveness and the Leontief Scarce-Factor Paradox," *American Economic Review,* 55: 131–139 (March 1965). The median response to Kreinin's survey regarding the Canadian-U.S. labor requirement to produce similar goods with similar organization and degree of mechanization was 100 percent; the mean response was 102 percent.

[10] *Costs and Competition: American Experience Abroad* (New York: National Industrial Conference Board, 1961), p. 54. Twelve percent of the N.I.C.B. respondents said that less Canadian than U.S. labor would be needed to produce a similar product with similar equipment; 78 percent said the same; and 10 percent said more.

ment on this point. Two suggestions in particular have been made that the quality of labor is lower in Canada than in the United States. Some have suggested that the labor force in the United States works harder and is more diligent than Canadian workers; it has also been pointed out that the level of education in the United States is higher than in Canada.

The hypothesis that the U.S. laborer is superior because he works harder is not easily tested. It is difficult to devise a better test than the surveys cited above, and these did not support the hypothesis. If the hypothesis were, nevertheless, correct, then an evaluation of the consequences of North American free trade would be more complicated because U.S. labor may work harder for two alternative reasons. First, they may be induced to do so by stronger competitive pressures. If so, then North American free trade might be expected to erode the differences between U.S. and Canadian labor: Canadians would be in the same competitive market. If they responded by working as hard as the Americans, the labor cost data of this study would still be relevant as an index of locational advantage for new industry; however, because Canadians would be giving up their relatively easy-going life, the estimates of the potential economic gains from free trade (Chapter 15) would have to be revised downward to take account of this loss of leisure.

Second, Americans may work harder because of fundamental differences in temperament: Canadians might conceivably work less hard as a result of an explicit choice and not because of differences in competitive pressures. If so, lower Canadian productivity might be expected to persist into a free trade situation. Canadian locations would thus become less attractive than they otherwise might be, with weaker free trade pressures for Canadian wages to rise or for the exchange value of the Canadian dollar to increase. Once again, the estimates of potential economic gain to Canada from free trade (Chapter 15) would have to be reduced, this time because of a smaller potential increase in Canadian money incomes.

But, as noted earlier, the best evidence indicates no such relative tendency for Canadian labor to "take it easy"; neither of these downward adjustments would therefore seem to be necessary. If the Young-Kreinin-N.I.C.B. studies may be extended with casual empiricism for a moment, it is our impression that, in general, the pressures on and attitudes of the two labor forces are quite similar. If there is a significant intercountry difference, it is at the entrepreneurial level: Canadian businessmen are under less competitive pressure and have smaller rewards open to them. The change in the "way of life" implied by free trade therefore would be confined primarily to Canadian businessmen: the level of competence required to survive might increase, with great rewards for those who meet the test.[11]

The other reason for suggesting that Canadian labor may be inherently inferior is its lower level of education. Recent research by the Economic Council of Canada provides evidence on comparative educational levels in the United States and Canada.[12] Their estimate is that lower educational attainment at all levels of management and in the labor force is the cause of over one third of the productivity difference between the two countries.

For several reasons one might speculate that the impact of educational deficiency may be concentrated heavily at the management level. It is likely that management efficiency would be more sensitive to this influence than worker efficiency — even if educational differences were equal at all levels. But they are not; the largest differences occur at the senior high school and especially the university level, whereas there is practically no difference between countries in the percentage of ten- to fourteen-year-olds in school.[13] For both reasons, the most marked educational effects should occur at the management level. No attempt has been made in this study to account for education-based productivity dif-

[11] This issue, and other related questions (cf. footnote 14) are extraordinarily difficult to evaluate; therefore, no attempt is made later on in this study to project quantitative changes in entrepreneurial income in free trade circumstances.

[12] Economic Council of Canada, *Second Annual Review* (Ottawa: Queen's Printer, December 1965), Ch. 4; and Gordon W. Bertram, *The Contribution of Education to Economic Growth* (Staff Study #22, Economic Council of Canada, 1965).

[13] See Economic Council, *Second Annual Review*, p. 83. This comparison seems to imply that the percentage finishing elementary school is the same in both countries, but it is not quite the case. Although Canadian performance is rapidly closing on that of the U.S., an 8 percent difference in recent elementary school completions still exists (p. 84, Table 4–5, first row).

ferences among production workers. Our working assumption is that inherent labor productivity is the same in both countries[14] — either because no educational effects are substantial at these lower levels or alternatively because any educational disadvantages are offset by advantages.[15] If educational differences are judged more important than this, the wage attraction of Canadian locations shown in Table 3 should be appropriately discounted.

There is one final reason for which wage rates in the two countries may not be strictly comparable: the exchange value of the Canadian dollar need not equal that of the U.S. dollar. This point will be dealt with in a separate section; it should be noted here, however, that the entire analysis of wage costs in this chapter (along with the analysis of other costs that immediately follow) is based on the assumption that the rate of exchange of the U.S. and Canadian dollars is parity. To the extent that the exchange rate may vary from this assumed level, wage differences between the two countries require inflation or discount by an appropriate percentage. In the base year 1958, the rate of exchange between the two currencies was fairly close to parity; however, at the present time the Canadian dollar is trading at a discount of about seven and one half percent. It is important to point this out because at present this discount gives Canadian industry an even more substantial advantage in terms of lower wage rates than the comparative domestic wage rates in Table 1 suggest.

[14] No attempt is made in this study to compare inherent management productivity in the two countries. Such a comparison would involve integrating differences in advanced education into our analysis; and this would be particularly difficult in any study of protection of the kind undertaken here. For example, it is not clear to what extent differences in higher education are "exogenous," and to what extent they may themselves be a result of tariff-induced economic separation between the countries. University education in particular is closely associated with research; research is an overhead, and therefore tends to be undertaken by large-scale enterprises with access to great markets. Because North American tariffs have resulted in a fragmentation of Canadian industry, it is possible that they may have discouraged Canadian research; thus, indirectly, tariffs may have had an (imponderable?) adverse effect on Canadian higher education.

[15] Of the type cited by Young above. For example, in response to Kreinin's questionnaire ("Comparative Labor Effectiveness," p. 136), employers cited a number of reasons why Canadian labor is superior and a number of offsetting reasons why it is inferior to U.S. labor. But lack of education was mentioned in only one questionnaire reply.

The reason that the exchange rate has not been explicitly used to discount figures on wage rates (and other costs) is that any change that might occur in the exchange rate would immediately throw the whole analysis out of date. Another reason it is useful to consider the exchange rate separately is that possible changes in this rate can be easily interpreted in terms of their regional impact on *total costs* — for example, a ten percent depreciation of the Canadian dollar provides Canadian producers with an immediate ten percent advantage in total costs.[16] Since other cost differences such as wages have also been reduced to the same total cost basis, it will be possible to compare directly the effects of changes in wage levels and the exchange rate.

Structural Analysis of Average Wage Rates

It has already been noted that a comparison of average wage levels between areas may be misleading. In a high wage area wages may not be high in any industry; the high average may be explained by the area's mix of high wage industries. An example has already been cited; wages in Ontario are higher on average than in the U.S. South; however, in almost all industries, wages in Ontario are *less* than comparable wages in the South. The explanation for this paradox is that employment in Ontario is more heavily concentrated in high wage industries, whereas in the South employment is concentrated in low wage industries. It is the objective of this section to develop an index of the variation of average wages between areas that will be independent of such structural differences in employment.

Table 3 shows the results of applying the wage pattern in each area to the employment structure of each area.[17] For example,

---

[16] This total advantage exists only if the import content of the product is negligible. If this is not the case, then the advantage of depreciation of the exchange rate is less than 10 percent — to a degree determined by the importance of import content.

[17] Specifically, the average wage rate when wages in area i are applied to the employment structure in area j is:

$$\frac{\sum_k (w_{ik}e_{jk})}{\sum_k e_{jk}} \qquad (k = 1 \ldots n, \text{ except for any industry in which } e_{ik} = 0)$$

in which w_{ik} is the wage rate in area i and industry k and e_{jk} is employment.

TABLE 3. *Average Wage Level Assuming Wage Rates in Row Area and Employment Structure in Column Area, 1958* ($1.00 U.S. = $1.00 Can.).

Areas	Maritimes	Quebec	Ontario	Prairies	British Columbia	Upper Midwest	West Lake	East Lake	Lower Midwest	Middle Atlantic	New England	South	Capital	Florida	Southwest	Mountain	Pacific Southwest	Pacific Northwest
1. Maritimes	1.41	1.50	1.53	1.38	1.31	1.58	1.64	1.66	1.47	1.57	1.54	1.43	1.54	1.42	1.46	1.17	1.51	1.35
2. Quebec	1.56	1.50	1.60	1.57	1.44	1.63	1.66	1.69	1.58	1.55	1.48	1.42	1.60	1.58	1.60	1.48	1.61	1.47
3. Ontario	1.67	1.61	1.73	1.69	1.60	1.80	1.81	1.86	1.71	1.69	1.62	1.51	1.74	1.69	1.74	1.57	1.76	1.64
4. Prairies	1.69	1.61	1.67	1.68	1.70	1.70	1.67	1.69	1.66	1.60	1.63	1.61	1.64	1.67	1.69	1.70	1.68	1.69
5. British Columbia	2.04	2.08	2.10	2.05	2.03	2.09	2.14	2.15	2.08	2.10	2.09	2.04	2.11	2.06	2.07	1.91	2.10	2.06
6. Upper Midwest	2.21	2.07	2.19	2.22	2.17	2.21	2.24	2.27	2.23	2.12	2.08	1.96	2.20	2.19	2.23	2.22	2.23	2.19
7. West Lake	2.23	2.11	2.28	2.28	2.14	2.26	2.37	2.44	2.44	2.21	2.12	2.00	2.31	2.19	2.23	2.19	2.33	2.19
8. East Lake	2.32	2.23	2.40	2.35	2.28	2.34	2.50	2.57	2.38	2.33	2.24	2.13	2.43	2.30	2.41	2.23	2.45	2.34
9. Lower Midwest	2.13	1.95	2.12	2.16	2.02	2.15	2.18	2.26	2.16	2.04	1.92	1.82	2.15	2.12	2.17	2.17	2.19	2.07
10. Middle Atlantic	2.22	2.11	2.27	2.27	2.15	2.26	2.36	2.42	2.28	2.21	2.11	2.02	2.30	2.19	2.31	2.18	2.33	2.21
11. New England	2.00	1.92	2.06	2.03	1.90	1.99	2.11	2.20	2.06	1.99	1.91	1.84	2.09	1.98	2.07	1.90	2.10	1.98
12. South	1.83	1.80	1.95	1.85	1.68	1.85	2.06	2.15	1.92	1.89	1.80	1.67	1.99	1.86	1.92	1.66	1.97	1.77
13. Capital	2.02	2.00	2.18	2.07	1.94	2.09	2.34	2.40	2.17	2.15	2.04	1.87	2.21	2.06	2.14	1.86	2.24	2.03
14. Florida	1.78	1.72	1.80	1.74	1.67	1.79	1.88	1.89	1.79	1.80	1.76	1.62	1.81	1.76	1.77	1.60	1.85	1.72
15. Southwest	1.92	1.85	2.01	1.95	1.77	1.91	2.10	2.21	1.99	1.93	1.82	1.69	2.05	1.96	2.05	1.74	2.07	1.88
16. Mountain	2.12	2.03	2.20	2.17	2.20	2.22	2.35	2.38	2.22	2.19	2.10	1.89	2.24	2.21	2.28	2.08	2.27	2.20
17. Pacific Southwest	2.40	2.23	2.40	2.40	2.40	2.43	2.49	2.53	2.41	2.34	2.27	2.14	2.42	2.34	2.43	2.34	2.48	2.42
18. Pacific Northwest	2.36	2.31	2.45	2.37	2.46	2.41	2.57	2.58	2.43	2.38	2.34	2.21	2.46	2.47	2.48	2.24	2.44	2.45

$1.53 in the Maritimes row and the Ontario column is the average wage if Maritimes' wage rates in all industries are weighted by the employment pattern in Ontario. Any element along the diagonal (in italics) in this table represents the simple average wage level of an area based on the weighting of its own employment structure. An unadjusted and often misleading estimate of how wage levels differ between areas is provided by comparing diagonal elements. For example, using an earlier illustration, the wage level in Ontario appears to be slightly higher than in the U.S. South ($1.73 compared to $1.67). This, however, is a biased figure. Wage levels in the two areas should be compared by holding employment structure constant, and this can be done in two ways. First, assuming the employment structure in Ontario (and reading up the Ontario column), the South (with a wage of $1.95) is a higher wage area than Ontario ($1.73). If employment structure in the South is used as a basis of comparison (and reading up the South column), then the picture remains substantially the same; the average wage in the South ($1.67) is substantially higher than the average wage in Ontario ($1.51). In this case the unadjusted diagonal comparison that suggests Ontario wages are higher is quite misleading. In fact, comparable wages in the U.S. South are from eleven to thirteen percent higher than in Ontario. The difference is explained by the fact that Ontario has specialized in high wage industries to a greater degree than has the South.

An examination of the diagonal values in this table might erroneously suggest that there is a region in the United States (the South) in which wages are actually lower than wages in Ontario; When appropriate discount is made for employment structure, however, it is evident that this is not the case. In fact there is no region in the United States in which comparable wages are as low as they are in Ontario, the area of heaviest manufacturing concentration in Canada. It should also be noted that wage rates in the United States are highest in the area immediately adjacent to Ontario with similar location characteristics in other regards — the East Lake area around Detroit and Cleveland. A diagonal comparison of wages in this area with Ontario wages suggests that the wage rate in the East Lake region ($2.57) is almost fifty percent higher than in Ontario ($1.73). However, if employment mix is held constant,[18] the difference in comparable wages is reduced to less than forty percent. The remainder is a reflection of the fact that the East Lake area has specialized to a higher degree in high wage industry. In comparing Ontario with U.S. regions, the South and East Lake represent the two extreme cases; therefore it may be concluded that comparable wages in U.S. regions range from ten to forty percent higher than wages in Ontario.

There are even greater surprises. For example, an unadjusted comparison indicates that East Lake wage rates are about fifty-five percent higher than wage rates in the South ($2.57 versus $1.67); but this apparent fifty-five percent difference reflects an actual difference of only about twenty to twenty-five percent in comparable

[18] It should be noted that, when employment mix is held constant, the implicit assumption is made that certain industries have high wages because of some inherent characteristics of the industry (e.g., rapid growth in markets or a requirement of highly skilled labor in the production process) but not because the industry happens to be centered in a high-wage area. The latter part of this assumption must be placed in question by the exhibited tendency for high-wage industries to be found in areas with high comparable wages. This suggests, in specific terms, that the auto industry has high wages not only because of its inherent characteristics (skill requirements, etc.) but also at least partially because it is concentrated in Detroit. Consequently, the complexity of the interplay between wages and location must be recognized: wages are high in Detroit because the auto industry is there; at the same time, wages may be high in the auto industry because it is located in Detroit. In Table 3, the potential importance of the former relationship is isolated.

It should also be observed that, at least to some degree, the wages an industry pays are likely to be a reflection of the overall wage pattern of the area in which it is located; consequently, any interarea comparison of wage averages made by a firm deciding between locations should involve more than just an examination of column elements in Table 3. For such a firm, a comparison of diagonal elements in Table 3 may also be useful — for the very reason that it does combine information on comparative wages and information on industry mix. Thus, a textile firm locating in the Middle Atlantic Area may wish to know that wages in comparable industries are 20 percent higher than in the South, and also that a large portion of the labor force in the Middle Atlantic is employed in high-wage industries, and any hiring this firm does at the expense of other industries may be at even higher cost.

For these purposes, the most definitive statement about wage averages is: The Middle Atlantic wage level is between 20 and 30 percent higher than the wage level in the South. (The former figure is based on column comparisons, the latter on the diagonal comparison.)

wage rates. The remainder is due to differences in industry mix.[19]

There are also surprises if Canadian regions are compared. For example, a diagonal comparison suggests that British Columbia wages are just over seventeen percent higher than wages in Ontario ($2.03 versus $1.73). But this apparent difference substantially underestimates an actual difference of from twenty to twenty-five percent in comparable wage rates in the two areas. The understatement is a reflection of the fact that, although wages in comparable industries are higher, British Columbia has an employment structure concentrated in low wage industries. An examination of the structure of B.C. employment makes this quite clear: by far the heaviest sector of employment in that province is the wood products sector; although British Columbia pays the highest wage rate in wood products in Canada, this is a sector in which wages are below average in all regions.

It is evident from an examination of this table that variations in employment mix between regions within the United States plays a substantial role in explaining interregional wage differences. The same is true in explaining interregional wage differences between regions within Canada. On the other hand, if this analysis is applied on an intercountry rather than interregional basis, the effects

[19] It should be noted that two means of comparing areas are used here, each appropriate to the industry mix of one of the comparison states. An alternative that is often used would be to derive a single measure of difference by assuming the North American pattern of employment and using this as the basis of all calculations. This is computationally attractive; however, for certain interarea comparisons the North American structure of employment may be relevant, but for others it may have little relevance. The latter would be the case if the North American pattern is dissimilar to the employment structure in either of the two areas being compared. In this event use of the North American employment structure is arbitrary; any employment mix more closely approximating those of the two comparison areas would be preferable. This suggests using the employment pattern of one of the comparison states — but it is evident from this analysis that the result would often depend on which of the comparison states is chosen. There is, of course, no difficulty if the employment structure of the two comparison areas does not differ greatly from that of North America. But in this case there would be little of the outside influence of employment mix to impound, and to assume this would be to assume the problem away. The greater the structural differences to be measured, the less appropriate is the method of using a North American base; consequently the success of this approach is inversely related to the importance of the problem.

of employment mix tend to disappear. In other words, differences in employment structure tend to be important in explaining wage differences between the Southwest and New England, between Ontario and British Columbia, or between Ontario and New England; however, differences in employment structure are *not* important in explaining differences in wage rates between Canada and the United States. This is illustrated in Table 4, in which precisely

TABLE 4. *Average Wage Level Assuming Wage Rates in Row Country and Employment Structure in Column Country, 1958 ($1.00 U.S. = $1.00 Can.).*

	Canada	United States
Canada	$1.65	$1.68
United States	2.15	2.19

the same analysis as previously described in Table 3 is applied to wages in two areas — Canada and the United States. It will be noted from this abbreviated table that the thirty-three percent difference in wage rates obtained by comparing the diagonal elements ($2.19 vs. $1.65) is approximately equal to the thirty percent difference yielded by a comparison of figures in either column. It is true that these figures do indicate that employment in Canada is slightly less heavily concentrated in high wage industries than in the United States. However, the overall similarity in employment mix in Canada and the United States is quite remarkable; this suggests that the Canadian industrial structure can be described as being a close reflection, on a much smaller scale, of the U.S. industry pattern. This similarity is perhaps not surprising, since Canadian protection historically has been aimed, at least in part, at ensuring diversification of industry. This has apparently prevented specialization in Canada in either high wage or low wage industries.

Returning to the analysis of wage differences between regions in Table 3, we may conclude that the U.S. Pacific Southwest is an area of relatively high comparable wage rates. This may be confirmed by an examination of the elements of the Pacific Southwest column in Table 3, which were computed by applying the wage pattern of each area to the Pacific Southwest employment structure.

The largest item in this column is on the diagonal (that is, the Pacific Southwest wage pattern yields the largest average wage); consequently by this measure the area has higher comparable wages than any other area in the United States or Canada.

Each column in Table 3 is subjected to the same type of examination[20] and the results are shown in Table 5.

TABLE 5. *Areas Ranked in Terms of Highest Comparable Wages, 1958* *($1.00 U.S. = $1.00 Can.).*

1. Pacific Southwest	10. Lower Midwest
2. Pacific Northwest	11. New England
3. East Lake	12. Southwest
4. West Lake	13. South
5. Middle Atlantic	14. Florida
6. Capital	15. Ontario
7. Upper Midwest	16. Prairies
8. Mountain	17. Quebec
9. British Columbia	18. Maritimes

The Pacific Coast region and the Chicago-Cleveland area show up with the highest wages; the lowest wage areas of the United States are New England and regions in the South. However, with one exception, all Canadian regions have comparable wages below even the lowest wage U.S. areas. This one exception is, of course, British Columbia; but even this province has lower wages than most U.S. regions, the exceptions being New England, the South, Florida, and the Southwest.

Since it has already been established that it is important to discount wage comparisons for differences in industry mix, it follows that certain areas must have employment concentrated in high wage industries to a greater degree than others. This may be

[20] In precise terms each column was examined to provide a count of the number of elements smaller than and larger than the diagonal element. The ratio computed by dividing the former by the latter was used as the basis of the rankings in this table. Thus, for example, the Pacific Southwest column yields a count of seventeen elements smaller than the diagonal value but no elements larger. This accounts for this area's top ranking. When this measure resulted in a tie between two regions (e.g., Pacific Southwest and Pacific Northwest), the region with the largest diagonal value was arbitrarily given precedence. An analogous treament of rows was used to determine rankings in Table 6.

confirmed by an examination of the East Lake *row* in Table 3. The elements in this row were computed by applying the fixed East Lake wage pattern to the employment structure of each area in turn. In each case the resulting average wage is lower than the East Lake wage — an indication that the East Lake area has an employment mix of high wage industries to a greater degree than any other region. Each area is subject to this type of row analysis and the results are shown in Table 6.

TABLE 6. *Areas Ranked by Employment in High Wage Industries, 1958*

1. East Lake	10. Upper Midwest
2. West Lake	11. Middle Atlantic
3. Pacific Southwest	12. Florida
4. Capital	13. Quebec
5. Southwest	14. Maritimes
6. Ontario	15. New England
7. Lower Midwest	16. Mountain
8. Pacific Northwest	17. British Columbia
9. Prairies	18. South

It should be noted that the ranking of U.S. areas in Table 6 exhibits some similarity to their ranking in Table 5. It is true that the relative position of the West Coast states and the Lake states is reversed in the two tables; however, both groups remain at the top of the list. Furthermore, the Southern states and New England retain their position in the lower half of the ranking. The one group of regions which does show a substantial change in the two sets of rankings is the group of Canadian areas. It is true that Quebec and the Maritimes retain their relatively low ranking. However, both Ontario and the Prairies are now in the top half of this ranking, and British Columbia, a medium wage region, is almost at the bottom of this latter scale.

It is interesting to consider how the rankings in the two tables compare if areas in the United States and areas in Canada are considered in two separate groupings. Considering the United States first, column and row rankings in the two tables are quite similar, indicating that areas in which comparable wages are low tend also to be those areas with an employment mix of low wage industries. Low income is associated with employment in low wage industries as much as with low comparable wage rates. If one examines Canadian regions in isolation, the same principle holds true; with one exception, rankings in the two tables are similar. Hence those areas in which comparable wages are low (e.g., Quebec and the Maritimes) are also those areas with an employment mix of low wage industries. Similarly, Ontario has both high comparable wages and a favorable employment mix. The one notable exception in the Canadian case is British Columbia, which has the highest comparable wages in Canada but the lowest wage employment mix in the country.

The analysis of average wages in Table 3 provides a basis for a number of quantitative wage comparisons between regions in Canada and the United States. Only those involving Canadian regions have been computed and are shown in Table 7. Three figures appear for each comparison in this table. The first two are computed by holding employment mix constant (by an analysis of columns in Table 3), whereas the figure appearing in parentheses below is the unadjusted estimate (derived by comparing diagonal elements in Table 3). The cases in which diagonal or unadjusted comparisons would be misleading can be easily identified in Table 7. For example, the potentially misleading comparison of wage levels in Ontario and the South cited earlier is verified in this table; the unadjusted comparison in parentheses suggests that wages in the U.S. South are three percent lower than in Ontario; however, the two preceding figures confirm that, when employment mix is held constant, wages in the South in comparable industries are eleven to thirteen percent higher than in Ontario. It is also evident from this table that if B.C. wages are compared with wage levels in other regions, in either Canada or the United States, B.C. wage rates will tend almost always to be understated — unless explicit account is taken of the employment mix of low wage industries in that province. For example, it appears from the unadjusted comparison in parentheses that West Lake wages are seventeen percent higher than B.C. wages; however, holding employment mix constant, West Lake wages are only five to eleven percent higher than wages in British Columbia. Similarly, it appears from the unadjusted comparison in parentheses that wages in the U.S. Southwest are slightly (one percent) higher than wages in British Columbia.

Absolute Advantage

TABLE 7. *Estimated Percentage that Average Wage Levels in Comparison Areas Are Higher (+) or Lower (−) than in Canadian Areas, 1958.*[a]

Comparison areas	Canadian areas				
	Maritimes	Quebec	Ontario	Prairies	British Columbia
Maritimes	−	−10 0 (−6)	−16 −12 (−18)	−18 −17 (−16)	−35 −31 (−31)
Quebec	0 +11 (+6)	−	−8 −7 (−13)	−7 −7 (−11)	−29 −28 (−26)
Ontario	+13 +18 (+23)	+7 +8 (+15)	−	+1 +4 (+3)	−21 −18 (−15)
Prairies	+20 +22 (+19)	+7 +7 (+12)	−3 −1 (−3)	−	−18 −16 (−17)
British Columbia	+45 +55 (+44)	+39 +41 (+35)	+21 +27 (+17)	+19 +22 (+21)	−
Upper Midwest	+40 +57 (+48)	+36 +38 (+47)	+23 +27 (+28)	+30 +32 (+32)	+6 +7 (+9)
West Lake	+45 +58 (+68)	+41 +43 (+58)	+31 +32 (+37)	+36 +42 (+41)	+5 +11 (+17)
East Lake	+55 +65 (+82)	+49 +52 (+71)	+38 +39 (+49)	+40 +52 (+53)	+12 +20 (+27)
Lower Midwest	+47 +51 (+53)	+30 +37 (+44)	+23 +26 (+25)	+29 +30 (+29)	0 +4 (+6)
Middle Atlantic	+41 +57 (+57)	+41 +43 (+47)	+31 +31 (+28)	+35 +38 (+32)	+5 +6 (+9)
New England	+24 +42 (+35)	+28 +29 (+27)	+18 +19 (+10)	+17 +21 (+14)	−6 −9 (−6)
South	+17 +30 (+18)	+18 +20 (+11)	+11 +13 (−3)	+4 +10 (−1)	−18 −17 (−18)
Capital	+43 +44 (+57)	+33 +38 (+47)	+26 +27 (+28)	+23 +35 (+32)	−4 +5 (+9)
Florida	+24 +26 (+25)	+11 +15 (+17)	+4 +4 (+2)	+4 +5 (+5)	−18 −15 (−13)
Southwest	+36 +40 (+45)	+23 +28 (+37)	+16 +18 (+18)	+16 +21 (+22)	−13 −1 (+1)
Mountain	+50 +78 (+48)	+35 +41 (+39)	+27 +32 (+20)	+22 +29 (+24)	+8 +9 (+2)
Pacific Southwest	+64 +70 (+76)	+49 +54 (+65)	+39 +41 (+43)	+43 +48 (+48)	+18 +18 (+22)
Pacific Northwest	+67 +81 (+74)	+54 +67 (+63)	+42 +49 (+42)	+41 +45 (+46)	+19 +21 (+21)

[a] There are three figures in each element in this table; the first two are computed by holding employment mix constant (by comparing column elements in Table 3). The third (in parentheses below) is an unadjusted estimate (taken by comparing diagonal elements in Table 3).

However, when employment mix is taken into account, wages in the U.S. Southwest turn out to be one to thirteen percent *lower* than in British Columbia.

The first five rows of this table may be examined in detail to establish quantitatively the precise position of the five Canadian regions: the Maritimes is the lowest wage area in Canada, with wages up to ten percent lower than in the next area, Quebec; British Columbia has the highest wages in Canada, about twenty-five percent higher than the next area, Ontario.

It is perhaps most enlightening to compare relative wage levels of adjacent areas in the two countries. Border regions presumably would be highly competitive in a free trade area, and whatever wage equalization might occur in free trade conditions is most likely to take place between such regions. (For example, in a free trade North American area a greater degree of wage equalization is likely to occur between British Columbia and the U.S. Pacific Northwest than between the Canadian Maritimes and the Pacific Northwest.) In comparisons of this kind, wages in adjacent U.S. regions run anywhere from twenty to forty percent higher than wages in the bordering Canadian areas: the wage level in the U.S. Pacific Northwest is twenty percent higher than in British Columbia; in the Upper Midwest thirty percent higher than in the Prairies; in the Middle Atlantic and East Lake areas thirty and forty percent higher than in Ontario; in the Middle Atlantic forty percent higher than in Quebec; and in New England twenty-five to forty percent higher than in the Maritimes. On average the wage level in adjacent U.S. areas is thirty-six percent higher than in Canada.[21] This difference should be contrasted with the earlier conclusion that the wage average over the whole United States is thirty percent higher than in Canada.

[21] If the comparison of Table 4 is run between Canada and the adjacent northern regions of the United States, the figures become:

	Canada	Northern U.S.
Canada	1.65	1.68
Northern U.S.	2.24	2.28

These figures indicate that Northern U.S. wages are 36 percent higher than in Canada, and that the U.S. North, like the rest of the country, has an employment mix only slightly more heavily concentrated in high-wage industries than Canada.

This fact that wages in the bordering northern regions of the United States are substantially higher than in the rest of the United States suggests that the Canadian wage advantage may be even more substantial than it might appear from first inspection of Canadian-U.S. wage differences. It also follows that Canadian wages would not have to rise as high as wages in neighboring U.S. regions for Canadian wage incomes to rise to the overall U.S. level; or to put it the other way around, if Canadian wages were to reach the levels of adjacent U.S. regions, wage income in Canada would rise above the average U.S. level. No judgment is being made at this stage on the likelihood or extent of such equalization; this question is deferred until Chapter 11.

Concluding Observations

The manufacturing wage level in the United States is thirty percent higher than in Canada; however, wages in the adjacent northern areas of the United States are thirty-six percent higher. Comparing regions within the United States, the Pacific Coast and Chicago-Cleveland areas are the high wage areas and New England and the South pay the lowest wages; within Canada, British Columbia and Ontario have the highest wages, and Quebec and the Maritimes the lowest. In comparing Canadian areas (except British Columbia) with U.S. areas, all Canadian regions have lower wages than all U.S. regions. For example, wages in U.S. areas run anywhere from ten to forty percent higher than in Ontario, the Canadian province of heaviest industrial specialization. Even the exceptional Canadian province, British Columbia, has a wage level lower than most U.S. regions, and much lower than the adjacent U.S. Pacific Northwest. Moreover, the present discount on the Canadian dollar effectively increases this Canadian wage advantage.

3

MARKET PROXIMITY

In a free trade North American area, Canadian locations would necessarily be forced to compete with possible industry locations in the United States. Because of geographical factors, it might be assumed that Canadian locations would be at a disadvantage in this competition in terms of the higher transport costs that firms located there would incur in moving goods into rich U.S. markets. The objective of this chapter is to evaluate the attractiveness of various Canadian locations as sites for servicing North American markets and compare their situation with similar locations in the United States that might be chosen as alternatives.

Before such an evaluation is possible, however, it is necessary to estimate the markets that a new firm entering an industry is most likely to capture. For example, it is not possible to conclude that Ontario is a better or worse location than California without some evaluation of the markets that might be serviced both from Ontario and California. It is certainly evident that firms in these two locations would not necessarily service identical markets: presumably a new firm locating in Toronto would service the Ontario and U.S. Midwest markets more heavily, whereas a new firm in San Francisco would service West Coast markets more heavily. It is simply not possible to evaluate the transportation costs that would be incurred, from either location, in shipping goods to market without a specific statement of where these markets are likely to be. Attention is therefore turned to what must be regarded as a keystone study of Part I — an evaluation of potential markets of a new firm locating in a specific area.

Proximity to markets has been recognized in classic location theory as one of the primary influences on the location of new firms. Moreover, it may be concluded from an examination of current literature that market proximity is now regarded (along with labor costs and conditions) as the most important location influence.[1] Nevertheless, present attempts by theorists to evaluate locations in terms of the market potential they provide have not reached an advanced stage.

There are probably many reasons for this. In the first place there is a considerable mix of diverse motives that might lead a firm to locate close to markets. The most obvious has already been pointed out: the transportation costs involved in shipping products to the point of sale will be less. But there are other reasons that are difficult to treat explicitly: the nearer the market, the more rapid the delivery and the more effective the service provided; on-the-spot knowledge of changing market conditions may allow faster and more efficient production changeover and tighter inventory control; there may be advertising advantages in having production facilities close to customers; the firm may be able, in a minor way, to take advantage of any parochial goodwill towards local manufacturing operations; and in some cases, local politicians and chambers of commerce may even become advertisers. Any one of these factors may or may not be too significant in any specific instance; however, it must be concluded that the tendency for firms to search out attractive markets is based on a mixture of motives. Probably the major reason for the limited theoretical advances in this area is that, with one exception, the above influences attracting firms to market do not lend themselves to quantitative measurement.

The one exception, of course, is transportation costs. But, as has been argued earlier, such an evaluation of transport costs requires a specification of the markets the new firm in a specific location is likely to service. The converse proposition is also true; little can be said about the firm's likely market without some reference to the transportation costs involved in shipping the product. Obviously, if a firm is producing a good with a heavy proportion

---

[1] See, for example, the results of questionnaire surveys of businessmen: "Plant Site Survey," Special Questionnaire, *Business Week*, 1961.

of its value going to transport costs, its market will be spatially limited as a consequence, but if the good involves minimal transport costs, then markets may be spread widely over space. The basic problem, therefore, is that transport costs cannot be estimated without a specific market pattern, and markets cannot be specified without reference to transportation costs. The simplest way of resolving this difficulty is to assume that the new firm will service an equal percentage of all markets. If Baltimore is considered as a location, it could be assumed that the firm might capture a fixed proportion of each market in the United States: by assumption, it would capture k percent of the Washington market, k percent of the Los Angeles market, and so on.

However, it should be recognized that, except in very special cases, this assumption is not realistic. The very nature of interspatial competition tends to contradict it. Because of its advantage of proximity, it is to be expected that the Baltimore firm will service the Washington market more heavily, leaving the Los Angeles market to firms located on the West Coast. This would result in lower total transport costs, both for the industry as a whole and for each firm individually. If this shortcut assumption of fixed market proportion is used, it will tend, to a greater or lesser degree, to result in an overstatement of transport costs. Such an assumption, therefore, can at best provide a basis for an extreme upper limit estimate, with the relevance of the estimate depending upon the reality of the assumption of fixed market proportions.

A more realistic specification of the markets that a firm in a specific location is likely to service is a basic problem that has been treated by one of the authors elsewhere,[2] and the model used is reproduced in Appendix E. This model is based on the assumption that a firm's ability to capture a market depends not only on the obvious transport cost advantages of closeness but also on all the other advantages cited above — servicing, advertising, and so on. It is recognized explicitly in this model that the motivation to get close to markets cannot be considered independently of the

[2] Ronald J. Wonnacott, *Manufacturing Costs and the Comparative Advantage of United States Regions* (Upper Midwest Economic Study, University of Minnesota, Study Paper 9, April 1963), p. 70.

spatial pattern of the firm's established competition. New York may have the richest total market; however, the accessible market for a new firm in Chicago may be greater if there are twenty competing producers already located in New York but none in Chicago. Consequently, the model in Appendix E is an attempt to advance location theory simultaneously in two directions — toward a more explicit recognition of the desire by the firm to get closer to rich markets and toward a more satisfactory description of the influence of existing patterns of established competition on the behavior of a firm.

The evaluation in this chapter of the relative attractiveness of various regions is the direct result of the application of the model in Appendix E to data on the Canadian and U.S. economies in 1958. It should be emphasized that this is designed to take account only of the influence of market proximity; it completely leaves out of consideration many other important location influences (such as labor costs), which are treated elsewhere. The solution is useful in two senses: it provides an independent evaluation of the relative desirability of various locations in terms of their market proximity; and it also yields the benchmark estimate of the spatial distribution of markets that is necessary to estimate transport costs.

For the purposes of this empirical investigation, the eighteen regions into which the North American economy was divided in Chapter 1 are used.[3] Each of these regions is considered to be both a demand (or market) center and also a supply (or industry location) center — although this equivalence of demand and supply points is not required by the model. It is obvious from the degree of aggregation that has been necessary that the sixteen industry grouping does not allow precise predictions on the behavior of a specific firm within any of these industrial sectors; however, such a rough breakdown does allow a test of how much these influences vary between broad industrial categories.

This model is now applied to estimate the possible spatial distribution of sales by a new firm locating in a specific Canadian re-

---

[3] In all empirical interregional studies the results are unavoidably dependent to some degree on the area definition. The present study is no exception to this rule.

gion, and in each of the other regions in the North American economy in turn. Before market shares can be estimated for a new producer, however, two sets of data are required: the location of the markets for each good and the place where the good is presently being produced.

The Location of Markets

The market for each good in each area was estimated by using exhibited patterns of interindustry and consumption demand, along with information on the spatial distribution of user industries and consumers. In addition it was necessary to take explicit account of the 1958 export-import flows between Canada and the United States.[4] The estimated percentage of total North American demand for (or sales of) each good in each area is shown in Table 8. The precise techniques in these computations are shown in Appendix F. The breakdown of these sales figures, both in terms of domestically produced goods and imported goods, is shown in Appendix G. The figure for imported goods consumed in Canada in each area is derived by taking the total imports of that good and distributing them to Canadian areas according to the spatial pattern of domestic Canadian consumption; the same method is used for distributing U.S. imports.

There are several observations that are warranted from Table 8 and Appendix G. The proportion of Canadian sales in the total North American market is very small indeed. In fact, the total Canadian market for every good is substantially less than the market in the largest U.S. region, the Middle Atlantic area. This difference is not surprising in view of the relative size of the Canadian and U.S. economies. The influence of relative size is important in explaining another outstanding feature in Appendix G. A large proportion of market demand in each Canadian region is satisfied by imports from the United States, but only a small percentage of each regional U.S. market is satisfied by imports from Canada. Whenever a small segment (in this case Canada) is cut out of a large economic area (North America), then the same pat-

---

[4] It was also assumed that the share of North American markets going to foreign (i.e., other than U.S. or Canadian) suppliers would remain constant.

TABLE 8. Estimated Percentage of the Market for Each Good in Each Region, 1958.[a]

Manufacturing sector[b]	Maritimes	Quebec	Ontario	Prairies	British Columbia	Upper Midwest	West Lake	East Lake	Lower Midwest	Middle Atlantic	New England	South	Capital	Florida	Southwest	Mountain	Pacific Southwest	Pacific Northwest
Food	0.4	1.5	2.5	1.2	0.6	3.3	10.1	8.9	7.0	21.2	4.3	11.1	2.3	2.1	8.3	3.4	9.2	2.4
Tobacco	0.5	3.4	4.1	1.3	0.8	3.1	8.9	8.4	7.2	20.6	3.7	10.3	2.2	2.0	7.6	4.9	8.9	2.3
Textiles	0.3	4.4	3.3	0.8	0.4	1.3	7.2	6.9	3.5	33.0	5.7	17.2	2.1	1.0	4.6	0.8	6.3	1.4
Apparel	0.4	1.4	2.2	0.9	0.6	2.4	10.0	8.0	5.3	27.5	4.5	11.2	2.7	1.9	7.7	1.9	9.1	2.4
Wood products	0.5	2.0	3.2	1.4	1.1	2.5	10.8	9.2	5.1	20.0	4.3	11.9	2.2	2.0	7.7	2.0	9.4	4.9
Paper	0.3	1.6	2.3	0.6	0.5	2.2	12.8	9.7	4.6	23.4	5.6	12.6	2.0	2.4	7.8	1.8	7.2	2.8
Printing	0.4	1.6	2.6	1.0	0.6	2.5	11.4	9.6	5.5	24.6	4.4	10.1	2.6	2.1	7.8	1.9	9.2	2.4
Electrical equipment	0.3	1.5	2.7	0.9	0.6	2.2	14.2	12.7	6.0	22.7	4.1	9.3	2.3	1.6	6.4	1.5	9.2	2.3
Chemicals	0.3	1.4	2.4	0.9	0.5	2.6	10.1	9.5	5.5	25.0	4.3	14.2	2.1	1.6	7.8	2.5	7.5	1.8
Petroleum products	0.5	2.1	3.6	1.8	0.9	2.4	11.3	8.5	4.7	19.3	2.6	7.2	1.9	1.3	17.9	2.0	10.2	2.0
Rubber and plastics	0.3	1.4	2.7	1.1	0.5	2.3	12.9	13.1	7.2	19.9	4.3	9.6	2.3	1.6	6.8	1.6	9.8	2.7
Leather goods	0.3	1.7	2.5	0.8	0.5	1.9	9.8	7.8	5.9	24.9	11.9	11.1	2.3	1.6	6.2	1.4	7.4	1.9
Nonmetallic mineral products	0.4	1.7	2.9	1.3	0.7	2.3	12.2	11.1	5.8	22.1	3.8	10.4	2.3	1.9	7.7	2.2	9.0	2.1
Metallic products	0.3	1.7	3.3	0.9	0.6	1.9	15.6	13.7	5.4	23.2	3.6	8.5	2.1	1.4	6.0	1.6	8.2	2.1
Transportation equipment	0.4	1.4	2.6	0.9	0.6	2.2	12.8	14.1	7.5	19.0	3.5	9.1	2.4	1.7	6.9	1.5	10.5	2.9
Miscellaneous	0.3	0.9	1.5	0.6	0.4	2.5	11.7	9.9	5.4	25.5	4.7	10.8	2.6	2.0	7.7	1.8	9.8	2.3

[a] A breakdown of these markets is presented in Appendix G.
[b] See Table 1, note a.

tern may be expected; the small area will have its markets heavily serviced by imports, but the large area will not. This would be just as true, for example, for California if that state were to break away from the United States.

Since final consumption accounts for a large proportion of the use of each good, markets tend to be associated fairly closely with regional income levels. There are, however, deviations from this general pattern due to the existence of important, regionally concentrated industries which constitute major markets for semifinished products. For example, the market for primary metals is heavily centered in the Chicago-Detroit-Cleveland area, the market for leather in New England, the market for textiles in the South, and the market for petroleum and coal products in the U.S. Southwest.

Deviations are also evident in the Canadian case: although markets for apparel are closely associated with final consumption, it is not true of markets in the textile sector, which produces semifinished products that are used as inputs by the apparel industry. Markets for textiles, therefore, are heavily centered in Quebec, where the apparel industry is concentrated, and the textile industry is almost absent from the Prairies and British Columbia.

The Pattern of Established Competition

The second set of data required for the model in Appendix E is the existing pattern of competitive producers. The spatial distribution of producers of each good [5] is shown in Table 9. It is evident that these figures on regional production levels are less closely associated with population and income than the figures on regional markets in Table 8 and are therefore less predictable and vary over a wider range. For example, market proportions for various goods

[5] There are three alternative indicators that yield approximately the same spatial distribution of production; the first, based on value of shipments of each good in each region, estimated from the 1958 U.S. *Census of Manufactures* and D.B.S., *The Manufacturing Industries of Canada,* 1958, Sections B to F, is shown in Table 9; the second, based on value added in each region, is used as the basis for the rankings shown in Table 13 below; and the third is based on employment in each area. The last was used as the data on spatial distribution for the model because information on average U.S. employment per establishment was available.

TABLE 9. *Estimated Percentage of Production of Each Good in Each Region, 1958.*

Manufacturing sector[a]	Maritimes	Quebec	Ontario	Prairies	British Columbia	Upper Midwest	West Lake	East Lake	Lower Midwest	Middle Atlantic	New England	South	Capital	Florida	Southwest	Mountain	Pacific Southwest	Pacific Northwest
Food	0.4	1.7	2.7	1.1	0.6	4.4	6.0	7.3	11.1	18.6	2.8	10.0	1.8	1.8	6.8	11.8	8.9	2.4
Tobacco	–	9.0	6.6	–	–	–	b	1.4	–	12.0	0.2	66.4	–	4.2	–	–	b	–
Textiles	0.1	3.8	2.9	0.2	0.1	0.3	1.8	1.4	b	20.8	11.3	54.8	0.4	0.4	0.8	b	0.9	0.2
Apparel	b	3.3	1.4	0.4	0.1	0.6	4.9	3.1	2.9	53.0	5.0	13.0	2.5	0.4	3.4	0.2	5.1	0.8
Wood products	0.5	2.2	2.5	0.7	4.0	2.1	9.2	6.1	2.3	11.3	3.6	18.7	1.0	1.6	6.4	1.9	10.2	15.5
Paper	1.1	4.4	4.4	0.4	1.3	1.8	13.3	9.3	2.3	18.2	8.0	15.0	1.0	3.1	7.1	0.1	4.2	4.8
Printing	0.2	1.6	3.0	0.6	0.4	2.2	15.1	9.0	5.0	35.7	4.6	5.5	2.8	1.2	4.1	1.1	6.8	1.3
Electrical equipment	–	1.3	3.5	0.3	0.1	0.8	22.9	13.6	3.7	30.1	5.7	7.4	1.4	1.8	1.6	0.2	6.7	0.6
Chemicals	0.1	1.6	3.1	0.3	0.3	1.5	11.2	10.3	3.8	25.2	2.1	18.3	2.4	1.8	10.9	0.8	4.9	1.3
Petroleum products	–	2.8	2.6	1.7	0.8	1.9	10.4	6.0	3.4	14.1	0.3	1.4	1.1	0.1	36.4	2.2	13.3	1.4
Rubber and plastics	–	1.2	4.4	0.1	b	0.4	12.5	28.2	1.0	20.5	10.8	8.5	2.5	b	2.1	–	7.7	–
Leather goods	0.1	2.9	3.1	0.1	0.1	–	6.8	3.0	8.6	29.5	31.1	9.9	1.4	0.3	1.2	–	1.9	–
Nonmetallic mineral products	0.2	1.7	3.0	0.8	0.2	1.7	12.6	13.6	5.6	22.0	3.1	11.6	2.1	2.3	7.8	1.9	8.4	1.5
Metallic products	0.1	1.6	3.3	0.2	0.3	1.1	21.5	18.4	3.3	27.0	3.5	5.9	1.8	0.6	3.8	0.9	5.5	1.0
Transportation equipment	0.2	1.0	4.0	0.2	0.1	0.5	15.2	26.9	10.3	11.8	1.2	4.2	2.1	0.3	3.3	0.2	14.3	4.1
Miscellaneous	0.7	0.6	1.5	0.3	0.1	2.6	12.0	7.8	2.8	38.7	8.1	2.9	1.0	0.9	1.8	1.7	16.1	0.3

Source: U.S. statistics were obtained from Department of Commerce, *Census of Manufactures, 1958*, Vol. III, Area Statistics. Canadian statistics were obtained from D.B.S., *Manufacturing Industries of Canada, 1958*.

[a] See Table 1, note a.

b More than zero, but less than 0.05.

in the U.S. Middle Atlantic area fall within the range of about twenty percent to just over thirty percent. However, production proportions in that region are much less stable — varying from a low of about eleven percent in the transportation equipment sector (which is concentrated around Detroit) to a high of fifty-three percent in the apparel industry (which is centered in New York City). Similarly, the East Lake area is the site of over one quarter of U.S. production of transportation equipment; however, only about one percent of U.S. textile manufacturing takes place in that area. Similar wide variations are evident in other regions; for example, well over one third of U.S. production of petroleum and coal products is centered in the Southwest, an area in which the textile industry is almost nonexistent. These regionally concentrated industries — textiles and apparel in New York and the South, petroleum and coal products in the Southwest, and transportation equipment in the East Lake area — all generate a heavy market demand for intermediate goods. This demand explains in turn the instances referred to above in which markets for intermediate goods deviate from regional income levels. This same phenomenon is shown in the Canadian example cited earlier; the concentration of the apparel industry in Quebec explains heavy market demand for textiles in that province.

Potential Sales in Each Market

The data in hand, it is now feasible to apply the model of competitive location in Appendix E.[6] Because it was not possible to

---

[6] Total market in each area (S^m) is substituted into the market potential equation (10) in Appendix E to compute the total sales potential of a firm located at k:

$$k_S = \sum_m S^m \left[1 + \sum_j n_j \left(\frac{k d^m}{i d^m} \right)^q \right]^{-1}.$$

The parameters in this estimating equation were derived as follows: the population center of gravity of each area was used to locate each of the eighteen areas on a single geographic point in space; highway mileage was used to represent distance between any pair of these points. Market center and production center of any area were assumed to be the same point. However, the distance involved in servicing the market in any area by a producer in that same area is not zero. (If it were, the model could not be applied.) Instead it is the average distance between the production center and the

specify precisely how important distance is as an influence on the sale of each good, three alternative assumptions were used: first, the limiting assumption that distance is of no influence; second, an assumption that distance is highly influential; and third, a median assumption falling between these two extremes.[7]

The results are presented in Table 10. It should be evident in applying such a theoretical model that it has been necessary to leave out of consideration many of the institutional influences (e.g., subsidiary-parent sales) that normally affect the spatial distribution of a firm's markets; therefore, the numerical results shown in this table should not be given precise interpretation, nor are they useful in predicting a firm's sales without specific reference to whatever institutional influences affect market behavior. Nevertheless, the model results do throw considerable light on the advantages or disadvantages of certain areas in terms of their market proximity.

The market potential from each comparison area is expressed in Table 10 as a percent greater ($+$) or less ($-$) than the potential market from the Ontario location. For every industry and comparison area there are three estimates, each based on one of the three alternative assumptions about distance orientation. However, only two of these estimates are shown in the table. The third estimate in each case is zero because we have made the assumption that distance does not influence markets; as a consequence, potential sales from all locations are equal, and all differences in market potential between locations become zero. *Although this set of zeros is not included in the table, it should be visualized as a bound.*

The two estimates for each location and industry that are in the body of this table are the median estimate (that markets are only

---

individual markets that have to be serviced in that area. (Note: each market is weighted by its population.)

For each industry the number of competitors already established in each area (n_j) was computed by dividing total area employment in that industry by the United States average employment per establishment. U.S. rather than Canadian employment per establishment was used as the basis of these calculations, in line with the assumption of this study that U.S. but not Canadian production is now rationalized to service the North American market.

[7] These assumptions are represented by setting q equal to 0, 1 and ½ respectively in equation (10) in Appendix E.

TABLE 10. Percentage That Estimated Market Potential from Comparison Area Is Greater or Less (—) than from Ontario, 1958.[a]

Manufacturing sector[b]	Maritimes	Quebec	Ontario	Prairies	British Columbia	Upper Midwest	West Lake	East Lake	Lower Midwest	Middle Atlantic	New England	South	Capital	Florida	Southwest	Mountain	Pacific Southwest	Pacific Northwest
Food	-36	-8	0	-33	-33	-14	21	9	-6	12	2	-6	16	-22	-20	-25	-24	-33
	-61	-6	0	-53	-21	-22	69	21	-7	30	18	-9	48	-32	-29	-38	-11	-34
Tobacco	-37	-8	0	-30	-26	-13	19	7	-4	5	-4	-10	8	-26	-19	-20	-15	-28
	-63	-19	0	-43	50	-14	92	15	1	5	-14	-23	20	-45	-25	-17	56	2
Textiles	-37	2	0	-40	-40	-25	8	4	-16	20	7	-10	20	-29	-30	-35	-31	-41
	-64	19	0	-59	4	-39	57	8	-24	38	11	-23	49	-49	-44	-48	14	-32
Apparel	-35	-9	0	-31	-29	-13	24	10	-5	13	1	-5	16	-22	-17	-23	-16	-28
	-61	-15	0	-45	47	-15	93	25	-1	19	4	-7	35	-30	-20	-27	32	3
Wood products	-37	-7	0	-35	-32	-18	18	8	-10	11	12	-9	15	-25	-23	-29	-26	-31
	-64	-6	0	-59	-41	-34	46	12	-21	29	12	-21	48	-43	-40	-48	-22	-44
Paper	-36	-8	0	-34	-33	-16	24	11	-7	13	4	-4	16	-21	-20	-26	-24	-32
	-60	-11	0	-52	-20	-22	69	24	-6	33	16	-2	49	-25	-23	-34	10	-23
Printing	-36	-8	0	-33	-31	-16	19	9	-7	13	2	-6	17	-22	-19	-25	-20	-31
	-60	-2	0	-50	7	-22	49	18	-8	28	13	-8	46	-28	-24	-34	13	-16
Electrical equipment	-37	-9	0	-34	-31	-16	22	12	-6	11	-1	-3	14	-24	-21	-24	-20	-31
	-62	-5	0	-49	40	-24	48	22	-7	22	-5	-11	41	-32	-26	-31	14	-5
Chemicals	-36	-9	0	-33	-33	-14	21	10	-5	11	2	-3	15	-22	-19	-26	-23	-33
	-61	-17	0	-50	2	-19	63	20	-5	24	19	-6	38	-34	-25	-35	12	-24
Petroleum products	-37	-7	0	-34	-33	-17	18	7	-9	9	-3	-10	12	-25	-17	-26	-24	-34
	-64	-2	0	-56	-14	-33	37	9	-22	9	4	-22	40	-43	-31	-45	-21	-39
Rubber and plastics	-37	-10	0	-31	-29	-13	25	12	-3	8	-2	-6	11	-23	-18	-23	-16	-27
	-61	-9	0	-44	50	-16	65	21	5	16	-1	-7	32	-30	-20	-29	26	13
Leather goods	-35	-8	0	-34	-32	-16	22	9	-6	12	8	-5	15	-23	-20	-26	-21	-32
	-60	-12	0	-46	45	-19	86	24	-1	20	11	-3	36	-28	-21	-29	41	-1
Nonmetallic mineral products	-37	-10	0	-33	-31	-16	22	10	-7	11	0	-7	15	-24	-21	-25	-22	-32
	-62	-19	0	-50	22	-24	59	19	-9	25	10	-12	43	-34	-28	-35	6	-18
Metallic products	-37	-9	0	-35	-33	-17	23	11	-8	10	-1	-9	13	-26	-22	-28	-23	-33
	-63	-8	0	-53	14	-28	56	18	-12	23	6	-15	39	-37	-32	-38	6	-20
Transportation equipment	-37	-9	0	-34	-33	-16	24	12	-5	10	0	-7	14	-24	-21	-27	-24	-33
	-61	-5	0	-54	-13	-25	68	21	-6	28	17	-11	47	-32	-31	-41	-15	-31
Miscellaneous	-37	-9	0	-35	-33	-17	23	11	-7	9	-2	-8	13	-25	-22	-28	-24	-33
	-62	-4	0	-54	3	-27	60	18	-9	22	9	-14	40	-35	-32	-42	-11	-27

[a] The first of the two estimates provided in each category is based on the assumption that markets are moderately influenced by distance (i.e., q = 0.5); the second estimate is based on the assumption that markets are more highly influenced by distance (i.e., q = 1). [b] See Table 1, note a.

moderately affected by distance), which appears first, and the other extreme estimate (that markets are highly influenced by distance), which appears below. It is evident that the first and second figures in each element generally exhibit some degree of difference and, in some cases, quite a marked degree of dissimilarity. Therefore, it may be concluded that the advantage or disadvantage of an area often depends on how strongly it is assumed that markets are distance oriented. Nevertheless, regardless of how heavily this distance orientation is assumed, certain broad conclusions are warranted on the basis of this analysis.

In terms of potential market penetration, the four areas (West Lake, East Lake, Middle Atlantic, and Capital) that fall along a broad axis running from Chicago to the eastern seaboard of the United States represent by far the most attractive locations.[8] The best Canadian region — Ontario — is geographically adjacent and ranks (along with New England) next in North America as an attractive location. Ontario and New England are similarly situated, since both lie on the northern border of this Chicago-New York axis.

To analyze the Ontario location in more detail: the geographical central point of this province has been specified[9] as a point close to Toronto because of heavy population concentration in that city. As a production location, there are only two minor disadvantages that prevent Toronto from being as well situated as any city between Chicago and New York: it lies somewhat to the north, and it is slightly isolated by the juxtaposition of the Great Lakes. These disadvantages, however, do not apply to the same degree to the area of Ontario lying to the south and west. In fact the broad axis running from Chicago to New York not only passes through Detroit and Cleveland; it passes through the area between Windsor and Niagara Falls in southwestern Ontario. As a potential location, therefore, this extremity of the province appears to be almost as well situated as the most attractive areas in the

----

[8] In addition to its proximity to large East Coast markets, another reason for the high ranking of the Capital area is the comparative absence of competitors in this area.

[9] See footnote 6.

United States, which are immediately adjacent. It is certainly more attractively situated with respect to market proximity than most areas of the United States — including the U.S. Pacific Coast, Mountain states, Southwest and the more distant regions in the Midwest.

In a few industries — under special assumptions — there are two areas on the Pacific Coast that represent exceptions to this proposition. The first is the Pacific Southwest (California); a comparison of Ontario with California indicates that, in certain industries, Ontario's situation is better if distance is assumed a minor influence but increasingly worsens as distance is assumed to be increasingly important. The former observation reflects the fact that Ontario is closer to the major U.S. markets; the latter reflects the fact that California has a much larger local market than Ontario. As distance is assumed to be more and more important — and as producers tend to be cornered in local markets — both Ontario and California increasingly lose sales in the major eastern U.S. markets. California producers are left to exploit their own substantial local markets, and Ontario producers are left with their smaller local markets. (It should be noted, however, that there are a number of industries in which this pattern does not hold and in which Ontario is preferred to California regardless of the assumption that is made about distance orientation. This is true of food and beverages, lumber and wood products, petroleum and coal products, and transportation equipment.)

The other exception is British Columbia. The same phenomenon seems to be at work in this case: the more distance is assumed to be important as a determinant of market penetration, the more British Columbia appears to be at an advantage rather than at a disadvantage vis-à-vis Ontario. The B.C. case, however, is not strictly parallel to the California case. Consequently, it must be explained, at least in part, in one of two other ways: relative to the size of its domestic market, there are very few producers in British Columbia; alternatively, the B.C. market is a much more concentrated market (centered in Victoria and Vancouver) than the market of the U.S. Pacific Northwest (which is spread over a number of large urban areas). In terms of available local market,

Vancouver appears to be an attractive production location. The local market around Vancouver is, of course, large; in addition, Vancouver is actually closer than many large Pacific Northwest cities to the largest single market in the Pacific Northwest around Seattle.

Quebec is somewhat less favorably situated than either Ontario or New England because it lies just beyond these areas in terms of the richest U.S. markets: Ontario is closer to Chicago, and New England is closer to New York. The Canadian Prairies and, to a lesser degree, the Maritimes are the least attractive Canadian regions in terms of market disadvantages; they are also less well situated than all U.S. areas. It should be noted, however, that the isolation of the Maritimes from adequate markets under free trade would almost certainly be substantially less than its isolation under present circumstances of North American protection. Current U.S. protection cuts it off from rich potential markets in Boston and New York. At the same time, it is too far from Toronto and Montreal for the Canadian tariff to provide compensating market advantages.

Conclusions

This chapter has been devoted to evaluating the desirability of various industry locations in terms of their proximity to markets. Two location influences have been simultaneously taken into account: the desire of producers to locate close to major markets and their desire to avoid areas already heavily serviced by competitors. On the basis of these criteria, Ontario and, to a lesser degree, Quebec are the best situated regions in Canada by a substantial margin. Ontario is at a disadvantage in comparison with only a limited area in the United States, that is, the heavily industrialized area from Chicago to the East Coast of the United States. Otherwise Ontario is to be preferred to all other regions of the United States — exceptions occurring only in certain isolated industries, given special assumptions about marketing behavior. In general, Ontario is favorably located for the production of goods that may be marketed widely over space because of its proximity to the richest North American markets along the Chicago-New

York axis. However, because of the relatively small size of the local Ontario market, the province is somewhat less favorably situated for the production of goods that must be distributed heavily in local markets.

In the next four chapters additional spatial and demographic influences will be analyzed in detail. Specifically, we shall continue to test the hypothesis that Canadian locations would face a substantial disadvantage in competition with the U.S. because of these influences. Readers with a superior grasp of North American demography and economic geography may wish only to scan these chapters at an accelerated pace. Similarly international trade theorists, accustomed to arguing factor proportions and prices, may wish to move rather quickly from the labor analysis to the discussion of capital in Chapter 8. But in laying out these road directions we are not recommending a complete detour around these chapters. They deal with key issues, and the chief conclusions of this book depend on the results of this inquiry. Indeed, these chapters should be carefully examined by Canadians who have become accustomed to accepting uncritically the notion that these influences prevent effective Canadian competition with the U.S.

4

MARKET TRANSPORTATION COSTS

In this chapter the extent to which differences in transportation costs may affect total costs between various locations is examined in detail. It should be recognized that the transport cost analysis of the optimal location of a specific firm or plant must take into account transport costs of shipping output to market and also costs of shipping in inputs and resources from their supply sites. For the firm, therefore, the geometrical analysis involving selection of the optimal production point within the space defined by resource sites and markets may be appropriate.[1] However, for the analysis that focuses not on a locating firm but on the relative desirability of various regions, such a procedure is quite out of the question. It is simply not feasible to work out the large number of solutions required, each specific to an individual firm or economic activity. Instead the problem becomes: Which North American locations are best situated in terms of low transport costs involved in shipping goods to market and in acquiring resource and material inputs? The first part of the question is dealt with in this chapter, and the latter in succeeding chapters.

In order to estimate the differences in transport charges incurred in servicing markets from various sites, it is necessary to estimate the total transport costs incurred from each location; the estimate of total transport costs requires a specification of transport rates and the markets it is presumed a new firm in each location might service.

[1] See, for example, M. L. Greenhut, *Plant Location in Theory and Practice* (Chapel Hill, University of North Carolina Press, 1956) pp. 115–116.

The Spatial Distribution of Markets

The spatial pattern of markets that a firm may exploit necessarily becomes a cornerstone in any analysis of transport costs. If a firm moves into a specific location, where is its output likely to be shipped? In answering this, the model of competitive location in Appendix E becomes relevant, and there are three cases that require careful distinction.

One limiting assumption is that distance is of no importance in influencing sales and that therefore the firm's shipments are dictated by the national pattern of demand for the product it produces. In this case the firm will incur maximum transportation costs. (Its transportation costs can be higher only if its sales tend to increase with distance and if, as a consequence, it services distant markets more heavily. In the absence of very special institutional arrangements — which have been assumed away in this study — there is no reason to expect this type of marketing pattern.) Consequently, the assumption that distance does not affect sales and that a firm will service all markets equally[2] is a reasonable basis for deriving maximum transport costs from each location.

Second, if the firm is able to take advantage of its proximity to increase its penetration of relatively close markets and consequently disregard its distant markets (in which the firms may be at a cost disadvantage), then its average transportation costs per unit of sales will necessarily be less. In the extreme case of a firm producing for an exclusively local market, its transportation costs will be less again, and it may safely be assumed that the difference in transport costs between two locations servicing local markets approaches zero. For example, the cost of servicing the Cleveland area from a Cleveland location might be assumed equal to the cost of servicing the Toronto area from a Toronto location.

However, a firm with a market that is completely localized in this way is by definition of almost no interest in a study of comparative advantage and changing patterns of production and distribution in a Canadian-U.S. free trade area. To the extent that such a firm is completely distance-protected, any existing interarea

---

[2] That is, the same proportion of the total sales in each market. (In equation (10) in App. E, q is set equal to zero.)

differences in labor and tax costs may also be assumed of no consequence in a comparative advantage study, and there is little point in analyzing the regional cost structure of such an industry. Firms will locate in a specific area not because of comparative cost advantages but because a local market exists there, and their approximate number and size may be predicted a priori by an examination of the size of the market in the region. Localized operations of this nature will not be affected by changes in commercial policy such as free trade because they are already regionally protected, and as a consequence their products would not in any case enter international trade.[3] The only effect of a change in commercial policy on such firms is a very indirect one: insofar as freer trade might result in a substantial expansion of *other* industries in the region, the resulting growth of the local market might generate an expansion of this type of firm. In the event of free trade, therefore, the changing position of these firms would not affect the overall pattern of industrial activity in either country; instead expansion or contraction of these firms would be entirely a result of changes that have occurred in the other industrial sectors that are subject to open competition in the two countries. Localized firms of this kind, therefore, are of no direct concern since their changing patterns should fall out of the solution derived for firms that are subject to interspatial competition; as a consequence the zero lower limit of differences in transport costs between regions applying to these firms is of little interest in this study.

Third, analysis of comparative advantage is relevant to firms that at least partially face outside competition in their own area and penetrate the distant markets of their competitors. Since these firms do service distant markets, transport cost differences between regions will exist. The question is: Can a useful minimum for interregional transport cost differences be defined for firms of this kind?

Given this objective, the behavior described in the market potential model in the previous chapter is relevant. Whereas any firm may service all markets to a degree, it is recognized that a firm will tend to service close markets more intensively than dis-

[3] An exception might be a firm producing a local good in a border city — for example, a bakery in Niagara Falls, Ontario.

tant markets, both out of preference and out of greater ability to compete on a price and service basis. Moreover, this preference for proximate markets may be assumed in a very strong form.[4] On this basis the firm's market penetration from any potential location may be estimated, and the cost of servicing this market becomes the basis for computing interarea differences in transport costs.

Basically, therefore, in this transport cost study the first and third assumptions about the spatial distribution of markets will be used: that all markets are serviced equally and that proximate markets are serviced more heavily.

Transport Rates

Turning to the other cornerstone requirement for such an analysis — transportation rates — we immediately encounter several rather perplexing difficulties. The complexities of the North American transport rate structure are well known. For example, in comparing two shipment points it is often the case that the closer point pays a per mile transportation rate which is not only higher

[4] That is, q is set equal to 1 in estimating equation (10) in Appendix E. In terms of the model of competitive location in the previous chapter, the three cases cited above reduced to the following:

(a) If q is set equal to 0 the result is the naive market assumption often used in location studies: all markets are serviced equally, generating a maximum estimate of transport cost differences between alternative locations.

(b) If q is set equal to ∞, this is the assumption of the Chamberlin-Hotelling approach; once a firm gets closer to a market than all competitors, it captures the entire market — and for precisely this reason all firms become cornered in their own local markets.

(c) If $q = 1$ it is recognized that firms concentrate heavily in local markets but still service distant markets as well. The estimate of transport cost differences in this case will fall beween the two cases above. In using this as a benchmark estimate of transport costs it is recognized that this places heavy reliance on distance as a determinant of market shares. However, it is true that distance might be assumed an even stronger influence — for example, q might be set equal to a value between 1 and ∞. Alternatively, a restraint might be imposed that only markets within a 500 mile radius may be serviced. The difficulty is that this solution will hinge on the definition of these arbitrary dividing lines. For example, if the Chicago market is centered 450 miles from the Upper Midwest, these Upper Midwest markets stand or fall on whether 400 or 500 miles is used as the arbitrary boundary.

but higher to a degree sufficient to drive total transport charges above those of a more distant area. There is a natural tendency for such a study to slide off into a morass of detail in examining peculiarities of individual transport rates. To avoid this, it has been necessary at a number of stages to make quite arbitrary assumptions in order to arrive at a solution, given the time and resources available for this study. Whenever feasible, alternative assumptions about transport rates were tested and it was encouraging that the results usually turned out to be roughly equivalent. This suggests that, in terms of total transport costs, vagaries in the transport rate structure are likely to be self-cancelling, or of secondary importance.[5]

Problems involved in transport costs are familiar; consequently they will simply be listed, along with the arbitrary assumption that was made in each case.

The first obvious difficulty is that goods may be shipped by several means — by rail, truck, ship, pipeline, or air; rail rates were used throughout this study on the ground that these were the only rates available in detail for industries and regions and because it is likely that transport charges incurred by other means of shipment (except by air)[6] are likely to be reasonably competitive.

(Moreover, if it was evident a priori that the rail rate was not the most relevant cost and if the appropriate alternative rate was both available and substantially different, then this other rate was used. For example, in Chapter 6 seaway rates were assumed for shipments of iron ore from Labrador up the St. Lawrence River, and pipeline rates were used for shipments of petroleum.)

Because of terminal loading and unloading charges, the cost per ton mile tends to decrease with length of haul. Nevertheless, for shipments of any length in the United States it was necessary to use one figure — the average cost per ton mile.[7] However, a more

---

[5] Even if the twists and turns of the present rate structure were important, it does not necessarily follow that they should be used in such a study; to the degree that transport costs are becoming less arbitrary and more closely related to distance, it may be unwise to base an analysis on nonpermanent peculiarities of the present rate structure.

[6] An insignificant proportion of freight is now shipped by this means.

[7] United States Inter-state Commerce Commission, *Carload Waybill Statistics, State to State Distribution*, 1956. Based on a one percent sample of shipments.

reasonable assumption was possible in the Canadian case. Substantial information on the regional rate structure is available in Canada[8] — for example, the average cost per ton mile in shipping a good from the Maritimes to Quebec, or from the Maritimes to British Columbia. Examination of this rate structure verifies two earlier observations: first, the longer the distance the lower the average cost per ton mile,[9] and second, the inconsistency and lack of pattern characterizing the rate structure.

There are three important subsidies built into the Canadian rail structure that should be recognized explicitly. Each is designed as a subsidy, not to the railroads but to specific industries or regions that benefit as a result of lower rail rates. The Maritimes Freight Rate Act allows for a subsidy for shipments from the Maritimes which terminate either in the Maritimes or points west in Canada. The Freight Rates Reduction Act of 1959 provides for a reduction in noncompetitive rail rates following an across-the-board increase in rail rates in late 1958. The Bridge subsidy of 1951 provides for a reduction in all Sudbury-Lakehead rates. The overall pattern of this legislation has clearly been designed to shrink Canada in an east-west direction. It should be noted that the recommendations of the 1962 Royal Commission on Transportation suggest that these subsidies (which do not apply to other com-

[8] Board of Transport Commissioners for Canada, *Waybill Analysis, Carload, All-Rail Traffic*, 1961.

[9] There are two reasons why cost per ton mile decreases with distance: the terminal charges referred to above, and the fact that the observed parcel of goods shipped between distant points is less likely to include goods with high transport costs. In addition it has been suggested that rail rates may have been designed to some degree to discriminate in favor of distant regions in order to "spread out" production and consequently ensure a larger market for transport services. As a consequence the method used in this chapter to compute transport costs may tend to overstate the disadvantages of distant locations. They may also be overstated because of the existence of milling-in-transit or stop-off privileges. (These allow a firm to process raw materials at a point off the direct line between the raw material site and market and to ship both the raw material and the processed good at the direct line raw material cost.) Such privileges have the effect of reducing the disadvantage of distant points in participating in the economic activity of the central area.

There are, however, several factors which tend to cause an understatement of the disadvantages of distance. These disadvantages include transportation costs proper as well as the delays in receiving payment and the inventory problems associated with distance. Both of these disadvantages cause higher carrying (interest) costs.

petitive forms of transport) should not be a permanent part of the Canadian rail rate structure.[10] As a consequence it is not clear that these subsidies should be taken into account in this analysis. This is, however, not an issue of any great importance, since the transport cost estimates (shown below in Table 11) were not noticeably different in a trial run in which these subsidies were included.

In order to test the importance of regional rate differences, two calculations were derived for the total transport costs incurred to service the entire Canadian-U.S. markets from various production locations. Both computations were based on U.S. rates for U.S. portions of haul; however, two alternative assumptions were used over the Canadian portion of haul. The first calculation was based on the detailed regional pattern of Canadian freight rates, and the second was based on the simple Canadian average cost per ton mile for each good. The two solutions were remarkably similar,[11] indicating little sensitivity of total transport costs to peculiarities in the rate structure. This indicates that regional rate differences, at least in Canada, tend to be self-cancelling to a large degree when total costs for a whole pattern of shipments are examined. This

[10] "But because transportation is no longer synonymous with railways, any decision to attempt to take care of regional or industry economic problems by means of transportation should consider the whole transportation environment. Under competitive conditions, the use of a single chosen instrument of transportation, rail or another, to achieve regional or national objectives may seriously distort the allocation of resources, may achieve the desired ends by unduly expensive means, or may prove to be of greater assistance to that chosen mode of transport than to the region or industry the policy is designed to assist. Such measures as the "Bridge Subsidy," the Freight Rates Reduction Act and the Maritime Freight Rates Act must be evaluated in the light of these considerations." *Royal Commission on Transportation* (Ottawa: Queen's Printer, 1961), Vol. 1, p. 33.

[11] For these and succeeding test computations it was assumed producers service all markets equally. Transport costs were estimated in two ways. Each involved applying U.S. rates to the U.S. section of haul; however, two sets of rates were applied to Canadian portions of haul: first, the detailed regional Canadian rate structure, and second, the average Canadian rates. On the basis of the second method, in all industries the transport costs incurred from each area (expressed as a percent of transport cost from the Ontario location) were generally within two percent of the transport costs computed on the basis of the first method. In the entire table made up of eighteen areas and sixteen industries there were only two exceptions, and these were within a range of ± 3.5 percent.

TABLE 11. *Estimated Percentage That Total Costs in Comparison Areas Are Higher or Lower (−) Than in Ontario Because of Transportation Costs, 1958.*[a]

Manufacturing sector[b]	Maritimes	Quebec	Prairies	British Columbia	Upper Midwest	West Lake	East Lake	Lower Midwest	Middle Atlantic	New England	South	Capital	Florida	Southwest	Mountains	Pacific Southwest	Pacific Northwest
Food	7.18 / 6.26	0.21 / 1.58	5.32 / 5.13	1.83 / 9.23	1.33 / 0.90	−1.45 / −1.04	−0.71 / −0.98	0.02 / −0.58	−1.16 / 0.11	−0.83 / 0.96	0.43 / 0.05	−1.60 / −0.19	2.17 / 2.75	1.82 / 1.95	2.34 / 3.16	0.19 / 8.01	1.91 / 8.28
Tobacco	1.12 / 0.79	0.16 / 0.19	0.55 / 0.65	−0.22 / 1.17	0.11 / 0.12	−0.32 / −0.12	−0.09 / −0.11	−0.03 / −0.06	−0.03 / 0.02	0.01 / 0.12	0.19 / 0.03	−0.11 / −0.01	0.55 / 0.38	0.22 / 0.27	0.13 / 0.41	−0.24 / 1.02	−0.01 / 1.05
Textiles	1.59 / 1.16	−0.14 / 0.23	1.35 / 1.55	−0.04 / 2.56	0.56 / 0.55	−0.12 / −0.01	−0.07 / −0.12	0.24 / 0.20	0.24 / −0.09	−0.09 / 0.08	0.27 / 0.11	−0.14 / −0.12	0.87 / 0.68	0.70 / 0.85	0.81 / 1.20	−0.12 / 2.41	0.41 / 2.34
Apparel	0.68 / 0.50	0.08 / 0.12	0.40 / 0.49	−0.14 / 0.84	0.08 / 0.12	−0.21 / −0.06	−0.09 / −0.07	−0.03 / −0.01	−0.07 / −0.01	−0.02 / 0.06	0.03 / 0.02	−0.12 / −0.04	0.19 / 0.24	0.11 / 0.22	0.17 / 0.33	−0.11 / 0.75	−0.01 / 0.76
Wood products	23.55 / 20.64	0.84 / 5.14	20.29 / 16.41	9.42 / 28.96	6.90 / 2.86	−4.19 / −3.51	−1.41 / −3.28	2.44 / −1.77	−2.99 / 2.31	−1.51 / 3.37	3.60 / 0.37	−4.39 / −0.62	10.10 / 9.39	9.15 / 6.79	12.39 / 10.33	3.67 / 25.83	10.52 / 25.77
Paper	11.27 / 9.23	0.89 / 2.23	8.73 / 9.15	1.91 / 15.79	2.18 / 2.27	−3.08 / −1.25	−1.45 / −1.39	−0.12 / −0.10	−1.86 / −0.06	−1.07 / −1.31	0.13 / 0.20	−2.51 / −0.50	2.53 / 4.38	2.30 / 4.10	3.87 / 6.29	−0.70 / 14.20	2.27 / 14.28
Printing	3.40 / 2.77	0.05 / 0.67	2.43 / 2.56	−0.16 / 4.46	0.65 / 0.59	−0.73 / −0.39	−0.34 / −0.42	0.02 / −0.10	−0.49 / −0.01	−0.26 / 0.39	0.13 / 0.10	−0.72 / −0.14	0.90 / 1.32	0.75 / 1.12	1.15 / 1.72	−0.26 / 3.93	0.41 / 4.02
Electrical equipment	2.55 / 2.04	0.09 / 0.51	1.74 / 1.86	−0.45 / 3.25	0.50 / 0.43	−0.51 / −0.31	−0.29 / −0.32	0 / −0.06	−0.29 / 0.03	−0.08 / 0.34	0.19 / 0.11	−0.47 / −0.06	0.76 / 1.02	0.59 / 0.86	0.86 / 1.29	−0.20 / 2.89	0.08 / 2.93
Chemicals	11.57 / 9.48	0.54 / 2.33	8.30 / 9.24	0.09 / 16.10	2.01 / 2.24	−2.79 / −1.26	−1.21 / −1.43	0.03 / −0.24	−1.79 / −0.08	−1.31 / −1.30	0.54 / 0.11	−2.30 / −0.57	4.05 / 4.38	2.84 / 3.99	3.62 / 6.29	−0.58 / 14.43	2.64 / 14.59
Petroleum products	50.88 / 44.47	0.49 / 11.52	39.73 / 31.07	4.70 / 58.72	14.37 / 2.91	−7.79 / −9.00	−2.32 / −7.48	4.80 / −7.83	−5.29 / 1.78	−1.23 / 8.49	8.01 / −0.64	−8.40 / −0.36	22.00 / 16.38	13.30 / 7.01	23.90 / 16.85	7.79 / 46.85	17.96 / 51.80
Rubber and plastics	2.08 / 1.62	0.13 / 0.41	1.20 / 1.37	−0.44 / 2.42	0.26 / 0.28	−0.52 / −0.27	−0.25 / −0.26	−0.15 / −0.10	−0.19 / −0.05	0.01 / 0.28	0.10 / 0.06	−0.33 / −0.03	0.57 / 0.78	0.34 / 0.59	0.54 / 0.90	−0.28 / 2.13	−0.15 / 2.18
Leather goods	1.27 / 0.89	0.12 / 0.19	0.80 / 1.03	−0.26 / 1.74	0.20 / 0.32	−0.38 / −0.06	−0.16 / −0.11	−0.05 / 0.07	−0.14 / −0.04	−0.09 / 0.08	0.03 / 0.08	−0.23 / −0.07	0.35 / 0.51	0.24 / 0.53	0.35 / 0.71	−0.24 / 1.58	0.01 / 1.59
Nonmetallic mineral products	61.19 / 50.76	0.62 / 12.66	43.30 / 44.65	−6.11 / 78.87	13.21 / 9.54	−13.35 / −7.84	−5.44 / −7.93	1.72 / −2.68	7.45 / 0.77	−4.06 / 8.11	6.03 / 1.59	−11.28 / −1.62	21.39 / 23.95	16.47 / 19.19	21.77 / 29.80	−1.10 / 69.66	9.45 / 71.01
Metallic products	16.18 / 13.05	0.24 / 3.22	11.91 / 12.34	−0.84 / 21.46	4.01 / 3.10	−3.27 / −1.80	−1.38 / −1.95	−0.78 / 0	−1.66 / 0.27	−0.40 / 2.22	1.93 / 0.94	−2.51 / −0.26	5.90 / 6.95	4.74 / 6.13	6.26 / 8.95	−0.58 / 19.40	2.47 / 19.43
Transportation equipment	4.28 / 3.83	0.12 / 0.99	3.46 / 3.10	0.29 / 5.48	0.93 / 0.56	−1.07 / −0.68	−0.46 / −0.64	−0.02 / −0.32	−0.56 / 0.13	−0.39 / 0.70	0.33 / 0.13	−0.85 / −0.05	1.35 / 1.78	1.23 / 1.28	1.95 / 2.00	0.50 / 4.77	1.16 / 4.90
Miscellaneous	1.68 / 1.34	0.12 / 0.32	1.16 / 1.25	−0.13 / 2.16	0.20 / 0.28	−0.49 / −0.20	−0.27 / −0.22	−0.12 / −0.06	−0.23 / −0.02	−0.07 / 0.18	−0.02 / 0.03	−0.37 / −0.09	0.32 / 0.61	0.25 / 0.52	0.51 / 0.82	−0.02 / 1.88	0.09 / 1.94

[a] Two estimates appear for each area and industry; the first assumes that sales are closely related to distance ($q = 1$), the second that sales are unrelated to distance ($q = 0$). [b] See Table 1, note a.

suggests but, of course, does not confirm that inconsistencies in regional U.S. rates may also be of secondary importance when an average transport cost involving a whole pattern of regional shipments is being computed.

Another perplexing question is how relevant a large portion of the Canadian rate structure would be in the event of the absence of any barriers to the free flow of goods over the North American continent; it is possible that there might be some tendency for equalization of rates in Canada and the United States in the face of the increased competition that this kind of change in commercial policy would involve.[12] To test the potential importance of such equalization, North American marketing patterns were evaluated in two ways: by using both the U.S. and Canadian cost per ton mile rates, with the Canadian rates being applied to the appropriate Canadian portions of haul; and by applying U.S. rail rates to *both* the U.S. and Canadian portions of haul. Once again the results turned out to be remarkably similar.[13] This is to be explained by the self-cancelling nature of individual rate differences when an overall transport cost is being determined and by the limited importance, in an integrated North American economy, of the Canadian portion of haul — for firms producing in the United States as well as for firms producing in Canada. To illustrate: in the present situation, goods produced in Ontario are shipped widely to British Columbia, the Maritimes, and other distant points in Canada. Consequently, present transport costs of Canadian goods are largely determined by Canadian rates. However, with free trade the bulk of Ontario goods would be shipped to Ontario markets and markets in the North Central and Midwest United States. And in such a shipment from, for example, Hamilton to New York,

[12] North American shipping costs would tend to be equalized by factors other than rate equalization. Present border delays involved in customs presumably would be eliminated. Present restriction on U.S. trucking lines originating or terminating in Canada might also be suspended.

[13] On the basis of the latter assumption, in all industries the transport costs incurred from each area (expressed as a percent of transport costs from the Ontario location) were generally within two percent of the transport costs computed on the basis of the former assumption. In the entire table made up of eighteen areas and sixteen industries there were only two exceptions, and these were within a range of just over three percent.

only a short section of the haul would be on the Canadian side of the border. Therefore, most of the shipping charges incurred by Canadian producers in a free trade area would be at U.S. rates for two reasons: first, sales by Canadian producers would be redirected to servicing proximate U.S. rather than distant Canadian markets; second, Canadian production points are generally closer to the border than are U.S. markets. There is obviously an even heavier reliance on U.S. rates by U.S. producers. Most of their shipments would be to U.S. markets; even their shipments to Canadian markets would generally involve only a short Canadian haul because Canadian markets tend to be located closer to the border than are U.S. production points.

In summary, the fact that Canadian economic activity is located along a narrow band just north of the border means that present differences between Canadian and U.S. transport rates would not substantially affect total transport costs in a free trade area. In terms of the overall costs examined in this study, possible Canadian-U.S. rate equalization is therefore not a critical question.[14] Moreover, for the sake of simplicity U.S. rates throughout may be assumed (as they will be in this analysis) with minimal risk of major error.

Alternative Estimates of Transport Costs

One estimate of transport costs is based on the assumption that markets are not influenced by distance.[15] In this case a firm will service a constant percentage of each market. Its transport costs *expressed as a percentage of total costs* will be the same regardless whether the firm services all markets completely or a small fixed percentage of each market. The strategy was to assume that the firm completely services all markets and, on this basis, to estimate transport costs incurred from each potential location. Each of

[14] This also implies that if explicit account is taken of the Bridge and Freight Rate Reduction Act, subsidies would not substantially affect total transport costs from various locations because the best estimate of the effect of these two subsidies is to reduce Canadian rates in most industries toward, but not beyond, U.S. rates.

[15] This is equivalent to setting q equal to 0 in equation (10) in Appendix E.

these transport costs was expressed as a percentage of total costs; in turn each percentage was compared with that incurred from the Ontario location. The precise estimating technique is set forth in Appendix H. Each of the resulting estimates is shown as the *second* figure in each element in Table 11.

The other set of transport cost estimates was derived by assuming that markets are heavily influenced by distance. As in the previous case, the market for each good in each area is used as the basic information to initiate the analysis. However, in this case markets are distributed by means of the market potential model developed in the previous chapter.[16] The resulting market pattern falling to a new producer in each potential location is used in conjunction with transport rates to determine the transportation costs incurred from that location. As in the previous method, each of these transport costs was expressed as a percentage of total costs, and each of these percentages was compared with that incurred from the Ontario location. The specific estimating techniques are set forth in Appendix I. Each of the resulting estimates is shown as the *first* figure in each element in Table 11.[17]

Inspection of Table 11 indicates that goods may be divided into three categories depending on the magnitude of shipping charges — high cost, intermediate cost, and low cost. The goods involving high transportation costs are lumber and wood products, petroleum and coal products,[18] and nonmetallic mineral products. Other

[16] By setting q equal to 1 in equation (10) in Appendix E.

[17] It is not surprising that the ranking of areas in this transport cost analysis is roughly similar to the ranking of areas in the market potential analysis shown as the second set of estimates in Table 10 of the previous chapter, since both are based on a common assumption about the influence of distance on markets. This similarity might a priori have been suspected but by no means guaranteed.

[18] It should be noted that products in the petroleum subsector are often shipped by sea or by pipeline; to this extent observed *rail* rates for the joint petroleum and coal products sector tend to be heavily weighted by shipments of coal products. The high transport costs in this sector may consequently be a reflection of the high cost of shipping coal products and the conclusions of this chapter apply more directly to coal products than to petroleum.

Comparable figures on various modes of transporting petroleum products are not available. However, this pattern of heavy shipment by pipeline is

things being equal, it is unlikely that these goods will be shipped as widely as goods with lower transport costs; consequently, the first estimate of costs in Table 11 (based on the assumption that distance influences sales patterns) is likely to be more appropriate.

The goods in which transportation costs are low are textiles and apparel, rubber and leather products, printing and publishing, transportation equipment, and electrical supplies and apparatus — as well as miscellaneous manufactures. In a parallel way it may be argued that because transportation charges involved in shipping these goods are low, they are more likely to be distributed widely to national markets. As a consequence, the second estimate in Table 11 (based on the assumption that distance does not influence sales) probably becomes more relevant for these industries than for the others.

In an evaluation of the relative standing of various regions shown in Table 11, there are several observations that should be kept in mind. The estimating procedure has probably resulted in a consistent overstatement of the disadvantages of distant locations.[19] Moreover, since only rail costs have been analyzed it is likely that the increased efficiency of the custom service now provided by truck lines has made a straightforward cost calculation of this kind less relevant than it may have been in the past.[20]

It is also important in evaluating these figures to note that there are two underlying factors that may make an area a low cost location. First, the area may be centrally situated to all North American markets, and the cost of servicing all these markets may be

clearly evident from comparative figures on movements of crude oil. Pipeline accounted for the bulk of shipments, with ships and railroads carrying a small proportion. In 1960, pipelines accounted for over 17 billion ton miles (D.B.S., *Oil Pipe Line Transport,* 55–201, 1960, p. 6); coastwise shipping for over 5 million tons — a figure that would necessarily require inflation by the mileage covered by an average shipment (D.B.S., *Shipping Report,* 54–204, 1960, Part III, p. 251); and railroads almost certainly the smallest proportion of less than 68 million ton miles (estimated from the one percent sample in Board of Transport Commissioners for Canada, *Waybill Analysis,* 1961, p. 13).

[19] For reasons, see footnote 9.

[20] For example, a more sophisticated analysis of marketing and transport cost by a firm now often involves recognition of the interplay of transit or transport costs proper with inventory costs.

low as a result. The extent to which a region is centrally located will be the key factor determining the ranking of an area in the second set of figures in Table 11 — which are based on the assumption that all producers service all markets equally. The influence of central continental location becomes less important as this assumption is abandoned in favor of the second factor — that producers concentrate heavily in servicing regional markets. In this case the effective size[21] and degree of spatial concentration of the regional market will heavily influence the relative attractiveness of a location and will largely determine the ranking of areas in the first set of estimates in Table 11. The fact that these conditions are quite independent of one another (and an area may rank high in terms of one, but low in terms of the other) will explain the ambiguities that are immediately evident in examining paired estimates in Table 11, which often disagree in both magnitude and sign. Only one region — the U.S. West Lake (Chicago) area — ranks high in terms of both characteristics. However, even this location is not optimal in terms of either; the East Lake Location is somewhat more central to all North American markets, and the Middle Atlantic area has a larger regional market.

In a specific comparison of regions in the two countries, it may be concluded that, almost without exception, the Ontario location involves lower transportation costs than any other location in Canada. It is somewhat superior to Quebec and markedly superior to either the Prairies or the Maritimes, regardless of the assumption about the influence of distance in determining market shares. Furthermore, it may be concluded that Ontario is generally preferred to British Columbia as a location. This is particularly true where there is a tendency for a producer to service all North American markets equally. However, if it is assumed that a producer's sales are concentrated in proximate markets (and the first set of figures in Table 11 then becomes more appropriate), the superiority of Ontario is no longer clearly evident. For many goods British Columbia now becomes a lower transport cost location since the B.C. producer would be servicing a market that is very heavily concentrated in space around Vancouver.

---

[21] That is, total size of the domestic market discounted for the number of competitors already established there.

In comparing Ontario[22] with potential U.S. locations, it may be concluded that Ontario is at least as well situated as most U.S. regions, but at a disadvantage when compared with several. Ontario is clearly to be preferred to six U.S. areas: the Pacific Northwest, Upper Midwest, South, Florida, Southwest, and Mountain regions. This conclusion holds regardless of which assumption about market distribution is used.[23] Ontario's advantage is particularly noteworthy if it is assumed that all North American markets are serviced equally because of the central location of the province — especially vis-à-vis the largest markets in the Chicago and New York areas.

On the other hand, Ontario is clearly at a disadvantage vis-à-vis three U.S. regions: the West Lake, East Lake and Capital areas. It should be noted in passing that Washington, D.C., is more central to all U.S. markets than New York. It is true that Washington is south of the largest markets, in particular those in New York and Chicago; however, it is far enough west of New York to be closer than New York not only to points in the U.S. West and South but also to Chicago and Seattle. It is also of some interest to compare the position of the West Lake and East Lake areas — both of which are preferred to Ontario. Because there is a heavily concentrated regional market around Chicago, the West Lake area appears to have an edge to the extent that markets are affected by distance. The East Lake area will have the edge because it is slightly more central (in most industries) to the largest U.S. markets if it is assumed that all U.S. markets are to be serviced equally.

A comparison of Ontario with any of the four other U.S. regions involves a certain degree of ambiguity. Given one assumption about market allocation, Ontario is preferred, but given the other assumption, the U.S. region is preferred. For example, the critical nature of the market assumption becomes evident in comparing Ontario with the Lower Midwest. If it is assumed that all markets are serviced equally, then the Lower Midwest has a slight edge

---

[22] Ontario is used as a basis for comparison because it is the most heavily industrialized Canadian region. This table is easily translated if another area is desired as the basis of comparison.

[23] The only exception to this generalization is provided by three industries in the Pacific Northwest, given the assumption that distance is important in influencing market shares.

because of its central location in the middle of the North American continent. However, if it is assumed that markets are highly influenced by distance and that producers concentrate on servicing their domestic market, Ontario becomes a lower cost location for many industries, largely because the domestic market in that province is spatially more concentrated than the domestic market in the Lower Midwest. It may be concluded that, as distance is assumed more and more important in affecting market distribution, Ontario becomes increasingly preferred to this U.S. area.

Precisely the opposite conclusion is appropriate in comparing Ontario with the remaining three U.S. areas — the Middle Atlantic, Pacific Southwest, and New England. Each of these regions enjoys an increasing advantage over Ontario as distance is assumed more and more important in the allocation of market shares. For example, if it is assumed that all North American markets are serviced equally, in some industries Ontario is preferred to the U.S. Middle Atlantic region, largely because of the more central location of the province to all markets on the North American continent. However, as markets are affected more and more by distance, and as producers concentrate increasingly on servicing their regional markets, the Middle Atlantic area becomes more and more preferred to the Ontario location. This tendency is even more pronounced for New England and the U.S. Pacific Southwest. In comparison with Ontario, either of these two U.S. regions is at a substantial disadvantage if all markets are serviced equally. However, as markets become increasingly dependent on distance, either U.S. area (with its larger regional market) becomes a lower cost location than Ontario for most industries.

Conclusions

Ontario is the best region in Canada in terms of minimizing transportation costs in shipping final output to the North American market. In comparison with the thirteen U.S. regions, Ontario ranks midway down the scale, regardless of what assumption about market distribution is used. However, a comparison of Ontario with any specific U.S. region is often not possible without specifying the spatial pattern of markets to be serviced. If all North

American markets are serviced equally by a producer in any location, Ontario is one of the five or six best locations on the North American continent, being clearly inferior only to the U.S. East Lake, West Lake, Lower Midwest and Capital regions. If a producer services regional markets more heavily than those at a distance, Ontario becomes less favorably situated and the province ranks below the regions mentioned above (except the Lower Midwest) and below the Middle Atlantic, Pacific Southwest and New England areas as well.

5

AGGLOMERATION
AND EXTERNAL ECONOMIES

In the analysis of market potential in Chapter 3 it was assumed, other things being equal, that new firms would tend to avoid regions where the ratio of present production to consumption is already high. It is reasonable enough to assume that such a heavy concentration of competitors would reduce the effective market that a new firm might hope to capture in such an area and, hence, would make this area less attractive on the demand side. Such an area, however, may be attractive for supply or cost reasons. The objective in this chapter is to examine those areas in which industry is now heavily centered; this concentration of industry may reflect substantial supply or cost advantages in these regions.

There are three broad categories of influences that may explain industry agglomeration. First, industry may concentrate in an area because of some spatial advantage analyzed in one of the other chapters of this study; for example, the area may be the unique site of a resource or may be spatially situated to allow a firm to service continental markets at minimum cost. Second, industrial concentration may result because of a spatial advantage not explicitly analyzed elsewhere in this study; perhaps a weather advantage for certain limited industrial activities (such as aircraft or textiles) or amenities provided by the area which allow firms to attract highly qualified personnel. It should be noted that either of the above attractive features of an area exists before the industry arrives. This is not true of the third group of attractions — external economies. This term is used to describe all the reasons why costs may be lower in an area simply because the industry exists there;[1] for example, apparel firms are attracted to New York because the present concentration of the industry there has resulted in easy accessibility of rental space, design facilities, etc.[2]

The first set of influences is dealt with explicitly in other chapters. In this chapter an attempt is made in a very rough-and-ready way to deal with the third set of influences: present North American areas of concentration in each industry are examined to provide an index of preferred areas for industries in which external economies may be significant.

There is an important observation that follows from the fact that external economies are related, not to any inherent characteristics of an area, but simply to the existence of an industry there. External economies cannot be used as an explanation of why an industry became established in an area in the first place; obviously the attraction of an existing industry cannot be made to explain an industry's initial existence. However, external economies may explain the continued existence of an industry — if its initial establishment resulted from pure chance, or some other influence that is no longer of any relevance.[3]

Some difficulties in interpretation arise when present areas of concentration are examined in both the United States and Canada.

[1] Some industries may, of course, face external diseconomies; that is, their costs may be higher in an area in which the industry already exists in force. The pressure on such an industry is to fragment into areas in which it is not now established. But such cases need not detain us; presumably a number of regions in the United States and Canada are equally attractive in the sense of providing locations in which the industry does not now exist.

[2] See Robert M. Lichtenberg, *One Tenth of a Nation* (Cambridge: Harvard University Press, 1960), p. 65. In the argument of this chapter it is assumed that external economies affect supply (by reducing costs). However, external economies on the demand side may exist. For example, the concentration of certain types of retailing may provide a larger — rather than a smaller — effective market for a new firm, if customers have been induced to congregate in this area of heavy supply.

[3] For example, an industry may have been initiated near a local source of funds. But its present growth to national stature — which allows it to raise funds on the U.S. capital market — means that this influence is no longer relevant.

Each country has developed an independent tariff policy, at least partially designed to influence the growth and pattern of industry. Consequently, the relevance of the industry pattern that has resulted must be questioned in an analysis designed to show the effects of the entirely different commercial policy of free trade. As a result, comparative advantage in a free trade continent may not necessarily be inferred by observing areas of present U.S. and Canadian concentration. Such an inference would be valid only if tariffs have been neutral in the sense of influencing the expansion or contraction of each industry in each country.[4] If the net effect of both the Canadian and U.S. tariffs has been to encourage Canadian industrial growth, then observed industry concentration in Canadian areas will tend to overstate the comparative advantages that Canadian regions would enjoy in a free trade situation; similarly, if North American protection has on balance discouraged Canadian industrial growth, then this analysis will give an inadequate statement of the comparative advantage of Canadian regions in a free trade area. In summary, this analysis of where industry is now concentrated probably gives a good indication of potential external economies; however, it is not as useful as an index of comparative advantage unless protection between the two countries has been neutral in the sense of nondiversion of production from one to the other. If protection has not been neutral, the ranking of *all* areas in one country will be biased as a result. In this case, the analysis provides some index of historical comparative advantage only between regions within each country — but not between countries.[5]

[4] It is possible, but admittedly very unlikely that both Canadian and U.S. protection have in sum been neutral — with the Canadian tariff (designed to stimulate Canadian industry) just offset by the U.S. tariff (designed to stimulate U.S. industry). It is surprising how often it is uncritically accepted that protection increases industrial activity in a country. This may be true of the tariff of the country concerned (although this is by no means assured); however, since a multicountry system of tariffs almost certainly reduces total income and industrial output, it will not cause a higher level of output for all countries, and may not even do so for any individual country.

[5] Even this qualified conclusion requires the further assumption that protection has not influenced the regional pattern of industry within a country. This question will be examined in some detail later in the argument.

Observed Areas of Industry Agglomeration

North American regions are ranked in Tables 12 and 13 according to their present concentration in each industry. Two sets of ranking are presented — the first, more relevant table, based on value added in the standard metropolitan area of heaviest concentration (Table 12) and the other based on value added in the entire region (Table 13). The reason the first is more significant is that limited meaning can be attached to value added in an entire region, since the resulting measure is arbitrarily determined by the area boundary — in particular, the number of large cities included. For example, two distant centers — St. Louis and Kansas City — are included in the Lower Midwest area. But a new firm attracted by external economies would have to choose between one or the other, and other things being equal, the city of heavier concentration would be the more attractive and, hence, would provide the appropriate measure of the attractiveness of the whole area. It is obviously inappropriate to take any sort of a sum of industrial concentration in both St. Louis and Kansas City, and the single city of heaviest concentration (used to compute Table 12) usually provides a preferred index. However, value added in an entire region may, under certain circumstances, have considerable significance — if it reflects a number of standard metropolitan areas of industry concentration clustered in one limited geographic region. External economies may be a function of the industry's concentration in this complex of cities, rather than in the single city of heaviest employment. This may be particularly important for regions in the urban complex running along the East Coast of the United States. In any event it should be noted that these two indexes generally yield a similar picture; the two or three significant exceptions will be singled out for attention later.

It is evident from the rankings in both tables that, in terms of overall manufacturing activity, Ontario and Quebec are in a median position. There are certain U.S. regions that obviously have a heavier degree of concentration in almost any activity: the Middle Atlantic area especially, and also the West Lake, Pacific Southwest, and East Lake areas. However, Ontario and Quebec are

TABLE 12. *Areas Ranked by Value Added in Standard Metropolitan Area of Heaviest Concentration in Each Industry, 1958.*

Manufacturing sector[a]	Maritimes	Quebec	Ontario	Prairies	British Columbia	Upper Midwest	West Lake	East Lake	Lower Midwest	Middle Atlantic	New England	South	Capital	Florida	Southwest	Mountain	Pacific Southwest	Pacific Northwest
Food	18	5	9	16	15	8	2	7	4	1	6	11	10	17	12	13	3	14
Tobacco	b	2	5	b	b	b	b	b	b	4	b	1	b	3	b	b	b	b
Textiles	b	4	6	15	14	11	5	8	16	1	2	3	9	12	13	17	7	10
Apparel	b	4	7	13	17	12	3	9	8	1	5	11	6	14	10	16	2	15
Wood products	18	10	9	17	4	8	3	5	11	1	13	7	12	15	14	16	2	6
Paper	b	13	6	17	15	9	2	10	7	1	5	11	8	14	12	16	3	4
Printing	18	10	5	17	16	7	2	6	9	1	4	12	8	15	11	13	3	14
Electrical equipment	b	8	5	17	15	10	1	4	6	2	11	13	7	16	9	14	3	12
Chemicals	18	11	9	10	16	12	2	6	4	1	10	7	8	13	5	14	3	15
Petroleum products	b	3	14	b	9	8	2	7	6	4	11	17	12	15	1	13	5	16
Rubber and plastics	b	10	6	12	b	9	4	1	8	2	5	13	7	12	11	b	3	14
Leather goods	b	5	6	16	13	b	3	8	4	1	2	9	7	10	11	b	b	b
Nonmetallic mineral products	18	8	12	17	17	6	2	5	6	1	10	11	7	14	9	15	3	13
Metallic products	b	11	10	17	15	9	1	3	6	2	7	12	5	16	8	14	4	13
Transportation equipment	b	11	13	17	14	12	5	2	6	3	10	9	7	16	8	15	1	4
Miscellaneous	b	9	7	17	15	8	3	5	6	1	4	11	10	16	12	13	2	14

Source: U.S. *Census of Manufactures,* 1958; work sheets provided by D.B.S.

[a] See Table 1, note a.

[b] Information on this industry in this area is inadequate.

TABLE 13. Areas Ranked by Total Value Added In Each Industry, 1958.

Manufacturing sector[a]	Pacific Northwest	Pacific Southwest	Mountain	Southwest	Florida	Capital	South	New England	Middle Atlantic	Lower Midwest	East Lake	West Lake	Upper Midwest	British Columbia	Prairies	Ontario	Quebec	Maritimes
Food	11	3	14	7	15	12	4	10	1	5	6	2	9	17	16	8	13	18
Tobacco	b	9	b	b	4	b	1	7	2	b	6	8	b	b	b	5	3	b
Textiles	12	8	18	9	15	10	1	3	2	17	7	6	11	16	14	5	4	13
Apparel	13	5	16	7	14	10	2	4	1	8	9	3	12	17	15	11	6	18
Wood products	2	4	14	7	15	16	1	9	3	11	6	5	13	8	17	10	12	18
Paper	7	10	18	6	12	10	2	5	1	11	4	3	11	14	16	9	8	15
Printing	13	4	15	8	14	10	5	7	1	6	3	2	12	17	16	9	12	18
Electrical equipment	13	4	15	9	14	9	5	6	1	7	3	2	14	17	16	8	11	b
Chemicals	13	6	15	4	11	16	2	10	1	7	5	3	12	17	16	8	12	18
Petroleum products	14	3	10	1	17	8	13	15	4	9	5	2	12	11	8	7	6	b
Rubber and plastics	b	5	b	9	13	10	6	4	2	10	1	3	12	b	b	7	11	b
Leather goods	b	9	b	11	12		4	1	2	3	6	5	b	15	13	8	7	14
Nonmetallic mineral products	15	5	14	6	11	10	4	9	1	7	2	3	13	17	16	8	12	18
Metallic products	13	4	15	9	14	10	5	6	1	8	3	2	13	16	17	9	11	18
Transportation equipment	7	3	16	6	14	10	9	11	2	5	1	4	13	17	15	8	12	18
Miscellaneous	15	2	9	8	11	12	7	4	1	6	5	3	16	18	17	10	13	14

Source: U.S. Census of Manufactures, 1958; D.B.S., 31-204, 31-205, 31-206, 31-207, 31-208.
a See Table 1, note a.
b Information on this industry in this area is inadequate.

preferred not only to the three other Canadian regions — British Columbia, the Prairies, and the Maritimes — but also to a number of U.S. regions, including the Mountain area, Florida, and (in most industries) the Pacific Northwest. In comparing Ontario and Quebec with the remaining U.S. regions it is difficult to generalize; in some industries there is heavier concentration in these Canadian provinces, whereas in others the U.S. regions have heavier concentration.

Comparison of these two tables confirms a previous observation; the ranking of areas is generally the same regardless which index is examined. However, there are some notable exceptions to this generalization. For example, the relatively low standing of the U.S. South should be noted in Table 12; the ranking of an area in this table is dependent on the size of the largest urban center in the region, and the South does not include within its boundary the largest cities in the United States. However, in Table 13 where areas are ranked according to manufacturing in the whole region, the standing of the South is improved substantially because the area is defined broadly enough to include a large number of cities. To a lesser degree, the U.S. Southwest and East Lake regions exhibit the same characteristics — neither has the largest U.S. centers of industrial concentration, but each has a number of sizable cities. The opposite characteristic may be noted for regions that have only one or two manufacturing centers of very large scale. For example, the Pacific Southwest has a relatively higher ranking when standard metropolitan areas of largest concentration are compared (in Table 12), but a lower ranking when entire areas are compared (in Table 13). The same is true of the Upper Midwest, Lower Midwest, Capital, and Quebec. This last province has its industrial activity concentrated almost exclusively around one city, Montreal. As a consequence, Montreal's ranking compared to other cities is generally higher than Quebec's ranking compared to other regions.

There are a number of exceptional industries which do not conform to the overall pattern of concentration described above. Tobacco products provide perhaps the most striking exception, with the industry centered in the South, Quebec, and Florida, as well as in the Middle Atlantic area. In the textile industry, New England

and the South are the centers of heaviest production. Both British Columbia and the U.S. Pacific Coast areas have heavy concentration in lumber and wood products. In petroleum and coal products the U.S. Southwest and, to a lesser degree, Quebec and the U.S. East Coast are the regions in which the industry is centered. (It should also be noted that the Canadian Prairies rank substantially higher in this activity than in any other.) Leather production is heavily centered in the Boston-New York area but not along the U.S. Pacific Coast to the same extent that other industries are located there. Finally, the transport equipment industry is concentrated in the East Lake and Pacific Southwest regions; the auto industry is centered in the Detroit area, and the aircraft industry around Los Angeles.

Despite these exceptions, there is a fairly clear overall pattern of industry concentration. Consequently, insofar as immeasurable implicit influences of comparative advantage or external economies *attract* firms to areas in which competitors are already heavily established, the U.S. Middle Atlantic and West Lake areas become the two most attractive locations on the North American continent for most industries. Strangely, these also turned out to be the two preferred regions when it was assumed, in the market potential analysis of Chapter 3, that firms seek out markets but *avoid* centers of established competition. Paradoxically, the conclusion that these are the two preferred areas follows from either of these two almost diametrically opposed sets of initial assumptions.

The paradox is easily explained. Insofar as external economies are important, the New York and Chicago areas are best situated because North American industry is most heavily concentrated there. However, precisely because of the concentration of industry in these regions, employment and income are also centered there. As a result, markets are heavily concentrated in these areas; and no matter how strongly it is assumed in the competitive location model that firms avoid other competitive producers when seeking out the most attractive markets, these areas remain most desirable because of their heavy market concentration. For exactly the same reason the least attractive areas in terms of external economies — Florida, Mountain, Prairies, British Columbia, and the Maritimes

— are also the least attractive areas in terms of the market potential analysis of Chapter 3. Because these areas lack established industry, they also have relatively limited domestic markets.

It may be concluded that, whereas there are certain specific industries and areas[6] that are exceptions, in general the rankings of both the most and least favorable locations in North America are roughly the same, given alternative assumptions about the influence of established competition. It should be recognized that this is partly fortuitous; this coincidence of results for North America cannot necessarily be expected in other regional analyses. If industries are not all heavily concentrated in one or two specific areas, then this result is unlikely to occur. This is illustrated by the two major industries that provide exceptions — tobacco and wood products. The tobacco industry is centered in the South rather than in the heavily industrialized areas around New York and Chicago. If it is assumed that firms wish to reach markets and avoid competition, the optimal locations are New York and Chicago; but if it is assumed that firms are attracted by external economies, optimal location is in the U.S. South, where the industry presently exists in strength.

The other exception is wood products. Chicago, one of the preferred areas in terms of market potential, is not a preferred area in terms of external economies. Such economies would be provided by areas on the Pacific Coast where the industry has already been established, presumably because of the attraction of resource supplies.[7]

With the exception of these two industries, it is possible to arrive at fairly strong conclusions if one considers only the two location influences, established competition and markets, examined in this chapter and in Chapter 3. The New York and Chicago regions provide preferred sites for new firms in most industries. Ontario

[6] Most notably the Pacific Southwest.

[7] It should be noted that only broad industrial sectors have been analyzed in this study. It is, of course, true that any conclusion on such a sector does not necessarily apply to all its component subindustries. One might speculate that as industries are examined on a less aggregated basis, the results might become less unambiguous — that is, as more clearly defined industries are studied, more exceptions like tobacco and wood products might become evident.

and Quebec — along with most other U.S. areas — are moderately well situated; but the Florida and Mountain areas in the United States, and the Prairies, British Columbia, and the Maritimes in Canada are less attractive regions. This conclusion holds regardless of which of the two conflicting motives is assumed to govern business behavior: either the attraction of external economies (analyzed in this chapter) or the desire of firms to avoid competition (analyzed in Chapter 3).

6

PROXIMITY TO RESOURCES

In the introduction to Chapter 4 it was pointed out that the typical firm should not choose a location solely with the objective of getting close to markets nor with the objective of getting close to resources. Instead, it should view both markets and resources (along with a number of other factors) as influences which codetermine its best location. For any firm, therefore, there is no solution to either the market or resource problem in isolation; both must be considered together as a single problem requiring a single solution. This solution involves the selection of the best point within the space defined by markets, resource sites, and other factors. The best location will be close either to resources or to markets, depending on the relative importance of transport charges on resource inputs compared to charges on finished product. These relative transport charges in turn depend on the transport rates charged on both inputs and outputs and the weight-losing properties of the production process.

This type of analysis is feasible for a specific product whenever market and resource sites can be specified in detail and when information is available on both incoming and outgoing freight charges. This interregional study of North America, however, focuses not on a particular product or process but on the relative attractiveness of various areas. It is not possible, having solved a large number of market-resource location problems of this kind for each industry, to infer by scanning these solutions the prospects of a specific region; moreover, the aggregate nature of industrial sectors under study does not provide a basis for an industry study at the level of detail that this inference would require. Instead it is necessary to evaluate each area in terms of its relative desirability for servicing North American markets (analyzed in Chapters 3 and 4) and in terms of its proximity to the most important resource supplies. The latter question is analyzed in this chapter.

If it could be assumed that the cost of a resource is similar at all extraction sites, then the problem of computing resource costs would be the relatively simple one of applying appropriate transport rates to the distance between each potential processing point and its nearest resource site. But the distance of a resource from its point of consumption or processing usually influences its price and thus generates a whole pattern of diverse economic "rents" at various resource sites. Consequently, the assumption that resources are similarly priced at all extraction sites is patently unrealistic. Insofar as the process of "rent" determination works itself out perfectly, resources coming from various sources to a single consumption point will all cost the same; that is, differences in transportation charges will be offset by differences in rents accruing to the resources. (The equal costs will apply only where qualities are equal, of course; per unit cost differences will persist where there are quality differences.)

Thus, if there were only one consumption point, resource prices would become a simple matter. Similarly, if there were several points of consumption but only one point of resource production,[1] resource prices would also be straightforward: at the points of consumption, prices would reflect differences in transportation costs. However, neither of these simple cases is likely to exist: the most usual situation is one of several points of production and several points of consumption.

To illustrate the difficulty, suppose we assume that for a specific resource there are two sources of supply, Virginia and Oregon, and two points of consumption, Baltimore and San Francisco. If competitive markets exist, three outcomes are possible:

[1] It is assumed that there are a number of competitive buyers (and sellers) at each consumption (and production) point. If resources are being produced by a single seller who acts as a discriminating monopolist, the conclusions of this section do not follow.

1. Baltimore may draw only from the Virginia source, while San Francisco will obtain the resource from both Oregon and Virginia. The resource will cost the same at San Francisco regardless of its source. Therefore, the price will be higher in Oregon than in Virginia by the amount of the transportation costs from Virginia to San Francisco less the costs from Oregon to San Francisco. The resource will also cost the same in Virginia regardless of its destination. Therefore, resource prices in San Francisco will exceed those in Baltimore by the Virginia-San Francisco transportation cost less the Virginia-Baltimore transportation costs. Since the present study is concerned with the location of industry rather than with the economic feasibility of resource exploitation, it is this second price differential (that is, the one between consumption points) that is of particular interest.

2. Baltimore may draw from both sources, while San Francisco draws only from Oregon. *Mutatis mutandis,* relative prices may be inferred from (1).

3. Baltimore may draw solely from Virginia, and San Francisco solely from Oregon. Here, relative prices will be indeterminate within the ranges set by (1) and (2). That is, the price of the resource in San Francisco may be greater than in Balitmore by any amount up to the Virginia-San Francisco transportation cost less the Virginia-Baltimore transportation cost, or it may be less than the price in Baltimore by any amount up to the Oregon-Baltimore cost less the Oregon-San Francisco cost.

Two issues are thus critical if resource cost differences are to be estimated. First, are the resource and user points integrated into an overall pattern, or is each resource site and its user industry isolated as in case (3) above? Only in the former instance will it be possible to calculate a differential; in the latter, the differential will be indeterminate within a range. Second, where the source-user pattern is integrated, it is necessary to identify the resource point from which a number of users draw; only if this is done will it be possible to determine which of the user points has the resource cost advantage.

To deal adequately with these points, it would be necessary to have a detailed breakdown of interregional resource shipments. This breakdown is not available, and therefore a less satisfactory procedure has been followed in arriving at the estimates shown in Table 14. Resource cost differentials are shown in pairs, the first being a minimum and the second a maximum.

First, the maximum estimate has been derived by calculating the transportation cost from the region of *greatest* resource concentration. For example, the area of greatest resource production for the petroleum industry is the U.S. Southwest. As the base area its cost differential is set at zero, and the higher cost for each of the other regions is simply the cost of shipping requirements of this resource from the Southwest.

Second, the minimum estimate is derived by calculating the cost from the *nearest* resource location.

The logical defects of this procedure should be noted. The area of greatest resource concentration is more likely than any other to be a major exporter, but there is no logical reason why it must export. Indeed, it is possible that this area might import the resource if its importance as a user were even greater than its importance as a source. If this were the case, then not only would the magnitude of the maximum shown in Table 14 be inaccurate; its sign would be wrong.

There is another possible defect to the data of Table 14, which were derived on the assumption of competitive conditions, that is, of "arm's length" transactions between resource suppliers and resource users. This assumption is clearly defective, as many resources are owned by the users. It is not clear, however, how or to what degree this difficulty biases the results of Table 14.[2]

[2] There is one more limitation to the analysis of resource costs. There are two advantages to being close to resources, just as there are two advantages to being close to markets. One advantage stems from the lower transportation costs and the other from the convenience of doing business at short range. In dealing with final markets, both the transportation costs (Chapter 4) and the convenience of proximity (Chapter 3) have been studied. In dealing with resources, only the transportation costs are considered. Since resources in general tend to be less important than markets as a locational factor, the omission of convenience of access to resources may be justified on the grounds that it is of secondary significance.

Certain other logical similarities between the resource and market problems might also be noted. The type of differential price analysis used in this resource chapter could also be applied to final markets. However, as market location tends to be much more diverse than resource location, a different (gravity-type) analysis has been used for markets.

Absolute Advantage

TABLE 14. *Estimated Percentage That Total Costs Are Higher in Comparison Areas Than in Regions of Mineral Supply Because of Difference in Mineral Costs, 1958.*[a]

Comparison areas	Metallic products			Petroleum and coal products	
	Primary iron and steel		Nonferrous metal products	Coal products	Petroleum products
	Iron ore (11%)	Coal (7%)	Base metals (17%)	Coal (61%)	Petroleum (53%)
Maritimes	0	0	0	0	6.81
	4.44	1.02	5.96	8.91	8.19
Quebec	0	0.39	0	3.36	5.30
	4.83	.46	4.33	3.99	7.34
Ontario	0	0.34	0	2.98	4.11
	5.62	0.46	3.43	3.99	6.43
Prairies	8.50	0	0	0	0
	16.58	1.73	3.87	15.15	6.81
British Columbia	17.41	1.05	0	9.16	5.63
	28.35	2.53	5.27	22.06	8.12
Upper Midwest	0	0.49	0	4.30	0
	10.77	1.02	2.41	8.88	5.52
West Lake	5.23	0	0	0	0
	7.82	0.51	2.36	4.41	5.48
East Lake	3.82	0	0	0	0
	6.27	0.31	2.82	2.65	5.89
Lower Midwest	5.51	0	0	0	0
	16.28	0.71	1.43	6.20	4.60
Middle Atlantic	0	0	0	0	0
	9.72	0.33	3.73	2.91	6.56
New England	0	0.24	0.58	2.06	2.60
	6.41	0.38	4.35	3.30	7.27
South	0	0	0	0	0
	11.74	0.40	2.25	3.50	5.36
Capital	0	0.14	0.35	1.24	1.72
	7.84	0.28	3.53	2.48	6.50
Florida	6.52	0.58	1.43	5.08	4.61
	9.31	0.95	2.66	8.33	5.72
Southwest	0	0.58	0	5.08	0
	12.65	1.18	0	10.34	0
Mountain	0	0	0	0	0
	22.65	1.53	2.19	13.33	5.38
Pacific Southwest	14.97	0.88	2.19	7.76	0
	27.64	2.37	3.29	20.73	6.26
Pacific Northwest	16.57	0.75	0	6.61	5.09
	28.96	2.24	4.86	19.53	7.80

[a] For estimating procedures, see Appendix J. The first figure in each element is the minimum estimate, the second the maximum.

To sum up: differential resource costs are extremely difficult to analyze because no reliable data is available indicating how resource costs vary in different locations. All that may be ascertained, in fact, is information on major sites of extraction, along with information on costs of transporting these resources. Theoretical manipulation of this information does not provide a basis for estimating precisely how resource costs may differ between areas; however, this information is sufficient to make tentative estimates of the bounding maximum and minimum limits on the variability of resource costs between regions. These limits are estimated by assuming that spatial arbitrage prevents resource costs in any area A from exceeding those in any other area B by more than the transport costs involved in shipping this resource from B to A. Indeed, it is only this assumption of effective spatial arbitrage that allows any analytical leverage on this question of resource costs.

The importance of resource cost to a firm depends not only on the price it may have to pay for a unit of resource but also on the importance of one unit of resource in the total cost picture of the user firm. The percentage of costs of each industry committed to the purchase of each resource is shown in table 14 at the top of each column in brackets next to the resource used.

An examination of the input structure of industry shown in the 1949 Canadian Interindustry Table[3] indicates that only a small number of manufacturing sectors have substantial resource purchases. In terms of the sectoral definition used in this study, only the seven sectors shown in Tables 14 and 15 are involved — along with the food processing and nonmetallic mineral products sectors discussed below; no other sectors make substantial purchases of resources.

It is difficult to specify the resource dependence of a manufacturing sector in the aggregate for one of two reasons. A sector may not be heavily dependent on resource supplies, but one of its subindustries may have substantial resource requirements (for example, the primary iron and steel subindustry in the metallic

[3] The input requirements of each sector could not be analyzed from the U.S. interindustry table because it generally aggregates resource extraction and secondary processing in a single sector, making it impossible to differentiate between the two.

TABLE 15. *Estimated Percentage that Total Costs Are Higher in Comparison Areas than in Regions of Resource Supply because of Differences in Resource Costs, 1958.*[a]

Comparison areas	Tobacco products Tobacco (37%)	Textiles Cotton (6%)	Wood products Furniture Lumber (6%)	Other wood products Lumber (37%)	Pulp and paper Lumber (26%)
Maritimes	0.91	0.33	0	0	0
	1.79	0.52	0.71	22.19	3.16
Quebec	0	0.23	0	0	0
	1.22	0.38	0.55	17.20	0
Ontario	0	0.13	0	0	0
	0.88	0.30	0.49	15.27	1.43
Prairies	1.43	0.27	0	0	0
	2.08	0.34	0.25	7.68	7.37
British Columbia	2.34	0.24	0	0	0
	2.91	0.46	0	0	11.43
Upper Midwest	0.59	0.11	0	0	0
	1.14	0.21	0.30	9.36	4.52
West Lake	0	0.08	0	0	0
	0.62	0.21	0.39	12.24	3.30
East Lake	0	0.11	0	0	0
	0.62	0.25	0.43	13.54	2.43
Lower Midwest	0.43	0	0	0	0
	0.73	0.13	0.36	11.27	4.65
Middle Atlantic	0	0.15	0	0	0
	0.79	0.33	0.52	16.39	1.55
New England	0	0.19	0	0	0
	1.00	0.38	0.55	17.13	1.25
South	0	0	0	0	0
	0	0.20	0.48	15.16	4.24
Capital	0	0.11	0	0	0
	0.59	0.31	0.48	15.53	2.25
Florida	0	0.13	0	0	0
	0.66	0.23	0.59	18.36	5.95
Southwest	1.06	0	0	0	0
	1.06	0	0.41	12.95	7.05
Mountain	1.62	0.19	0	0	0
	1.62	0.19	0.25	7.74	7.89
Pacific Southwest	2.93	0	0	0	0
	2.93	0.29	0.22	6.82	11.88
Pacific Northwest	2.73	0.20	0	0	0
	2.73	0.43	0	0	10.45

[a] For estimating procedures, see Appendix J. The first figure in each element is the minimum estimate, the second the maximum.

products sector requires large supplies of both iron ore and coal). Alternatively, a sector may be an aggregate of two or more sub-industries with quite independent resource requirements. For example, the petroleum products subindustry requires petroleum inputs, while the coal products subindustry requires coal; both are combined in the petroleum and coal products sector. For both these reasons, it generally makes less sense to analyze resource dependence on a sectoral basis than on the more detailed sub-industry basis shown in Tables 14 and 15.

Table 14 illustrates that, within the metallic products sector, two subindustries have heavy resource requirements: the primary iron and steel subindustry is dependent on iron ore and coal supplies, and the nonferrous metal products industry is dependent on base metal inputs. The possible impact on differential costs of each resource is shown in this table for each of these subindustries; the first estimate is the minimum figure, the second the maximum derived by the method discussed in the previous section.

The iron and steel industry is the subindustry in the metallic products sector through which both iron and coal resources are channelled and, therefore, iron and coal resources loom much more important for the iron and steel subindustry than for the metallic products sector in the aggregate. Iron ore and coal represent eleven and seven percent respectively of the costs of the iron and steel subindustry but less than one percent of the cost of the aggregate metallic products sector; as a consequence, proximity to resources is important only for the iron and steel industry but not for the sector; if columns (1) and (2) are recomputed to show the sensitivity to the cost of coal and iron ore of the metallic products sector as a whole, rather than the primary iron and steel industry alone, all cost differences become very small indeed. Table 14 also indicates that as the best North American source of iron ore shifts from the Mesabi range to the Labrador area,[4] iron ore may become a more critical cause of cost differences between areas than coal. This is partially explained by the fact that coal production, centered in the Pennsylvania-West Virginia area of the United States, is far more central to North American regions than is iron ore extraction in the Labrador area.

[4] This area was used as the basis for determining all maximum prices.

The other resource requirement of the metallic products sector is base metals. (It should be noted that the U.S. Mountain area, as the region of greatest production, was used as the base of reference in determining maximum cost differences. Insofar as the Canadian Laurentian shield is a supply source of equally low cost, these maximum estimates greatly overstate the cost disadvantage of many regions.) The observation of the iron requirements for the iron and steel industry has a parallel in the base metal requirements of the nonferrous metals industry: the potential base metal cost differences shown in column (3) appear to be important for the nonferrous metals subindustry because seventeen percent of its costs go into base metals; however, potential base metal cost differences lose significance if the metallic products sector as a whole is considered, since only about six percent of its costs are devoted to base metals.[5] There are a number of other subindustries in the metallic products sector; because they are engaged in later stages of metal fabrication, they are not resource oriented — except insofar as they are influenced by the location of the primary iron and steel or nonferrous metal industries. (This indirect dependence on resources is analyzed in Chapter 7.)

Two aggregate sectors which do show heavy resource requirements are the tobacco and textiles sectors shown in Table 15; thirty-seven percent of the costs of the tobacco products sector go into raw tobacco purchases, and six percent of the costs of the textile sector are devoted to cotton. Yet, paradoxically, each of these sectors shows little spatial sensitivity to differing resource costs because transport costs for these resources are low; as a consequence, they may be shipped to potential production locations anywhere in the North American economy without greatly affecting the total cost of production.[6] There is a major difficulty involved in estimating the sensitivity of the textile industry to cotton supplies because cotton is only one of several moderately

[5] To compute the sensitivity of the metallic products sector to base metal costs, each estimate in column (3) should be multiplied by about 0.36, a factor representing the relative size of the nonferrous metal products subindustry in the metallic products sector.

[6] The maximum estimates for tobacco were derived by using the U.S. South as the pricing point of reference, and estimates for cotton by using the U.S. Southwest.

substitutable inputs, the others being wool and synthetics.[7] Unfortunately, an examination of this sector on a less aggregative basis does not help, since its subindustries are classified in terms of consumers' goods (men's clothing, women's clothing, etc.), rather than by resource use (cotton goods, woolens, etc.). Hence the maximum cost estimate in the textile column may be overstated for an additional reason: inasmuch as there are substitutes for cotton, the textile industry may be less sensitive to cotton supplies than these figures suggest. At the same time it should be recognized that any specific subindustries in this sector that concentrate on cotton goods rather than woolens or synthetics may be more sensitive to cotton supplies than is the sector as a whole.

The other important resource used by the textile industry is wool. Wool enters Canada duty free but pays a substantial tariff entering the United States. Since imports account for such a large proportion of the domestic consumption of wool in the United States,[8] it is likely that the U.S. domestic price is influenced, if not determined, by the tariff. Given the importance of third countries as suppliers and the fact that Canada affords more favorable tariff treatment to wool imports than the United States, it seems likely that Canadian textile manufacturers enjoy a substantial advantage over their U.S. competitors in terms of lower wool price. It is not clear, however, that such differential resource tariffs would be maintained by the two countries in the event of reciprocal free trade.

Subindustries in the petroleum and coal products sector are potentially very sensitive to resource costs. Both the petroleum products and the coal products subindustries have heavy resource requirements, and in both cases, substantial differences in cost between areas are evident. This suggests that there may be considerable cost advantage for firms in the coal products industry locating near centers of coal production, especially in the Pennsylvania-West Virginia area. There is likely to be a similar advan-

[7] Cotton accounts for about one half the fibre used in the textile industry, whereas wool and synthetics together account for most of the other half.
[8] In 1958 imports represented about 57 percent of domestic U.S. consumption and about 42 percent of Canadian consumption. See *United States Commodity Yearbook*, 1962, and *Trade of Canada*, 1958.

tage for firms in the petroleum products area locating in the regions of greatest resource supply — especially in the Texas, California, and Alberta areas.

The resource dependence of wood-using industries (wood products and pulp and paper) is less easily generalized, and the figures in Tables 15 must be interpreted with great care. In each case the minimum is zero, indicating that the wood resource required by these industries is available in all North American regions. Insofar as wood prices are similar in all regions, there might, in the extreme case, be no difference in costs between areas. However, the *maximum* estimate indicates that at the other extreme resource costs may conceivably be very important for these industries — to the extent that resource prices in each region are determined by adding transport costs from the region of greatest production and export. Because of relatively high transport charges, it is quite expensive to ship wood between North American regions; hence, these maximum bounding estimates are generally quite substantial. It cannot be argued that these are not valid *bounding* estimates. The problem is that they are often too large to be useful in providing any sort of fix on resource costs.

From an examination of the second and third last columns in Table 15 it is evident that the furniture industry, because of its limited lumber requirements, is less sensitive to differential lumber costs than the rest of the wood products sector. It should also be noted that the pulp and paper sector shows a considerable degree of potential sensitivity to wood costs. It must be pointed out that the major source of supply of lumber for the wood products sector (and, hence, the point of reference for the maximum estimates) is the British Columbia and United States Pacific Northwest region, whereas the major source of supply of wood for the pulp and paper sector is Quebec. This could be due to the fact that a different kind of wood is required by each sector; or, more likely, it may be explained by the influence of large markets in the northeast United States on the location of both the pulp and paper industry and its wood supplies. Concentration of logging in Quebec to supply the pulp and paper sector may, therefore, have resulted *not* because Quebec is the cheapest source of wood but because Quebec is located adjacent to the large markets for pulp and paper in the eastern United States and Canada. Insofar as proximity to markets is a factor determining the present use of resources, resource costs in British Columbia for the pulp and paper industry may not be higher than in Quebec. This complication associated with market proximity provides another reason for recognizing that the maximum may overstate resource cost differentials. Areas of greatest resource supply and export may be determined by market factors rather than lowest resource costs. As markets develop in other regions, such as the Pacific Coast, then a growing pulp and paper industry there might find that wood supplies are no more expensive than in Quebec. Thus, the maximum resource cost estimate may be irrelevant, since it is computed by using Quebec — the present site of heaviest resource extraction and export — as the base for all spatial price calculations.[9]

Along with the sectors shown in these tables there are two others with substantial resource requirements in their input structures. The first is nonmetallic mineral products. Available statistics on subindustries in the sector using sand, clay and gravel (including the cement, concrete products and artifical abrasives industries) imply that, if these inputs are to be shipped long distances in the North American economy, total costs of these subindustries will increase by forty percent, and in many cases much more. This explains why nonmetallic mineral production is located close to resource supplies. Paradoxically, it does not necessarily mean that resources determine location; because many nonmetallic

[9] The same difficulty may distort the maximum estimate in the nonferrous metal products industry. The figures in column (3) of Table 14 suggest that base metals costs in the Laurentian shield areas of Ontario and Quebec may be higher than in many U.S. regions because this maximum estimate was computed by using the present area of heaviest base metals extraction — the U.S. Mountain area — as the point of reference from which resource costs in all other locations were computed. If this U.S. Mountain region is the area of greatest production and export, not because resource costs are lower there, but because the U.S. tariff prevents greater production and export from Ontario and Quebec, then this maximum estimate will tend to overstate the free trade cost differential. If tariffs were eliminated, the Canadian Laurentian shield might be a much lower cost source of base metals than these estimates suggest.

resources are available in all regions, locating firms are indifferent on this account and their location tends to be determined instead by markets. For example, the sand and gravel used by many subindustries in this sector are available almost anywhere. This broad availability, coupled with the high cost of shipping the output of this sector, combine to force subindustries to locate close to markets; in the cases in which resources are broadly available, therefore, points of both resource extraction and processing tend to be determined by markets.

The relevant conclusion for this sector is that considerations of transport costs (both on the required resource and the finished product) are sufficient in most subindustries to eclipse other cost considerations such as wages, taxes, etc. Whenever required resources are in abundant supply (as is often the case) resource-using subindustries tend to locate close to markets. If required resources are not available in all locations, then both market and resource sites determine location.

The other sector that is undoubtedly heavily dependent on resources but is not shown in either table is food processing. It is excluded for several reasons. In view of the large number of processing activities included in this sector, a long list of resources is used, each relating to a specific subindustry. Generalizations on the resource orientation of the sector are, therefore, difficult. Moreover, resource restrictions may not be critical for the food-processing industry to the degree that most agricultural products, like many nonmetallic minerals, are available in supply in all regions in North America.

The other seven manufacturing sectors analyzed in this study do not require significant resource inputs. One of the excluded industries that might be expected to show some resource dependence is the leather products industry, which requires animal hides. However, the leather industry is not significantly dependent on this resource, since only about three percent of its costs represent purchases from the agricultural sector. The tannery subindustry is, of course, more dependent on hides than the leather products sector. An examination of industrial categories in sufficient detail will show that a subindustry with heavy resource requirements can be found in any manufacturing sector.

Conclusions

It is almost impossible to get an accurate measurement of differences in resource costs between areas. Hence, it has been necessary to compute the limits on resource cost differences between areas allowed by the possibility of interarea arbitrage, given relevant transport costs for each resource. Two extreme estimates have been computed; together they have been designed to bracket the actual cost differences between areas that this type of arbitrage would allow. Resource cost differences between areas can hardly be less than the minimum used in this study because this is taken to be zero for all areas with resource supplies; for any area without a local resource supply, the cost of shipping it in from the nearest supply source is used. The actual cost differences between areas can hardly be more than the maximum figure used in this study because this estimate is simply the cost involved in shipping the resource to any area from the area of present heaviest concentration and export. (Costs in any area cannot rise above this because purchases can always be made in the final resort from this export source.)

Obviously the extreme assumptions used ensure that both the maximum and minimum estimates are likely to be quite unrealistic. This suggests that actual costs fall well within these two bounds; however, an additional problem must be kept in mind. There is no guarantee that the region with greatest production of a resource will not also import the resource; thus, the signs of the differential shown in Tables 14 and 15 could conceivably be incorrect. In spite of these methodological difficulties, certain generalizations are possible.

Interarea differences in petroleum and coal prices could have a very important impact on costs in the petroleum and coal products sector. For example, to the extent that coal prices are determined by the West Virginia-Pennsylvania price plus transport costs, total costs in the coal products subsector may as a direct consequence range as much as twenty percent higher in some North American regions (for example, in British Columbia) than in others (for example, in the Middle Atlantic region). Costs in the petroleum products industry may also be sensitive to regional petroleum price differences, although to a much smaller degree. Similarly, costs in the pulp and paper and wood products sectors may be sensitive to interarea differences in wood and lumber costs.

Coal, petroleum, and lumber are the only resources whose costs can explain substantial interarea differences in production costs in broad manufacturing sectors, and thus only three of the sectors analyzed in this study would be significantly affected as a result: petroleum and coal products, pulp and paper, and wood products. However, the fact that transport costs may *allow* such interregional differences in total costs does not mean that these interregional cost differences do exist. They may or may not, and judgment on them is therefore withheld.

A much firmer conclusion is possible for all other resources and producing sectors. The wide availability of nonmetallic minerals in all areas seems to preclude wide interregional variations in these resource costs. Otherwise, spatial arbitrage prevents interregional resource cost differences from substantially affecting total costs of any of the other manufacturing sectors under study. The maximum impact in any case would be to raise total costs of a producing sector in the most distant area by about two percent, and probably much less. It is true of the tobacco products and textile sectors with their heavy requirements of tobacco and cotton. It is also true for the metallic products sector, although in this case, as in any other, subindustries within the sector can be found (for example, primary iron and steel) that could be much more sensitive to resource costs.

It should be emphasized that formal calculations of this nature abstract from institutional practices. Such arrangements may be very important in the resource area because of the close parent-subsidiary ties that often exist between extraction activities and processing. Such ties of course allow a regional price system to exist outside the bounds derived in this study. This should be recognized, but the potential importance of such arrangements should be evaluated carefully. If a regional price of a resource falls outside the limits allowed by spatial arbitrage because of institutional arrangements, then three possibilities must be considered: first, that the price is strictly an accounting convention used by a parent to subsidize or tax a resource subsidiary, with the location of its activities based on a more sophisticated shadow accounting with more realistic prices, which in fact do fall within these limits; or second, that the firm has miscalculated — a condition which is difficult to analyze; or third, that resource extraction is so heavily bound up in monopoly arrangements that competitive resource markets simply do not exist. Only the second possibility, in the short run, and the third are significant for a location analysis; but these possibilities should be kept in mind in any evaluation of these resource estimates.

In terms of proximity to resources, Canadian regions are well situated (with certain exceptions). There are two producing sectors — textiles and tobacco products — in which Canadian regions are apparently at a disadvantage since both cotton and raw tobacco production are concentrated in the southern United States. However, these are resources with low transport costs; hence, any location disadvantages tend to lose significance. Petroleum production is also centered in the South. Unlike cotton and tobacco, required petroleum supplies are more expensive to transport; as a consequence, some Canadian (and U.S.) areas may be at a cost disadvantage vis-à-vis Texas, California, and the Canadian Prairies. However, as North America is a net petroleum importer, seaboard areas (including the Great Lakes regions) may also be favorable locations for petroleum-based manufacturing.

The situation of eastern Canadian regions is relatively attractive in terms of proximity to a likely future major source of iron ore in Labrador. These regions are less attractively situated in terms of coal. However, the Canadian steel industry in Hamilton, Ontario, is situated not far distant from the largest sources of coal in the Pennsylvania-West Virginia area of the United States. British Columbia is, of course, not well situated in terms of proximity to North American sources of either coal or iron ore.

Canadian areas are at least as well situated as comparable U.S. areas in terms of proximity to lumber supplies; British Columbia is an area of heavy lumber extraction for the wood products sector, and Quebec is the major source of wood for pulp and paper.

In summary, Canada has a reputation for being a country in which resources are available in large quantities; as a consequence, it is not surprising that the country is well situated in terms of supplies of all resources. The only resources which may provide a substantial competitive edge to U.S. production locations are petroleum and coal; and even in these cases it should be noted that the Canadian Prairies have recently become a major source of petroleum supply, and the eastern industrial center of Canada is relatively close to North American coal concentration in Pennsylvania and West Virginia.

7

PROXIMITY
TO MANUFACTURED SUPPLIES

A firm has two types of material input: resources and semiprocessed manufactured goods supplied by other industries. In considering a new location, a firm must consider its proximity to sources of both these materials. Resources have been considered in detail in the preceding chapter; in this chapter North American locations will be ranked in terms of their proximity to supplies of manufactured goods.

The very close relationship of these two influences may best be illustrated by the following hypothetical example. Suppose the tobacco industry (which we shall refer to in this context as a secondary industry) uses two inputs: raw tobacco and paper. The first is a resource, the second a manufactured or "intermediate" good. On reflection, however, the distinction becomes less significant because paper — the intermediate good — can be considered a resource (wood) that has passed through several stages of processing. Since resources in a processed form become indistinguishable from intermediate supplies, the analysis of this chapter can, at least on the theoretical level, be looked upon simply as an extension of the resource analysis of the previous chapter.

Direct and Indirect Costs of Acquiring Processed Resources

The first approach that should be considered is a simple extension of the resource analysis. Using the example of the tobacco industry, it would be quite feasible to examine the importance of paper as an input requirement, along with the cost of shipping paper from the least cost source. The computations would be strictly parallel to the analysis of the raw tobacco requirement in the previous chapter; the location of the manufactured supply (paper) would be considered as one datum and the location of the basic resource (tobacco) as another. However, the analysis of manufactured supplies would not be reduced to a resource problem. In order to do this, it would be necessary to push back the analysis one stage to examine the wood input used in paper manufacturing, along with the cost of shipping wood and distances from wood sources. In this framework of analysis, only resource sites (for example, wood) are considered fixed; intermediate manufacturing supply sites (for example, paper) are not.

On purely theoretical grounds there is an attractive symmetry involved in handling both problems of location of the intermediate supplying industry (paper) and the secondary user industry (tobacco) as extensions of resource analysis. Moreover, in the long run it is likely that to a substantial degree, industry location is determined in this way — with the location of both intermediate and secondary manufacture dependent on proximity to resources and to markets. Theoretically, therefore, the location of the intermediate supplying industry and the secondary user industry should be simultaneously determined from a single, complex solution, with only market and resource locations given a priori.

Problems of simultaneity of this kind have been encountered before in this study. Ideally, all locations of every activity in this analysis (including, for that matter, even markets and the resources that are exploited) should be determined as parts of one general simultaneous solution. However, it is not feasible, for practical reasons relating both to the theoretical inadequacy of any applicable model and to the statistical problems involved in defining the large number of simultaneous relationships involved; instead, the problem must be broken up into parts, with each part isolated by simplifying assumptions.

Simplifying assumptions must also be made in analyzing the influence of intermediate manufactured supplies on the location of secondary industry. Because most goods pass through many stages of fabrication, there is generally not one supplying intermediate industry, but many; and as the number of stages in the analysis increases, the computations become more and more entangled,[1] and resource content becomes less important and more difficult to define. In addition, the circular interindustry flow of goods and services makes it impossible to distinguish unambiguously between intermediate and secondary industries. In the exchange of one good, *A* may be the intermediate supplying industry and *B* the secondary user industry; but in the exchange of another good their roles may be reversed.

In order to simplify, no attempt is made to trace back directly and indirectly the resource content of any intermediate supply; nor is any attempt made to evaluate possible changes in the location of present intermediate supply sites. Instead present sources of intermediate industrial supplies are taken as given, and each potential location for manufacturing is evaluated in terms of its proximity to the given pattern of its own intermediate suppliers.

Manufactured Supply Potential

Since in this analysis no attempt is made to evaluate resource availability facing the intermediate supplying industry, one dimension of the problem is clearly restricted. However, this restriction allows a broader and more detailed analysis in other directions. In terms of the example of the tobacco industry, all intermediate manufactured inputs may be studied; and the entire value of each input (for example, paper) may be considered and not just its resource (for example, wood) content.

A specific secondary industry is assumed to have preferences of approximately the following kind. Each of its potential locations may be evaluated in terms of its proximity to each required intermediate supply by a gravity, or potential, function. This evaluation involves examining the spatial distribution of present sources of this particular intermediate supply and discounting the supply availability at each source by the distance from the potential location being considered by the secondary industry. How-

---

[1] This conclusion also depends on the degree of vertical integration in an industry.

ever, because a secondary user industry requires many intermediate manufactured supplies, a gravity index of this kind may be derived for each intermediate input. The problem becomes one of finding appropriate weights for combining these indexes. Obviously, a firm should be more concerned about its proximity to some intermediate supplies than to others. Specifically, it should be most sensitive to an input that it must purchase heavily and that is expensive to ship. These two influences are combined to provide an appropriate weight to indicate the importance a firm attaches to getting close to each intermediate input; thus, if input *A* is twice as important in the input structure as input *B,* but input *B* is twice as costly to ship, then it is assumed that the firm is equally interested in getting close to either input *A* or input *B.*[2]

The assumptions involved in applying a gravity model to each intermediate input supply pattern should be clarified. First, it is assumed that the firm is interested in all supply sources of an input but much more interested in close sources. This is analogous to the assumption, in any market gravity or potential model, that the firm may be prepared to sell in all markets, but it is especially interested in large, close markets because of the expectation that it will be able to exploit these more heavily. This assumption may be questioned, since a firm's relation to its sources of supply seems to be quite different; presumably it is interested in only one (that is, the least cost) source of supply. As soon as it can be established that a source is "least cost," the firm may effectively disregard the location of all other suppliers.

The problem in an analysis of this kind is specifying such least cost sources. No information is available on differences in prices of supplies at various locations; thus, the only reasonable a priori

[2] Formally, the supply desirability index of location p for the production of secondary good j is:

$$\sum_i \sum_k \left(\frac{q_i{}^k}{{}^k d^p} \right) t_i a_{ij}$$

in which $q_i{}^k$ = proportion of industry i located in area k, as estimated in Chapter 3.
   ${}^k d^p$ = distance from k to p, as estimated in Chapter 3.
   t_i = cost per dollar mile of shipping intermediate good i, as estimated in Chapter 4.
   a_{ij} = proportion of total costs of industry j devoted to purchase of intermediate good i.

assumption is that if price differences do exist, the lower price is likely to be found in the areas in which this good is now heavily produced and exported — rather than in (import) areas of limited production. The supply potential model used in this chapter inclines firms toward these areas of heavy intermediate supply and may, consequently, be regarded as an indirect way of introducing likely price patterns.

There is another reason that areas of heavy supply may be preferred. Given the level of industry aggregation used in this study, there is some production of goods in each aggregated industrial sector in each region. However, each of these broad industrial categories includes a large number of diverse products; and certain of the specific products in this category may *not* necessarily be produced in each region. It would seem reasonable to argue that, for any area, the greater the level of production in an aggregated industrial sector, the more likely it is that all or most of these intermediate subcomponent goods are produced. Similarly, the smaller the production level in an aggregated industrial sector, the less likely it is that all required supplies of subcomponents will be available. The fact that figures on aggregated industrial sectors are the only indexes that can be used in this study may obscure the fact that a firm may be unable to acquire all its intermediate subcomponent requirements in any area; and as a firm is forced to turn to more than one source of supply, it will find, other things being equal, that the most attractive areas are those that provide the best mix of available subcomponent intermediate goods.

The rationale of the assumptions of this model — that firms are interested in the whole spatial pattern of supply, but especially the closest sources of heaviest supply concentration — may be summarized as follows. Specific intermediate supplies are not necessarily represented in each industrial aggregate used in this study, and firms will be interested in the overall pattern of all available supplies, especially the locations of heaviest supply that are likely to provide the widest range of product mix. The cost of supplies may vary with their source, and the firm will be interested in the heaviest sources of supply (since these are likely to be low price export points) and in the most proximate sources (since they involve lower transport costs).

The use of a potential model, therefore, is based on implicit recognition of two problems which cannot be evaluated explicitly because of data limitations: the problem of aggregation of intermediate industries and the problem of differing possible prices at various supply sources. When these problems do not exist all locations become equally desirable in terms of their proximity to intermediate manufactured supplies because in these circumstances all supplies would be produced in all areas, and any new firm would minimize its only relevant cost — transport charges — by drawing all its supplies from its own domestic area. It is not necessary to pass firm judgment on the importance of these problems. When they are not important, all locations are equally desirable; when they are important (and the authors incline to this view), the attractiveness of areas in terms of their closeness to intermediate supplies will vary. And the application of this model seems to be a reasonable way of deriving a first estimate of this location influence.

Comparison of North American Regions

Two important observations should be remembered in evaluating the empirical results presented below. First, it should be noted in examining the input requirements of any industry that it is necessary to consider supplies of the *same* intermediate good, as well as supplies of *other* goods because many industries rely heavily on inputs produced by their own industry — for example, textile manufacturers are heavily dependent on textile supplies. The greater the level of aggregation, the more likely it is that both suppliers and producers will be aggregated together in the same industrial grouping causing this phenomenon,[3] and it should be

[3] In the extreme, if an industry used only goods produced by the same industry, then this supply potential study would reduce to an analysis parallel to the study of agglomeration and external economies. In both cases firms would be attracted to areas of heavy concentration of industry producing the same good. Such an extreme case can be dismissed. However, to the extent that firms do rely heavily on supplies produced within the same industry (that is, to the extent that the interindustry flow table shows heavy concentration on diagonal elements), the results of the two studies will tend to be similar.

observed that there is a very high level of aggregation used in this study.

Second, a careful examination of the model employed (see footnote 2 above) indicates that an area may be judged attractive because of one or both of the following characteristics: it may be an area in which there is a heavy concentration of intermediate suppliers; alternatively, it may be centrally located to all other North American sources of supply. The empirical results,[4] which provide the ranking of all North American regions in each industry shown in Table 16, illustrate these two influences.

In terms of proximity to available sources of intermediate supplies, the best regions in the North American continent are the familiar U.S. areas lying along the Chicago-New York axis: the West Lake, Capital, Middle Atlantic, and East Lake areas. The next most attractive areas are those lying on the periphery of this axis of central activity: New England, followed by Ontario and Quebec. It should be noted that both these Canadian provinces rank ahead of the U.S. South and all other U.S. areas. It should also be noted that the Canadian Maritimes and Prairies are the least attractively situated areas on the North American continent.

---

[4] It seems reasonable to combine the last two influences in the model equation in footnote 2 (i.e., the relative importance of each input, a_{ij}, and its shipping cost, t_i) by simple multiplication. However, it is more difficult to justify multiplying the product of these two by the gravity factor made up of supply concentration (q_i^k) and distance from each supply point ($^k d^p$). To reduce the arbitrary nature of these computations, the resulting index was tested for sensitivity to a number of alternative assumptions. The first set of alternative assumptions is that the relative importance of each input, (a_{ij}) or its cost of shipment, (t_i) — or both — should be multiplied by a scalar. However, this would simply change the supply potential index for each area by the same scalar, and would leave the rankings of all areas unchanged. The rankings in Table 16 are therefore independent of scalar multiplication of the component influences. This is not true of another test — changing the exponent (s) of the gravity factor $(q_i^k/^k d^p)^s$. Exponent values for s of 2 and ½ were also tested, along with the exponent 1 (implicit in the equation in footnote 2). For almost all of the eighteen areas and fifteen industries relative standings remain unchanged or are altered by only one or two ranks. The greatest observed changes in ranking involve moving an area up or down by three or at most four positions. None of these changes is substantial enough to affect the overall pattern of conclusions discussed in the text. The three complete sets of rankings, based on these three different exponent values are shown in Appendix K.

TABLE 16. Regions Ranked in Terms of Proximity to Intermediate Manufactured Supplies, 1958.[a]

Manufacturing sector[b]	Pacific Northwest	Pacific Southwest	Mountain	Southwest	Florida	Capital	South	New England	Middle Atlantic	Lower Midwest	East Lake	West Lake	Upper Midwest	British Columbia	Prairies	Ontario	Quebec	Maritimes
Food	16	13	15	12	11	2	9	5	3	8	4	1	10	14	18	6	7	17
Tobacco	14	17	15	13	11	3	8	6	4	9	5	1	12	10	18	7	2	16
Textiles	17	14	15	12	11	2	8	5	3	9	4	1	10	13	18	7	6	16
Apparel	18	15	14	12	10	2	6	1	3	9	7	4	11	17	16	8	5	13
Wood products	9	12	16	14	15	3	10	6	4	11	5	1	13	2	17	8	7	18
Paper	12	15	16	14	13	2	9	4	5	10	6	1	11	8	18	7	3	17
Printing	14	16	17	13	12	2	8	3	4	9	6	1	11	10	18	7	5	15
Electrical equipment	16	14	15	13	12	2	9	5	3	8	4	1	10	11	18	6	7	17
Chemicals	17	13	15	11	15	2	9	6	3	8	4	1	10	14	18	7	5	16
Petroleum products	16	10	14	8	11	2	11	9	4	7	5	1	12	13	17	6	3	18
Rubber and plastics	18	13	14	12	11	2	8	5	3	9	4	1	10	16	17	7	6	15
Leather goods	16	14	15	12	11	2	9	3	4	8	5	1	10	13	18	7	6	17
Nonmetallic mineral products	17	13	14	12	11	2	9	5	3	8	4	1	10	15	18	6	7	16
Metallic products	17	13	15	11	12	2	9	5	4	8	3	1	10	14	18	6	7	16
Transportation equipment	17	12	15	11	13	2	9	6	4	8	3	1	10	14	18	5	7	16
Miscellaneous	15	14	16	13	12	2	8	5	3	9	4	1	10	11	18	6	7	17

[a] For the derivation of these rankings, see footnote 2, Chapter 7.
[b] See Table 1, note a.

There are exceptions to this overall pattern in several industries. British Columbia has a relatively high rank in the lumber and wood products industry largely because of the concentration of that industry there and because a large proportion of the supplies used by this industry is its own product. This same phenomenon may be observed in the high ranking of the New England area in the leather industry.

Conclusions

An industry that is interested in its proximity to sources of intermediate manufactured supplies will be attracted to those North American areas of heaviest industrial concentration along the Chicago-New York axis, which includes the West Lake, Capital, Middle Atlantic, and East Lake areas. These regions are well endowed with almost all lines of manufacturing and, hence, provide the best selection of available inputs. The heavy concentration of production in this central area in almost all industrial lines — along with the employment and income generated as a direct result — combined with the fact that this area is centrally located to the North American continent in purely spatial terms make this a preferred area in terms of proximity to intermediate manufactured supplies and in terms of a whole group of location influences analyzed in previous chapters: proximity to markets, external economies, and minimization of market transportation costs. Furthermore, the conclusions in this chapter about the next best source of intermediate supplies are again roughly parallel to those of the same previous chapters: those areas on the periphery of this region of central concentration — New England, Ontario, and Quebec — are next preferred. Almost without exception, they are superior to other U.S. regions in the south and west. Parallel conclusions also follow on the least attractive North American regions. In supply potential, as well as in proximity to markets, external economies, and transportation costs, the Canadian Maritimes and Prairies are least favored.

8

CAPITAL COSTS

Capital costs in Canada may currently be different from those in the United States for any of the following reasons: initial costs of purchasing machinery and equipment may be higher in Canada on account of Canadian protection of these items; initial costs of plant facilities may differ in the two countries because labor and materials costs differ; the cost of carrying debt may be higher in Canada because of higher interest rates; and there may be some similar additional cost on equity capital necessary to attract investment funds to Canada. Some of these higher Canadian costs would tend to disappear automatically with free trade (for example, higher machinery prices attributable to Canadian duties); these influences are evaluated in Appendix L. The objective of this chapter is to analyze the higher Canadian capital costs that would continue into a period of free trade.

Initial Costs of Machinery and Equipment

The present Canadian tariff on machinery and equipment tends to raise costs to Canadian firms undertaking investment. The average Canadian tariff on machinery is about twelve percent; however, this tariff varies substantially between items in various categories. This twelve percent duty allows machinery prices in Canada to be that much higher; however, it does not guarantee it, since Canadian domestic producers may sell machinery at a price below the maximum allowed by the tariff. In any case, in the event of free trade and the elimination of the Canadian tariff on machinery imports, the cost of machinery would tend to be equalized in the two countries.[1] In terms of this particular item, therefore, it is assumed that capital costs in the two countries would be equal.

Initial Costs of Plant

It is by no means clear that construction costs are now either higher or lower in Canada than in the United States. Best available evidence[2] suggests that in 1954 brick and lumber costs were lower in the United States, but cement and labor costs lower in Canada. With free trade, costs of materials would tend to be equalized in the two countries,[3] leaving a difference in costs attributable to lower Canadian wages. The effects of lower labor costs in the construction industry are evaluated in this chapter; however, insofar as higher Canadian materials prices, like higher machinery prices, are a result of Canadian protection, they would not persist in a free trade area. Hence, their evaluation is deferred until Appendix L.

Costs of Carrying Debt

Interest rates in Canada have traditionally been substantially higher than in the United States. The basic reason for this is that the supply of domestic savings in Canada has not been adequate to service investment requirements, and Canada, as a consequence, has acquired the additional investment funds from the nearest and best source, the United States. Any restraints or rigidities that have prevented a free flow of capital north into Canada have been reflected in higher interest rates in Canada than in the United States. Therefore, any explanation of higher interest rates in

[1] The difference in price that might remain because of differing tax treatment in the two countries is evaluated in the next chapter.

[2] F. A. Knox, *The Canadian Electrical Manufacturing Industry: An Economic Analysis* (Canadian Electrical Manufacturers Association, 1955), p. 41.

[3] Differences in costs of materials in the two countries would also persist because of differences in taxes; these are evaluated in the next chapter.

Canada or any judgment on whether they would persist in a free trade scheme involves a detailed examination first, of the effects of free trade on the Canadian excess demand for investment funds, and, second, of the restraints on the free flow of capital from south to north across the border. The possible effects of free trade on Canadian supply and demand conditions for capital are considered in Chapter 11. The institutional restraints or rigidities may be classified as follows:

Foreign Exchange Risk. An important restriction on the free flow of capital is that Canada and the United States do not form a common currency area. Since the relative value of the Canadian and U.S. dollars is not permanently fixed, any resident investing in the other country undertakes a substantial degree of risk, which he would not face if he were to invest his funds domestically. This is the risk of the windfall gain or loss that occurs whenever one currency is revalued in terms of the other. Specifically, the American investor buying a Canadian bond runs the risk of gain or loss from a revaluation of the Canadian dollar because it would cause a sudden change in the value of the U.S. funds that he would receive from the repayment of his principal and interest. As a result, he will lend his funds in Canada only at a premium; the Canadian borrower must pay a higher interest rate, and the incidence of the exchange risk is shifted onto the Canadian borrower.[4]

Political Considerations. One of the reasons capital may not flow freely between countries is the possibility of unexpected political changes that may affect the status of the foreign investor. For example, a foreign country may pass tax legislation discriminating

[4] If Canadians borrow by selling bonds expressed in U.S. dollars in New York, the same risk is involved, and the incidence, even more clearly, is borne by the Canadian borrower.

For a more detailed discussion of Canadian-U.S. interest rate differentials, see Gerald K. Helleiner, "Connections between United States' and Canadian Markets, 1952–1960," *Yale Economic Essays*, 2: 351–400 (Fall 1962); G. L. Reuber and R. J. Wonnacott, *The Cost of Capital in Canada* (Washington: Resources for the Future, 1962), pp. 54–67; Rudolf R. Rhomberg, "A Model of the Canadian Economy under fixed Exchange and Fluctuating Exchange Rates," *Journal of Political Economy*, 72: 1–31 (February 1964); and Paul Wonnacott, *The Height, Structure and Significance of Interest Rates* (Ottawa: Royal Commission on Banking and Finance, November 1962).

against foreign investors as a means of increasing domestic ownership of industry and resources; in the face of a severe deterioration
of its balance of payments, a foreign government may temporarily
freeze repayment of capital and interest abroad; or, in extreme circumstances, it may simply repudiate its debt.

It is quite true that some of these adverse actions, for example,
the raising of taxes, might be instituted against U.S. investors by
their own government. The real issue, therefore, is the extent to
which foreign investment is viewed as involving a greater risk than
domestic investment. If this greater risk — whether real or imagined — discourages the American investor from supplying his
funds to Canada, the interest rate will be higher in Canada than
in the United States, and there will be a premium sufficient to
compensate the borrower for these risks. Again the incidence of
this risk is, in the long run, mostly[5] shifted onto the Canadian borrower who has to pay a higher price for funds.

It is important to note that the evaluation of risk (and the associated higher Canadian interest rate) is a subjective decision by
the U.S. investor. The "objective risk" involved in lending money
to Canada may not in reality be as important as the subjective
evaluation of risk by the U.S. investor. Mild discriminatory
legislation against U.S. investment has already been attempted by
Canada; if it is viewed by U.S. investors as a portent of things to
come, this legislation may be very important in deterring these investors from entering the Canadian capital markets. Therefore, the
impact on Canadian interest rates (and consequently on production costs) may be much greater than the direct quantitative importance of this legislation suggests.

Institutional Conventions. There are certain rule of thumb devices that may be used by large American lending institutions,
such as implicit limits on the funds that are allocated to foreign,
as opposed to domestic investment. As these restrictions become
important in allocating the flow of funds, they result in higher

---

[5] Logically, the imperfection in international capital flows might also
fall partly on the U.S. suppliers of investment funds. However, because the
U.S. capital market is so much larger than the Canadian, any interruption
in Canadian-U.S. capital flows will have a much greater effect on Canadian
than on U.S. interest rates.

interest rates on foreign, as compared to domestic, U.S. securities. In addition, the fact that there may be close contact and confidence between U.S. borrowers and lenders may mean that these borrowers can raise funds on more favorable terms than Canadian borrowers.

Special Factors. Finally, the simple element of geography and physical distance may influence interest rate differences. Even though there may be no evidence of greater risk involved, interest rates tend to rise with any spatial movement away from a capital export area into areas of excess demand for capital. In the last century interest rates were related to distance from the London capital market; today interest rates tend to rise as one moves from New York west, or from Toronto west. The element of distance may help explain why interest rates are higher as one moves from the New York market north into Canada.

It is extremely difficult to measure the importance of these spatial effects. Interest rates are higher in California than in New York, and higher in British Columbia and Alberta than in Toronto. However, it is not possible to derive any estimate of the effect of space alone on interest rates from these observations because of all the other factors influencing the structure of interstate and interprovincial interest rates. For example, Alberta rates are probably higher than they would be otherwise because of the repudiation of provincial debt during the depression; and, at least in the opinion of the Canadian financial community, B.C. provincial interest rates are higher than they would be otherwise because of the unorthodox "elimination" of the provincial debt that has taken place.[6] It is, therefore, extremely difficult to measure in isolation the impact of geography on interest rates. It should be remembered that costs of capital may vary interregionally, as well as internationally; however, these interregional differences need be borne only by firms that raise capital in regional markets. A firm that is able to raise funds on the New York capital market through a head office there for investment in California presumably does not encounter this cost differential.

[6] By transforming direct provincial debt into indebtedness of various public facilities in the province.

The question is whether the same is true for an international company that is able to raise funds on the New York market for investment in Canada. The answer is no: although the firm is raising funds in New York at low rates, a cost is involved insofar as the firm must attach a premium internally to those funds transferred into Canada, to cover the risk of exchange revaluation. It is assumed in this study that the market's evaluation of this risk — as reflected in the higher Canadian interest rate — provides the best estimate of the premium that firms are likely to attach to such an international lending operation; consequently, if funds for Canadian expansion are provided by a U.S. parent at the U.S. interest rate, some sort of implicit subsidy is involved.

How far would the current difference in interest cost between Canada and the United States persist in the event of free trade? The most important of the above causes of the interest differential is probably the foreign exchange risk. This risk will remain regardless of changes in commercial policy; it would be eliminated only if the two countries joined in a common currency area. Furthermore, it is likely that the other causes of the interest differential would remain to much the same degree in the event of free trade. Hence, differences in interest costs would tend to remain with any change in commercial policy, unless the two countries were to establish a common currency area, or unless free trade affected Canadian excess demand for capital. These two points are considered in Chapter 11.

Equity Costs

The final, extremely important question is whether the cost of raising equity funds is higher in Canada than in the United States. This cost would be reflected, for example, in the price of a comparable stock issue being lower in Canada. The lower receipts by the issuing firm would have the same effect as raising costs; this situation is directly parallel to the higher effective interest rate the firm must pay if it is forced to sell a bond issue at a discount.

It should be expected that international flows of equity capital — as well as debt capital — are influenced by all the barriers catalogued in the previous section; and for all these same reasons differences in equity costs are likely to persist in a free trade area. Since equity markets tend to be less perfect than bond markets, it would not be surprising if the higher cost of raising equity capital in Canada exceeded the higher cost of raising debt capital. There is, however, an important pressure operating in the other direction. There is a capital gains tax in the United States, but not in Canada. The tax free status of capital gains presumably makes equity for the Canadian investors more attractive vis-à-vis debt than it is in the United States. For this reason one would expect that the difference in equity costs between the two countries might be less than the difference in debt costs. Complications arising from the different tax treatment of capital gains in Canada and in the United States make it very difficult to estimate empirically the difference in effective costs of raising equity in the two countries.[7]

It follows that, in analyzing capital costs in the two countries, different equity costs must remain an important undefined variable. To provide a range indicative of the relative importance of this variable, two estimates of capital cost differences have been computed — one ignoring differences in equity costs, and the other including possible effects of higher equity cost in a somewhat arbitrary way.

Capital Cost Estimates

When costs in two countries are compared, it is not always clear whether production techniques in one country or the other should be used as the basis of comparison. However, in line with the argument that, under free trade, U.S. techniques and industrial and financial organization are more likely to be appropriate than

---

[7] To the degree that equity capital is more expensive to raise in Canada, stock prices in that country should be lower (relative to earnings) than in the United States. Equivalent price-earnings ratios for common stocks in Canada and the United States should throw light on this question in the future. Unfortunately, historical comparisons are not possible because Canadian price-earnings ratios were not published prior to 1964. The admittedly far too limited evidence of 1964 shows no substantial difference in the two countries and hence seems to imply that the influence of exchange risk in raising Canadian equity capital costs may be roughly

the Canadian, U.S. debt-equity ratios[8] and investment rates in each industry were used throughout as the base to which capital cost differences were applied.

These capital cost differences for each industry are shown in Table 17; the total impact on all industries is shown in the bottom row of this table. An examination of this row indicates that in 1958 depreciation of plant in the United States in all manufacturing sectors was over $2 billion. At Canadian wage rates the initial cost of construction of this plant could be about nine percent lower; since this lower cost would reduce depreciation charges by the same proportion, capital costs could be as much as $182 million lower.[9] (The lower capital costs imply that total costs might be almost 0.06 percent lower in Canada as a result.)[10] Outstanding

---

offset by the influence of Canadian capital gains treatment in lowering capital costs:

Price Earnings Ratios

	Canada (Toronto Stock Exchange Industrial Index)	United States (Dow Jones Industrial Average)
June 30, 1964	19.2	18.8
September 30, 1964	18.7	19.2

(from *Barron's; Toronto Stock Exchange Monthly Review*.)

[8] The U.S. debt and equity structure in 1958 in each manufacturing industry is shown in Appendix M.

[9] Canadian wage rates in construction are approximately thirty-five percent lower than in the United States; about twenty-seven percent of total construction costs goes to wage payments.

[10] Derived from the formula:

percent difference in total manufacturing costs =

$$W_c \left[\frac{L_c}{VS_c} \right] \left[\frac{D_M}{VS_M} \right]$$

in which W_c = percent difference in wage rates in the construction sector

L_c = labor costs in construction

VS_c = value shipped (total costs) in construction

D_M = depreciation of plant in all manufacturing sectors

VS_M = value shipped in all manufacturing sectors.

The computations for each industrial sector were identical except that depreciation and value shipped figures for each industry replaced the manufacturing totals above.

These estimates are subject to two conflicting biases: the cost advantage in Canada will be less to the degree that the construction industry in Canada is less efficient than in the United States; the cost advantage is greater because savings on initial investment involve savings on interest carrying costs.

TABLE 17. *Estimated Percentage That Total Costs Would Be Higher in Canada Than in the United States Because of Higher Capital Costs (1958 U.S. Base).*

Manufacturing sector[a]	Lower costs of construction		Higher carrying costs — Debt				Equity		Estimated percentage	
	Estimated depreciation on plant (1)	Lower capital costs of construction (@ 9%) (2)	Bank loans (3)	Higher cost of bank loans (@ 0.89%) (4)	Other debt outstanding (5)	Higher cost of other debt (@ 1.19%) (6)	Equity (7)	Higher equity cost (@ 2.4%) (8)	Excl. equity (9)	Incl. equity (10)
	$ millions								Percent	
Food	198	18	1,680	15	2,958	35	12,893	307	0.05	0.52
Tobacco	3	b	293	3	560	7	1,900	45	0.61	3.35
Textiles	33	3	463	4	918	11	5,875	140	0.10	1.26
Apparel	21	2	283	3	183	2	1,877	45	0.02	0.35
Wood products	104	9	506	5	542	6	3,953	94	0.02	0.79
Paper	121	11	289	3	1,347	16	6,089	145	0.06	1.07
Printing	73	6	196	2	335	4	2,539	60	–	0.48
Electrical equipment	112	10	573	5	1,520	18	8,093	193	0.07	1.07
Chemicals	201	19	776	7	2,582	31	14,493	345	0.08	1.58
Petroleum products	263	24	1,372	12	3,784	45	26,128	622	0.21	4.11
Rubber and plastics	38	3	146	1	697	8	2,668	63	0.10	1.11
Leather goods	4	b	116	1	154	2	1,033	25	0.08	0.76
Nonmetallic mineral products	99	9	268	2	661	8	5,408	129	0.01	1.27
Metallic products	557	50	2,281	20	7,101	85	38,479	916	0.08	1.38
Transportation equipment	129	12	1,039	9	1,886	22	14,336	341	0.05	1.00
Miscellaneous	67	6	373	3	530	6	4,053	96	0.02	0.73
Total, all industries	2,023	182	10,654	95	25,758	306	149,817	3,566	0.07	1.15

Sources: See text and Appendix M.

a See Table 1, note a.

b Less than 0.5 million but greater than 0.

debt in the same manufacturing sectors was $36,412 million; at higher Canadian interest rates this debt would have involved a higher carrying cost of $401 million. (This figure was estimated by applying the higher Canadian prime bank rate (0.89 percent)[11] to $10,654 million of bank loans, and the higher Canadian interest rate on industrial bonds[12] (1.19 percent) to $25,758 million of bonded indebtedness.) Higher Canadian interest rates could consequently increase total costs by as much as 0.13 percent.[13] Considering the offsetting effects of lower construction costs and higher carrying charges on debt (but not equity), manufacturing costs could as a result be as much as $219 million higher at Canadian prices; these two influences could result in total costs being about 0.07 percent higher in Canada than in the United States.

To account for the possibility that equity returns in Canada may, like bond interest rates, have to be higher than in the United States in order to encourage and maintain the south to north flow of equity capital, it was assumed that the difference in equity yield to the investor in the two countries was similar to the bond differential of approximately 1.2 percent. However, because of corporate tax rates in the two countries of about fifty percent, this difference implies a higher yield (before corporate tax) of roughly 2.4 percent. The higher cost involved in making equity returns so much more attractive could run as high as $3,566 million, or roughly 1.08 percent of total manufacturing costs. Comparison of the substantial cost of $3,566 million with the much lower $401 million that might result from differences in debt carrying charges indicates the relatively heavy cost a firm may face in making equity returns more attractive.

A breakdown for each industry of the higher capital costs in Canada is shown in the balance of Table 17. Several observations

[11] Bank rate on short-term business loans for nineteen U.S. cities (*Federal Reserve Bulletin*) was compared with the prime bank loan rate provided by the Bank of Nova Scotia.

[12] Derived by comparing Moody's *Aaa Industrial Bond Rate* for the United States and McLeod, Young and Weir's *10 Industrial Bond Rate* for Canada.

[13] Estimated by dividing the higher carrying cost of $401 million by total costs (value shipped) of all manufacturing sectors. The incidence of higher equity cost was derived in the same way. Moreover, the same technique was used to estimate all figures for individual industries.

are warranted. Each individual industry shows a much greater potential sensitivity to equity effects than to debt effects. The explanation is similar in each case: equity is a far more important source of funds than debt, and the corporate income tax forces a firm to earn more on equity in order to pay a similar yield to investors. Examining subcategories of debt, it is evident that (the apparel sector excepted) bank loans represent a much less important source of funds for business than other forms of debt.

Lower labor costs of plant construction in Canada explain only a relatively minor part of capital cost differences in the two economies; these labor cost savings do not even offset higher Canadian debt costs, and they represent only a small portion of possible higher equity costs. The industry that is the most sensitive to higher Canadian capital costs is petroleum and coal products, and the least sensitive is apparel.

Conclusions

Interest costs in Canada exceed those in the United States by just over one percent. This higher Canadian interest rate is largely to be explained in terms of exchange rate risk and other restraints on the free flow of capital between the two countries. Interest differentials would be reduced if the two countries were to establish a common currency area; however, they should remain substantially unaffected by tariff reductions. It has been estimated that this higher interest carrying cost of debt could, under free trade, keep total costs for firms producing in Canada higher than in the United States by about one tenth of one percent.

If, in order to attract and hold equity in Canada, the rate of return on equity must be higher to the same degree as interest returns, then total Canadian manufacturing costs could as a consequence be raised by somewhat more than one percent, with some industries being substantially below this, and others considerably above. The fact that possible equity costs far exceed debt costs is due to two influences: firms generally rely much more heavily on equity than on debt as a source of funds, and the corporate income tax means that a firm's additional earnings before tax must be roughly double any increase in after-tax returns. It is by no means clear, however, that the costs of raising equity funds are in fact as much higher in Canada as interest costs. The restrictions on the free flow of capital between the two countries strongly suggest that returns to equity in Canada must exceed U.S. returns in order to attract and retain U.S. capital. However, the absence of any Canadian capital gains tax presumably makes equity for the Canadian investor more attractive vis-à-vis debt than it is in the United States; thus, the difference in equity costs between the two countries is likely to be less than the difference in interest costs.

Initial investment costs, as well as carrying costs, may vary between the two countries. Costs of building materials and machinery and equipment may be higher in Canada because of protection; however, these cost differences would disappear with free trade. In the short run, lower Canadian wage rates would tend to keep Canadian construction costs below U.S. levels, but this influence on total cost is minor, since labor cost savings in Canada are sufficient to offset only a small proportion of higher carrying costs of debt. Differences in federal taxes also affect initial investment costs; these are analyzed in Chapter 9.

9

FEDERAL TAXES

In addition to labor costs, transportation costs, capital costs, and proximity to markets and sources of supply, the location of industry may be influenced by differing levels of taxation in different areas. Logically, all categories of taxation — federal, provincial or state, and local — may influence location decisions. Because of the mass of detail that a consideration of all categories of taxation would require, the present study will concentrate on the federal level, to give some picture of the difference in the tax structures between the two North American countries.

In analyzing differing taxation systems, there are problems that arise because of the volume of detail; there are also basic conceptual questions. If the influence of taxation on location is to be studied, logic would seem to indicate that the other side of public finance should also be considered: the effects of government-provided amenities. It is not simply through taxation but through its total "fiscal residuum" of fiscal benefits minus taxation that the government influences location decisions.[1] However, in the present work, the amenities and advantages provided by government expenditures will be ignored, and attention will be turned exclusively to the taxation side. There are a number of justifications for this procedure. In the first place, insofar as government expenditures make possible less expensive transportation facilities, the effects will

[1] See James M. Buchanan, "The Pure Theory of Government Finance, A Suggested Approach," *Journal of Political Economy,* 57: 496–505 (December 1949).

show up in the analysis of transportation costs. More fundamentally, the greater part of government expenditures — such as those for defence and health and welfare — contribute generally to the amenities of living in the countries concerned and thus may be classified broadly with such amenities as climate and cultural environment. These amenities may have considerable influence on locational decisions because they influence the possibilities of recruiting highly qualified employees; however, they are not easily quantified and, having been mentioned, may be dropped out of the discussion.

Because indirect taxes are generally[2] rebated on exported goods and applied to imports, whereas direct taxes fall on exports as well as on domestic production, relatively great dependence on indirect taxation, in contrast to direct taxation, has been taken as a contributing factor in the international competitiveness of a country's industry.[3] In this respect, the structure of the Canadian tax system is more favorable for the international competitiveness of industry than the U.S. system. As may be seen from Table 18, U.S. direct taxes provide approximately eighty percent of federal tax revenue, compared to approximately sixty percent in Canada.[4] The most noticeable difference in the federal taxation systems of the two countries lies in the area of indirect taxation: the United States has nothing to compare with the eleven percent general manufacturers' sales tax in Canada.

[2] An exception arises because duties on imported materials used in the manufacturing process are normally not remitted where the materials are included in manufactured exports.

[3] This point is discussed in Walter S. Salant, "The Balance of Payments Deficit and the Tax Structure," *Review of Economics and Statistics,* 46: 131–138 (May 1964). Salant concluded (p. 138) that the desirability of changing the composition of taxation should be determined on the grounds of its domestic effects and "not on the grounds of its supposed favorable effect on the balance of payments."

[4] The same general picture emerges if state and local taxation are included. For all levels of government, approximately 66 percent of tax revenue in the United States is derived from direct taxes, compared to approximately 47 percent in Canada. See Ronald Robertson, *Tax Aspects of Canada's International Competitive Position* (Montreal: Canadian Trade Committee, Private Planning Association of Canada, 1963), Table 3, p. 6. Of 35 countries included in Robertson's table, the United States derived the second highest percentage of total tax revenue from direct taxes; Canada was nineteenth.

TABLE 18.   *Major Sources of Federal Government Tax Revenues, United States and Canada, Fiscal Years 1961–62.*[a]

Source of revenue	U.S. millions of dollars	Percent of total tax revenues	Canada millions of dollars	Percent of total tax revenues
Personal income tax[b]	45,571	55.4	1,793[c]	35.1
Corporate income tax[b]	20,523	24.9	1,202[c]	23.5
Customs import duties	1,142	1.4	535	10.6
General manufacturers' sales tax[b]	–	–	760	14.9
Other sales and excise duties and taxes	12,286	14.9	625	12.2
Alcoholic beverages	3,248	3.9	210	4.1
Tobacco	2,022	2.5	368	7.2
Motor fuel	2,451	3.0	–	–
Other	4,565	5.5	47	0.9
Death, estate and gift taxes	2,016	2.5	85	1.7
Other tax revenues	724	0.9	112	2.2
Total tax revenues[b]	82,262	100.0	5,111	100.0
Other general (budgetary) revenue	9,754		618	
Old age fund receipts	12,289		644	
Old age tax on personal incomes			259	
Old age tax on corporate incomes			100	
Old age sales tax			285	

[a] United States: fiscal year July 1961–June 1962.
  Canada: fiscal year April 1961–March 1962.
[b] Excluding Old Age Tax, entered separately below.
[c] Excluding withholding tax on dividends and interest going abroad which are included in "other tax revenues."

However, it is not the proportion of total revenue derived from direct taxes but rather the rates of direct and other nonrebatable taxes that determine the taxation influences on the location of industry. Two items are of primary importance here: the level of corporate income taxes and the newly imposed eleven percent manufacturers' sales tax on construction materials and machinery. These recent taxes on machinery and construction materials are not like the eleven percent general manufacturers' sales tax on consumer goods because they may fall upon exports as well as upon domestically consumed goods. It is true that, if Canadian-built machinery and construction materials are exported, the sales tax is not imposed; nevertheless, this tax does in part fall on exports: it is applicable to machinery and construction materials used by Canadian manufacturers in the production of exports.

TABLE 19. *Corporate Income Tax Rates (in percent).*

Canada[a]		United States			
			1963	1964	1965
On first $35,000	23	On first $25,000	30	22	22
On the rest	52	On the rest	52	50	48

[a] Basic Canadian corporate rates are 18 percent and 47 percent; to these rates the old age security tax of 3 percent must be added. Dominion rebates of 9 percent in Ontario and 10 percent in Quebec are allowed, but these are more than offset by provincial taxes of 11 percent and 12 percent respectively. Thus, Dominion-Provincial arrangements add another 2 percent to the total tax, giving rates of 23 percent for profits up to $35,000 and 52 percent thereafter.

It might seem that the difficult question of the incidence of taxes should be addressed before significance can be attached to any specific tax rates. However, the question of incidence is not strictly relevant to this study of costs. It is true that, in an equilibrium situation, taxes may fall partly on factors and partly on purchasers, with the exact proportions being very difficult to determine.[5] However, if equilibrium adjustments are to be considered, then the question of "incidence" arises regarding *all* the cost items considered in this part. Thus high transportation costs (like taxes) may fall partly on labor (in the form of lower wages), partly on other factors of production, and partly on the purchaser in the form of higher prices. In brief, taxes may be looked on as a cost similar to wages or transport charges; and the problem of incidence applies equally to all these components of cost. With the exception of the case where indirect taxes are rebated on exports, taxes will affect the competitive position of industry just as any other cost. In the following chapter, taxes are considered to be different from other costs of production; this difference does not, however, depend on the incidence issue. Rather, it arises because tariff changes are the subject of this book, and tariffs themselves are taxes with public finance implications, particularly in Canada. Therefore, if tariffs are changed, there may be direct pressures to change other taxes in order to compensate for the change in revenue.

[5] It is difficult to determine the incidence of income taxes, as well as that of indirect taxes. See Marian Kryzaniak and Richard A. Musgrave, *The Shifting of the Corporation Income Tax* (Baltimore: Johns Hopkins Press, 1963).

Corporate Income Taxes

At the beginning of 1964, the corporate income tax rate in Canada was very close to that in the United States; with the U.S. tax reduction, U.S. rates will become somewhat lower than those in Canada. The effective corporation tax rates beginning in 1965 are shown in Table 20.

TABLE 20. *Comparison of Effective Rates of Corporation Income Tax in Canada and the United States (in percent, U.S. federal taxes at 1965 rates).*

Taxable income of corporation	Tax in Canada, including Ontario tax	U.S. tax in states without corporate tax (13 states)	Combined federal and state tax in New York and California (5.5% state rate)
$100,000	41.9	41.5	44.4
$1,000,000	51.0	47.4	50.2
$3,000,000	51.7	47.8	50.6

Source: Debates, House of Commons, March 16, 1964, p. 1003.

The maximum differential in tax rates between Canada and the United States will be four percent and will apply only to those states without corporate income taxes.

An estimate may be made of the effects on economic "costs" of this maximum differential of four percent. Although profits are, of course, not a cost in the accounting sense, they are an economic cost in the sense that returns to equity capital are necessary to attract and hold such capital. If Canadian after-tax returns of capital are to remain in the same relative position to U.S. returns prior to the tax cut, Canadian before-tax equity returns must rise to 52/48 of their previous rate to compensate for the four percent tax differential; that is, Canadian returns must rise by one twelfth.

This one-twelfth rise in the return to equity necessary to maintain the relative after-tax position of Canadian capital will increase the economic "costs" of Canadian industry. This increase may be estimated by examining equity and total costs of each industry, along with supplementary data on the normal rates of return to equity in the United States and Canada.[6] In Table 21, estimates are presented of the upper limits of Canadian disadvantage in total economic costs attributable to income tax differentials between Canada and the United States.

There are a number of assumptions in the derivation of Table 21 which should inspire caution in their use. In the first place, the results are based on U.S. rates in states without income taxes; this is true for only thirteen states. If Ontario were to be compared to New York, a state with an income tax, the percentage tax differential would be in the neighborhood of one percent rather than four percent; thus, the figures of Table 21 would have to be divided by four. Furthermore, it is by no means clear that the equity re-

[6] The increase of one twelfth will be:

$$\frac{\text{Canadian before-tax rate of return to equity}}{12} \left(\frac{\text{equity}}{\text{value shipped}} \right).$$

The equity-value shipped ratios for the sixteen manufacturing categories were found in Chapter 8. We may reuse those data, which are available on three bases: the 1958 U.S. figures and Canadian ratios for 1958 and 1961.

Because of year-to-year fluctuations in profits, it is notoriously hard to estimate the normal rate of return to equity. However, an estimate of the normal Canadian rate may be made by adding the average rate of profits in the United States to the Canadian-U.S. equity return differential derived in Chapter 8. This (after-tax) differential was assumed to be approximately equal to the long-run corporate bond yield differential, that is, 1.2 percent. For the United States, 6 percent may be taken as the average after-tax rate of return to equity; this is close to the rate (measured as a percentage of book values) found for U.S. manufacturing corporations for the 1940–1958 period by George J. Stigler, *Capital and Rates of Return in Manufacturing Industries* (Princeton: Princeton University Press for the National Bureau of Economic Research, 1963), p. 12. It should be noted that the 1.2 percent and 6 percent are aggregate data, not broken down by industry. We will assume that the normal interindustry return differentials are small compared to the interindustry capital-output ratio differentials, and will multiply industry capital-output ratios by the overall equity return in order to evaluate the expression above.

Because the average corporation tax is approximately 50 percent, the after-tax return must be doubled to get the before-tax return. Thus,

$$\frac{2(6 + 1.2)}{12} \left(\frac{\text{equity}}{\text{value shipped}} \right) = 1.2 \left(\frac{\text{equity}}{\text{value shipped}} \right) \text{ percent.}$$

It will be noted that this is one half of the expression used to compute the effects of higher equity returns on total costs in Chapter 8.

TABLE 21. *Estimate of Upper Limit of Percentage Canadian Disadvantage in Total Economic Costs Attributable to 1965 Corporation Income Tax Differences if Canadian-U.S. Differential in After-Tax Equity Returns Remains Unchanged.*[a]

Manufacturing sector[b]	Percent
Food	0.24
Tobacco	1.37
Textiles	0.58
Apparel	0.16
Wood products	0.39
Paper	0.51
Printing	0.24
Electrical equipment	0.50
Chemicals	0.75
Petroleum products	1.96
Rubber and plastics	0.51
Leather goods	0.34
Nonmetallic mineral products	0.63
Metallic products	0.65
Transportation equipment	0.48
Miscellaneous	0.36

Sources: As in Table 17. Derivation explained in footnote 6, Chapter 9.

[a] Basis of these calculations: 1958 U.S. figures on equity and value shipped. Assumptions: 1. Equity returns net of taxes are 6 percent in the United States and 7.2 percent in Canada, both before and after U.S. tax reduction. 2. There is no state corporation income tax in the United States (true in thirteen states). For a comparison of the disadvantage of Ontario in comparison with New York, a state with an income tax, the figures in this table should be divided by four. (See Table 20 for rates of income taxation in New York State.)

[b] See Table 1, note a.

turn differential between Canada and the United States would tend to remain unchanged after a movement toward free trade. Nevertheless, the figures in Table 21 may be taken as indicating the general significance of the income tax differentials.

Manufacturers' Sales Tax on Machinery and Building Materials

The second area of taxation particularly relevant to the international competitive position of Canadian industry is the tax on building materials and machinery. The manufacturers' tax on consumer goods is not an important factor in the international competitive position of industry. It is not applied to exports and is imposed on imports; thus it is applied to goods sold in Canada, regardless of their source, whereas it is not applied to Canadian goods sold in the United States. As a consequence, it does not discourage industry from locating in Canada (except insofar as it limits local markets in Canada). The tax on building materials and machinery, however, becomes part of the cost of production and thus enters into the cost of exports as well as domestically sold goods. In a sense, this tax represents a double tax: not only is the final good subject to the manufacturing sales tax, but the machinery to produce the good is subject to the tax. Thus, even from the point of view of a closed economy, the tax could be objected to on the grounds that it tends to distort productive processes away from capital-intensive toward labor-intensive methods of production. However, it is the international implications of the tax which will concern us here.

As was the case with corporate income taxes, it is necessary to look forward to 1965 to evaluate the possible effects of manufacturers' sales tax already enacted. The full eleven percent Canadian tax on building materials and machinery is not to become effective until January 1, 1965; the rate was only four percent between June 14, 1963, and March 31, 1964; and eight percent between April 1, 1964, and December 31, 1964.[7]

Machinery. The sales tax on machinery will add eleven percent to its cost. The extent to which the sales tax is judged to increase total costs will depend in part on how capital is held to influence cost. The most obvious answer — through future depreciation changes — does not seem unreasonable, and therefore the ratio of depreciation to total costs is taken as a basis for constructing the estimates in Table 22.[8]

---

[7] *Debates, House of Commons,* July 8, 1963, p. 1952.

[8] The addition to costs attributable to the sales tax on machinery is estimated on an industry-by-industry basis as the ratio .11 multiplied by depreciation on machinery and equipment to value shipped of the specific industry.

Because industry-by-industry depreciation data on machinery and equipment is not readily available, we have estimated it from available statistics by assuming that the net expenditure on machinery and equipment may be determined for each industry by multiplying the gross expenditures on machinery and equipment for the industry by the ratio of net to gross expenditure on all types of fixed investment in that industry, including investment in buildings. Thus, depreciation on machinery and equipment in a specific industry is equal to gross expenditure on machinery and equipment

TABLE 22.   *Estimated Minimum Addition to Total Costs from Eleven Percent Canadian Tax on Machinery (fully effective in 1965).*[a]

Manufacturing sector[b]	Estimate based on Canadian depreciation and value shipped data (in percent)	
	1958	1961
Food	0.144	0.157
Tobacco	0.102	0.063
Textiles	0.224	0.207
Apparel	0.092	0.116
Wood products	0.156	0.168
Paper	0.521	0.562
Printing	0.156	0.239
Electrical equipment	0.187	0.169
Chemicals	0.463	0.540
Petroleum products	0.028	0.017
Rubber and plastics	0.162	0.421
Leather goods	0.052	0.092
Nonmetallic mineral products	0.353	0.550
Metallic products	0.239	0.167
Transportation equipment	0.156	0.160
Miscellaneous	0.188	0.130

Sources: Value shipped: for 1958: D.B.S., *Manufacturing Industries of Canada*, Sections B–F, 1958. For 1961: *ibid.*, Section A, 1961.

Depreciation data from (a) gross expenditures on machinery and equipment: Department of Trade and Commerce, *Private and Public Investment in Canada, Outlook 1960; ibid.*, 1963; (b) depreciation on machinery, equipment and buildings: Department of National Revenue, *Taxation Statistics*, 1960 and 1963; (c) gross expenditures on machinery, equipment, and buildings: *ibid.*

[a] For method of deriving figures in this table, see footnote 8, Chapter 9.

[b] See Table 1, note a.

This is not, however, the only possible way to consider the costs of capital. Insofar as growth is financed out of current receipts, increases in the costs of capital will in the long run add to depreciation charges and to the current costs of capital formation. It does not seem reasonable to assume that capital formation is financed entirely from current receipts; indeed, such an assumption would be inconsistent with the assumption made earlier that rates of return must be maintained to attract new capital. Nevertheless, as

in that specific industry, multiplied by the ratio of depreciation to gross expenditures on machinery, equipment, and buildings in that same industry.

Since machinery generally depreciates at a more rapid rate than buildings, the solution may be expected to result in an underestimate in a growing economy. This gives one more reason in addition to those given below in the text for considering the figures in Table 22 as minimum estimates.

there may be some tendency to consider expansion as a necessary part of carrying on business, the figures in Table 22 based on depreciation charges alone may be taken as minimum estimates.

There is a second reason for considering these data to be minimum estimates. Because the eleven percent tax falls on capital equipment, this will not only add to depreciation charges in the future but will also raise carrying costs, for example, total interest costs.[9]

Building Materials. The addition to total costs attributable to the eleven percent tax on building materials may be found by a method analogous to that for machinery. However, there is an additional complication because the eleven percent tax does not apply to all building costs but just to building materials. In deriving the figures in Table 23 on the addition to costs, this difficulty was attacked by adjusting the figures with the ratio of total materials costs to total building costs, derived from 1949 input-output data.[10]

Various sources of bias are introduced into Table 23 by the method of estimation. Once again, as in the machinery case, the

[9] There is also a third reason for a downward bias noted in the immediately preceding footnote.

In the case of the estimate in Table 22 based on the 1961 data, however, there is a possible offsetting upward bias because of an increase in depreciation rates permitted by the budget of June 1961. That budget introduced a special investment incentive in the form of a 50 percent increase in the first year in the rates of capital allowance applicable to new assets acquired for use in Canada between June 21, 1961, and March 31, 1963, inclusive. (*Debates, House of Commons,* June 20, 1961, p. 6,658.) This change presumably accounts for the fact that for one industry (nonmetallic minerals) the 1961 ratio of depreciation to gross investment exceeded one. (It was 1.03; see Appendix N.)

[10] Table 23 is based on the following formula: addition to total costs attributable to tax on building materials for specific industry is equal to .11 of the product of the ratio of building materials costs to total building costs for all industries and the ratio of depreciation on buildings to value shipped of specific industry.

Once again, industry-by-industry depreciation of buildings is not available; it is therefore estimated by using a formula analogous to the one in footnote 8. That is: depreciation on buildings for a specific industry is equal to gross expenditures on building for that specific industry multiplied by the ratio of depreciation to gross expenditures on machinery, equipment and buildings for the same industry.

The more rapid depreciation of machinery than of buildings introduced a downward bias in the estimates for machinery; it introduces an upward bias in the estimates for buildings.

tax will add to the cost of capital goods and will thus add to the carrying charges by increasing the debt or equity required to finance capital equipment; the omission of these carrying charges

TABLE 23. *Estimated Addition to Total Costs from Eleven Percent Canadian Tax on Building Materials (fully effective in 1965)*[a]

Manufacturing sector[b]	Estimate based on Canadian depreciation and value shipped data (in percent)	
	1958	1961
Food	0.028	0.034
Tobacco	0.022	0.007
Textiles	0.011	0.021
Apparel	0.003	0.014
Wood products	0.025	0.029
Paper	0.052	0.067
Printing	0.042	0.024
Electrical equipment	0.025	0.023
Chemicals	0.109	0.085
Petroleum products	0.204	0.046
Rubber and plastics	0.020	0.032
Leather goods	0.006	0.007
Nonmetallic mineral products	0.079	0.080
Metallic products	0.053	0.023
Transportation equipment	0.028	0.026
Miscellaneous	0.022	0.020

Sources: Building materials as a proportion of total building costs: D.B.S., *Supplement to Interindustry Flow of Goods and Services, Canada, 1949.*
Value shipped: as in Table 22. Depreciation data: as in Table 22.
[a] For method of deriving figures in this table: see footnote 10, Chapter 9.
[b] See Table 1, note a.

results in a downward bias. On the other hand, an upward bias in the estimate of the importance of the eleven percent tax on total building costs will possibly result from the derivation of the building materials to total building cost ratio from input-output data; it is not clear that the tax will apply to all materials included in the input-output estimate. In addition, the 1961 data are disturbed by the change in depreciation regulations introduced in June.[11] For these several reasons, the figures in Table 23 should be interpreted only as rough approximations.

[11] See footnote 9.

Taxes: Are They Basic Costs?

In the first part of this work, attention has been paid only to the basic regional costs that help to determine the present location of industry and that would continue to influence the location of industry in the event of a reduction of barriers between Canada and the United States. It is true that not all the factors dealt with in this part are completely independent of present tariff levels; Canadian wages, for example, respond to general demand and supply conditions, which would be altered by a change in tariff levels. Nevertheless, the present level of wages may be used as a point of departure in investigating the probable direction of adjustment forces in the event of free trade.

This assumption is not necessarily applicable in the case of taxes. Taxation is directly determined by governments; an abolition of tariffs would affect the revenue-expenditure situation facing the government; therefore, adjustments in tax rates might be considered more or less an integral part of the process of removing tariffs. Because the Canadian government receives over ten percent of its revenue from import duties while the United States government derives less than two percent of its revenue from this source (Table 18), a tariff reduction might be expected to have much greater repercussions on public finance in Canada than in the United States. How the Canadian government would respond to the loss in customs duty revenues is not clear.

Because of this large element of uncertainty, because taxes are a policy variable, and because the cost data presented in Tables 21, 22, and 23 represent estimates of future rather than historical costs, the taxation estimates are being treated as separate data and are not being integrated in the summary chapter with the labor, transportation, and other costs in developing an overall picture of the competitive position of Canadian industry.

10

A SUMMARY OF LOCATION PRESSURES
IN A FREE TRADE AREA

There is a central industrial heartland in the North American continent. This may be roughly defined by drawing a triangle from Chicago on the west to Boston and Washington, the two terminal points of the band of heaviest industrial activity along the eastern seaboard. This has already been referred to as the Chicago-New York axis; it should be recognized, however, that it is an ever-widening axis as one moves west to east. This "North American Triangle" represents only slightly more than five percent of the area of the United States, and about two and one half percent of the area of the North American continent. Nevertheless, approximately thirty percent of the population of Canada and the United States is in this area. Moreover, ten of the fifteen largest North American cities are located in this triangle: New York, Chicago, Philadelphia, Washington, Baltimore, Boston, Cleveland, Detroit, Pittsburg, and Newark. In addition, Buffalo is on its border. This area includes only a small Canadian section — the southernmost strip of southwestern Ontario. Toronto and Montreal lie just to the north.

In terms of many of the location influences considered in Part I, it is a superior region for several reasons. It is the area of heaviest central concentration of industry; as a consequence, it is attractive both for firms that may be drawn by external economies to concentrations of firms in their own industry and for firms seeking best sources of a wide variety of manufactured supplies. Because it is the area of heaviest industrialization, it is also the area of greatest concentration of employment and income. Firms seeking rich markets find it attractive as a consequence. In purely spatial terms this area is also fairly centrally located to the North American economy. (Both the West Lake and the East Lake regions are among the most centrally located areas in North America.) The concentration of markets in this area along with its fairly central location together ensure that this region is one of the best areas from which to service North American markets at minimum transport costs. These advantages have allowed firms in this area, competing with firms less favorably situated elsewhere, to pay higher wages. As a result, its relatively high prevailing wage level now represents the one offsetting disadvantage of this area.

The preferred situation of this area is illustrated in Table 24, which is a compendium of the three location influences that cannot be reduced to a quantified cost analysis: the attraction of markets; the attraction of external economies, which leads firms to seek out present areas of heaviest concentration in their own industrial sector; and the attraction of intermediate supplying industries. In Chapters 3, 5 and 7 respectively, all North American regions were ranked in terms of these characteristics. The summary ranking for each industry shown in Table 24 is derived by comparing each area with Ontario. Since there are three sets of rankings involved, there are four possible outcomes shown down the left-hand side of this table: the comparison area may be preferred to Ontario by all three criteria; the area may be preferred to Ontario by two criteria but not by the other one; it may be preferred to Ontario by one criterion only; or it may not be preferred to Ontario in any way.

The five areas falling in whole or in part within this North American industrial heartland are the five areas that are most favorably situated by these criteria. They are the Middle Atlantic, West Lake, East Lake, New England, and Capital areas of the United States. The very high ranking of the Chicago and New York areas across the board should be noted. The same reasons that make the regions in this triangle most attractive also make the regions that are adjacent to them the next most attractive locations. Hence, the next most favored areas are the Canadian prov-

TABLE 24. *Standing of Comparison Areas Relative to Ontario in Terms of Market Potential, External Economies, and Manufactured Supply Potential, by Industry, 1958.*[a]

	Manufacturing sector[b]					
	Food	Tobacco	Textiles	Apparel	Wood products	Paper
Area rankings						
Areas superior to Ontario in all 3 rankings.	W. Lake Mid. Atl. E. Lake N. Eng.	Mid. Atl.	Mid. Atl. W. Lake N. Eng. *Que.*	W. Lake Mid. Atl. Cap. N. Eng.	W. Lake Mid. Atl. E. Lake	W. Lake Mid. Atl. N. Eng.
Areas superior to Ontario in 2 rankings but inferior in 1.	Cap.	*Que.* (W. Lake)[c] (Cap.) (E. Lake)	E. Lake Cap.	P. SW *Que.* E. Lake	Cap. *Br. Col.* N. Eng.	Cap. E. Lake P. SW
ONTARIO						
Areas inferior to Ontario in 2 rankings but superior in 1.	*Que.* L. Midw. P. SW Up. Midw.	South Fla. (*Br. Col.*) (N. Eng) (L. Midw.) (P. SW) (P. NW)	South P. SW *Br. Col.*	L. Midw. South *Br. Col.* P. NW	*Que.* P. SW P. NW Up. Midw.	*Que.* P. NW
Areas inferior to Ontario in all 3 rankings.	South SW *Br. Col.* Fla. Mount. P. NW *Prair.* *Mar.*	(Up. Midw.) (Mount.) (SW) (*Prair.*) (*Mar.*)	Up. Midw. L. Midw. P. NW SW Fla. Mount. *Prair.* (*Mar.*)	Up. Midw. SW Fla. Mount. *Prair.* (*Mar.*)	L. Midw. SW Fla. Mount. *Prair.* Mar.	South L. Midw. SW Up. Midw. Fla. Mount. *Br. Col.* *Prair.* (*Mar.*)

TABLE 24. *Continued*

	Manufacturing sector[b]				
	Printing	Electrical equipment	Chemicals	Petroleum products	Rubber and plastics
Area rankings					
Areas superior to Ontario in all 3 rankings.			W. Lake Mid. Atl.	W. Lake Cap.	
	W. Lake Mid. Atl. N. Eng.	W. Lake Mid. Atl. E. Lake	Cap. E. Lake	Mid. Atl. E. Lake	W. Lake E. Lake Mid. Atl.
Areas superior to Ontario in 2 rankings but interior in 1.	Cap. E. Lake P. SW	Cap. N. Eng. P. SW	N. Eng. P. SW	*Que.* N. Eng.	Cap. P. SW N. Eng.
ONTARIO					
Areas inferior to Ontario in 2 rankings but superior in 1.				SW L. Midw. P. SW	
			L. Midw. South *Que.*	Br. Col. Up. Midw. Mount.	L. Midw. *Que.* P. NW
	Que. Br. Col.	Br. Col.	SW Br. Col.	Prair.	(Br. Col.)
Areas inferior to Ontario in all 3 rankings.		*Que.* L. Midw. South			
	L. Midw. South Up. Midw. SW P. NW Fla. Mount. *Mar.* Prair.	Up. Midw. P. NW SW Fla. Mount. Prair. (*Mar.*)	Up. Midw. Fla. Mount. P. NW Prair. Mar.	South Fla. P. NW (Mar.)	Up. Midw. South SW Fla. (Mount.) (Mar.) (Prair.)

(continued on next page)

TABLE 24. *Continued*

Area rankings	Manufacturing sector[b]				
	Leather goods	Nonmetallic mineral products	Metallic products	Transportation equipment	Miscellaneous
Areas superior to Ontario in all 3 rankings.	W. Lake Mid. Atl. N. Eng.	W. Lake Mid. Atl. Cap. E. Lake N. Eng.	W. Lake Cap. Mid. Atl. E. Lake N. Eng.	W. Lake E. Lake Cap. Mid. Atl.	W. Lake Mid. Atl. E. Lake N. Eng.
Areas superior to Ontario in 2 rankings but inferior in 1.	Cap. E. Lake *Que.*	P. SW	P. SW	N. Eng.	Cap.
ONTARIO ———————					
Areas inferior to Ontario in 2 rankings but superior in 1.	L. Midw. *Br. Col.* (*P. SW*)	L. Midw. *Que.* Up. Midw. South *Br. Col.* SW	L. Midw. Up. Midw. SW *Br. Col.*	L. Midw. *Que.* P. SW South SW P. NW Up. Midw.	L. Midw. *Br. Col.* P. SW
Areas inferior to Ontario in all 3 rankings.	South Fla. SW *Prair.* (Up. Midw.) (P. NW) (Mount.) (*Mar.*)	Fla. P. NW Mount. *Prair.* *Mar.*	*Que.* South P. NW Fla. Mount. *Prair.* (*Mar.*)	*Br. Col.* Fla. Mount. *Prair.* (*Mar.*)	*Que.* Up. Midw. South SW P. NW Fla. Mount. *Prair.* (*Mar.*)

ᵃ The three rankings on which this table is based are: market potential (derived from Table 10); external economies (from Table 12); and manufactured supply potential (from Table 16).

ᵇ See Table 1, note a.

ᶜ Parentheses signify no record of an industry in that area. Since it seems reasonable to assume that areas with no record of production have less production than areas with such records, these areas are considered inferior to Ontario in the external economies ranking. (There is a record of production in Ontario in all sixteen sectors.)

inces of Ontario and Quebec, lying along the northern border of this triangle. The only exception to this generalization is the U.S. Pacific Southwest, which ranks somewhat above Ontario in some industries but just below in others. The reason a clear-cut comparison cannot be made between these two regions is that Ontario has the advantage of closeness to Chicago and New York, but the Pacific Southwest has heavier internal concentration of industry and economic activity. Because of the size of the San Francisco and Los Angeles Standard Metropolitan areas, the Pacific Southwest is a better location in most industries for firms seeking external economies within the immediate environs than Ontario; at the same time it is less attractive than Ontario as a location for acquiring intermediate manufactured supplies; hence, the Pacific Southwest ranks either above or below Ontario, depending on the relative ranking of the two regions in the market potential analysis.[1]

In evaluating the free trade prospects of Ontario and Quebec, as compared to this U.S. industrial triangle, it is necessary to consider how the nonquantitative U.S. advantages cited above may be offset by those advantages of Ontario and Quebec (such as wages) that can be quantified in terms of total costs. A cost ranking of all North American areas in each industry is shown in Table 25; along with Table 24, this provides a complete summary of all the location influences considered in Chapters 2–8. The following cost differences are included in the totals in Table 25: labor costs, transport costs on final product, resource costs, and capital costs.[2]

[1] It should be noted that several estimates of market potential were made in Chapter 3, given various alternative assumptions about the degree to which firms service local as opposed to national markets. The estimate used for these summary purposes was one in which it was assumed that firms service local markets heavily. If it is alternatively assumed that all North American markets are serviced equally, the U.S. Pacific Southwest compares less well with Ontario and would fall below it in almost all industries in this table.

[2] When there were several estimates for a specific cost component, the figure was chosen that showed Canadian locations at the greatest disadvantage, in line with the general strategy of this study; the more the estimating procedure is biased against Canadian locations, the greater the confidence in the conclusion of this chapter that Canadian locations are in a favored cost position. Thus, the capital cost estimate included in this table was the one which was based on the assumption that equity capital

TABLE 25. *Estimated Percentage That Total Costs in Comparison Areas Are Lower (−) or Higher (+) Than in Ontario, by Industry, 1958 ($1.00 U.S. = $1.00 Can.).*[a]

Percent	Manufacturing sector[b]							
	Food	Tobacco	Textiles	Apparel	Wood products	Paper	Printing	Electrical equipment
−10								
−9								
−8								
−7								
−6		W. Lake, N. Eng., Fla., Mid. Atl., E. Lake						
−5		P. SW, South						
−4								
−3					*Que.*			
−2				*Que.*			*Mar.*	
−1	Cap.	L. Midw., Cap., SW, *Que.*	*Que.*, Mount., SW		Cap.	Cap., Mid. Atl., W. Lake, N. Eng., *Que.*	*Prair.*, *Que.*	*Que.*, *Prair.*
Ontario[c]	*Que.*, South, N. Eng., W. Lake	Mount., Up. Midw.	L. Midw.	*Prair.*		E. Lake		*Mar.*
+1	Mid. Atl., E. Lake	*Mar.*, *Prair.*	South	South, SW	South	L. Midw., Up. Midw.	South	N. Eng., South

+2	Fla., SW, L. Midw., *Br. Col.*		Fla.	Fla., L. Midw.	W. Lake	South	N. Eng., SW, L. Midw.	Fla., L. Midw., Mount., SW, *Br. Col.*
+3		P. NW			N. Eng.			
+4	Mount., P. SW, Up. Midw.	*Br. Col.*	Cap.; *Mar.*	Mount.			Cap.; *Br. Col.*	W. Lake, Mid. Atl., Up. Midw.
+5	P. NW		N. Eng., Up. Midw.	Cap.	Mid. Atl.			P. SW
+6	*Mar.*		W. Lake, Mid. Atl.	N. Eng., Up. Midw., W. Lake, *Mar.*, P. NW		Fla., Mount., P. SW, SW	Fla., E. Lake, W. Lake, Mid. Atl., Up. Midw., Mount.	E. Lake, Cap.
+7	*Prair.*		P. SW, P. NW, E. Lake, *Prair.*	P. SW, Mid. Atl.	L. Midw.			P. NW
+8					SW			
+9				E. Lake, *Br. Col.*	E. Lake		P. SW	
+10			*Br. Col.*		Fla., *Br. Col.*[d], Up. Midw., P. SW, *Mar.*, *P. NW*[d], Mount., *Prair.*		P. NW	
+20						*Prair.*, *Br. Col.*[d], *P. NW*[d], *Mar.*		
+30								
+40								
+50								
+60								

(continued on next page)

TABLE 25. *Continued*

Percent	Manufacturing sector[b]							
	Chemicals	Petroleum products	Rubber and plastics	Leather goods	Nonmetallic mineral products	Metallic products	Transportation equipment	Miscellaneous
−10		Cap.						
−9		W. Lake						
−8		Mid. Atl.			W. Lake			
−7		E. Lake			Cap.			
−6		N. Eng.						
−5			*Que.*		*Br. Col.*		*Que.*	*Que.*
−4			Fla.	*Que.*	Mid. Atl.	*Que.*		South
−3								*Mar.* / *N. Eng.* / SW
−2	Cap. / W. Lake	L. Midw.	*Prair.*					
−1	Mid. Atl. / *Que.* / N. Eng.		*Mar.*		N. Eng. / E. Lake			
Ontario[c]			Cap. / L. Midw.					
+1	E. Lake / P. SW / L. Midw. / South	*Que.* / South	N. Eng. / Up. Midw. / *Br. Col.*	SW		N. Eng.	Fla. / *Prair.* / *Mar.*	*Prair.*
+2	Up. Midw. / *Br. Col.*		Mid. Atl. / SW	South		W. Lake / L. Midw.	*Br. Col.*	Cap. / W. Lake / *Br. Col.*

+3		P. SW	W. Lake			Cap. Mid. Atl.	South Mount. L. Midw. W. Lake N. Eng.	L. Midw.
+4	Fla.		South					Up. Midw. E. Lake
+5			P. SW Mount.	L. Midw. Fla.		*Br. Col.*	Up. Midw. Mid. Atl. Cap. P. NW P. SW E. Lake	Mid. Atl. Fla. P. NW
+6		SW		*Mar.*	P. SW L. Midw. South	South E. Lake Fla.		
+7	SW Mount. *Prair.* P. NW		P. NW E. Lake	Up. Midw. Mid. Atl. Mount. N. Eng. *Prair.* Cap.		SW Up. Midw.	SW	
+8		*Br. Col.*		W. Lake E. Lake P. NW P. SW				
+9	*Mar.*			*Br. Col.*		P. SW	P. SW	
+10		Up. Midw. P. NW Fla. Mount.			Up. Midw. SW Fla. Mount.		Mount.	
+20		*Prair.*				*Prair.* Mount. P. NW *Mar.*		
+30		*Mar.*			*Prair.*			
+40 **+50** **+60**					*Mar.*			

ᵃ The following costs are included: labor costs, transportation costs, resource costs, and capital costs. For sources, see Appendix O.
ᵇ See Table 1, note a.
ᶜ Ontario = 0.
ᵈ The poor rankings of B.C. and P. NW are a result of the assumptions — in these cases very unrealistic — regarding the pricing of resources. See Chapter 6.

Two cost differences are not included in Table 25: differences in taxes and the effect of the present exchange rate discount on Canadian costs. Taxes are excluded because they are best treated as a residual policy variable. In addition there is little evidence that tax rates prior to 1963 significantly affected the competitive position of Canadian industry relative to that of the United States. Recent changes in 1963 and 1964 were not fully effective until 1965; they have been analyzed in Chapter 9, and it should be noted that these taxes in combination are likely to raise costs in Canada by only about one percent or less. The effects of the exchange rate are considered later in this chapter and in Chapter 11.

What can be said of the relative importance of those location influences in Table 25 that can be reduced to a common cost measure? The figures shown in earlier chapters indicate that capital costs and resource costs are of secondary importance in almost all industries. As a consequence, the comparison of Canadian and U.S. regions in this table tends to be reduced to an evaluation of how lower Canadian wages are offset (or augmented) by differences in transport costs on final products. Specifically, in comparing Ontario (and Quebec) with the five heartland regions of the United States, the issue becomes the extent to which lower Ontario wages are offset by higher transport costs from the Ontario location; because of the relatively central location of Ontario, transport cost disadvantages of the province generally are not sufficient to offset the substantially lower wage in that province.

Before examining this table in detail, an important caution is required. In the analysis in Chapter 4 it became evident that there are three manufacturing sectors that have particularly heavy trans-

---

— like debt — is more expensive in Canada. (This almost surely overstates higher Canadian costs, since the limited available evidence in footnote 7 of Chapter 8 suggests that equity costs may be no higher in Canada than in the United States.) In the case of both resource costs and transport costs, a median estimate was used, since — unlike capital costs — it is not possible to generalize that all U.S. regions are lower cost than Canadian regions. On balance in the case of transport costs, U.S. regions may tend to be better situated, whereas in terms of resource costs there may be some overall tendency for Canadian regions to be preferred. There are, however, so many exceptions to this conclusion that median cost estimates were used in both cases. There was only one estimate of labor cost differences, and it was used throughout.

port costs on shipments of their aggregate products: petroleum and coal products, nonmetallic mineral products, and to a lesser degree, lumber and wood products. Transport costs, especially for the first two sectors, tend as a consequence to swamp all other costs and become the major determinant of the relative cost position of each area. The magnitude of the transport cost differences explains why the range of cost estimates in Table 25 is greater for these three industries than for the others. It also tends to make regions close to the biggest markets preferred cost locations. Thus, the five regions in the U.S. industrial heartland are preferred locations.[3] But because of the dominance of transport costs, these goods will tend to be produced for local markets, and the location of these industries may be largely predicted from an examination of the local market in each region. For this same reason, their potential impact on international trade patterns, given any change in commercial policy, is limited. Consequently, the apparent cost advantage of the U.S. heartland regions in two of these cases, and Ontario and Quebec in the other, should not be regarded as highly significant. These three industries are of secondary interest in a study of comparative advantage, and major attention should be directed to the other manufacturing sectors.

In almost all other industries Ontario is a lower cost location than all or most of the five favored U.S. regions. The only exceptions are the tobacco products and pulp and paper sectors; it should be noted that the former is the only industry in which Canadian wages are already as high as those in the United States. In the chemical products sector, Ontario and Quebec costs are almost identical to those in the five industrialized U.S. areas. In all ten remaining sectors Ontario and Quebec are preferred cost locations.

This conclusion becomes even stronger when the cost advantage of just over eight percent provided by the present discount on the Canadian dollar is considered.[4] Since no account is taken in Table

[3] This is clearly evident in petroleum and coal products and nonmetallic mineral products; it is less evident in lumber and wood products because transport costs are somewhat less significant in this sector than in the other two, and are offset by substantial wage advantages in Ontario and Quebec.

[4] The discount of 7.5 percent on the Canadian dollar means that the U.S. dollar is 8.1 percent more expensive than the Canadian dollar.

25 of this discount, it means effectively that every U.S. region should be shifted down in this table by a maximum of 8.1 percent, while leaving each Canadian region in its present position. The extent of this downward shift cannot exceed 8.1 percent and will be less insofar as each Canadian industry would require imports from the United States; however, even discounted in this way the net Canadian cost advantage should be substantial enough to ensure that Ontario and Quebec would be low cost locations in most industries.

It might appear that the production of goods in Canada for sale in U.S. markets would involve some "trading" risk premium to cover a possible revision in the exchange rate.[5] It is true that this sort of risk is involved; but, paradoxically, it is possible that exchange risk will reduce rather than increase the total risk pattern involved in Canadian production. If a U.S. owned firm in Canada undertakes sales in the United States, the trading risk of exchange revaluation should tend to offset the "capital repatriation" risk discussed in Chapter 8 because the "loss" from repatriating investment funds from Canada to the United States after a depreciation in the Canadian dollar would be partly or wholly offset by increased profits accruing to the Canadian company because of the increase in its revenue from sales in the United States.[6] To the extent that trading risk offsets capital risk, the capital cost dis-

[5] If North American markets are to be serviced, this exchange risk cannot be entirely avoided even by locating in the United States — since in this case an exchange risk becomes associated with sales in *Canada*. However, because of the relative size of the Canadian and U.S. markets, there is less exchange risk involved for a producer in the United States than for a producer in Canada.

[6] This would generally, but not always, be true. It follows, for example, provided that the import content of Canadian production is less than sales for export and provided that the prices of both import components and export sales are determined in the U.S. In extreme cases "trading" risk may more than completely offset "capital" risk, and there thus arises a risk of an exchange rate movement in the other direction. Suppose, for example, that Canadian production is devoted completely to export to the United States and involves no import content. Suppose the firm's export prices are determined on the U.S. market; further suppose that all its accounting is done in Canadian dollars. The stability of the firm's costs (which are all Canadian) means that, with a depreciation of the Canadian dollar, any increase in its revenue from sales in the United States would increase its profits by an even greater proportion; consequently, even after repatriation into U.S. funds, these profits would be increased.

advantage already attributed in this analysis to Canadian locations will overstate the net effects of exchange rate risk, and as a consequence Canadian costs may be somewhat more favorable than Table 25 and Appendix O suggest.[7]

More will be said of exchange rate effects in the next chapter. At this stage it is sufficient to note that the present discount on the Canadian dollar will give Canadian producers an additional cost advantage, thus strengthening the following tentative conclusions of Part I.

The prospects of Ontario and Quebec in a free trade area cannot be confidently compared with those of the five adjacent regions in the U.S. industrial heartland because there are no firm guidelines for trading off the agglomeration advantages of these U.S. regions shown in Table 24 with the cost advantages (especially wage advantages) of Ontario and Quebec reflected in Table 25. Only limited conclusions of the following kind are justified: if free trade specialization takes place between these two areas, Ontario and Quebec may be expected to attract labor intensive industries, whereas the U.S. areas will be attractive for industries sensitive to whatever agglomeration pressures may be generated by market attractions, external economies, and so on.[8]

[7] In pursuing an argument this complex, it should be remembered that the premium that is in fact attributed to risk is dependent on a subjective evaluation by the businessman. Therefore, true objective risks evaluated logically may be of little consequence, if the entrepreneur thinks the risks involved are quite different.

[8] In general it is easier to compare any other Canadian region with its adjacent U.S. region. The Canadian Maritimes, and to a smaller degree the Canadian Prairies, compare unfavorably with New England and the Upper Midwest, respectively. In each case the Canadian region is less centrally located in terms of the indexes used in Table 24; moreover, each of these Canadian regions has no offsetting clear advantage in costs (in Table 25), largely because higher transport costs tend to counteract the effect of lower wages. However, British Columbia does compare favorably with the U.S. Pacific Northwest. Vancouver is so close to Seattle that the Canadian province suffers no significant disadvantage in terms of relative proximity to markets. Since transport costs tend to be equal from either location, British Columbia's lower wage level makes it a preferred location. The free trade prospects for these three Canadian regions — British Columbia, the Maritimes, and the Prairies — therefore closely reflect their past industrial experience in a protected Canadian economy; for British Columbia the outlook is favorable, but for the Maritimes and Prairies it is less so. Differences in the prospects facing each Canadian region will be analyzed in greater detail in Chapter 11.

Firmer conclusions may be reached in comparing the prospects of Ontario and Quebec with all U.S. regions except those lying in the Chicago-New York heartland. In terms of both the rankings of Table 24 and the explicit costs summarized in Table 25, Ontario and Quebec are preferred locations. They provide lower wages (and costs) and better access to the central North American concentration of industry and income. On the basis of this comparison, it may be predicted that the prospects of these two provinces in a free trade area are likely to be at least as good as the prospects of those U.S. regions which do not lie along the Chicago-New York axis. The proven ability of these U.S. regions to maintain prosperous conditions and high rates of growth within the U.S. "free trade area" should provide grounds for considerable optimism concerning the (even more favorable) prospects of Ontario and Quebec.

The U.S. area that is most likely to provide an exception to this general rule is California. The wage and cost disadvantage of California vis-à-vis Ontario (in Table 25) may be offset in specific industries by advantages of heavier local industry concentration in the state (shown in Table 24). The West Coast industrial complex still cannot be compared with that of the U.S. eastern industrial heartland — because it is smaller in absolute size and because it is more widely dispersed along the western seaboard. However, more rapid growth is taking place there than in North America as a whole, and this growth would almost certainly be reflected in a more favorable ranking for California in Table 24 were more recent figures available.

There are two substantial reasons for this California growth, neither of which has been analyzed in preceding chapters. Each is important in explaining past and likely future growth in the state as well as in tempering Canadian optimism on the outcome of free trade.

The first is the attraction for industry of regional amenities. Such diverse influences as physical surroundings, climate, or local cultural attractions may tend to draw industry. Because of regional amenities a firm may find its costs are indirectly lower; for example, a manufacturer of electronic equipment may find that engineers and mathematicians may be hired more easily, or at lower salary levels, in a certain area because they are attracted by its amenities. Alternatively, if the firm's management is sensitive to these attractions, an area with amenities may be chosen as a location, even though higher costs may be incurred there. The reason amenities are not analyzed in detail in this study is that industry or regional generalizations are very difficult, partly because these influences cannot be measured; nor can it even be concluded that a specific set of amenities will attract rather than repel. For example, there is no problem, other things being equal, in regarding low wages in an area as an attraction, since lower costs may be regarded as an unambiguous advantage for any industry. But warm, sunny weather every day of the year may attract some businessmen while repelling others who prefer a change of climate and season. Conclusions, therefore, cannot be strong; but, judging from recent migration of the retired and footloose, it might safely be assumed that California and Florida may offer amenities sufficient to stimulate some degree of growth, both past and future. A more precise statement is not possible because preferences can neither be measured nor compared, nor is there even any general agreement on what is an amenity and what is not.

The second reason for rapid growth in California is defense expenditure by the U.S. federal government. This is perhaps best classified as one of those special institutional arrangements not directly analyzed in this study. Admittedly there may be certain weather advantages enjoyed by southern U.S. regions that may be important for the aircraft and space industries; however, the choice of a specific location for defense expenditure is often made on political or other noneconomic grounds — in such a way as often to defy or contradict economic pressures. For this reason Canadian regions may not achieve rates of growth enjoyed by U.S. regions that are otherwise similarly or even less attractively situated — except of course insofar as these Canadian regions are able to attract Canadian federal expenditures. Certainly free trade, like our present protection system, does not in any way ensure a reasonable degree of equality in North American defense sharing for Canadian regions. Equal treatment in this regard for Canadian industry would seem to require policy developments that are, at least in part, independent of tariff changes; such developments might be along the lines of recent intergovernment agreements regarding the location of defense expenditures. It is sufficient at this stage to note that the regional pattern of U.S. defense expenditures would remain unaffected by tariff reductions per se; this pattern would be subject to change only if more drastic commitments between the two countries were undertaken. Finally, it should be noted from the differential experience of various regions in the United States that simply being part of that economic union by no means ensures that a region will get a "fair share" of federal defense commitments.

Although much of the discussion in the above pages has dealt with the free trade prospects of Ontario and Quebec, it should not be concluded that the rest of Canada would be adversely affected by free trade. Rather, Ontario and Quebec have been the center of attention because they may be expected to remain the most industrialized of the Canadian provinces — whether there is free trade or not. The experience within the U.S. "free trade area" in the past decades is instructive in this regard: the "manufacturing belt" in the broad Chicago-New York axis has remained "the very heart of the national economy," [9] in spite of the many changes occurring since 1900. At the same time, however, there has been some tendency for manufacturing employment to shift toward the West and the South, and there has been a gradual decline in regional wage differentials.[10] The capital generated in the core areas has been used to fill out other regions. The free trade prospects of the Canadian West and Maritimes will be considered below (esp. under interregional aspects of the adjustment process in Chapter 11); for the present, it will suffice to stress that the generally favorable prospects of Ontario and Quebec should not be used as a basis for concluding that other Canadian areas would be left behind.

It should also be emphasized that in the location decision there must always be a large element of chance. The lack of pattern that is evident if only U.S. regions in Tables 24 and 25 are compared

[9] Harvey S. Perloff, Edgar S. Dunn, Eric E. Lampard, and Richard F. Muth, *Regions, Resources, and Economic Growth* (Baltimore: Johns Hopkins Press, 1960), p. 50.
[10] *Ibid.*, pp. 263, 384.

emphasizes the importance of chance factors. It also provides a caution on too rigid an interpretation of cost figures aggregated over broad industrial sectors. Obviously, cost disadvantages that apply to an aggregate sector do not necessarily apply to individual subindustries. There are many instances of growth in subindustries in regions where sector costs appear to be relatively high; it follows that overall sector cost disadvantages have not prevented regions from effectively specializing in more favored subindustries. This satisfactory experience of specialization by less favored U.S. regions should be remembered in evaluating the prospects of low wage areas such as the Canadian Prairies and Maritimes; the cost disadvantages they face in a manufacturing sector because of their distance from markets may not prevent them from effective specialization in labor-intensive subindustries.

In summary, for all these reasons it is simply not possible to make firm predictions on the future patterns of industry location. It is only possible in an economic study of this kind to analyze the economic pressures that will tend to draw industries into various areas. In terms of these basic cost conditions it may be concluded that, given the present value of the Canadian dollar and present relative wage levels in the two countries, the Canadian industrial complex in the Windsor-Quebec City area would be very favorably situated for expansion in most industrial sectors in the event of free trade. The implication is that the long-run process of international adjustment would involve some rise in Canadian wages relative to U.S. wages or an appreciation of the Canadian dollar or both. Part II is a detailed study of this adjustment process.

PART II

Comparative Advantage:
The International Adjustment Mechanism

11

THE PROCESS OF ADJUSTMENT

TO FREE TRADE

Part I has involved a comparison of potential Canadian and U.S. costs under free trade, assuming exchange parity and present wage rates. It was concluded that Canadian locations would be potentially in a strong competitive position in these circumstances. The overall picture of factor prices in Canada is favorable; wage advantages generally more than offset disadvantages such as higher capital costs.

This, of course, does not imply that *present* Canadian costs of production are lower. In fact, they are generally higher, with favorable factor price conditions more than offset by higher costs resulting from protection-induced inefficiencies — for example, fragmented production runs.[1] In this chapter, we consider the question of how Canadian business would rationalize in response to free trade; it would involve the elimination of (protection-induced) inefficiencies in order to take advantage of generally favorable factor price conditions.

Once the question of adjustment is raised, it must be recognized that general equilibrium issues have been introduced. As a response to free trade, there would be pressures on businesses to modify their organization of production to take account of the new situation; there would also be fundamental adjustment forces operating on the underlying wage and exchange rates. Because of the general equilibrium nature of the adjustment process, the di-

[1] Higher present Canadian costs are broken down in detail in Part III.

rection and strength of the forces that operate on any one sector or economic variable would depend in part on the outcome of the pressures operating on other sectors or variables. Although it is logically possible to construct a system of equations to deal with many economic forces simultaneously, a number of the important issues in this chapter are not susceptible of simple algebraic formulation. They must be dealt with less formally, and, because of the limitations of verbal exposition, they must be divided into topics. Because the topics are interrelated, a brief overall view of the picture presented in this chapter is in order before attention is turned to the details of adjustment.

There are two main sects of forces in the adjustment process. One set operates on the structure of the economy, and one operates toward the maintenance of balance-of-payments equilibrium. In its simplest form, international trade theory indicates that a country will, under free trade conditions, specialize in the goods in which its comparative efficiency is greatest and import the goods in which its comparative efficiency is least. The dividing line between the goods that will be exported and those that will be imported will depend on the forces operating through changes in the exchange rate and relative domestic factor and output prices.

In past discussion of the Canadian-U.S. case, it has generally been concluded that with free trade there would be a major adjustment between the raw material and manufacturing sectors. Canada would specialize in raw materials, which she has traditionally exported, and would greatly increase her net import of manufactures; thus Canadians would become "hewers of wood and drawers of water" for their American neighbors. But the argument is deceptive. It cannot simply be concluded that the primary effect of free trade would be a stimulation of the export of products whose present costs are lowest; the difficulty arises because free trade may significantly alter cost conditions. In the section below that deals with raw materials in the adjustment process, it is concluded that no major tendency toward Canadian raw material specialization is likely; there would be no general collapse of Canadian manufacturing. Rather, the major forces would operate *within* the manufacturing sector, pressuring Canadian manufacturers toward fewer and longer production runs. The reorganization of industry and the associated pressures on international capital flows are studied under the industrial sector below, although detailed empirical confirmation on reorganization is delayed until Chapters 13 and 14. In the section on Canadian-U.S. wage and exchange rate equilibrium, it is concluded that, because of the possibilities of Canadian reorganization and the resulting lower costs, the pressure on the relative Canadian wage rate and the Canadian dollar would be in an upward direction. Finally, some special interregional and interindustry aspects of the adjustment process are considered in the last section.

Raw Materials in the Adjustment Process

Because of the special problems associated with farm programs, the agricultural sector is being excluded from detailed consideration in this study. This is not to suggest that the agricultural sector could be left unchanged in the event of a Canadian-U.S. free trade arrangement in manufactured goods: for example, if there were to be free trade in flour, economic rationality would imply that the price of wheat to U.S. and Canadian mills should be equalized.[2] Thus, subsidies equivalent to those on exports might be extended to U.S. domestic users of wheat along the lines of the recent changes in the cotton program, which were designed to eliminate the disadvantage of U.S. textile manufacturers because of high-priced U.S. cotton.[3] However, this is only one of many possible ways of dealing with the farm question. Because of the direct intervention in the domestic and international markets that the farm programs have involved, it is difficult to foresee accurately what would happen in this area under Canadian-U.S. free trade.

If minimal changes occur in agricultural protection and domestic farm programs, little change may be expected in trade flows in these goods. But, even if agricultural products were included in a free trade scheme, the effects on Canadian-U.S. trade in such products are unlikely to be large compared to changes in other areas. If U.S. support programs were retained, and U.S. quotas on agricultural imports eliminated, Canadian exports (for example, of wheat) would of course increase by a vast amount. But this situa-

---

[2] See the discussion of wheat flour costs, below, p. 265.

[3] See the discussion of cotton gray costs, below, pp. 264–265.

tion could hardly continue because in the process the U.S. tax-payer would be heavily subsidizing the Canadian farmer. Consequently, free trade would force abolition or drastic revision of these programs; and in these circumstances it is by no means clear that trade flows would increase greatly in either direction.

From Table 26, it is evident that Canadian-U.S. trade is dominated by processed and semi-processed materials rather than agricultural goods; both the present situation and the trend that has occurred toward trade in manufactures result from basic economic forces that may be expected to continue whether there is a movement to free trade or not. With the rise in per capita incomes, agricultural products play a declining relative role in economic activity. Thus, in the overall scheme of things, agricultural adjustments due to a movement toward Canadian-U.S. free trade would be unlikely to play a primary role. This conclusion is strengthened by the pattern of natural markets for agricultural products: unlike the case in minerals and manufactured goods, the best agricultural markets for the two North American countries are not one another but third countries. This is particularly true for wheat, where the United States and Canada are natural competitors.

On somewhat different grounds, it may be anticipated that non-agricultural raw materials will also play a relatively limited role in the overall adjustment process. In this area, present restrictions are relatively low: about two thirds of Canadian resource exports to the United States and approximately ninety percent of U.S. resource exports to Canada are already duty free. The most notable exception to the general policy of low resource restrictions is oil, which is the subject of government policies in both countries. Free trade in resources would have a direct effect only in selected areas of this kind. Otherwise, the volume of change in resource trade is likely to be small: elasticities in the resource area are relatively low, and these low elasticities would be operating in conjunction with small changes in relative prices.[4]

[4] The competitive position of Canadian and U.S. resource producers would also be affected by any general equilibrium adjustment in relative wage and exchange levels. Since the Canadian wage and dollar are likely to rise (see the last section of this chapter), the elimination of the U.S. tariff on Canadian resources would tend to be offset. (That is, wage-exchange adjustment would reduce the relative importance of natural resources in Canada's export trade.)

TABLE 26. *Canadian Balance of Payments with the United States, and with all Countries, 1958 ($000,000 Canadian).*

	With the U.S.		With the world	
	Credit[a]	Debit	Credit	Debit
I. CURRENT ACCOUNT				
A. RAW MATERIALS	909	394	1,701	889
Wheat (1)	15	—	446	—
Other agricultural goods (1)	272	168	364	286
Cotton (3)	—	29	—	45
Lumber (5)	41	10	49	11
Coal (10)	3	88	3	94
Crude petroleum (10)	73	5	73	274
Nonmetallic minerals (13)	57	14	67	15
Iron ore (14)	78	28	108	29
Aluminum (14)	—	1	—	35
Uranium (14)	263	—	277	—
Other metals (14)	48	1	148	4
Miscellaneous	59	50	166	96
B. SEMI-PROCESSED AND PROCESSED[b]	1,919	3,178	3,125	4,303
Food	109	100	264	286
Tobacco	—	1	—	2
Textiles	8	163	20	328
Apparel	—	—	—	—
Wood products	513	56	636	70
Paper	606	61	724	66
Printing	3	78	4	88
Electrical equipment	8	187	25	240
Chemicals	78	172	176	210
Petroleum products	5	85	7	138
Rubber and plastics	5	113	29	126
Leather goods	6	9	12	22
Nonmetallic mineral products	54	105	101	162
Metallic products	446	1,267	856	1,546
Transportation equipment	24	412	155	542
Miscellaneous	54	369	116	477
TOTAL, MERCHANDISE TRADE	2,828	3,572	4,826	5,192
Adjustment factor			61	−126
C. OTHER TRANSACTIONS	1,102	1,743	1,692	2,644
Tourist and travel	309	413	349	542
Interest and dividends	100	500	168	612
Other items	693	830	1,175	1,490
TOTAL CURRENT ACCOUNT	3,930	5,315	6,579	7,710
II. CAPITAL ACCOUNT	1,195	243	1,471	340

Sources: D.B.S., *Trade of Canada,* 1958; *Canada Year Book,* 1962.
a Commodity exports, capital imports.
b See Table 1, note a.

Moreover, in the process of international adjustment, there is little prospect that rising employment and wages in the resource sector will pull the present Canadian labor force out of manufacturing. Increased output in this sector would be limited for the reasons mentioned above, and in addition, any increase in output tends to result in a relatively small increase in employment in resource extraction. This is, of course, not true in agriculture, which does involve substantial employment. But most agricultural labor is self-employed and hence does not earn wages; moreover, wage-earners in agriculture already have wages so far below industrial wages that it is difficult to conceive of any circumstances in which agricultural wages would rise sufficiently to pull the labor force back to the farm.[5]

Thus, in the event of a free trade arrangement, there would be relatively little adjustment *between* the resource sector (including agriculture) and the manufacturing sector. Furthermore, *within* the resource sector, a relatively small degree of adjustment might be expected, in sharp contrast to likely adjustments within the manufacturing sector. In manufacturing, present North American tariffs have resulted in fragmented production runs in Canada. In the event of free trade, the competitive pressures from U.S. enterprises and the possibility of free entry into the U.S. market would give Canadian manufacturers a major incentive to specialize. In contrast, the current low Canadian tariff and heavy exports of resources imply that Canadian resource industries are already internationally competitive, and at or near the optimum degree of specialization. In resources, therefore, there would be little pressure on individual producers to modify their methods of production.

The same generalization is also true in agriculture: although there are major economies of scale at the farm level, the size of the total domestic market in either Canada or the United States has not limited the realization of these economies. Because of the increasing mechanization of agriculture, there are major pressures for the consolidation of small farms. However, for almost any type of farming, substantially all the benefits of large scale farming are obtained on a farm of a few hundred acres or, at most, a few thousand. Thus, the size of the domestic market has not been a limitation on the organization and size of individual farms in either country.

---

[5] The most likely long-run effect would be that higher returns to the self-employed in agriculture might reduce migration from the farm to the city, and this change would indirectly influence employment patterns.

The Industrial Sector: Reorganization and Capital Flows

Since it has often been presumed in Canadian policy debate that Canadian manufacturing would contract with free trade, this possibility must be addressed. In view of the favorable manufacturing cost conditions established in Part I, the impetus under free trade would be toward manufacturing expansion rather than contraction, provided Canadian industry is successfully reorganized. The limits on this expansion will have to be discussed, since an appreciation of relative wages and the exchange rate modifies Canadian cost advantages. However, before proceeding, we must digress to take up one important point: the survival of manufacturing in Canada does not depend on the accuracy of our favorable conclusions regarding free trade costs and the reorganization of industry. Even if one or both of these conditions were not met, and if Canadian manufacturing costs were unfavorable, Canadian industry would not collapse. It is true that it would initially contract under pressure from import competition. But the resulting deterioration in the balance of payments would result in a decline in the Canadian exchange rate[6] until the unfavorable balance-of-payments effects were offset by an increase in capital inflow, a decrease in imports, an increase in primary exports, an improvement of the service and travel accounts, or an increase in manufactured exports.

These changes may be taken one at a time. If capital inflows increase, the level of aggregate demand required to maintain Canadian full employment will rise and for two reasons: first, aggregate demand will have to be sufficient to permit the full employment of domestic factors and sufficient to cover the current account deficit associated with the capital flow; second, if full employment policies are followed, the international monetary capital inflow is likely to be associated with an increase in Canadian real capital formation and hence in productive capacity. Because of the increase in the full employment level of aggregate demand, an increase in Canadian imports of manufactures associated with a

---

[6] If it is allowed to fluctuate. If the rate is pegged, it would eventually have to be devalued. The advisability of exchange flexibility is considered below, pp. 203–206 and 327–329.

monetary capital inflow need not involve a decrease in the Canadian market for Canadian-produced manufactures; indeed, if full employment is maintained, an increase in this market may occur.

The second possible response to a fall in the value of the Canadian dollar would be a decline in the level of Canadian imports. But most Canadian imports are manufactured goods. Hence, in this case, the initial free trade increase in manufactured imports will be offset through the exchange rate mechanism by a secondary decrease in manufactured imports (and probably by some decrease in nonmanufactured imports).

The third possibility is an increase in primary exports. The resulting expansion of the primary sector of the Canadian economy is the type of adjustment foreseen in the oversimplified free trade theory, with Canada having a comparative advantage in primary goods and a general comparative disadvantage in manufactures. However, for reasons noted earlier, the expansion of employment in the primary areas of the Canadian economy is likely to be limited. Similarly, the potential response of the service and travel accounts is limited; these items are relatively less important in the balance of payments, and they are already freely traded. The fifth possibility is an increase of manufactured exports; with increases in such exports, the level of manufacturing activity will tend to be maintained.

Thus, even if the most unfavorable situation for Canadian manufacturing is considered, and if it is assumed that the initial reaction to a reduction in tariffs would be a deterioration of the Canadian balance of trade in manufactured goods, the exchange rate mechanism would operate to prevent a collapse of Canadian manufacturing. With the decline in the Canadian dollar, the Canadian manufacturer would find his costs falling relative to those in other countries. This exchange decline would improve his ability to export and to compete with imports.

There are, however, reasons for believing that this unfavorable initial reaction would not occur;[7] that Canadian industry could reorganize in the face of a larger market; that the lower Canadian in-

---

[7] If both Canadian and U.S. tariffs are eliminated together. But this initial reaction is a distinct possibility if Canada unilaterally abolishes her tariff. (See Chapter 15.)

put costs studied in Part I of this book would place Canadian manufacturers in a favorable competitive position; and that the basic initial pressures would work toward an expansion of Canadian manufacturing output and an appreciation of the Canadian dollar. It is to these central issues that we now turn.

Possible Reorganization of Canadian Manufacturing. The possibilities of Canadian industry improving its efficiency through reorganization in the event of free trade center on the question of economies of scale. The inherent complexity of such economies is perhaps the explanation for the prevalence of two contradictory propositions in the discussion of the Canadian tariff: first, that tariffs are necessary to protect Canadian industry because it cannot reduce costs to world levels with the present limited size of the domestic market; second, that multilateral free trade would wipe out Canadian secondary industry because its costs generally exceed world levels. Logically, if a limited domestic market is the explanation for the present higher level of Canadian costs, then free trade would itself help to eliminate these higher Canadian costs by opening up foreign markets and, therefore, the possibility of extended production runs.

There are a number of published works which throw light on the problem of economies of scale. Of these, three in particular might be mentioned: Joe S. Bain's study of economies of scale in the United States, H. Edward English's study of the significance of Canada's industrial structure in her international competitive position, and Tibor Scitovsky's discussion of the importance of economies of scale in Western European integration.[8]

Bain concluded that the size of plant necessary to achieve substantially all economies of scale was generally not very large compared to the total U.S. market. Even in steel, the optimal scale of a fully integrated plant was estimated at only one to two and one half percent of U.S. national capacity, with conflicting evidence on whether there were further cost advantages in multiplant opera-

[8] Joe S. Bain, *Barriers to New Competition* (Cambridge: Harvard University Press, 1956), especially pp. 245–254; H. Edward English, *Industrial Structure in Canada's International Competitive Position* (Montreal: Canadian Trade Committee, Private Planning Association of Canada, 1964); Tibor Scitovsky, *Economic Theory and Western European Integration* (Stanford: Stanford University Press, 1958), Chapter III.

tions. Technological advances since Bain's study would seem, if anything, to have decreased the size of plant capable of achieving lowest cost levels. Thus, it would seem to be possible for a steel plant to achieve substantially all economies of scale even if it were confined to the Canadian market. (Parenthetically, it might be noted that steel has been a product in which the Canadian competitive position has greatly improved in recent years.)

In four of the twenty products he studied, Bain's data indicated that there might be disadvantages for a plant confined to a market of the size of that in Canada.[9] Bain found the optimal scale of a tractor plant to be between ten and fifteen percent of U.S. national capacity or 50,000 to 75,000 units per annum, with costs only slightly higher at half the minimum optimal size, and only "moderately" higher at a fifth or even a tenth of it. U.S. production at much less than one percent of the U.S. market seemed rare. For typewriters, ten to thirty percent of the national market was judged necessary to achieve optimum plant size, or roughly 150,000 to 450,000 units per annum. Costs would be substantially higher if capacity were only five to seven and one half percent of the U.S. national market. The optimum size of a fountain pen plant would require five to ten percent of the U.S. market.

The fourth product, automobiles, presented a particularly difficult case because of the variety of models and the varying characteristics of parts production. However, Bain found that, in general, "300,000 units per annum is a low estimate of what is needed for productive efficiency in any one line; there are probable added advantages to 600,000 units . . . Costs would be 'moderately' higher at 150,000 units, or 5 percent of the [U.S.] low-priced field, substantially higher at 60,000 units, and uneconomical at smaller scales."

One of the problems which present themselves in a particularly noticeable form in the automobile industry is the number of different models. Some of these models are very similar to one another, with many interchangeable parts; these automobiles may even be produced on the same assembly line. On the other hand, some of the models have relatively little in common, even though

---

[9] The size of the Canadian market has traditionally run about 7 percent of the size of the U.S. market.

they may be produced by the same manufacturer. The result is that it is very difficult to estimate economies of scale because for some parts, the relevant output may be the entire output of automobiles in the economy; for other parts, the relevant output may be only the output of the specific model in question.[10]

The problems created by the number of models and the number of producers of manufactured goods in Canada form a major theme of English in his study on the *Industrial Structure in Canada's International Competitive Position*. He notes that in all but a few products, the size of the Canadian market is greater than that necessary to sustain the smallest efficient plant. Moreover, the geographical distribution of the Canadian market does not generally prevent the attainment of plants of optimum size: for most products, the geographically centralized Ontario-Quebec market is sufficiently large to absorb the output of at least one plant of the most efficient size.[11]

A market barely sufficient to support one producer at optimal scale is, however, not large enough in three respects. The monopoly position of a single producer would allow him to sell his product at a relatively high price, regardless whether or not he produces at minimum cost.[12] Moreover, although he may be pro-

---

[10] Tibor Scitovsky has stressed an additional complication: because of the interrelations among segments of the economy with varying optimum sizes, the overall magnitude of the economy needed to achieve substantially all the advantages of size may be considerably greater than would be deduced by looking at any individual segment. See his "International Trade and Economic Integration as a Means of Overcoming the Disadvantages of a Small Nation," in E. A. G. Robinson, ed., *Economic Consequences of the Size of Nations* (London: Macmillan, 1963).

[11] Of the four products in which the total Canadian market was deficient for an optimum size plant according to Bain's estimates, tractors provide the greatest problem of geographical dispersion of demand. Although Quebec and Ontario combined have approximately 63 percent of the Canadian population, only 48 percent of the 23,765 farm tractors sold in Canada in 1962 were sold in these two provinces; Bain estimated that the economies of scale could be fully gained at a minimum of 50,000 units. Although there are no North American tariffs on farm tractors, no tractors are produced in Canada; Canadian agriculture machinery output is concentrated on other items, particularly combines.

[12] The existence of monopoly affects not only consumption; since the output of almost any industry is the input of another, an economy comprised of monopolists could involve substantial productive inefficiencies, even if each producer operated at optimum scale.

ducing at the minimum point in his cost curve, increased competition could cause a downward shift in his entire cost curve. Furthermore, a single seller is unlikely to satisfy the public's desire for variety.

H. Edward English attributes the inefficient Canadian industrial structure in large part to the Canadian tariff, which encourages and enables a broad spectrum of U.S. manufacturers to set up branch plants in Canada in order to gain a share of the Canadian market; thus, Canadian industry becomes a small-scale replica of U.S. industry. But explanations are in order for behavior that prevents the achievement of optimum-scale production, and English offers a solution along the following lines. Price competition among producers, which would eliminate the weaker firms and permit the stronger to extend their scale of production toward internationally efficient levels, is discouraged by two characteristics of the industrial scene. In the first place, most producers have the extensive resources of American parents behind them; therefore, the prospects of eliminating rivals through price competition in the Canadian market are not good. Secondly, the Canadian tariff structure permits many small-scale producers to survive and supplies each industry with an obvious formula for eliminating price competition without overt collusion, or, indeed, any direct communication. The obvious price is the U.S. price plus the Canadian tariff.[13] Industries which follow this pattern gain a high measure of security; it is true that they are less efficient, but this cost is borne by the Canadian consumer. Thus, although the size of the Canadian market for most consumer durables does not preclude production at or near optimum scale, actual Canadian production is at suboptimum scale because of the industry characteristics caused by the Canadian tariff.

On this analysis by English, a strong argument for enthusiastic Canadian participation in international rounds of tariff reduction may be built; his thesis indicates that Canadian gains from tariff reductions may flow as much from Canadian tariff cuts as from foreign tariff cuts. A tendency for reductions in Canadian tariffs

[13] English, *Industrial Structure,* p. 36. English notes that, after the 1962 devaluation, the full effect of exchange rate changes was not immediately reflected in the application of this pricing formula.

to be followed by vigorous price competition and by a rationalization of Canadian industry would mean that, although the costs of adjustment to tariff reductions might be high, the potential gains would likewise be high. Moreover, the major adjustments need not involve the collapse of large numbers of Canadian producers. It would seem as likely that producers would be driven out of the production of specific lines as out of all production. Thus, after rationalization, there might be almost as many firms, with each specializing in a restricted range of products but producing large numbers within this restricted range and doing so at low cost levels.

Before this line of reasoning may be accepted as a strong argument in favor of free trade, however, a logical difficulty must be dealt with. It is not clear that the dropping of some lines by Canadian manufacturers in the face of foreign competition would permit them to specialize in a few long production runs. The threatened imports might materialize, with the result that the remaining lines of the Canadian producers could not, in fact, be lengthened. This outcome might be particularly pronounced in industries where Canadian production is in the hands of U.S. subsidiaries. As Canadian manufacturers close down the production lines of some goods, they might wish to offer a full line of products by importing the discontinued lines. As the Canadian market is carved up by imports, cost reductions in lines of Canadian specialization would not be realized, and even these lines might be unable to compete with imports. Is the protectionist, therefore, justified in his two major fears about free trade: that is, that import competition would eliminate much of Canadian industry, and that there would be few or no favorable effects on Canadian efficiency?

With a *unilateral* Canadian tariff cut, the first fear would not be justified, but the second might have partial validity. Because of the exchange rate mechanism outlined in the previous section, Canadian manufacturing would not collapse even if it were initially in a position of higher costs. As long as the exchange rate were allowed to adjust, the Canadian dollar would fall on the international exchanges until Canadian manufacturing became competitive. But the precise extent of this fall cannot be predicted; and even if it could, there would be no way of knowing the degree to which Canadian industry would be reorganized. The limit of the exchange rate fall may, however, be specified: it cannot fall by as much as the full amount of tariff abolition. If it were to do so, Canadian industry would find itself with equal domestic protection (albeit in a different form), and at the same time, Canadian firms selling in U.S. markets over the U.S. tariff would find their position strengthened.[14] Substantially increased efficiency of Canadian manufacturing could result from any such Canadian specialization for the U.S. market. The difficulty is that the extent of Canadian exchange depreciation, industrial reorganization, and entry into U.S. markets are closely related; but none can be precisely predicted under unilateral Canadian tariff cuts.[15]

However, if the U.S. as well as the Canadian tariff is eliminated, neither protectionist fear is justified. In this case, the total size of the market open to Canadian producers will not shrink. Indeed, the opposite will tend to happen: with the decrease in U.S. tariffs, an enormously enlarged market will be opened to Canadian producers. Where their costs are competitive, they will be able to sell throughout North America. Therefore, even though the Canadian share of the Canadian market may be shrinking, Canadian producers will have the possibility of cost-cutting, large-scale production open to them. This line of argument, it should be noted, supports the widespread Canadian viewpoint that it is the U.S., rather than the Canadian, tariff that is the major barrier to rationalization of Canadian manufacturing.

Free access to this large U.S. market is not the only condition required for reorganization; the other is that Canada would be an attractive production point for servicing this market, that is that Canadian industry, by reorganizing and scaling up, could reduce its costs to U.S. levels or below. The evidence in Part I is that, at the present wage and exchange rate, such competitive cost levels could be achieved in many industrial lines in Canada. This possibility is confirmed in the sample industry studies in Part III; in

[14] Canadian exchange depreciation can be regarded as similar in its price effects to an export subsidy.

[15] For a more detailed discussion of unilateral Canadian tariff reduction, see Chapter 15.

addition, these studies suggest that the cost reductions that could be achieved by Canadian reorganization are substantial.

The chances appear to be very good, therefore, that these incentives would outweigh any influences that might inhibit free trade reorganization in Canada. The most important of these inhibiting factors would be the risk that a rationalized Canadian operation would be made obsolete if the free trade arrangement broke down; thus, it is important that specific guarantees be included in any free trade agreement. A second inhibiting factor would be any residual American nonprice preferences for U.S. rather than Canadian goods. This is a factor which cannot be dismissed out of hand as trivial; however, there are reasons for believing that it would not be of major importance.[16] If the European experience may be taken as a guide, the establishment of a free trade area would itself tend to break down previous national purchasing preferences. Furthermore, the fragmentary evidence we have been able to glean on this problem suggests that the difficulty lies in the initial introduction of the Canadian product into the U.S. market and declines rapidly after sales have continued for any length of time. Thus, the problem also implies economies of scale: because initial sales often require a significant selling effort, they can be justified only for sizable and continuing sales.

In conclusion, then, there are strong reasons for believing that Canadian industry could and would be rationalized in the event of free trade.[17] The last section of this chapter will show that this

[16] Except where government purchases are concerned. The outcome in this area would be very much dependent on the nature of a free trade agreement.

[17] One further complication regarding industrial organization should be noted. As Scitovsky has pointed out in his *Economic Theory and Western European Integration* (pp. 110–135), economies of scale may have an important implication for the pattern of growth. Even if a country is large enough to support one or a few producers of optimum size, there may be still another problem (in addition to those already discussed) in achieving optimum scale of production. In a period of one or two years, the growth in the market will be insufficient to support an additional producer of optimum size. Thus, a dilemma will result: if a new unit of long-run optimum size is created, production will be at less than capacity, and therefore inefficient until demand grows; if, however, a new unit is constructed with a design aimed at meeting the current small level of unsatisfied demand

rationalization toward U.S. levels of efficiency would be likely to result in a substantial appreciation in both the Canadian dollar and Canadian income level. But before pursuing this main line of the argument, we digress briefly to consider the important implications of rationalization on the Canadian demand for capital — from both domestic and foreign sources.

Industrial Organization and the Demand for Capital. Past Canadian excess demand for monetary capital has resulted in very sizable net inflows from other countries, particularly from the United States. Therefore, the changing Canadian demand for foreign capital under free trade would be an important determinant of balance-of-payments equilibrium.

If the demand for capital is to be studied, an apparent paradox in the present Canadian use of capital must be explained. Interest rates and the price of capital goods are generally higher in Canada than in the United States; on the other hand, Canadian wage rates are significantly lower than U.S. wages. Thus, there is reason to expect that more labor and less capital would be used in productive processes in Canada than in the United States. Hence, on

---

most efficiently, then the economy will be saddled with a productive unit of less than optimum size in the longer run. The greater the size of the market compared to a single optimal-size producer, the shorter the time period necessary for market growth to justify an additional unit of long-run optimum size. Thus, the larger the market, the smoother and more efficient the growth process.

This may be taken as an additional explanation of English's paradox of a number of Canadian producers all operating at suboptimal scale even though the Canadian market is large enough to support one or more optimal-size producers. These suboptimal units may be the historical result of the establishment of a series of production units, each designed to meet the limited demand created by a period of growth and each, as a consequence, having higher minimum costs than would a larger-scale producer. But even though this may be taken as a contributing factor in the fragmented Canadian industrial picture, it can scarcely be taken as the whole explanation: specifically, it does not account for the simultaneous rush of U.S. subsidiaries to gain a foothold in the Canadian market (e.g., in television receivers), nor does it explain why suboptimal facilities have been replaced on depreciation rather than reorganized into larger units.

Clearly, this argument has limitations. But to whatever extent it is valid, it suggests a gain from tariff elimination. If Canadian producers could operate within a North American, rather than a national, framework, this growth problem would be greatly eased, as Canadian manufacturers could set up fewer, but longer and more efficient production lines.

theoretical grounds, one would anticipate that the capital-output ratio would be lower in Canada than the U.S. However, as may be seen from Table 27, this theoretical expectation is not borne out by the facts.

TABLE 27. *Canadian and U.S. Capital-Output Ratios, by Industry, 1958.*

Manufacturing sector[a]	Canada	U.S.
	A. Capital-value shipped	
Food	0.48	0.36
Tobacco	0.51	0.66
Textiles	0.66	0.61
Apparel	0.44	0.32
Wood products	0.63	0.57
Paper	1.07	0.75
Printing	0.55	0.48
Electrical equipment	0.59	0.50
Chemicals	0.76	0.72
Petroleum products	1.06	1.08
Rubber and plastics	0.65	0.62
Leather goods	0.48	0.39
Nonmetallic mineral products	1.00	0.81
Metallic products	0.91	0.75
Transportation equipment	0.46	0.52
Miscellaneous	0.61	0.55
All manufacturing	0.71	0.62
	B. Capital-value added	
All manufacturing	1.55	1.35

Sources: For the U.S.: *Census of Manufactures,* 1958, Vol. II, Part 1; Federal Trade Commission, *Quarterly Financial Report for Manufacturing Corporations,* fourth quarter, 1958, and second quarter, 1959. For Canada: D.B.S., *Manufacturing Industries of Canada,* 1959; Department of National Revenue, *Taxation Statistics,* 1960. The data from *Taxation Statistics* are based on a sample of about one seventh of the incorporated firms in each sector; it is necessary to assume that these are reasonably representative of all corporate and noncorporate firms in each sector.
a See Table 1, note a.

The data of Table 27 are presented on two bases.[18] At the top of the table, the capital-value shipped ratios are shown for each

[18] Neither base is the same as that of Wm. C. Hood and Anthony Scott, *Output, Labor and Capital in the Canadian Economy* (Ottawa: Royal Commission on Canada's Economic Prospects, 1957), p. 259. Hood and Scott included construction, machinery, and equipment as capital in each sector. Since the focus in this study is on the use of financial capital broadly defined, assets included in the calculation of Table 27 are those used by Hood and Scott, plus cash, receivables, land, and inventories.

industry. In fourteen of the sixteen industrial groups, and in the overall average, the Canadian capital-output ratios exceed those in the United States. There is, however, one major theoretical limitation of these ratios based on value shipped: they are sensitive to the degree of vertical integration of industry. Nevertheless, the higher Canadian ratios cannot be attributed to different degrees of integration: when the integration difficulty is removed by a calculation of the capital-value added ratio (Table 27, Part B), the Canadian ratio still exceeds that of the United States.

Nor can these higher Canadian ratios be explained by the fact that both numerator and denominator are expressed in value terms rather than in more appropriate physical units. Differences in the Canadian and U.S. valuation of a physical unit of output seems to be roughly similar to the difference in their valuation of a physical unit of capital. Manufactured products in Canada have prices which average somewhere in the neighborhood of five to ten percent higher than those in the United States; the higher price of capital goods in Canada is probably in the same general range.[19] Since both the numerator and denominator of each Canadian capital-output ratio in Table 27 are similarly overvalued, these monetary ratios should provide a good comparison of physical ratios in the two countries. It may be concluded, therefore, that Canada is a more capital-intensive country than even the United States, a conclusion that is confirmed by recent findings of the Economic Council of Canada.[20]

There are several lines along which the paradoxically higher Canadian capital-output ratios might possibly be explained. It

[19] The range of 5 to 10 percent is a rough approximation based on an unweighted average of a number of selected manufactured products whose Canadian-U.S. price differentials are given in John H. Young, *Canadian Commercial Policy* (Ottawa: Royal Commission on Canada's Economic Prospects, 1957), Appendix A. There are two reasons for believing that the price differential for capital is of the same general magnitude: capital consists largely of manufactures and, therefore, would tend to have the same price characteristics as other manufactures. Secondly, much Canadian capital equipment is imported; some of this equipment enters tariff free, whereas the rest is subject to M.F.N. duties ranging up to 22.5 percent.

[20] In its *Second Annual Review* (Ottawa: Queen's Printer, December 1965), pp. 59–61. The Council's conclusion — that capital stock *per employed person* is higher in Canada — is an even more surprising one than ours.

could be argued that the decade of the 1950's was a period of overinvestment in Canada based on excessive optimism. However, only limited weight should be put on overinvestment of this type. By 1958 it was becoming evident that the earlier expectations were not being realized; therefore, the overinvestment arising from unrealistic expectations occurred only for a limited time. Yet, if overinvestment is to make a sizable difference in the overall capital-output ratio, it must continue for an extended period of time, since investment in any year represents only the addition to capital stock whereas the capital-output ratio includes the total capital stock.

A more fundamental explanation for the higher Canadian capital-output ratios lies in the characteristics of Canadian industrial organization discussed in the previous section. Because production runs are generally short and inefficient compared to U.S. runs, Canadian industry tends to use more of *both* capital and labor in producing a unit of output. While the real capital-output ratio in Canadian manufacturing exceeds that in the United States by approximately fifteen percent,[21] the real labor-output ratio in Canadian manufacturing is roughly thirty-six percent higher than in the United States.[22] Although more capital is used in Canada in producing a unit of manufactured output, relatively more labor is employed; the Canadian labor-capital ratio exceeds that of the United States. Thus, the paradox of the higher Canadian capital-output ratio may be solved by considering this ratio as the combined result of two opposing forces. First, because of the higher relative price of capital in Canada, there is a tendency to substitute labor for capital in the productive process; this shows up in

[21] Derived from Table 27 by comparing the average of 0.71 and 0.62 or those of 1.55 and 1.35, and noting that these value ratios reasonably approximate real ratios.

[22] The ratio of Canadian wages and salaries in manufacturing to Canadian value added in manufacturing in 1958 was 0.49; in the United States it was 0.52 (from D.B.S., *Manufacturing Industries of Canada,* 1959; *U.S. Census of Manufactures,* 1958, Vol. II, Part I). Higher priced output in Canada can be reduced to the U.S. base by multiplying the Canadian value-added figure by 0.9; lower Canadian wages and salaries can be adjusted to the U.S. base by multiplying by 1.3. (See Chapter 2.) Thus, the physical labor-output ratio in Canada is roughly 136 percent that of the United States (i.e., 0.49/0.52 × 1.3/0.9).

the higher labor-capital ratio in Canada. Second: because of the restricted scale of Canadian production, it takes more of both labor and capital to produce a unit of output in Canada than in the United States. The fact that the capital-output ratio is greater in Canada than in the United States implies that the second influence outweighs the first.[23]

With free trade, and the end of artificial restrictions on the length of Canadian production runs, it is to be expected that Canadian production efficiency would approach that of the United States, and the quantity of Canadian capital employed in the production of a unit of output would fall toward the U.S. level.[24] With this fall in the Canadian capital-output ratio, the following changes might be expected in the numerator and denominator: first, the absolute amount of capital used in Canada would be likely to *rise* because Canadian wage rates would tend to be pulled up by a free trade arrangement (a proposition established elsewhere in this chapter); but Canadian capital costs would not rise. Thus, as long as full employment policies are pursued, there should be an increase in the amount of capital used in Canada

[23] Canadian production runs tend to be shorter; this does not mean, however, that Canadian firms are smaller. In his *Concentration in Canadian Manufacturing Industries* (Princeton: Princeton University Press, 1957), pp. 82–84, Gideon Rosenbluth presents evidence that average firm size in the two countries is similar. The greater economies of scale in the United States are thus associated with greater concentration of production within the firm. (That is, an individual Canadian firm tends to produce a broader range of goods than does an individual U.S. firm.)

The conclusion that Canadian small-scale production tends to be capital intensive may seem strange in the light of cross section data (drawn from single economies) indicating that small enterprises tend to be less capital intensive than large enterprises. In part, this apparent paradox may be explained by the fact that, although Canadian production runs are relatively small, Canadian enterprises are not. In addition, within a single economy, the efficiency of management may determine both the size of enterprise and capital intensity. However, in comparisons between American and Canadian operations, the key issue may not be differences in managerial competence so much as market limitations. That is, shorter Canadian production runs are not so much an indication of incompetence as a reflection of the more severe market limitations under which Canadian producers operate.

[24] In the long run, the Canadian capital-output ratio could even fall below the U.S. level if interest rates remain higher in Canada.

per unit of labor.[25] Second, the absolute amount of output in Canada should rise even more. An increase in output follows from the scaling up of Canadian production to service wider markets.[26] Moreover, a falling capital-output ratio implies that Canadian output would rise even faster than capital use.

The increase in the absolute quantity of capital demanded in Canada seems at first glance to imply that Canadian capital imports would increase with free trade. However, this conclusion does not follow because the international capital flow does not provide the total supply of Canadian capital but only the difference between the domestic demand and domestic supply. The most important element in the supply of Canadian capital is domestic savings, and this is dependent on income. It has already been concluded that, as Canadian production runs became longer and output increased, the Canadian capital-output ratio would tend to fall. Because output is a good proxy for income, and because savings are related to income,[27] a falling capital-output ratio implies a falling capital-domestic savings ratio. Thus, domestic savings would rise relative to the demand for capital, and *free trade in the long run would cause a fall rather than an increase in the net inflow of capital into Canada.*[28]

This decrease does not mean that the net inflow would fall to zero. The above argument has involved only the manufacturing sector and has not dealt with the natural resource sector where capital inflows have traditionally been important. In the event of free trade, a continued (absolute) growth in the demand for raw materials might be expected, and U.S. as well as Canadian capital might be attracted into Canadian resource development. Thus,

[25] It is also necessary to assume that Canada doesn't lose population through emigration. This seems reasonable enough because, under free trade, employment opportunities in Canada should increase and existing Canadian-U.S. differences in income levels would be narrowed. (See the next section below.)

[26] The free trade increase in Canadian factor incomes discussed in the next section is a direct corollary of the increase in Canadian output.

[27] This argument becomes even stronger if the ratio of savings to income rises as income rises.

[28] More precisely, a fall in the net inflow of capital relative to Canadian income.

although the net demand for capital inflows would tend to fall in the long run under free trade, some capital inflow and a corresponding current account deficit might well persist.

Although free trade would result in a decrease in the net Canadian demand for international capital in the long run, the probable short-run effects are by no means clear. In the period during which Canadian production was being reorganized, the net demands for capital would depend on a number of factors besides the general equilibrium mix toward which the economy was moving. An important question here is the adaptability of present Canadian machinery. Even though present equipment is used for short production runs, some of it would be adaptable to efficient extended runs. Insofar as this is the case, the demands for capital during the adjustment period would be less than otherwise.

Also important is the nature of the temporary adjustment arrangements included in a free trade agreement. If, for example, the suggestion of the Canadian-American Committee were followed and U.S. tariffs were lowered over a five year period while the Canadian reductions were staged over a ten year period, Canadian producers would for several years have the combined advantages of access to U.S. markets and a partially protected Canadian market. The higher prices which could be charged in the domestic market would provide them with a source of funds for capital renovation and reduce their demands on the capital market.[29]

Canadian-U.S. Wage and Exchange Rate Equilibrium

The examination of manufacturing costs in Chapter 10 has suggested that at the present exchange rate and relative wage levels, Canadian producers might enjoy some cost advantages in a free trade continent, provided they could set up rationalized operations approaching U.S. levels of efficiency. In the preceding section of this chapter, the feasibility of rationalized production in Canada was established (although the empirical evidence supporting the

[29] Other possible arrangements might have the same effect. The automobile agreement of 1965, for example, provided Canadian automobile producers with an increased source of profit explicitly designed to provide investment funds.

case has been delayed until Chapters 13 and 14). In the present section, it is recognized that favorable cost conditions in Canada would result in substantial industry expansion in that country. In the process, offsetting pressures would tend to build up: to the degree that the Canadian labor force became subject to demand pressures generated by these new employment opportunities, wages in Canada would tend to be bid up toward U.S. levels; and to the extent that low cost Canadian producers increased exports by effectively competing in U.S. markets, Canadian accumulation of foreign exchange reserves would create pressure toward an appreciation of the Canadian dollar. In either case, Canadian costs would rise relative to U.S. costs.

In this process, some of the industries in which Canada originally enjoyed a cost advantage would find that their advantage would slip away. Eventually this adjustment would run its full course when relative costs between the two countries had shifted to the point where there was balance-of-payments equilibrium and when marginal costs[30] were equated between the two countries. Then lower Canadian costs would be evident only in a proportion of manufactured products; Canada would specialize in these products because she produces them efficiently by international standards. Such specialization, with the attendant increased exports to the United States that it implies, would result in a balance-of-payments credit to offset increased Canadian imports from the United States in other lines in which Canada would not specialize.

It is important to recognize that adjustment pressures on wages and the exchange rate would build up to temper Canadian economic growth. Failure to understand this adjustment mechanism would lead to a quite unwarranted optimism concerning Canadian future growth prospects in the same way that, had Canadian costs in Part I turned out to be higher than in the United States, there might have been undue alarm regarding Canada's free trade prospects. The adjustment process tends to worsen the relative cost position of the country with the initial cost advantage and improve the position of the country with initial cost disadvantages. Thus,

---

[30] That is, costs of the marginal units in increasing-cost industries and average costs of the marginal producers in decreasing-cost industries.

in the long run, reasonable levels of performance tend to be achieved in both, provided that the international adjustment mechanism does not interfere with the maintenance of full employment.

If the adjustment mechanism permits the pursuit of full-employment policies, it makes no sense to talk about a general collapse in the volume of industrial production in Canada; nor does it make sense to talk of the size of Canadian industry doubling in the short run at the expense of U.S. producers. (With continued growth, Canadian industrial production will, of course, double in an extended period of time.) Present cost levels are of interest only in analyzing questions of a less extreme nature — for example, how do the levels of productive efficiency compare in the two countries? And, in the event of free trade, which country's relative wage level (and exchange rate) would be likely to rise?[31]

The cost comparisons in Chapter 10 suggest that Canada will be the country with the appreciation of its currency and wage level. And the United States will be the country that may have to deal with short-run unemployment and balance-of-payments problems. This is obviously fortunate for Canada; but even from the viewpoint of both parties, it may be relatively fortunate. It means that Canada, the country on which the short-run costs of reorganization fall most heavily, is the country which can expect initial growth and demand pressure on its labor force because of its favorable cost conditions. Furthermore, short-run employment and balance-of-payments improvements that occur may appear substantial from the Canadian point of view. However, the unfavorable short-run employment effects on the United States are unlikely to be large because of the relative size of the two economies, and because of the tendency for U.S. export and import industry adjustments to be overshadowed by other larger adjustments continually occurring in the American economy. Because of the importance of Canada as a trading partner of the United States, the balance-of-payments effects on the United States are likely to be

---

[31] It should be emphasized that real income will rise in one country because of an appreciation of its currency or relative wage level. In addition, in the process of multilateral tariff reductions, real income would increase in *both* countries because efficiency is increased.

greater than the employment effects. Even here, however, the probable outcome is not particularly undesirable: an increase of Canadian exports to the United States will have a favorable effect on the Canadian balance of payments that will be relatively greater than its unfavorable effect on the U.S. balance.

The Process of Wage Determination in North America. Before detailed attention is given to the extent of change in wage levels with free trade, it is important to consider the assumptions that are being made in this analysis about wage determination and labor mobility. The key assumption is that labor is immobile to a degree — between nations, between regions, and between industries. The assumption is not that labor is completely immobile but that labor migration occurs only in response to substantial differences in income levels. This assumption seems reasonable enough because differences in wage levels do now exist in fact — between Canada and the United States, between regions within each country, and between industries within regions.

It is also assumed that the wage rate reflects the marginal product of labor. This assumption is not to argue that productivity is the sole determinant; trade union activity and other influences may cause some departures from the productivity-dictated pattern. Nevertheless, productivity is undoubtedly the predominant long-run influence in the determination of wages. According to this argument, higher wages in a specific location tend to reflect some economic advantage of that location: for example, the advantage may be proximity to markets, involving lower transport costs than competitors in other regions must pay, or tariff free access to markets that producers in another country do not enjoy.

To consider a concrete instance: suppose we compare two firms producing the same good, one in a location which is very close to markets, the other in a more distant location. If their product is priced at the market, then the revenue (after shipping charges are deducted) for the closer firm is greater than for the distant firm. In this way, the factors of production in the closer location become more productive. And the greater net revenue accruing to the closer firm allows higher rent and quasi-rent payments to scarce and specialized factors, including labor.

If labor were perfectly mobile, such a productivity and wage difference between regions would be eroded. Faced with a difference in return, labor would flow out of the low wage area into the high wage area until marginal productivity and wages were equalized between all regions.[32] In the process quasi-rents to labor would disappear; and the only quasi-rents arising from locational advantage would go to other factors, such as land. It may be observed from U.S. and Canadian experience that there is some tendency for labor to move to high wage areas, but mobility is not perfect. The reluctance of workers to move and the costs involved in moving allow labor in high-productivity areas to continue to receive a higher income. Therefore, to the degree that this theory holds, wage differences may be regarded as differential payments going to a factor of production (labor) that is partially fixed in supply in each location.

International and interregional wage differences on the North American continent are broadly consistent with this theory. Historically Canadian migration to the United States has been a result of higher returns to labor in the United States; nevertheless, the continued existence of this wage difference suggests that labor is immobile internationally to some degree. The higher U.S. wage represents a "rent" differential reflecting the advantage of American labor in producing in a tariff free market — along with any other advantages (such as proximity to the richest markets) that the U.S. labor force might enjoy even in a free trade situation.

This theory also provides a partial explanation of regional wage differences within each country. It is evident from Table 1 that wage rates in Canada tend to fall with distance from Ontario; similarly, in the United States, rates tend to fall with distance from the New York-Chicago axis. In both countries the higher wage rates in the core area may be regarded as rents accruing to a labor force in an area in which transportation costs are less; in each case these rents are protected by the imperfect mobility of labor into these areas.

There are two major exceptions to this pattern that should be noted. Wages remain considerably lower in the U.S. South than

[32] Some wage differences might persist even if there were perfect mobility; these differences could result from differing amenities (e.g., weather) or differing costs of living (e.g., high real estate prices).

might be expected on the basis of transportation costs to markets. It is true that in recent years the South has attracted new industry; however, this has not been sufficient to raise wages in the area to a level where remaining differentials may be explained by transport costs. The reasons for this are not clear; however, it is likely that they are, in part at least, sociological. Such differences between the South and other parts of the country may have partially inhibited the out-migration of labor and the in-migration of industry.

The other major exception to the transportation-differential explanation is the West Coast both of Canada and of the United States. B.C. wages are the highest in Canada, and California wages are about as high as wages in any other U.S. area. To a large extent, this high wage may be because California has now passed a threshold level of growth and is now an area of market and production concentration sufficient to become — like the Chicago-New York area — a region generating its own independent attractions. This observation, however, does not answer the fundamental question of how such a level of growth has been possible in the past for this distant, high wage area. Part of the explanation may be that California is generally regarded as a high amenity area.[33] More important, California has had a number of productivity advantages because of her natural resources and climatic conditions — for example, in the production of gold a century ago and in aircraft (and electronics) more recently. Another contributing factor in California growth has undoubtedly been the attraction of the area for retired people.[34]

---

[33] This observation seems to raise about as many questions as it answers: if the labor force is prepared to forgo income on this account, wages should be *lower* in California than in other areas. Since this contradicts observed levels of California wages, it does not provide a solution to this question. However, employers rather than laborers may like to lie in the sun. If this is a sufficient attraction, then industry may have been drawn to California despite high wage costs there. The attraction of amenities for employers does, perhaps, partially explain rapid growth in a high wage area.

[34] The unique characteristic of the retired population is that it increases the demand for goods and services and hence for labor; however, precisely because this population is retired, it does not add to the supply of labor. Such immigration, therefore, exerts upward pressure on a region's wage level.

In spite of these exceptions,[35] there is substantial evidence of this mechanism of spatial determination of wage structure. However, the pattern is a somewhat ragged one and it is evident that wage differences cannot be fully explained or predicted in terms of natural location advantages alone; there appear to be substantial friction and slippage in the working out of this process.

The Limits to Wage and Exchange Rate Adjustment. It is by no means clear how upward pressure on the Canadian wage level caused by increased demand for labor might affect the interindustry and interarea structure of Canadian wages. Ideally one should consider the changing pattern of labor demand generated by free trade with the pattern of available supply. Any estimate of changing pattern derived in this way, however, requires information about the mobility of labor between areas and industries that is not presently available in any form. Lack of information is not the only problem: the pattern of industry specialization is dependent on wage (and other cost) differentials between areas; but, at the same time, the whole interindustry pattern of wage adjustment may depend partially upon the initial selection of industries in which businessmen decide to specialize. In other words, the pattern of specialization depends on wage structure, and wage structure depends on the pattern of specialization. For these reasons, it is not possible within the scope of this study, to predict changing patterns in the interindustry and interarea wage structure as international wage levels become aligned; consequently, it is assumed for the present that the Canadian wage structure would retain its present interindustry and interregional pattern in the event that demand pressure pushed the whole Canadian wage level upward toward the prevailing U.S. level.

It is by no means clear how the effect of demand pressure on the Canadian economy either would or should be divided between higher wages and a higher value of the exchange rate. The issue will be considered later in this chapter; but for suggestive purposes

---

[35] Another partial exception is the city of New York. One might expect wages there to be among the highest in the United States rather than the median level that they have actually reached. It should be noted that salary incomes in this area are high; the low wage is undoubtedly to be explained, at least in part, by the continuous influx of unskilled labor into the city.

it will be assumed for the moment that the exchange rate effect is limited to a rise in the Canadian dollar to parity with the U.S. dollar, and any additional adjustment required occurs in a revision in the Canadian wage level.

It may be recalled that the comparison of relative costs in Canada and the United States shown in Table 25 in the previous chapter was based on the exchange parity assumption; the preferred cost position of the Canadian manufacturing regions of Ontario and Quebec suggests that, in addition to full parity in the exchange rate, a further adjustment in terms of higher Canadian wages is quite possible.

What is the limit to the rise in the Canadian wage level? The greatest increase one might contemplate can easily be rejected as too extreme — that is, a rise in the wage level in each Canadian region to the level of the adjacent U.S. region. (It was noted in Chapter 2 that such a wage revision would result in the average Canadian wage exceeding the average U.S. wage because wages in the U.S. North are higher than those in the South.) Underlying economic conditions simply do not warrant a Canadian wage that is so much higher; with this sort of upward wage revision each Canadian area would be left at a disadvantage vis-à-vis its counterpart U.S. region in terms of transport costs and capital costs.

A more modest rise would be involved if the average Canadian wage were to rise to the level of the average U.S. wage. This would leave Canadian regions with some labor cost advantage over adjacent regions in the high-wage U.S. North. It is not clear whether such a Canadian wage revision would be possible or not — that is, it is not evident a priori whether or not this remaining wage advantage of Canadian regions over the adjacent regions in the United States would offset capital cost and transportation cost disadvantages. This possibility is tested: Table 28 shows a comparison of total costs, given the assumption that Canadian wages (on average) rise to the U.S. level.[36]

It is evident from this table that such a degree of wage equaliza-

[36] Specifically the Canadian average wage is equated to the U.S. average wage *in each manufacturing sector*. Because industry mix in the two countries is similar (see Chapter 2), it also implies that the all-sector Canadian and U.S. averages are approximately equal.

TABLE 28. Estimated Percentage That Total Costs in Comparison Areas Would Be Lower (−) or Higher (+) Than in Ontario (Assuming that the Average Canadian Wage Rises to the Average U.S. level), by Industry (1958 base).[a]

Percent	Food	Tobacco	Textiles	Apparel	Wood products	Paper	Printing	Electrical equipment
−10								
−9								
−8								
−7		W. Lake, N. Eng., Fla., Mid. Atl., E. Lake						
−6				South, SW			South	
−5	Cap.	P. SW			Cap.			
−4	South	South	Mount., SW, L. Midw.	Fla., L. Midw.	South	Cap.		N. Eng., South, Fla., L. Midw., Mount., SW
−3	N. Eng., W. Lake		South, N. Eng., Fla.	Mount.		Mid. Atl., W. Lake, N. Eng.	N. Eng., SW, L. Midw.	
−2	Mid. Atl., SW, Fla., E. Lake	Cap.		Cap., N. Eng.	*Que.*, W. Lake, N. Eng.	E. Lake	Cap., *Mar.*	W. Lake, Up. Midw.
−1		L. Midw., SW, Up. Midw.	Cap., *Que.*	Up. Midw., W. Lake, *Prair.*		L. Midw., Up. Midw.	Fla., E. Lake, *Prair.*, W. Lake, Mid. Atl., Up. Midw., *Que.*, Mount.	*Que.*, Mid. Atl., P. SW

Ontario°	Que.	P. NW	Que.	Prair.
+1	Que., L. Midw., P. SW	Mount., Mar. / P. SW	South	Mar., E. Lake, Cap.
+2	Mount.	Prair. / Up. Midw. / W. Lake, Mid. Atl.	Mid. Atl., Que. / Mid. Atl.		P. NW
+3	Up. Midw., P. NW	P. NW / P. SW, P. NW, E. Lake	E. Lake / L. Midw.		Br. Col.
+4	Br. Col.	Br. Col.	SW		
+5		Mar.	E. Lake		
+6	Mar.		Mar. / Fla. / Mount., Fla., P. SW, SW		
+7	Prair.	Prair.			
+8					
+9			P. NW[d]		
+10		Br. Col.	Up. Midw., P. SW, Br. Col.[d], P. NW[d], Mount., Mar., Prair. / Prair., Br. Col.[d], Mar.		
+20		Br. Col.			P. SW / P. NW / Br. Col.
+30					
+40					
+50					
+60					

(continued on next page)

TABLE 28 *Continued*

Percent	Chemicals	Petroleum products	Rubber and plastics	Leather goods	Nonmetallic mineral products	Metallic products	Transportation equipment	Miscellaneous
−10		Cap. W. Lake Mid. Atl. E. Lake	Fla.					
−9								
−8								
−7								
−6	Cap.	N. Eng.			W. Lake Cap.			South
−5	W. Lake			SW	Mid. Atl.	N. Eng.		N. Eng. SW
−4	N. Eng. Mid. Atl.		Cap. L. Midw. N. Eng. Up. Midw. *Que.*	South L. Midw. Fla.	N. Eng. E. Lake	W. Lake	Fla.	
−3	E. Lake P. SW L. Midw. South	L. Midw.	Mid. Atl. SW W. Lake South	*Que.*	*Br. Col.*	Cap. Mid. Atl.		W. Lake Cap.
−2	Up. Midw.		P. SW Mount. *Prair.*	Up. Midw. Mid. Atl. Mount.		L. Midw.	South Mount. L. Midw. W. Lake Up. Midw. N. Eng. Mid. Atl. Cap. P. NW *Que.*	L. Midw. *Que.* Up. Midw.
−1	Fla. *Que.*			N. Eng. Cap.		South *Que.* Fla. E. Lake	P. SW E. Lake	E. Lake Mid. Atl. Fla. *Mar.* P. NW

Ontario[c]	South	Mar.			SW	SW	SW	Prair.
+1	Que.	P. NW / E. Lake / Br. Col.	W. Lake / E. Lake / P. NW / P. SW	P. SW / L. Midw. / South Que.	P. SW		Prair. / Mar.	Prair.
+2	Br. Col. / SW / Mount.				P. SW	Br. Col.	Br. Col.	Br. Col.
+3	P. SW							
+4	P. NW							
+5	SW	Mar.	SW	Up. Midw. / SW / P. NW / Fla.	Br. Col. / Up. Midw.			P. SW
+6				Mount.	Mount. / P. NW			Mount.
+7	Prair.	Prair.	Prair.					
+8	Up. Midw. / Br. Col.				Prair.			
+9	Mar.				Mar.			
+10	P. NW / Fla. / Mount.	Br. Col.	Br. Col.	Prair. / Mar.				
+20			Mount.					
+30	Prair.	Prair.						
+40	Mar.	Mar.						
+50								
+60								

[a] The following costs are included: labor costs (assuming that the average Canadian wage is equal to the average U.S. wage); transportation costs (first set of figures in Table 11); resource costs (Tables 14 and 15); capital costs (Table 17). Raw figures are given in Appendix P (item #2).
[b] See Table 1, note a.
[c] Ontario = 0,
[d] See Table 25, note d.

tion would drop Ontario and Quebec from the preferred cost position they generally enjoyed prior to this wage adjustment. These two Canadian provinces would, under these circumstances, drop roughly to a median position when compared to U.S. regions, although this does not hold strictly for all industries. (British Columbia, the Maritimes, and Prairies also drop down into an even less favored cost range.) Therefore, it may be concluded from this table that, were this degree of wage equalization to occur, any cost advantage of Ontario and Quebec established in Table 25 would disappear.

There are several reasons why some uncertainty must remain regarding the exact degree of wage equalization. Tables 25 and 28 are based on the assumption that the demand and supply conditions for capital after an establishment of a free trade area would result in the same Canadian-U.S. difference in capital return as existed in the late 1950's. As was noted in the previous section, reorganization under free trade is likely to decrease the gap between the Canadian demand for and supply of capital and would thus tend to reduce the interest rate differential between Canada and the United States, improving the position of the Canadian regions shown in Table 28.

On the other hand, there may be some tendency for Tables 25 and 28 to overstate the relative attractiveness of Canadian regions if these regions are unable to match the centripetal pull to industry of regions in the U.S. industrial heartland.[37] It is by no means clear how important these effects may be; but they cannot be critical because they have not prevented peripheral U.S. areas from prospering in a free trade system. And it should be noted from Table 25 that this prosperity has often existed despite additional cost disadvantages of the peripheral U.S. regions.

One plausible explanation for the prosperity of peripheral U.S. regions is to be found in the level of aggregation involved in this study. Each sector involves a wide range of subindustries. If, as seems likely, there is a substantial variation in comparative costs across these subindustries, then cost conditions in a peripheral

---

[37] See Table 24. In some cases (e.g., autos) Canadian regions (e.g., Ontario) may be better situated in terms of external economies than most of the central U.S. regions.

region may be lower than costs in the central U.S. heartland in the small number of subindustries in which this area may specialize — even though average sector costs in this region are above the heartland level. To restate: the fact that average sector costs in a peripheral area may be high does not prevent an area from specializing in selected subindustries in which it may enjoy a cost advantage. And the smaller the peripheral area, the more likely it is to be able to maintain employment on this selective subindustry basis.

As an example of how a region may specialize in selected products within an industrial sector, consider the U.S. Upper Midwest. This region is not as centrally located as areas along the Chicago-New York axis; as a consequence transport costs of firms located there are relatively high. At the same time it enjoys some cost advantage over these central regions because of lower wages. One of its activities of specialization is electrical machinery — in particular the electronic equipment produced by Minneapolis-Honeywell. Specialization in this subindustry has been possible in this region, presumably encouraged by relatively low transport rates on these components and other favorable conditions (for example, lower wages) in the area; yet this subcomponent specialization has occurred even though, in the aggregate electrical machinery and apparatus sector, the Upper Midwest has no cost advantage over most other U.S. areas.

At this level of aggregation, it is not possible to specify comparative advantage across whole sectors within the United States, nor can Canadian and U.S. comparative advantage be specified. Instead, specialization within, rather than between, industrial sectors is to be expected and is confirmed by the roughly symmetrical distribution of U.S. and Canadian regions in each industrial sector in Table 28; there seems to be no broad industry category in which Canadian subindustry specialization might not occur.[38]

Compared with central U.S. areas, Canadian regions are relatively small, like the Upper Midwest. Consequently, there is no reason why they might not effectively maintain employment on

---

[38] The least likely sector seems to be tobacco products, in which there is no substantial initial Canadian wage advantage. But even in this sector, some areas may be found for Canadian specialization.

such a selective basis, despite sectoral cost conditions that are not particularly favorable. This conclusion is afforded further support by the observation that, as a large net exporter of raw materials, Canada's long-run balance-of-payments equilibrium is likely to involve substantial net imports of manufactured goods. This tends to reduce further the necessary range of selected subindustries in which Canada need enjoy a cost advantage.

Imprecisions resulting from the high level of aggregation mean that a sizable range of error should be assumed in interpreting the estimates in Table 28. Nevertheless, the central position of Ontario and Quebec indicates that wage parity is at least consistent with free trade equilibrium. It is possible that, with exchange parity, the Canadian equilibrium wage level might be less than the U.S. level; but it also could conceivably be higher, with its upper limit defined by the prevailing wage in each adjacent U.S. region.[39]

Whereas this may be a plausible enough explanation of the Canadian *equilibrium* wage level in a free trade area, it should not be interpreted as a *prediction* of the Canadian wage level that would quickly result. Strictly speaking, this is an analysis only of the underlying cost conditions that *allow* changes of this nature in (exchange and) wage levels. Other conditions are also necessary — for example, Canadian labor productivity[40] and management efficiency to match U.S. levels. And even if these conditions were fully met, the adjustment toward wage equilibrium would be a long-term process, partially and temporarily blocked at many junctures by a number of rigidities and restraints in the labor market.

---

[39] Since the process of international adjustment is also dependent on service and resource trade flows and capital movements, this conclusion should be qualified even further. If a substantial Canadian surplus continues in these accounts — in the form of net resource exports and net capital imports — balance-of-payments equilibrium may be maintained despite a deficit in manufacturing trade of the same amount. And it is conceivable that such a deficit in manufacturing might allow an even higher Canadian exchange and wage level.

[40] This analysis may be interpreted either as an examination of the equilibrium Canadian wage level assuming labor productivity in the two countries is equal or as an analysis of the equilibrium efficiency wage in Canada — that is, the payment to a labor unit with the efficiency of one U.S. worker. In Chapter 2 it was argued that Canadian labor is as productive as U.S. labor; thus, we believe that the equilibrium wage level interpretation is plausible.

Wage in Contrast to Exchange Rate Adjustment. Adjustment of the exchange rate or the relative wage level may be viewed as two alternative means of international adjustment. In either case, costs in the two countries are brought into line. In addition, the country experiencing the appreciation finds itself in an improved position — either from the increase in labor income resulting from a wage increase, or from an improvement in the terms of trade following an exchange appreciation. Two interesting questions arise in the Canadian-U.S. case: Which means of adjustment is more likely to occur? And which means is to be preferred?

If the exchange rate is flexible, it will tend to play the dominant role in the adjustment process because a flexible exchange rate tends to respond immediately to balance-of-payments pressures, whereas wage response to demand pressure on the labor force involves a lag.[41] If, however, the exchange rate were to be pegged, this would allow time for pressure to build up on the Canadian wage level. Concurrent pressure would, of course, fall on the U.S. balance of payments with the loss of foreign exchange reserves to Canada during this period. Because of their increased reserves, the Canadian authorities would be under pressure to revalue the Canadian dollar upward; if they did so, it would have the same general effect as a more gradual appreciation of a floating rate. It is not clear to what extent the Canadian authorities would be able to resist this pressure; but to the degree that they did, they would be indirectly forcing some of the adjustment pressure back onto the Canadian wage level. However, the speed of this wage adjustment would be inversely related to the level of cyclical unemployment in Canada. For example, if free trade were introduced in a period of heavy Canadian unemployment, demand pressure on the labor force would tend initially to increase employment, rather than wages. In these circumstances, the U.S. balance of payments would be placed under pressure for a considerable period prior to any relief in the form of rising Canadian wages.[42]

[41] For a discussion of the lags involved in wage adjustments between regions within the U.S. (free trade) area, see Richard Easterlin, "Long Term Regional Income Changes: Some Suggested Factors," *Papers and Proceedings, Regional Science Association,* 1948, pp. 313–325.

[42] There would, of course, be some immediate relief in the form of increased Canadian imports from the United States resulting from the higher Canadian employment (and income) level.

Thus, the exchange rate could accomplish the job of realigning international costs if the authorities were prepared to let it fluctuate. Alternatively, if it is fixed, some of the adjustment process would be fed back into domestic wage revisions. However, it is not clear how long the authorities might be able to hold the Canadian rate fixed in the face of rising reserves and increasing U.S. balance-of-payments embarrassment. The issue of whether the Canadian dollar should be allowed to fluctuate freely can be reduced to the question of which form of international adjustment — exchange or wage rate — is preferred. If an exchange rate adjustment is preferred, the rate should be turned loose to do the job. If a wage adjustment is preferred, then the exchange rate should be held fixed for as long as possible.

Exchange rate flexibility is obviously the simplest and fastest method of realigning international costs and finding a new wage and price equilibrium between two economies. A freely floating exchange rate reacts immediately, and in addition, there are no barriers to its movement in either direction. But, there are barriers to wage revision; the existence of unemployment limits upward flexibility, and labor unions prevent downward flexibility. Forcing revisions in relative wages in the face of these restraints is almost certain to result in some short-run unemployment in the country in which wages are initially relatively high.

Whereas either an appreciation of the Canadian dollar or an upward revision in Canadian wages would increase Canadian real income, their impact on domestic income distribution would differ. Obviously, an increase in the wage level in Canada would directly benefit the labor force. On the other hand, an appreciation of the Canadian dollar would raise real incomes in Canada, especially for individuals purchasing imports and traveling abroad. To some degree, the same individuals might benefit from either change, but not entirely; for example, those holding debt instruments specified in Canadian dollars would be better off if the Canadian dollar rather than the wage rate were to rise. Thus, judgment on the desirability of these alternative policies cannot be made entirely independently of the issue of income distribution.

The question of exchange variability is, of course, an important one regardless of the decisions made about the future course of commercial policy. A movement toward free trade would, however, accentuate a number of the arguments on both sides of the issue. In particular, it has been argued that a flexible rate increases the uncertainty and risk of international trade and investment; hence, one argument for a fixed rate is that it would minimize this risk during a period in which major disturbances of other kinds would be occurring. Planning guidelines of business would be changing rapidly with the major restructuring of industry under free trade; therefore, it may be argued, businessmen should be left with some fixed guidelines, such as the exchange rate. However, a fixed exchange rate might increase the possibility that an industry with an absolute advantage at the present exchange and wage level, but *not* a comparative advantage, might embark on an expansion program which will eventually prove uneconomic. In short, the advantage of a flexible rate is that the businessman is told as quickly as possible about balance-of-payments pressures. The risk is that he may be told too much and become confused.

In general, the case for flexible exchange rates is strongest when major structural changes[43] are taking place in the economy. At such times, balance-of-payments pressures are particularly hard to predict, and therefore it is especially difficult to know whether (and how far) to change a pegged-but-adjustable exchange rate. Furthermore, if wage adjustment is chosen in preference to exchange flexibility, the upward movement of Canadian wage rates required to establish balance-of-payment equilibrium may create a momentum that will make it difficult to stabilize wages as the adjustment process approaches completion. Thus, even though the maintenance of a fixed exchange rate would lead to a downward movement of the general Canadian price level in the initial stages because of the abolition of duties on imported products, it might nevertheless lay the basis for a wage-price spiral problem in the longer run.

However, once again the case for a flexible exchange rate may be balanced with contrary arguments. Free trade is likely to require a revision in the structure of wage rates between industries and regions within each country. Although no attempt can be made in this study to specify these necessary changes, they may

[43] That is, shifts in demand and supply as functions of price.

be substantial.[44] If the entire international adjustment comes in the form of an exchange revision, overall Canadian costs (in all regions and industries) will tend toward overall U.S. costs, but no change would result in the regional and industry wage structure. There would remain residual upward pressure on wages in some regions and industries and downward pressure in others. Because of downward stickiness of money wages, however, pressures in this direction will tend to generate unemployment and other major strains. Relative price adjustments seem to take place more smoothly under the umbrella of an upward movement of average prices;[45] similarly, relative wage adjustments among regions and industries may be expected to take place more smoothly if the overall wage level is rising. Thus, a major advantage may be gained by allowing at least some of the adjustment pressure to be exerted through an appreciation of the overall Canadian wage level.

When all these pros and cons are considered, a case can be made for an intermediate system, with the adjustment taking place partly through the exchange rate and partly through a rise in the relative Canadian wage level. This outcome may be achieved by exchange fund activity to resist but not completely prevent exchange movements. Guidelines for, and issues associated with, such exchange fund activity are presented elsewhere.[46]

[44] For example, consider the U.S. South. Its favorable cost position in Table 28 may be traced to its low wage rates. If, under free trade, wages were to remain low in this area while Canadian wages were adjusting upward, the U.S. South would become the lowest wage region on the North American continent. This implication is in the assumptions made in deriving Table 28, and the resulting cost pattern should be questioned as a result. The problem is that, whereas this table reflects an assumed equalization of U.S. and Canadian wages, it does not account for any change that might occur during this period in the interregional pattern of wages within either the United States or Canada. The question is: Would not wages in the U.S. South (as in Canada) tend to rise toward the average U.S. level during the interim period of free trade adjustment? The answer is quite likely to be yes. This rise might be partially the result of changing commercial policies; but, more important, it would simply be a continuation of the (admittedly somewhat erratic) process of wage adjustment that has been historically taking place within the continental United States.

[45] See, for example, Charles L. Schultze, *Inflation in the United States* (Washington: Joint Economic Committee of Congress, 1959).

[46] Paul Wonnacott, *The Canadian Dollar, 1948–1962* (Toronto: University of Toronto Press, 1965), Ch. XII.

Interregional and Interindustry Implications

Interregional Aspects of the Adjustment Process. The comparisons made in the summary Tables (25 and 28) are most valid for contiguous regions because the problems least amenable to satisfactory treatment have been associated with transportation costs. With respect to transportation costs to market, alternative assumptions were made in Chapter 3 regarding the relationship between sales and distance to markets; but Tables 25 and 28 had to be constructed on the basis of only one of these assumptions (albeit a reasonably representative one). However, as may be seen from Table 11, the relative position of the West Coast regions as compared to the Great Lakes regions is particularly sensitive to changes in this assumption.

With respect to resource transportation costs, much depends on the realism of the assumption that the area containing the major supply of the resource is the major exporter and pricing point for that resource. In the absence of direct information on resource export flows, this is the most reasonable assumption that can be made, and it does provide adequate grounds for concluding that resources cannot be a critical cost factor in most industries. But in the few industries in which resources may be important, it does not always provide a meaningful guide in defining regional advantage. The most pronounced illustration of this difficulty occurs in estimating the position of British Columbia in pulp and paper products. The cost figures in Table 28 include a B.C. cost disadvantage of five to six percent attributable to higher wood costs. This cost disadvantage represents the average of two bounding estimates. The problem is that one of these limiting estimates is based on an untenable assumption — that is, that because Quebec is the most important single source of wood for producing pulp and paper, it may be taken as the base for calculating wood costs in other regions. Thus, wood costs in British Columbia were estimated as the Quebec cost plus transport charges from Quebec to British Columbia. This limiting estimate is useful in the sense that the B.C. cost cannot exceed this level; the problem is that the cost won't even approach this limit. There is no prospect whatsoever that wood might actually be shipped from Quebec to British

Columbia. Part of the difficulty is removed in the process of averaging this bounding estimate with an estimate that is extreme in the other direction; yet in this specific case, a substantial range of error almost certainly remains.

Thus, although Tables 25 and 28 give a reasonable enough overall view of basic costs in most industries, some problems undoubtedly remain in special cases of this kind. Hence, the data should not be used as the basis for detailed regional analysis; if the regional prospects for specific industries are to be studied, it is important to double back to reconsider the problems of transport costs to market for most industries, and differential resource costs for those few industries in which they have been established as important.

Subject to these caveats, some tentative generalizations may be made regarding regional prospects in the event of free trade. Ontario and Quebec would generally be preferred to other Canadian regions in most industrial activities — largely because of the market proximity and attendant lower transport costs from these two provinces. Therefore, these provinces would remain the most favored for secondary industry in Canada under free trade — as under protection. Industrial expansion in British Columbia, the Prairies, and Maritimes would be limited under free trade, as it has been limited under protection.

There are, however, industry exceptions in which the least favored Canadian regions — the Maritimes and Prairies — would apparently enjoy favorable cost conditions: printing and publishing, electrical machinery, and rubber and plastics. In addition, the Prairies would be in a favorable cost position in the apparel industry. To some degree, this advantage may be offset by the external economies that other regions may enjoy because of their present heavy concentration in these activities. Therefore, whatever specialization might occur in these two Canadian regions would almost surely be in subindustries in which the pull of present concentration is not a strong one.

In one respect, the Maritimes is in a special situation. The opening of the U.S. market might have far-reaching effects for this area, especially in products with easy and inexpensive access (especially by sea) into New York, Boston, and other large urban centers on the northeastern U.S. seaboard; these cities are closer and in this sense more "natural" markets than the present Maritimes markets in Montreal and points west in Canada.

It is difficult to generalize about the prospects in British Columbia because its West Coast position greatly increases the uncertainty associated with the treatment of transportation costs. It will remain a relatively unattractive location for producing goods that must be distributed widely to all North American markets. But rich markets in the U.S. Pacific Northwest would be opened, and its prospects for producing goods that are localized within this sort of geographical range appear to be good. Even in the limiting case in which the exchange rate would rise to parity and the average Canadian wage level would rise to full equality with that in the United States, the B.C. competitive situation would be close to that of U.S. West Coast regions in most industries. It is true that British Columbia cannot expect to attract the aircraft industry, on which much of the U.S. Pacific Northwest economy is based; but it might become a component supplier. Otherwise, the best prediction of B.C. prospects seems to be the present pattern of the U.S. Pacific Northwest. Moreover, minimal risks are involved for B.C. secondary industry from duty free import competition because the region has so little secondary manufacturing at present. Free trade in manufactures, therefore, seems to be an almost risk free venture for both British Columbia and the Prairies. Almost no risk is involved from imports displacing employment in secondary manufacturing; but lower prices are a certainty as a result of Canadian tariff elimination.

In the very long run, the prospects for British Columbia, along with those for the adjacent regions of the United States, appear to be excellent because of resource endowments. Even though an attempt has been made to include the pull of resources in our cost estimates, it involved a procedure with severe limitations noted above. In addition, any cost calculation, no matter how precise, may provide a seriously inadequate index of resource availability. Thus, the pulp and paper industry may find British Columbia an attractive location not because of the cost of timber but because it is one of the few regions in which a sufficient supply may be found.

In addition, it should be recognized that the importance of resources as a location pull increases with time. Over short periods of time, the pattern of population is unlikely to change and is important in determining the market advantages of various locations. In the long run, however, population tends to move, and with it go markets. Resources constitute one of the major attractions for population. Thus, if optimum industry locations in the coming decade are to be identified, the present location of population (and therefore markets) is a matter of prime importance; if, however, the outlook for the next hundred years is to be considered, the location of natural resources (defined broadly, to include weather and other amenities) gains in significance. As time has passed, the historical accident of North American settlement from the east has been of declining importance as a locational factor, and this decline may be expected to continue.

Interindustry Aspects of the Adjustment Process. It has already been argued that Canadian specialization is to be expected in selected subindustries in all, or almost all, broad industrial sectors. But, in view of the level of aggregation used in this study, no inference can be made as to which specific subindustries are likely to be involved.

It is, however, possible to identify some influences that will come into play in determining Canadian specialization. Canadian prospects are not good in declining industries; Canadian, rather than U.S., plants may be closed down first, even though Canada might be a favorable location in terms of low operating costs. For example, a U.S. parent faced with the decision to close up some of its facilities may close up its Canadian subsidiary, even though a rationalized Canadian operation could be run at lower cost. The point is that the Canadian plant would not initially be rationalized; and the costs of reorganization may outweigh the Canadian operating cost advantage that would follow reorganization. (There would be a tendency for a similar outcome in any declining industry, whether or not parent-subsidiary ties exist.)

In expanding industries, the management decision is not which plant to close down but where to expand next. And in these circumstances, the potential costs addressed in this study become the governing factor, and any Canadian advantages should come

into full play. This difficulty is therefore restricted only to declining industries; but it implies somewhat more serious short-run
adjustment problems for the Canadian economy. It also implies
that eventual Canadian specialization would tend to be concentrated in growth industries.[47]

The eventual pattern of Canadian specialization is also likely
to be influenced by marketing considerations and the ability of
Canadian management to sell in the United States. With free
trade, Canadian firms in many industries would lose the bulk of
their Canadian sales to low priced U.S. imports, in favor of increased sales of specialized commodities in the U.S. In these
latter lines, in which Canada enjoys a comparative advantage,
Canadian firms would have no problem in keeping their production costs competitive — *provided* they can increase their production volume on the basis of new sales in their "natural" U.S.
markets. Invading these U.S. markets will be a major problem
for Canadian firms in this period of rapid change — because these
are precisely the markets in which many of these firms currently
have inadequate marketing facilities, or no facilities at all.

The problems that arise in sorting out "natural" markets in a
period in which market patterns are changing rapidly have encouraged many observers to recommend special marketing arrangements — at least during the short-run period of reorganization.
Such schemes typically involve marketing agreements between
firms to ensure that those with a comparative cost advantage but
limited financial resources are not eliminated by cutthroat price
competition in the shakedown period. For Canadian subsidiaries
with U.S. parents, this type of market sharing arrangement would
automatically occur under the aegis of the firm. For example, if
General Motors decides to produce transmissions — or Buicks —
in Canada, the North American marketing of these Canadian-
produced items is assured within the G.M. sales organization. As
a consequence, there may be substantial advantages involved in
the transition period for Canadian firms with U.S. affiliates. Not
only are marketing arrangements feasible within the parent-sub-

---

[47] This growth-industry bias in Canada could be partially offset by Canadian specialization in labor- rather than capital-intensive activities — as
a result of the higher capital costs that may persist in Canada.

sidiary structure of the firm; in addition, the parent has a substantial vested interest — in its ownership of the Canadian subsidiary — in solving these problems in a way that will involve operation of Canadian plants whenever this can be done profitably.

On the other hand, Canadian firms without these close ties will face much more difficult marketing problems. There are at least two ways in which these difficulties may be overcome: by an agreement with a competing U.S. producer to produce jointly a specialized line to be distributed in each country through the domestic marketing facilities of each firm; or by an agreement with a major wholesale or retail outlet in the United States. For example, a small Canadian furniture manufacturer, forced by the price competition of U.S. imports to specialize in certain designs, could agree to coordinate its production lines with those of a U.S. furniture manufacturer; these could be distributed through the United States via the U.S. firm's marketing facilities, and the U.S. firm's output might be distributed in Canada through the established marketing facilities of the Canadian firm. Alternatively, the Canadian firm could approach a major U.S. wholesaler or retailer (such as Sears Roebuck and Co.) to promote a new, distinctive line of furniture; this might be designed either by Sears or by an independent Canadian or U.S. designer for production by the Canadian manufacturer.

Although marketing problems of this kind are likely to be the chief obstacle Canadian-owned firms must hurdle,[48] they are not insuperable by any means. In fact, because of the general inclination to think in terms of consumer trademarks, there is a natural tendency for these difficulties to be overestimated. These problems would be far less critical in the sale of industrial components than in heavily advertised consumer goods. And in this latter category, the problem is reduced because of the close affiliation that already exists between Canadian and U.S. firms.

Conclusions

The major free trade adjustment is likely to occur within manufacturing rather than between manufacturing and nonmanufactur-

---

[48] There are also potential problems arising from antitrust legislation (especially in the United States) that would have to be avoided.

ing. Moreover, Canadian specialization is likely to occur within broad industrial sectors, rather than between them. Thus, there is little danger of Canadians becoming "hewers of wood and drawers of water" in the event of reciprocal tariff elimination. This conclusion holds regardless of the direction of change in wage and exchange rates.

Present high Canadian costs of manufacturing may be attributed largely to fragmented production lines, which are in turn a result of North American protection. Free trade would create pressures for reorganization and specialization of Canadian industry. With such reorganization, the Canadian capital-output ratio would decline toward the U.S. level, thus decreasing the gap between the Canadian demand for and supply of capital. Thus, in the longer run, the Canadian import of capital would be diminished by a free trade arrangement. The extent of the international capital flow in the adjustment period is uncertain: it would depend in part on detailed adjustment provisions of a free trade agreement.

With the reorganization of Canadian industry, there would be upward pressures on the Canadian dollar and on the relative Canadian wage rate. The precise degree of change is uncertain, but it might carry the exchange rate to parity and the average Canadian wage as high as the average U.S. wage (but not as high as average wages in adjacent regions of the United States).

Because of methodological difficulties associated with transportation costs, the differential regional impact of free trade is uncertain. Because some restructuring of regional (and industry) wage rates may be required, the authors favor a combination of wage and exchange rate adjustment, in preference to placing the whole burden of international adjustment on either the exchange rate or the relative wage rate.

PART III

The Incidence of Tariffs:
Analysis of Present Prices, Costs
and Money Incomes

12

PROTECTION
AND THE PRESENT STRUCTURE
OF INDUSTRY COSTS: INTRODUCTION

In Parts I and II American and Canadian costs as they would exist under free trade were compared. An important element of the analysis was the proposition that Canadian industry could reorganize to eliminate substantially the elements of higher cost that exist because of North American protection. But there has not yet been any empirical examination of these present elements of higher Canadian cost; it will be undertaken in Part III. In the following chapters relative Canadian-U.S. costs in fourteen sample industries will be broken down in detail. This will allow us to evaluate to what extent differential Canadian-U.S. costs can be attributed to North American protection and to what degree they are independent of tariffs and hence would persist under free trade.

The latter group of "inherent" or "basic" cost differences will provide the basis for an inference on the free trade absolute advantage of each sample industry. Because this part of the analysis is similar to the section on aggregated industrial sectors in Part I, it will be no surprise that the results are comparable.

The major new contribution of this section will be the evaluation of cost differentials because of protection. This will be useful in two ways: first, as an indication of the degree to which each sample industry may be forced to reorganize and of the potential cost reductions that may be realized; and second, as a basis for estimating how North American protection has involved costs to Canada, for example, in terms of inefficiency and limited scale in Canadian manufacturing. This leads to an evaluation in the last chapter of Part III of how these costs have been shifted onto the Canadian public in the form of a reduction in per capita income.

The dual objective in this section requires much more cost detail than that collected in the less complicated free trade analysis of the first two parts. Hence, costs for only fourteen sample products could be considered, one chosen from each of our broad industrial sectors (excepting tobacco and miscellaneous products). Because of the additional data requirements of this section, no attempt was made to break out these comparisons by region. Instead there is in each case only one comparison, that is, between the industry in its present major location in Canada, and the present industry in the United States. This comparison is reasonable enough because in Part III our interest is centered at least as much on present costs as on hypothetical free trade costs.

Each sample industry, along with the sector from which it was chosen is shown in Table 29. In choosing a specific product from each sector four criteria were used: the availability of data; the product's share of total production in the sector; the representativeness of the product; the geographical breadth of the market.

TABLE 29. *Products Chosen for Study.*

Manufacturing sector[a]	Product
Food	Wheat flour
Textiles	Cotton gray osnaburg
Apparel	Men's clothing
Wood products	Plywood and veneer
Paper	Wrapping paper
Printing	Trade books
Electrical equipment	Electrical industrial equipment
Chemicals	Synthetic resins
Petroleum products	Gasoline
Rubber and plastics	Tires
Leather goods	Upper shoe leather
Nonmetallic mineral products	Asbestos products
Metallic products	Steel pipes and tubes
Transportation equipment	Automobiles

[a] See Table 1, note a.

(Such items as newspapers in the printing sector and dairy products in the food sector were excluded from consideration on the grounds that their markets tend to be localized, and they are unlikely to be important in international trade even if there are major international cost differences.) Because there were often conflicts between these criteria, experts with a detailed knowledge of the various sectors will undoubtedly be able to find some grounds for challenging our choices in a number of instances. We suspect that this will be the case in the textile industry, for example, where cotton gray is not particularly representative of the industry as a whole; in this instance, the first criterion was the controlling consideration.

In Parts I and II, free trade prospects were inferred from aggregate data covering all industrial sectors. In comparison, Part III deals only with a limited sample of products (albeit a broad spectrum); hence, it cannot present a comprehensive view of the possible effects of free trade between the two North American economies. Rather, these studies should be interpreted as sample confirmation of the results of Part I and as illustrations of the possible prospects, opportunities, and difficulties a number of selected industries would face.

But by sacrificing comprehensiveness and moving closer to the basic data, the present section derives offsetting gains. The issues dealt with come closer to the specific problems which the businessman must face during a period of adjustment, and the difficulties of aggregating and averaging are diminished.[1]

The analysis of costs involves several stages. The initial estimate is the extent to which the Canadian product price exceeds that of the U.S. price; to this is added Canadian cost advantages (for example, lower wages). In combination these two elements indicate the advantages of producing in Canada for that generally higher priced market. The question is: Where does the margin go? First, it goes to cover those inevitably higher costs of production in

---

[1] These latter problems are not, of course, entirely avoided; as may be seen from the products listed in Table 29, several of them (for example electrical industrial equipment) are categories of products rather than specific, unique items. Some reasonable compromise had to be reached between the goal of representativeness and the risks of losing detail through aggregation.

Canada due to inherent Canadian disadvantages (such as transport costs and capital costs). When these are calculated and deducted, there remains a margin attributable to protection, which in turn can be broken down into two components: higher costs which are directly due to protection and which can be measured — for example, the higher cost of protected inputs; and higher costs attributable to all the diseconomies associated with producing in a limited market. The latter cannot be calculated directly but may be estimated as the residual left when all the other above calculations are completed.

The detailed pattern of this cost analysis is shown in Figure 4; and the data are given in Table 30. All estimates indicate the percentage by which Canadian costs and prices differ from the U.S. level, represented by the heavy reference line running horizontally through the center of Figure 4.

The first estimate is of different product prices in the two countries. Where information is available, the percentage difference between average Canadian and U.S. wholesale prices (excluding

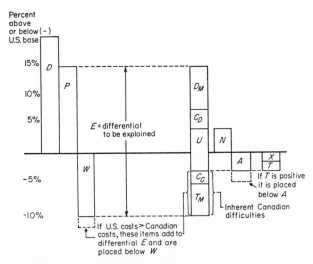

Figure 4. Method of analyzing Canadian protection and a comparison of Canadian and U.S. free trade costs, by industry (see Table 30). The baseline represents U.S. wholesale price excluding indirect taxes.

indirect taxes) is entered (P); where price data is not available, the Canadian tariff (D) is used as an upper estimate of the extent to which Canadian prices can be quoted above those in the United States. From left to right, W represents the percentage cost advantage provided by lower Canadian wage rates.[2] Thus, $P + W$ may be taken as an estimate of the margin of advantages of producing in Canada, or the differential to be explained (E).[3]

In the next column, the factors explaining this differential are entered. The first set, shown at the bottom, are those "inherent" Canadian cost disadvantages that would survive into a period of free trade.[4] These are the higher Canadian carrying costs of capital (C_G), that is, higher Canadian interest rates and returns to equity[5] and the excess of Canadian transport charges over U.S. transport charges on inputs (T_M). (In any instances in which a Canadian industry incurs lower transport costs on inputs, T_M is entered below W and increases the differential to be explained.)

The next set of influences are those higher Canadian costs that are due to the tariff and that can be measured; they are entered at the top of the unexplained differential. They include higher costs because of protection on materials (D_M) and duties on capital equipment (C_D).

Since this is the first attempt in this study to measure protection-induced costs, it is appropriate to consider the two major alternatives that may be used in these calculations. The first involves estimating only duties paid on actual imports. This is likely to underestimate costs because it ignores the degree to which equivalent Canadian-produced materials are more expensive because of the protection they receive. Another problem involved in this method is that a distinction must be made between an industry's use of an import and the domestically produced equivalent; and the distinction cannot be estimated satisfactorily from published

[2] Computed by the technique outlined in Chapter 2.

[3] Where Canadian prices are lower than U.S. prices, P will lie below the line, and the margin will be W minus P rather than the sum of W and P. See the example provided by the upper leather industry in Chapter 14 below.

[4] Except insofar as they might be modified by the adjustment process.

[5] See Chapter 8 for a discussion of how these capital cost differences were computed. The possible effects of free trade on these differences are discussed in Chapters 8, 11, and 17.

statistics. The second general approach is to recognize explicitly the degree to which Canadian-produced materials may be more expensive because of the protection they receive; Canadian materials producers may raise their price by the full degree of protection offered by the Canadian tariff. In this case no cost distinction need be made between the purchase of an import and the domestic equivalent. Insofar as materials producers use less than this full amount of protection, the second approach will overstate higher Canadian costs. In spite of this limitation, the second method was generally used.[6]

This method is also used in estimating higher Canadian machinery costs due to the tariff (C_D); average tariff rates are applied to all Canadian machinery purchases, whether imported or not. Hence, it may be argued that, like input costs, the machinery estimate is also a maximum. However, in another sense it is a minimum. In this study the extra costs due to the tariffs on machinery have been applied only to depreciation; but if growth is considered necessary for survival in the modern world, it may be argued that the tariff costs on gross machinery investment rather than just on depreciation should be included as a charge against current output.

When higher costs due to protection (D_M and C_D) and "inherent" Canadian difficulties (C_C and T_M) are subtracted from the differential to be explained (E), there remains only an unexplained residual (U). This will be taken as a first approximation of the diseconomies in Canada attributable to the more limited market. Economies of scale in this context are defined broadly, to include not only economies of scale from an engineering point of view, but also possible differences in profit margins allowed by a differential exercise of oligopoly power in the smaller market, and possibly, any differences in managerial effectiveness that may have resulted from the distractions of fragmented production runs in Canada and the enervating influence of a less competitive milieu.

Even when the concept of "economies of scale" is defined broadly, caution must be used in interpreting the unexplained residual as the Canadian disadvantage from small-scale operations. In the first place, the errors in estimating all the cost differences that

[6] Exceptions, such as the auto case, are noted where they occur.

could be identified and that were used in computing U will fall into this residual estimate; these errors may tend to offset each other, but they may not. Second, this residual will also reflect any cost differences that have not been accounted for in this study. Third, this residual also represents differences in labor productivity. If productivity differences reflect differences in the organization of production — as assumed in this study[7] — rather than some intrinsic quality of the labor force, they are correctly regarded as one form of diseconomy of a small market. But if permanent intrinsic differences in labor quality do exist, U will partially reflect these and hence will overstate diseconomies of a small market.

Thus, we present the unexplained residual as an estimate of differing economies of market size with an acute sense of its limitations. Our only defense is that we are unaware of preferable ways to estimate this very important but very elusive element. We should also like to stress that the details of our conclusions are to be considered as tentative, particularly as they apply to specific industries.

If, as assumed, this unexplained residual may be traced to diseconomies of a small market, then it will tend to disappear in the event of free trade *provided that* Canadian firms can successfully enter the large markets. But this requires that two conditions be met. First, Canadian firms must have a free trade cost advantage over U.S. competitors. This advantage (A) is computed by deducting Canadian free trade cost disadvantages $(C_C + T_M)$ from the Canadian wage advantage (W). Second, this net advantage (A) must more than offset any transport cost disadvantage (T) of shipping Canadian products to North American markets.[8] The difference in A and T is shown as X; if it appears below the base line (as in Figure 4), it indicates an industry in a strong competitive free trade situation, with a cost edge over its U.S. competition. At present relative exchange and wage levels, this provides incentive to expand into U.S. markets.

[7] For the grounds for this assumption, see Chapter 2.

[8] Calculated by the method outlined in Chapter 4, setting q equal to one. In cases in which the Canadian producing area has a transport cost advantage over its U.S. competition, T is *added* to the other net Canadian advantage A. Thus it is entered below A on this diagram, and X becomes the *sum* of A and T.

TABLE 30. *Analysis of Canadian Protection and Comparison of Canadian and U.S. Free Trade Costs, by Industry (in percent).*[a]

Products[b]	D	P	W	FP	E	D_P	D_M	C_D	U	C_0	T_P	T_M	N	A	T	X
Automobiles	17.50	9.50	3.90	—	13.40	4.20	—	0.20	7.70	0.80	0.50	—	5.10	2.60	−0.50	2.10
Upper shoe leather	15.53	−6.03	7.67	—	3.96	—	0.17	0.09	2.82	0.88	—	−2.32	−6.29	9.11	−0.18	8.93
Electrical industrial equipment	22.20	N.A.	3.69	—	26.14	—	2.65	0.16	22.50	0.83	—	−0.25	19.39	3.11	−0.18	2.93
Asbestos products	16.02	N.A.	6.24	—	23.67	—	1.48	0.20	20.41	1.58	—	−1.41	14.34	6.07	−0.60	5.47
Tires	22.50	N.A.	4.41	—	27.28	—	2.40	0.02	23.84	1.02	—	−0.37	20.08	3.76	−0.27	3.49
Plywood and veneers	16.55	N.A.	4.30	—	20.87	—	1.91	0.16	18.30	0.50	—	−0.02	14.48	3.82	0	3.82
Men's clothing	27.80	N.A.	5.59	—	33.60	—	9.80	0.06	23.15	0.59	—	−0.21	17.94	5.21	−0.23	4.98
Trade books	10.00	N.A.	6.33	—	16.33	—	7.26	0.07	8.14	0.86	—	0	2.67	5.47	0	5.47
Wrapping paper	22.50	16.90	1.82	—	18.81	—	0.09	0.84	15.21	2.67	—	−0.09	15.97	−0.76	−0.51	−1.27
Synthetic resins	13.83	N.A.	2.02	—	15.85	—	2.00	0.46	10.75	1.84	—	0.80	11.37	−0.02	−0.35	−0.37
Steel pipes and tubes	13.90	N.A.	1.73	—	16.09	—	4.12	0.17	9.97	1.83	—	−0.46	9.61	0.36	−0.71	−0.35
Gasoline	5.50	N.A.	0.88	5.04	6.38	—	0	0.58	3.31	2.49	—	0	4.92	−1.61	0	−1.61
Cotton gray[c]	20.00	N.A.	2.56	—	27.60	—	5.90	0.15	19.19	1.52	—	0.84	13.95	0.20	0.34	0.54
Wheat flour[c]	4.57	N.A.	2.14	18.18	24.89	—	0	0.17	24.02	0.70	—	0	4.40	1.44	−0.28	1.16

[a] D, tariff protection; P, Canadian–U.S. price differential, i.e., percentage by which Canadian wholesale price exceeds U.S. price. If Canadian price is less than U.S. price, P appears below baseline; W, Canadian cost advantage due to lower wages; FP, Canadian cost advantage due to U.S. farm program; E, differential to be explained — i.e., combined advantages to Canadian producer of higher price and lower wage program; D_P, Canadian cost disadvantage due to duties on parts; D_M, Canadian cost disadvantage due to protection of material inputs; C_D, Canadian cost disadvantage due to duties on capital equipment; U, unexplained residual; C_C, Canadian cost disadvantage due to higher capital carrying costs; T_P, Canadian cost disadvantage due to transportation of parts; T_M Canadian cost disadvantage due to transportation of material inputs; N, net Canadian protection used. (Where relative price data are unknown, this item becomes net Canadian protection available.) A, deduced Canadian basic advantage, i.e., estimated cost advantage to Canadian producers in a free trade area, at given exchange rate and wage levels; T, Canadian cost advantage or disadvantage (−) in shipping products to North American markets; X, estimated Canadian absolute advantage in free trade situation, i.e., Canadian incentive to expand into U.S. markets at given exchange rate and wage levels.

[b] Automobile prices and costs are for the 1964 model year (exchange rate: $1.00 U.S. = $0.925 Can. = $1.00 U.S.).

[c] Industries with farm support.

It must be stressed that even if X falls below the reference line, this Canadian *absolute* advantage under free trade would not necessarily guarantee that the Canadian industry will capture and retain U.S. markets over the long term. Reservations must be based on the possibilities of erroneous computations and on the fact that, in the long run, comparative rather than absolute advantage determines the course of international trade. Thus, a small X might be more than offset by a premium on the Canadian dollar on the exchanges or by an upward trend of Canadian wage rates compared to U.S. rates. Nevertheless, there is a presumption that, the greater the absolute advantage X, the more favorably will that Canadian industry be situated in the event of free trade.

There is another interesting estimate that may be deduced from Figure 4. The difference between the higher Canadian price due to protection (P) and the difficulties due to protection $(D_M; C_D)$ yields the net protection[9] used by the Canadian industry (N).[10] Since N is generally less than P, Canadian industry receives less protection than its own tariff rate suggests. N may even be negative and lie below the base line. In these circumstances a Canadian industry is more harmed than aided by Canadian protection; furthermore, the Canadian industry could survive in the event of free trade even if it did not reorganize to reap the advantages of large-scale production. For such an industry free trade would provide two benefits: first, it would remove the negative protection imposed by the Canadian tariff; second, it would open new U.S. markets by eliminating the U.S. tariff.

[9] "Net protection," as the term is used here, is measured as a fraction of the import price of the product. Thus, it is not the same concept as the "net protection" discussed by Corden and others, which is measured as a percentage of the value added by the industry. See W. M. Corden, "The Structure of a Tariff System and the Effective Protective Rate," *Journal of Political Economy*, 74: 221–237 (June 1966). Since Corden's formula for net protection involves a multiplication by the reciprocal of the fraction of value added, "net protection" in his sense is frequently greater than the tariff rate on the product in question.

[10] In cases where price data is unavailable, N represents net protection *available;* how much of it is used by the Canadian producer is unknown.

13

THE AUTOMOBILE INDUSTRY

Our first sample industry, automobiles, is singled out for special, detailed treatment in this chapter for a number of reasons: it is an extremely important segment of the Canadian economy and is often regarded as a "bellwether" industry; imports used by the industry may be relatively easily identified because content regulations imposed on this industry provide useful detail on maximum import content and because the major item, auto parts, is a specific category appearing in the trade statistics; last and most important, this industry has recently been subject to major tariff changes designed to promote its efficiency and rationalization.

Because current interest surrounds this industry, a special effort was made to update this analysis; consequently this study is based on the 1964 model year. The reader will note that this involves use of a $0.925 Canadian exchange rate — rather than the parity rate used for the other industry studies based on the 1961 period. It should also be noted that in 1964 the new limited free trade arrangement in autos had not yet been introduced. Some of the implications of this new agreement will be discussed at the end of this chapter; however, a reasonably complete analysis of its effects cannot yet be undertaken because reactions have not yet been clearly defined, and recent data are not yet available. But the major result of this plan — a movement towards a rationalization of North American auto production — is already apparent. It comes as no surprise; what is surprising is that rationalization did not occur before. Hence the analysis in this chapter of the auto industry prior to this scheme may be more enlightening than a study of its (more predictable) reactions since. To simplify the exposition, the present tense is used throughout. The reader should not be misled; except for the last section, this chapter describes the industry's situation prior to the limited free trade plan.

The Difference in Canadian and U.S. Auto Prices

The Canadian tariff on completed automobiles imported from the United States (M.F.N. rate) is 17.5 percent.[1] Thus the U.S. price plus 17.5 percent may be taken as the approximate[2] ceiling on Canadian prices. This ceiling is not absolutely rigid; at least one exception has come to our attention. This occurred in the late 1950's when the Canadian dollar was at a premium.[3] With the

[1] Duty free imports of completed automobiles could be gained by increasing exports of automobiles or parts under the Order-in-Council of October 22, 1963 (P.C. 1963 — 1/1544). This possibility was not used by the automobile companies because of the greater profit in applying export credit to parts imports dutiable at 25 percent. See Appendix A, where the 1962 and 1963 auto tariff amendments are discussed.

[2] As explained in a footnote to Table 31, the effective Canadian tariff may exceed 17.5 percent; in the cases dealt with in that table, it amounted to 17.9 percent.

[3] Importation of the cheaper corresponding U.S. model by Canadian dealers was discouraged at that time by administrative impediments placed by the U.S. parent companies on refunds of U.S. excise taxes on exports to Canada.

There are other exceptional circumstances that might explain a Canadian price above this ceiling. For example, any decided "buy Canadian" tendencies on the part of Canadian purchasers would open the possibility of a continuing excess of prices of Canadian-built autos over U.S. prices plus duty.

In correspondence with one of the major Canadian automobile producers, we have been informed that "experience with low volume models has shown that of two identical vehicles, one imported from the U.S. and one made here, and both priced at the same level, the Canadian vehicle will outsell the American on the Canadian market. This is due to national loyalty and higher dealer aggressiveness associated with a 'Made Here' vehicle, and customer fear of a longer waiting period and poorer service with an imported vehicle."

Nevertheless, it is difficult to substantiate Canadian national preferences with the evidence provided by the used car markets. From time to time, Canadian manufacturers have marketed similar models, one corresponding to an American-built car and the other identical in practically every respect except for a Canadian nameplate and distinctive grille. At times these Canadian nameplate vehicles have commanded higher used car prices than the corresponding Canadian-built car with U.S. nameplates; at times they have sold at lower prices on the used car markets.

decline of the Canadian dollar on the international exchanges, the Canadian-U.S. automobile price differential of the late fifties has declined. Prices of automobiles in a recent model year (1964) indicate that the excess of Canadian prices over U.S. prices is well within the range set by the 17.5 percent Canadian tariff, as may be seen from Table 31.

TABLE 31. *Prices of Canadian and Imported American Automobiles, 1964 Model Year.*

	Automobile A[a]		Automobile B[a]	
	U.S. dollars	Canadian dollars	U.S. dollars	Canadian dollars
1. U.S. list price	1,822.00[b]			
2. U.S. factory price (excl. tax) of U.S. auto	1,439.00[b]		1,931.10[b]	
3. Handling	6.00[b]		6.00[b]	
4. Holdback[c]	36.00[b]		46.00[b]	
5. Value for duty[d]	1,481.00[b]	1,599.50[b]	1,983.10	2,141.80
6. Canadian duty[e]		279.90[b]		374.80[b]
7. Canadian federal tax (11% of duty-paid value)		206.70[b]		276.80[b]
8. Freight to Windsor	9.00[b]	9.70	13.00[b]	14.00
9. Refund of holdback[e]	−36.00	−38.90	−46.00	−49.70
10. Factory price of imported auto				
(a) Including tax and tariff		2,056.90		2,757.70
(b) Excluding tax and tariff		1,570.30		2,106.10
11. Factory price of Canadian-built auto				
(a) Excluding tax		1,719.00[b]		2,207.20
(b) Including tax		1,907.80[b]		2,450.00
12. List price of Canadian-built auto		2,364.80[b]		3,210.10
13. Tariff protection used; i.e., excess of Canadian price (11a) over U.S. price (10b)		9.47%		4.80%

[a] Automobile A is a compact with standard transmission produced by one of the big three.

Automobile B is a full size car with automatic transmission also produced by one of the big three.

[b] Figures provided by manufacturer. Other figures were calculated from data provided by manufacturer.

[e] Holdback of 2 percent of the U.S. list price is added to invoice at time of payment and refunded at periodic intervals. Duty paid on holdback is not refunded and is part of total duty paid together with duty on bare wholesale and handling. As duty is collected on a figure exceeding the final wholesale cost, the effective duty (17.9 percent) exceeds the nominal rate (17.5 percent).

[d] Exchange rate: $1.00 Can. equals $0.9259 U.S.

Information on a broader sample of Canadian autos is not presently available for the 1964 model year. However, pre-tax price data for the 1962 model year, presented in Table 32, indicate that

TABLE 32. *Percentage Excess of Canadian Wholesale Automotive Prices Over Corresponding U.S. Prices, 1962 Model Year (excluding excise taxes, at exchange rate $1.00 Can. = $0.97 U.S.).*

	Percent	
Type of vehicle	Manufacturer A	Manufacturer B
Automobiles		
1. Compact	17.7	17.6
2. Large compact	15.9	17.4
3. Full size, low price	15.9	17.1
4. Luxury model of (3)	17.3	17.4
5. Medium price	15.0	17.5
Average — all automobiles	16.2	17.3
Trucks		
1. Light	13.7	13.8
2. Medium	15.1	14.8
3. Heavy	12.4	12.4
Average — all trucks	13.6	13.5
Average — all vehicles	15.8	16.8

the excess price in this earlier period was more nearly the 17.5 percent maximum allowed by the Canadian tariff.[4] Since estimates of

[4] An interesting question is why the price gap narrowed in the period 1962–1964. This can be partially explained by the depreciation in the Canadian dollar. Between the summer of 1961 and the summer of 1963 when the prices of the 1962 and 1964 models were being determined, the Canadian dollar fell by nearly 5 percent; however, with only 60 percent of the final car being produced in Canada, this change in the exchange rate would have a direct total effect of only 3 percent on the relative cost of the Canadian car. Thus, even if the lowest price difference for 1962 (15 percent) and the highest for 1964 (9.5 percent) are considered, there remains a change of 2.5 percent in the relative price position of Canadian and U.S. automobiles that cannot be explained by changes in the exchange rate (that is, the total change, 15 to 9.5 percent, less than 3 percent change that can be explained by the exchange rate). Part of this 2.5 percent unexplained reduction in the relative Canadian price may perhaps be attributable to increased economies of scale of the Canadian industry: in the calendar year 1963, during which the prices of the 1964 models were set, the output of the Canadian automobile industry was 60 percent higher than in 1961, when 1962 model prices were determined.

Canadian prices shown in Tables 31 and 32 are between 4.8 percent and 17.7 percent higher than equivalent U.S. prices, the 1964 estimate of 9.5 percent on automobile A is regarded as reasonably typical of most recent pricing practice and is entered as excess price (P) in Figure 5.[5]

We turn now to the question of how differing costs in the two countries explain this higher Canadian price.

Differences in Canadian and U.S. Costs

Costs will be compared between Ontario and the U.S. East Lake Region, the present centers of auto concentration in the two countries.

Wages. In 1963, auto wages in Ontario were approximately 30 percent less than in the U.S. East Lake Region.[6] Multiplying this

[5] It is also interesting to note the substantial variation in excess price between models in either the 1962 or 1964 samples shown in Tables 31 and 32. No close relationship between the quantity of each model produced and its excess Canadian price was apparent; hence it is difficult to argue that economies of scale are important in determining relative prices of specific Canadian models, although they may raise the price of the entire range. This is not altogether surprising, since the prevalence of joint costs makes the pricing of each model somewhat arbitrary. (Because trucks are involved in the joint costs of the industry, data on relative U.S. and Canadian truck prices are included in Table 32. However, trucks will not be examined further; passenger automobiles only are dealt with in the balance of this chapter.)

[6] Regional industry data for 1961 have been used for this estimate:

U.S. East Lake wage rate in motor vehicles and parts in 1961 = $3.13 U.S.
Ontario wage rate in motor vehicle industry in 1961 = $2.39 Can.
Ontario wage rate in motor vehicle parts industry in 1961 = $2.13 Can.
Combined Ontario wage rate (weighted by man hours) = $2.26 Can.

From Department of Commerce, *Annual Survey of Manufactures, 1961,* and D.B.S., *Review of Man-Hours and Hourly Earnings, 1945–62.* These data have been updated to 1963 by multiplying the 1961 East Lake figure by the ratio of the U.S. motor vehicles and parts wage in 1963 to the U.S. motor vehicles and parts wage in 1961 (i.e., 3.10 divided by 2.99), and by multiplying the 1961 Ontario figure by a similar ratio (2.41 divided by 2.22) for Canada (*from Survey of Current Business* and D.B.S., *Man-Hours and Hourly Earnings, with Average Weekly Wages*). In deriving the final wage differential between Ontario and the U.S. East Lake region, the exchange rate of $1.00 Can. = $0.925 U.S. was used. The resulting estimate is that the average automotive wage in Canada was 28 percent less in 1963 than the average in the United States.

percentage by the ratio of wages to total costs[7] yields a Canadian cost advantage (W) of approximately 3.9 percent. When this is added to the higher Canadian auto price of 9.5 percent, the result is a 13.4 percent margin of advantages that the Canadian industry enjoys in producing for the Canadian market; this is shown as $E = P + W$ in Figure 5. How is this differential to be explained by offsetting Canadian cost disadvantages?

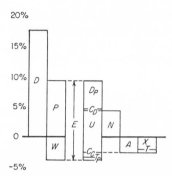

Figure 5. International differences in automobile prices and costs, 1964 model year (see Table 30). The baseline represents U.S. factory price (excluding indirect taxes). Exchange rate: $1.00 Can. = $0.925 U.S.

Higher Cost of Inputs Due to Canadian Protection. The most important input component of the Canadian auto industry is auto parts. A large proportion of Canadian parts are imported, with these imports coming almost exclusively from the United States. The Canadian tariff law requires that the major Canadian automobile producers include 60 percent Canadian content in their automobiles.[8] If this is done, then an extended list of parts may be imported duty free. This exemption does not, however, extend to all parts. In 1961, for example, Canadian producers paid a total of $27.46 million in duties on automobile parts imports of $289.53

---

[7] In calculating this ratio, 1961 data collected for Part I were used. Specifically, the total wage payment was divided by the value shipped of the auto industry, yielding a labor content of 12.84 percent of total costs.

[8] This content was required during the 1964 model year under consideration. The regulations have been changed since that time. See Appendices A and B.

million.[9] This amounted to an average of about $85 per automobile, or 4.2 percent of Canadian value shipped in the automobile industry. Since 1961 data are the most recent complete set available, this 4.2 percent is taken as an estimate of the additional costs of the 1964 model attributable to Canadian parts duties and is entered as D_P in Figure 5.

It should be noted that the standard procedure of this study — applying published tariff rates to the total input requirement of the industry — was *not* used in this auto study because auto parts duties are partially avoided by Canadian firms which meet specified content requirements. Therefore, in the exceptional case of the auto industry, actual duties paid rather than tariff rates may be taken as the more accurate indicator of the higher costs due to protection on parts. Furthermore, the usual problem of sorting out which industry receives this specific input does not exist to the same degree. Except for replacement parts, all imported auto parts are used by the auto industry.

In the estimates made in this chapter, the Canadian auto industry is defined to include parts as well as assembly. The definition of the industry is an important issue; for if the industry were to be defined to include only assembly (a procedure which does not seem very reasonable to us), an additional item would logically have to be included with D_P, that is, an estimate of how higher prices of Canadian-produced parts add to higher costs of assembling Canadian cars. This would narrow the size of the unexplained residual in Figure 5 but would also narrow its meaning; it would become an estimate of the costs of Canadian inefficiency only in automotive assembly, rather than in the whole auto industry.

The other empirical difficulty is how Canadian protection may

[9] *From* D.B.S. data reported in Harry G. Johnson, "The New Tariff Policy for the Automotive Industry," *Business Quarterly* (University of Western Ontario), 29: 54 (Spring 1964).

In the following year, 1962, the duties collected were particularly great on automatic transmissions and engines. This was only partly due to the increase in automobile production between 1961 and 1962. It was also partly attributable to the new enforcement of the transmission duty in late 1962 and the decision of one of the big three to import a newly introduced engine pending the establishment of an aluminum engine block plant in Canada.

increase the cost in Canada of inputs *other* than parts (for example, steel). An upper estimate of a 4.9 percent increase in total costs was derived by assuming that all such inputs (whether imported or domestically produced) were higher priced in Canada by the full amount of their protection. However, because this figure was computed from the total input structure of the auto industry,[10] it cannot be used in conjunction with the 4.2 percent parts estimate above, as the combination would amount to double counting. Fortunately, this complication does not arise in other industries.[11] However, it cannot be avoided in the auto case. The only conclusion, therefore, is that Canadian protection on inputs raises Canadian costs by at least 4.2 percent (D_P). Inasmuch as there are higher priced inputs other than parts, Canadian costs will be even higher. Another 4.9 percent is an estimate of the maximum additional cost that can be involved for this reason, but the actual figure is certain to be very much less. Since only D_P is entered in Figure 5, it should be regarded as a minimum estimate of the addition to Canadian costs because of input protection.[12]

High Machinery Costs Due to the Canadian Tariff. In Part I it was concluded that differences in building costs were not sufficiently great to affect capital costs; they were, therefore, ignored in this analysis, and all the industry studies that follow. Tariffs on machinery were estimated to add a maximum of 0.17 percent to the cost of producing autos in Canada in 1961; this figure was taken as an approximation to the 1964 figure, and accordingly 0.2 percent was entered as item C_D, in Figure 5.

These are the two major Canadian cost disadvantages due to protection that may be identified specifically; both would disappear with free trade. We now turn to an analysis of those higher Canadian costs that reflect inherent Canadian disadvantages, and

[10] Specifically, from the eighty-one sector U.S. interindustry table for 1957.

[11] Because they do not have content provisions similar to those on the auto industry.

[12] Logically, Canadian costs may also be higher if the U.S. parent overcharges on any parts exported to the Canadian subsidiary. Because it is difficult to define overcharging and because there was no information on this subject, this possibility has not been evaluated. See the section below on the response of an oligopolistic industry to protection.

that would, therefore, persist even under free trade (except insofar as they might be modified in the adjustment process).

Higher Costs of Capital in Canada. It is not clear to what degree the returns on equity and debt in the Canadian automobile industry must be higher than in the United States in order to attract and hold capital because the greater part of the financing of the Canadian industry is directly from the United States. However, following the methods outlined in Part I, estimates of this differential have been computed. These estimates, based on 1961 data, indicate that total Canadian costs could have been higher by about 0.02 percent because of higher debt charges and by about 0.82 percent because of higher opportunity costs on equity capital. Thus, the total differential due to carrying costs may be estimated as just over 0.8 percent. Although no great confidence may be placed in its accuracy, this estimate of 0.8 percent is entered as C_C in Figure 5. Because of the small size of this item, the problem of possible inaccuracy is relatively insignificant.

Transportation Costs on Parts. The most recent annual data available (1961) indicate that parts imports amounted to approximately 40 percent of Canadian costs in the automobile industry. The additional transportation costs arising from the shipping of these parts from their center of production in the Detroit area to the center of the Canadian industry (the Toronto area) add just over one percent to parts costs,[13] or approximately 0.45 percent to the total costs of automobile production in Canada. It should be noted that Toronto is further from Detroit than Windsor, another center of the Canadian industry. Hence, this estimate of the costs due to transportation charges on parts may be taken as a maximum estimate, and is entered as item T_P in Figure 5.

Economies of Scale and the Higher Canadian Price

We are now in a position to estimate roughly the effects of a limited market on Canadian costs of production. On the auto model with a 9.5 percent higher Canadian price, the Canadian producer also enjoyed a 3.9 percent cost advantage due to lower

---

[13] Cost per dollar mile of parts shipments is calculated on the basis of 1959 U.S. transportation costs, as described in Part I.

wages, leaving a differential of 13.4 percent to be explained. This differential was partially dissipated in higher capital and materials costs, which were estimated to increase total cost by 5.7 percent. This leaves an unexplained residual (U) of 7.7 percent,[14] which may be taken to represent the estimated degree to which Canadian costs are higher because of diseconomies of a limited market. As has already been pointed out, this is the least satisfactory estimate in this chapter because it also represents the accumulation of errors in previous computations, plus the effects of any cost influences omitted from this study.

It should be noted that this does *not* mean that large-scale production in the United States is only 7.7 percent more efficient than Canadian production. Since only 60 percent of the car is made in Canada, and since this 7.7 percent is a percentage of total costs, the higher costs attributed to a smaller market amount to approximately 13 percent when taken as a fraction of the Canadian-produced content alone.

The picture, therefore, is as follows: Canadian producers are selling a product at about 9.5 percent above the U.S. price. Higher Canadian costs other than those attributable to market size explain very little of this price differential, since the Canadian wage advantage almost offsets other Canadian disadvantages. Thus, most (7.7 percent) of this 9.5 percent higher Canadian price is to be explained by diseconomies of a small market, that is, either by higher costs of production due to limited scale[15] or by higher pricing by firms operating behind protection in the less competitive Canadian market.

The Response of an Oligopolistic Industry to Protection

High Price and the Proliferation of Models. In order to weight the two alternative explanations (suggested in the previous paragraph) of the higher Canadian price, it is necessary first to ex-

[14] Or less because of the higher Canadian cost of (non-parts) inputs. This additional input cost will, however, be at least partially offset to the degree that C_D, C_C, and T_P represent overestimates.

[15] This limited scale may include both economies of scale from an engineering viewpoint and possible lower levels of managerial efficiency attributable to the distractions presented by fragmented production runs.

amine the pricing practice of the Canadian auto industry. One hypothesis that has been suggested to explain Canadian pricing is that the tariff provides protection and an obvious formula for a higher Canadian price. There are none of the problems of communication usually faced by oligopolies when it is tacitly agreed to charge the U.S. price plus the Canadian tariff.

There are two limitations to this explanation in the auto case: first, 1964 Canadian prices were not apparently set by any automatic formula, since they fell well below the level allowed by the 17.5 percent Canadian tariff;[16] second, if the higher Canadian price did represent greater exercise of oligopoly power in the Canadian market, then per unit profits of the Canadian producers should be higher than per unit U.S. profits. This does not appear to be the case. Although consistent and meaningful comparative profit data are very difficult to obtain and interpret — and, indeed, the problems in this area are so great that no direct profits data will be presented — such information as is available indicates that, if anything, per unit profits in the Canadian automotive industry have tended to lie below those in the United States. (This generalization applies to basic automobiles only, and not to automotive accessories.) Thus, the price differential may not be explained simply by a difference in profits, but it seems to represent a difference in costs.

There is a variant of this simple oligopolistic argument that might possibly explain part of the price difference, even if Canadian per unit profits are no higher than U.S. profits. It is possible that the oligopolistic profits accrue to the U.S. parent rather than to the Canadian subsidiary. This might happen if the U.S. parent were to use its relationship with the subsidiary and the protection offered by the Canadian tariff to overcharge the subsidiary for parts. Needless to say, information that might be used to test this hypothesis is not the sort of data that is easily acquired. Even if information were available its interpretation would involve prob-

---

[16] The "automatic price" formula seems to be a better explanation of prices in the 1962 model year; however, even in this case it is not a completely consistent explanation. Moreover, Canadian price seemed insensitive to the exchange depreciation between the 1962–1964 model years; hence in this sense at least it was not "automatic."

lems. With the prevalence of joint costs, it is difficult to determine whether the cost estimates for a specific part are "correct." And even if the problem did not exist, the reasonable price in a parent-subsidiary transaction is by no means obvious. How, for example, should research and other overhead charges of the parent be distributed between its Canadian and U.S. operations? It must be concluded that it is just not possible to evaluate empirically the "parts pricing" variant of the simple oligopolistic argument.

A more sophisticated explanation suggested by Professor H. Edward English[17] involves recognition of both the oligopoly structure of the auto industry and the existence of economies of scale. English argues that the margin opened by the Canadian tariff and by the obvious oligopolistic pricing formula that it provides will not be reflected primarily in Canadian profits but rather will attract additional entrants into the market until possible oligopoly profits are frittered away on fragmented, high-cost production processes. With the three largest companies dominating the Canadian automobile market, English's proposition regarding additional entrants may be put primarily in terms of additional models rather than additional companies, although the entry of American motors and Volvo, the Canadian expansion of Studebaker, and the possible future entry of one or more French companies may have some significance.

The major difficulty in this argument is that it raises fundamental questions about the rationale of behavior of the Canadian automobile companies. English's proposition that oligopolistic behavior will attract new entrants that will tend to split the market and eliminate above-normal profits creates no particular logical problems in general; unless there is a high degree of common ownership or overt collusion among the companies, there is little reason for a new entrant to hesitate on the ground that his actions will adversely affect the profit positions of the established companies. However, English's proposition does involve logical problems if it is applied, as in the auto case, to the entry of new models rather than new firms. Why would a Canadian auto company introduce new models when in the process it fragments its production proc-

[17] See Chapter 11.

esses and raises its costs? This model proliferation would tend to wipe out the high levels of profit made possible by the Canadian tariff.

An oligopoly pattern can be postulated that will explain this sort of behavior. It may be that the oligopolists are sufficiently well disciplined to restrict price competition but not sufficiently well disciplined to restrict model competition. Alternatively, the same outcome could result, even if all oligopolists act without any reference whatsoever to their collective interest or to the chain of competitive reactions they may initiate. This could occur if consumers place a greater premium on choice than price. Thus the individual producer might not cut price by specializing in a single model because he would expect to attract fewer customers by his lower price than he would lose because of his more limited range of models. Consumer preference for choice rather than price is difficult to test; U.S. evidence on this subject is of limited relevance because the further price reductions that might be achieved by increasing scale in that country are minor (or nonexistent) compared to possible reductions in Canada. Furthermore, even in Canada, feasible price reductions through specialization may be very limited. Increasing scale, by say 50 percent, for expansion in the Canadian market may decrease costs by only a small proportion of the 7.7 percent estimate derived by comparing Canadian scale with that of the United States; and this decrease may be more than offset by even a weak consumer preference for choice.

There are a number of less theoretical ways of explaining why the auto companies market such a wide range of models in Canada. Management may feel under great pressures to "play it safe," which in this context means following the pattern of models set by the U.S. parent. This, at best, can be only a partial explanation because there are some specifically Canadian models produced in Canada whereas some U.S. models are not produced there. Alternatively, management in the short run may be prepared to sacrifice profit in order to improve relative market position — and the best way of increasing market share is to increase the range of models offered. But here again, it must be assumed that the customer places a heavy premium on range of choice compared to lower price.

This line of argument may be recapitulated, as follows: higher Canadian auto prices reflect higher cost due to shorter production runs which result when oligopolists compete by increasing the number of models rather than by reducing price. Presumably, they act in this manner because Canadian consumer preference is for a wide range of choice rather than reduced price.[18] Oligopoly power by the Canadian companies may or may not be exercised in covering inefficiency and in determining the range of models and consequently auto prices, but this oligopoly power is apparently not used to extract higher profits in Canada than in the United States.

What Prevented North American Rationalization of Auto Production? The apparent existence of economies of scale in Canadian production raises another important question. Why did manufacturers not gain economies of scale and a wide range of models simultaneously by concentrating Canadian production on one model, by importing the other models, and by maintaining the total quantity of Canadian production through exports of the model produced in Canada?

Such a line of action would involve certain obvious problems: most clearly, if the Canadian producer sold his model more cheaply in the United States than in Canada, difficulties might arise because, technically speaking, dumping would be involved. However, the Studebaker case indicates that the United States is not particularly sensitive to such export pricing by U.S.-owned companies in Canada.[19] In what follows immediately below, we will assume that Canadian producers maintain production by new ex-

---

[18] If consumers have this preference for choice rather than lower price, then not only would individual Canadian companies face the possibility of loss if they restricted the number of models, but the Canadian industry as a whole might decline. This would follow if two conditions were met: first, if consumer demand for variety in the face of restricted choice among Canadian-built vehicles resulted in an increase in imports; and second, if protection blocked exports to the United States of the models in which Canada specialized. This second issue is dealt with directly.

[19] They have, however, been sensitive to the Export Incentive Plans of 1962 and 1963, whereby indirect government subsidies rather than company pricing policies were the stimulus behind Canadian exports. Even in this case, American objections have been confined primarily to the exports of independent Canadian parts producers, rather than to exports of the large, integrated automobile producers.

ports (of the model in which they specialize) equivalent to the increase in imports (of all other models).[20] Let:

  s = savings as a fraction of total production costs if Canadian production is restricted to only one model, but total output is maintained at the present level,
  x = rise in Canadian imports in response to the limited choice of Canadian models (as a fraction of total Canadian sales of the producer in question).

Because of our balance of payments assumption, the rise in Canadian exports of completed autos (as a fraction of total Canadian sales of the producer in question) will also equal x.

The advantage of such Canadian specialization would be s. The disadvantages would be the U.S. and Canadian duties which must be paid.[21] Thus, with U.S. and Canadian automobile tariffs of 6.5 and 17.5 percent, concentration of Canadian production would take place if the advantages were at least equal to the two duties paid on auto imports and exports, that is, if

$$s \geq 0.175x + 0.065x$$

or

$$s \geq 0.24x. \tag{1}$$

If Bain is correct in his conclusion that optimum efficiency for any model may be approached at 300,000 units, and that costs are only moderately higher at 150,000 units,[22] and if our earlier 7.7 percent estimate of U is attributed exclusively to higher Canadian costs due to limited scale, then s may approach this 7.7 percent for the two largest Canadian producers, General Motors and Ford. (Ford production in calender year 1963 was approximately 142,-000; for General Motors the figure was over 264,000).

If this policy is undertaken, a firm will minimize its duty payments by minimizing x (the proportion traded). This would be accomplished by Canadian specialization in the model with heaviest

[20] This balance-of-payments restriction will be relaxed shortly.

[21] It might seem that there is an additional disadvantage in selling Canadian-built cars competitively in the United States, that is, at a price lower than in Canada. There will, however, be an offsetting advantage from selling an equivalent amount of U.S. cars in the high-priced Canadian market. Thus, total duties paid constitute the total disadvantage.

[22] See Chapter 11.

sales in the domestic market. The Ford Motor Company could choose the Galaxie, with a 38 percent (i.e., 54,233 divided by 142,270) share of the market (see Table 33). The balance of the

TABLE 33. *Canadian Motor Vehicle Production, by Model, Calendar Years 1962 and 1963.*

Type of vehicle	1962	1963
1. AMERICAN MOTORS: TOTAL CARS	21,928	30,167
2. CHRYSLER		
Chrysler	11,129	11,999
Dodge	12,295	21,401
Plymouth	12,156	21,442
Valiant	14,980	31,963
TOTAL CHRYSLER CARS	50,560	86,805
3. FORD		
Ford Galaxie	32,638	54,233
Fairlane	25,038	21,121
Falcon	15,651	14,253
Mercury	15,911	21,188
Meteor	15,849	17,761
Comet	13,103	13,714
TOTAL FORD CARS	118,190	142,270
4. GENERAL MOTORS		
Chev./Chevy II/Corvair/Chevelle	105,896	117,986
Acadian	16,503	17,857
Pontiac	85,086	97,336
Oldsmobile	12,923	16,761
Buick	9,252	14,383
TOTAL G.M. CARS	229,639	264,341
(G.M. trucks)	37,579	43,883
5. STUDEBAKER: TOTAL CARS	7,948	8,190
6. VOLVO: TOTAL CARS	–	1,139
7. (INTERNATIONAL TRUCKS)	10,285	11,539
TOTAL CARS	428,265	532,912
(TOTAL TRUCKS)	79,816	98,454

Source: Canadian Automobile Chamber of Commerce.

Canadian market would be satisfied by imports; hence $x = 1 - 0.38 = 0.62$. Therefore, provided the Galaxie share of the Canadian market remained constant through this change,[23] the company would incur roughly a 15 percent cost in the form of Cana-

[23] The Galaxie share might increase if some of the cost savings of producing this model were to be passed on to the Canadian consumer, or if Canadian consumers have "buy Canadian" biases. See footnote 3, above.

dian and U.S. duties. (That is, the right side of the expression (1) would become $(0.24)(0.62) = 0.149$.) This disadvantage more than offsets the maximum estimated cost savings (7.7 percent) that could be achieved through economies of scale.

Therefore, it is no surprise that Ford did not rationalize its Canadian operations, even though cost savings would have resulted from specialization.[24] The existence of the Canadian and U.S. tariffs was more than adequate to explain fragmented production runs in Canada. It may be seen from equation (1) that the sum of the Canadian and U.S. tariffs would have to be reduced to about 12 percent (or roughly half their level of 0.24 shown in that equation) for serious consideration of Canadian rationalization to take place.[25] This means that rationalization of the industry could occur if tariffs were reduced; their complete elimination is not necessarily required.

But even if necessary condition (1) were met, certain risks might still prevent Canadian specialization — unless the gains outweighed the costs by an appropriate margin. The major risk would be the rather pronounced year-to-year variation in the relative popularity of the various models marketed by the automobile companies. By placing all their eggs in one (model) basket, the Canadian manufacturers would be increasing their vulnerability to year-to-year fluctuations in their output and employment; in addition the necessary profit condition for this policy (equation 1) might no longer be satisfied if there were a substantial change in model popularity and market share.

In order to minimize possible political repercussions to Canadian rationalization, a balance-of-payments restraint equating increased imports and exports has been assumed for each firm. But such a pattern might not maximize profits; for example, it might be more profitable for a firm to increase imports more than exports. In the face of the resulting unfavorable shift in the Canadian

[24] Corresponding calculations for General Motors are more difficult, since the production of the most popular "models" may not be identified from their aggregate production data. (Chevrolet, Chevy II, Corvair, and Chevelle are distinct models.)

[25] If most (or all) economies of scale could be achieved by Canadian specialization in several models, the necessary condition for rationalization (equation 1) could more easily be satisfied, since x would be smaller.

balance of payments, the Canadian government might react by raising tariffs and thus undercut the ability of the automobile companies to offer a full line to their customers.

Alternatively it may be profitable for a firm in Canada to increase exports more than imports; this raises the possibility of an entirely different sort of rationalization of Canadian facilities. Why should a firm not specialize in one line (for example, Galaxie) for North American distribution, while providing Canadian customers with a full range by continuing present (inefficient) Canadian production of all other models? Since imports from the United States would not increase as Canadian exports (of Galaxies) increased, a favorable change in the Canadian balance-of-payments and auto employment picture vis-à-vis the United States is implied. In this case, it would be the U.S. balance of payments that would deteriorate, and the pricing policy for Canadian Galaxies in the two markets could become a critical issue.

Suppose, first, that Galaxie sales in Canada were to continue at the present high price. It would be in Ford's interest to increase Canadian production to efficient scale $Q + Z$ (where $Q =$ present production for domestic sales and $Z =$ exports) provided that the scale savings on Q (i.e., $UQ = .077Q$) more than offset the higher cost of producing Z in Canada rather than in the U.S. This latter is estimated as $.088Z$, to include both the U.S. tariff ($.065Z$) and the higher costs[26] in Canada $[(D_p + C_D + C_c + T_p - T - W)Z = .023Z]$. This question cannot be answered without detailed knowledge of efficient scale,[27] and thus the relative size of Q and Z; but if efficient scale involves production at about double the present Canadian level (Q) or more, such rationalization in Canada for U.S. export would not be profitable.

But even in the unlikely case that U.S. scale efficiencies could be achieved by less than doubling Canadian output, there are other impediments to such a scheme which cannot be included in this type of simple calculation. Pressure on both the U.S. balance of payments and employment would be generated by Canadian dumping in the U.S. market. Dumping in the United States may be

[26] For details, see Table 30.

[27] Again, this analysis is complicated if Canada now imports Galaxies, and/or parts costs change with rationalization.

ignored if it has small employment or balance-of-payments effects. But this type of dumping would scarcely be overlooked, and the risks of a defensive reaction by the U.S. government would undoubtedly be sufficient to deter the substantial long-term investment that would be required in Canada.

Dumping problems could be avoided, of course, by selling Galaxies in Canada at the U.S. price. In this instance costs cannot be shifted onto high priced Canadian sales; and the net advantage in producing in Canada (X shown in Figure 5) would not cover the combined disadvantages of both the U.S. tariff [28] and the higher costs of capital (C_D), parts (D_P) and other (non-parts) inputs.[29]

It may be concluded that the major restrictions inhibiting Canadian specialization have been the Canadian *and* U.S. tariffs,[30] and the risk that either government might invoke defensive measures in the face of employment or balance-of-payments difficulties.

The Response of an Oligopolistic Industry to Protection: Summary. Both Bain's estimates and the cost data of this chapter indicate that at least some of the higher cost of Canadian automobiles is attributable to the proliferation of models that is made possible by the Canadian tariff. The question is raised why the Canadian auto companies do not limit the number of models they produce and thus reap the oligopolistic profits allowed by the protection of the Canadian tariff. This puzzle can be solved along any one of several lines: for example by assuming the companies are at least as interested in their share of the market as in short-run profits; by assuming that Canadian management chooses

[28] Again yt as in equation (2). The present level of the U.S. tariff is 6.5 percent but the relevant figure would be its expected level. The latter might be considerably higher, if the U.S. tariff is to any degree a protectionist device. Recall that the policy of Canadian specialization under consideration here implies substantial deterioration in the U.S. balance of payments.

[29] And there are other possible disadvantages. The lower price (relative to other models sold in Canada) might be expected to cause a shift in consumption toward Galaxies. This would tend to reduce y; but it also might increase costs (by decreasing scale) in the production of other models in Canada.

[30] This restricting influence was recognized in the Canadian Export Incentive Plan, which encouraged rationalization of the industry by allowing rebates of Canadian tariffs for companies increasing their exports. The limited free trade scheme that has replaced it does recognize that elimination of both U.S. and Canadian tariffs are highly desirable objectives.

the safety of following the pattern of the U.S. parents; or by assuming that lower prices are a relatively weak attraction compared to wide choice among models.

The existence of economies of scale also raises the possibility that Canadian companies might limit the number of models produced in Canada, export these models over the U.S. tariff, and (perhaps) import other models from the United States. However, failure of the Canadian companies to act along these lines can be explained: potential economies of scale in Canadian production are more than offset by the costs of the U.S. and Canadian tariffs, and by the risk of an unfavorable reaction by either government to employment or balance-of-payments problems.

The Free Trade Prospects of the Canadian Auto Industry

In the event of free trade, several major elements of Canadian cost would disappear. Most obviously, the tariff cost on parts (D_P) and on other inputs would no longer apply. Higher costs because of Canadian protection on machinery (C_D) would also disappear. Provided that Canadian producers were able to enter the U.S. market, the costs attributable to the smaller Canadian market (U) would decline and possibly disappear.

Would such exports to the United States be likely? On the basis of available data, prospects appear to be favorable. It is true that some of the cost disadvantages estimated above — transportation costs on parts (T_P) and higher carrying costs of capital (C_C) — would remain. However, these two higher costs do not offset the Canadian wage advantage; consequently Canadian producers are left with an advantage of about 2.6 percent in total costs (A) over their U.S. counterparts. This would be sufficient to overcome any minor cost disadvantage of transporting Canadian cars to U.S. markets (T).[31]

Thus the best estimate is that there would be about a 2 percent Canadian absolute advantage in auto production; this indicates

[31] Two limits to this transport cost disadvantage were computed by using the market distributions that result from setting q equal to zero and one in the model of Chapter III. The upper limit was estimated as 0.7 percent; but if Canadian companies enter those U.S. markets where their transport disadvantage is least, this extra cost was estimated at 0.54 percent.

that at current wage and exchange levels, rationalization and continued production of this Canadian industry would be likely under unrestricted free trade. The major reservation to this favorable conclusion is that, in the long run, resources might be bid away from this sector by some other Canadian industry with an even more favorable competitive position under free trade.

Addendum: The Limited Free Trade Plan in Autos

No attempt is made here to describe or analyze this plan,[32] which was introduced after this chapter was in draft form. However, the above analysis does throw interesting light on this scheme.

Because this plan allows duty free imports only by auto manufacturers and not by independent importers, Canadian prices have remained above U.S. levels. This has provided the auto companies with a financial reward in return for their commitment to invest and continue production in Canada. This reward comes in the form of an increased profit potential because of several separate reductions in cost resulting from this plan. The auto companies no longer pay a Canadian tariff on parts imports (D_P). Elimination of the U.S. tariff allows Canadian scaling up for North American markets; consequently, higher costs due to restricted scale of production in Canada (U) will be progressively eliminated.

For these two reasons alone, the profit potential of Canadian production could be increased by roughly 12 percent of total costs;[33] such substantial cost savings may be expected to have a major effect on a company's Canadian earnings unless large amounts of capital are quickly written off and Canadian prices are lowered.[34]

In addition, there are two other savings of this scheme; although

---

[32] For an analysis of this program, see Appendix B.

[33] $D_P + U = 4.2 + 7.7 = 11.9$ percent.

[34] It may be inferred from the Annual Income Statement of Ford of Canada that a 12 percent decrease in costs could have increased the company's before-tax earnings in Canada by almost five times in 1964 and by two to three times in 1963. Ford of Canada, of course, has operations in several countries; although these cost savings might increase the profitability of its Canadian operations by this degree, they will have no effect on its overseas operations.

they are not directly related to the production of autos in Canada (and therefore do not appear in Figure 5), these savings do go to the auto companies in their international operations. There is a gain of up to 17.5 percent on the Canadian sales of completed autos imported from the United States. The Canadian price of these cars previously covered the Canadian tariff; now that this has been removed, this margin will go either to the consumer (if prices are lowered), or to the auto companies which act as sole importers at the duty free rate. This saving of the duty on completed autos is likely to save the auto companies an amount equal to more than one third their savings from the remission of duties on parts.[35] Lastly, there is a saving from the elimination of the U.S. tariff on Canadian parts exports. It is not clear whether this benefit accrues to the parents or to the Canadian subsidiaries. A portion of this saving will also go to independent Canadian auto parts producers developing markets in the United States.

All the above cost savings by the auto companies are automatic — except for the elimination of U with increased Canadian scale, which requires rationalization and new investment. The partial insulation of the Canadian market has been defended as a means of providing incentives for this new investment. The issues raised by the details of the modified free trade agreement are considered in Appendix B.

[35] In 1962, duties collected on auto parts (almost all of which came from the United States) amounted to over $41 million. Duties on autos imported from the U.S. were approximately $13 and a half million. (These estimates based on figures in Johnson, "New Tariff Policy," p. 54.)

14

OTHER INDUSTRY STUDIES

The additional thirteen sample industries examined in this chapter illustrate other possible situations Canadian firms would face with free trade. It should be emphasized again that, in all cases, it is absolute advantage, rather than comparative advantage that is under consideration; and the competitive position of many industries is likely to change as wages and the exchange rate adjust to a new free trade equilibrium. (In the industries dealt with below, 1961 data and an exchange rate of $1.00 Can. = $1.00 U.S. are used; in contrast, the automobile study in Chapter 13 was based on more recent (1963–64) data and an exchange rate of $1.00 Can. = $0.925 U.S.) Moreover, it should be pointed out that the classification of industries in the following chapters is based on imperfect and incomplete information; the description must therefore be considered a rough sketch rather than a precise picture.

Canadian Absolute Advantage under Free Trade: No Reorganization Required

There are two types of Canadian industry that could successfully meet free trade competition without reorganization. The most straightforward is an industry in which basic Canadian advantages are reflected in a lower present price of the product in Canada than in the United States. The second is an industry with negative net protection (N lies below the baseline in Figure 4). Its product price would be forced down by tariff removal, but its costs would fall even more with the elimination of protection on its inputs.

A firm of the first type can be recognized if it is already selling its product in Canada at a price below the prevailing U.S. price. (It may or may not now be exporting to the United States, depending on the height of the U.S. tariff.) Its ability to market its product in Canada at this low price indicates that in all probability it is an industry in which Canadian producers enjoy a natural advantage.[1] Moreover, it is already sufficiently well organized to survive without tariff protection from U.S. competitors;[2] as a consequence, no further rationalization of this Canadian industry is necessary. Moreover, exports to the United States may be expected with U.S. tariff elimination. It should also be noted that any Canadian protection now provided to this industry is irrelevant. The Canadian producer does not use this protection by raising domestic price; nor does the Canadian tariff exclude U.S. exports from the Canadian market because they would be unable to compete in Canada even in the absence of tariffs.[3]

The sample Canadian industry falling in this category was the tanning of upper shoe leather (Figure 6). The best estimate is that the Canadian industry priced its product about 6 percent below the U.S. price.[4] The Canadian tariff of about 15.5 percent was

[1] An exception might occur if U.S. tariffs on inputs were responsible for the higher U.S. price.

[2] Although such an industry is relatively efficient, it cannot be concluded that it has necessarily achieved an optimal level of efficiency. A certain degree of inefficiency may remain, in the sense that access to the U.S. market would make possible even lower per unit costs. In this event, the industry would be in an even stronger position in a free trade area.

[3] If there is significant product differentiation, this conclusion requires substantial qualification. In this case, it is possible that the Canadian tariff may exclude some U.S. exports to Canada that otherwise would be able to compete in the Canadian market because of special non-price characteristics (for example, style or design).

In the specific case dealt with below (upper shoe leather), product differentiation of this kind seems unimportant.

[4] Somewhat surprisingly, however, there were major differences in the competitive positions of the various segments of the tanning industry, and Canadian sole leather prices exceeded those in the United States by about 4 percent in 1961. In recent years, imports and exports of unmanufactured leather have been each in the neighborhood of $10 million per annum. As

obviously disregarded because the Canadian price was about 21 percent below that allowed by the duty.

The lower Canadian wage results in potentially lower costs in Canada of about 7.5 percent; in addition, costs may be more than

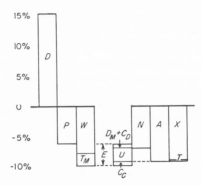

Figure 6. Cost analysis for 1961: upper shoe leather (see Table 30). The baseline represents U.S. wholesale price. Exchange rate: $1.00 Can. = $1.00 U.S.

2 percent lower because the Canadian industry is closer to required input supplies.[5] In total, Canadian advantages may reduce costs by almost 10 percent. A large part of this lower cost is passed on to the consumer in the form of a 6 percent lower price; consequently, a margin of advantages of only about 4 percent is left to the Canadian producer.

This margin is partially offset by higher Canadian capital costs (C_C and C_D) and higher costs in Canada due to Canadian protec-

might be expected, Canadian exports tended to be concentrated in the area where Canadian prices were relatively low: the two major exports were upper leather made from calf hides, and upper leather NOP. Canadian imports were concentrated on other lines of leather, the most important two categories being dressed leather including reptile leather and leather for the manufacture of gloves and leather clothing.

[5] The largest center of the Canadian tanning industry is Hamilton, which is very close to the Toronto stockyards, the major source of Canadian hides. The U.S. tannery industry is centered around Lowell, Mass., close to the shoe industry but distant from the major slaughtering centers in the Midwest. Since the Canadian industry is located much closer to input supplies, but farther from the largest markets, it has a cost advantage over its U.S. competition in terms of the former (T_M) but a disadvantage in terms of the latter (T).

tion of required inputs (D_M).[6] The result is that in this industry there is a small unexplained residual U (less than 3 percent) to be attributed to inefficiencies such as diseconomies of scale; hence, there seems to be little margin for reducing costs by scaling up to the larger North American market opened by free trade.

With free trade, the Canadian industry would enjoy initial absolute cost advantages of almost 10 percent over its U.S. competition because of lower Canadian wages and greater proximity to input supplies. In a free trade system these would be only slightly offset by higher Canadian capital costs and somewhat higher costs involved in shipping the final product to market, leaving a net cost advantage (X) of about 9 percent to the Canadian industry. Because the analysis above suggests neither the necessity (P negative) nor major advantages (U small) of reorganization, the Canadian industry should initially expand with little reorganization in the event of free trade.

With one exception, this sort of Canadian-U.S. price comparison is a good index of the free trade reorganization required by an industry: a lower present Canadian price indicates an industry that requires no reorganization to compete, whereas a higher present Canadian price indicates an industry that either cannot compete or must reorganize in order to do so. The one exception to this rule of thumb is, however, an important one. It arises from the possible existence of negative protection for an industry — in the sense that its costs are higher because necessary inputs are protected. If this influence is strong enough, it may result in a situation in which a Canadian industry with a natural advantage, and requiring no reorganization to compete under free trade, is nevertheless forced to sell its product in Canada at a higher price than in the United States; in effect, an efficiently organized industry may be driven to use all or most of its Canadian protection simply to offset the negative protection levied on it through duties on its inputs. An extreme case of a chemical product for which this negative protection on inputs exceeds the protection on the final prod-

[6] Hides, which constitute the largest single input, are not subject to Canadian duty; this helps to explain the low addition to costs (only 0.17 percent) attributable to duties on inputs. Although Canada imports substantial amounts of hides and skins, she exports more of this raw material than she imports.

uct (an item with negative *net* protection) has been brought to our attention.[7] However, since detailed cost data for this product could not be obtained, no diagrammed substantiation can be presented. It is surprising that such a firm even exists; its existence implies substantial offsetting Canadian advantages. The normal result of this type of protection would be to discourage Canadian production. Hence, one would expect to find it occurring in goods that are *not* produced in Canada, rather than those that are. The existence of such an industry implies that negative net protection probably occurs in a number of other cases, which go unnoticed because the industry has long since ceased to exist in Canada or has never been established because of the negative protection.

It is difficult to justify overall Canadian protection in such a case unless the earlier stages of production are considered inherently superior to the later stage. Paradoxically, it may be *Canadian* protection which keeps firms of this kind out of U.S. markets. They cannot export now because their costs are higher, but if Canadian protection were to be unilaterally abolished, Canadian producers would find their costs below U.S. costs; as a consequence, they might be able to export into the U.S. market, provided the additional problem of the U.S. tariff could be overcome (that is, provided their resulting cost advantage exceeded the U.S. tariff).[8]

Canadian Absolute Advantage under Free Trade: Reorganization May Be Required

The second type of industry, like the first, would be in a strong competitive position in the event of free trade (X lies below the baseline). However, on the basis of its current techniques, the Canadian industry would be unable to compete unless it were to

[7] In this case the net protection *available* to the industry is negative. In the leather industry above, the net protection available is positive; however, the reader will note that, because of its apparent efficiency, the leather industry doesn't *use* any of this protection; in fact its price is so low that the net protection it uses is negative.

[8] Moreover, because it is negative, Canadian protection tends to *reduce* rather than to increase Canadian money wages in such an industry; see Chapter 15 below.

√ reorganize to approach U.S. levels of efficiency. Diagrammatically, its free trade advantage, combined with its present high level of protection and high domestic Canadian price, means that its unexplained residual attributable to inefficiencies of a small market (U) straddles the baseline. As long as U exceeds the Canadian basic advantage, this industry cannot compete under free trade unless the exchange rate changes or Canadian wages or other costs fall. But if U were to be reduced to less than the basic advantage, the industry would be in a strong competitive position. If free trade were introduced, the threat of low priced imports from the United States and the accessibility of rich U.S. markets would provide the pressure and incentive for this reorganization.

The most difficult data to acquire in this analysis are comparative prices in Canada and the United States (P). This information was not available for the six industries included in this category. But tariff information was available; hence, it was possible to approximate roughly the *maximum* Canadian price allowed by protection (the U.S. price plus the Canadian tariff).[9] The diagrams are based on this calculation; but the conclusions of this section follow as long as these industries use *any* (or all) of their available protection. Evidence of previous studies is that Canadian industries generally do use at least some of their available protection;[10] indirect supporting evidence is also provided below for one of these industries (electrical equipment).

However, it is quite possible that one (or more) of these six industries does *not* use any of its available protection. In this case it should be classified in the first category above; consequently, it would be able to compete without reorganization and presumably should support any move toward general free trade on the grounds of its improved access to U.S. markets.

The industries shown in Figures 7 to 9 exhibit the same overall pattern, illustrated by the electrical industrial equipment industry,

[9] This approximation cannot be taken as a firm limit on the maximum, but it is a reasonable estimate. The Canadian industry may also receive "protection" from distance and transport costs.
[10] See John H. Young, *Canadian Commercial Policy* (Ottawa: Royal Commission on Canada's Economic Prospects, 1957); and H. Edward English, *Industrial Structure in Canada's International Competitive Position* (Montreal: Canadian Trade Committee, 1964).

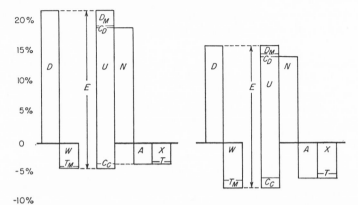

Figure 7. Cost analysis for 1961: (left) electrical industrial equipment; (right) asbestos products (see Table 30). The baseline represents U.S. wholesale price. Exchange rate: $1.00 Can. = $1.00 U.S.

shown in Figure 7. This industry,[11] which takes in about 20 percent of the total Canadian electrical machinery and apparatus sector and includes such items as electric dynamos, generators, motors, transformers, meters, switches, and electric welding apparatus,

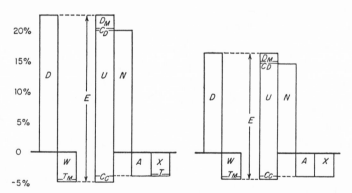

Figure 8. Cost analysis for 1961: (left) tires; (right) plywood and veneers (see Table 30). The baseline represents U.S. wholesale price. Exchange rate: $1.00 Can. = $1.00 U.S.

[11] As defined in D.B.S., *Standard Industrial Classification Manual*, 1960. This sector is roughly comparable to the following U.S. four-digit industries: 3611 to 3613, and 3621 to 3623.

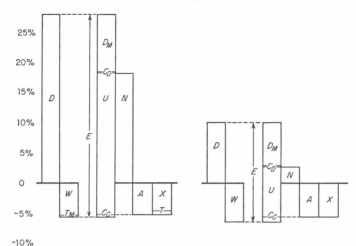

Figure 9. Cost analysis for 1961: (left) men's clothing; (right) trade books (see Table 30). The baseline represents U.S. wholesale price. Exchange rate: $1.00 Can. = $1.00 U.S.

is protected by an average Canadian tariff of over 22 percent.[12] In addition, Canadian producers have advantages of about 4 percent, owing largely to lower Canadian wages. There are offsetting disadvantages of about one percent attributable to higher interest rates and other capital carrying costs and about 3 percent owing to protection on inputs.[13] In addition, there are costs attributable to the differences in organization and efficiency of the Canadian and U.S. industries.

[12] With the exception of steam turbo generators and electric welding apparatus, both of which are subject to M.F.N. duties of 20 percent (Canadian tariff item 446), the products listed have Canadian duties (item 445) of 22.5 percent.

[13] The general method of estimating the costs of protection of inputs in the industry studies has been to assume that Canadian producers of the inputs use the full amount of their protection. This procedure has not been followed for the aluminum input for the electrical industry, since Canadian prices of aluminum are about 10 percent less than U.S. prices, in spite of the Canadian tariff of about 20 percent. See Clarence L. Barber, *The Canadian Electrical Manufacturing Industry* (Ottawa: Royal Commission on Canada's Economic Prospects, 1956), p. 57. Instead, the Canadian aluminum advantage has been subtracted from the tariff disadvantages to give the net figure of 2.65 percent shown in Figure 7.

In the previous section and in the chapter on automobiles, the "unexplained residual" (U) could be attributed to errors of estimate and differences in efficiency between the two countries. Because comparative price information is not available, the unexplained residual for electrical equipment includes a price component as well, that is, the difference between the actual price of Canadian goods and the U.S. price plus Canadian duty. If the Canadian producer is not now using all his available protection, this price component in U is increased, and the unexplained residual attributable to differences in efficiency is reduced.[14]

In the absence of price data, therefore, it is not possible to estimate differences of efficiency even in the imperfect way in which this was done in the previous section. Some idea of the probable range of comparative prices may, however, be gained indirectly. Table 34 shows that more than one quarter of new Cana-

TABLE 34. *Import Share of Canadian Market for Selected Electrical Products (in percent).*

Product	1937	1950	1952	1958	1961
Instruments and meters	15.3	29.3	40.2[a]	26.6[a]	25.7
Motors and parts	23.7	22.4	31.6	27.0	29.0
Generators and parts	54.1	35.7	50.8	31.9	42.6
Switchgear and protective equipment	21.1	16.5	19.1	N.A.	28.7
Transformers and parts	4.4	5.2	7.0	11.6	13.2
Industrial control equipment	34.1	44.3	38.0	N.A.	36.7

Sources: F. A. Knox, *The Canadian Electrical Manufacturing Industry: An Economic Analysis* (Canadian Electrical Manufacturers Association, 1955), p. 11; Clarence L. Barber, *The Canadian Electrical Manufacturing Industry* (Ottawa: Royal Commission on Canada's Economic Prospects, 1956).
[a] The decline in this category between 1952 and 1958 can be explained by a change in trade classifications in this period.

dian electrical industrial equipment was imported for all major categories except transformers (and, in some years, switchgear). This large percentage of imports suggests that Canadian prices

[14] The definition of N in these diagrams also must be interpreted differently. Since it is calculated from the maximum price allowed by the Canadian tariff, it represents the maximum net protection *available* to the producer. How much of this he actually *uses* cannot be estimated because there is no information on his selling price.

are close to the maximum[15] permitted by the U.S. price plus the Canadian duty. Such a conclusion is not, however, a logical necessity: with a wide range of specialized products being manufactured by the industry, it is possible that imports could be concentrated on specialized items not made in Canada. Nevertheless, it seems reasonable, on the basis of the limited information available, to conclude that much or all of its Canadian protection is used by this industry, and hence to conclude that most of the unexplained residual is attributable to differences in efficiency between the U.S. and Canadian industries and, specifically, to the greater degree of specialization by U.S. producers.[16]

With free trade, this unexplained residual will tend to disappear if Canadian producers successfully concentrate production and if they export to the United States the relatively limited range of products in which they specialize. The feasibility of this sort of specialization is suggested [17] by the absolute advantage the industry would enjoy under free trade: the basic Canadian advantage of approximately 4 percent (owing mainly to lower Canadian wages)[18] outweighs basic disadvantages of approximately one percent.

The other five subsectors studied in this section (tires, asbestos products, plywood,[19] men's clothing, and trade books) are in a

[15] In fact, the Canadian price could slightly exceed this limit, to the degree that administration or transport costs might raise the price of competing imports above the U.S. price plus Canadian duty.

[16] The wider range of products manufactured by Canadian firms, and the consequent higher costs of tooling for small-volume production runs, are discussed by F. A. Knox, *The Canadian Electrical Manufacturing Industry: An Economic Analysis* (Canadian Electrical Manufacturers Association, 1955), pp. 44–45.

[17] But by no means insured; see the concluding section of this chapter.

[18] Canadian wage rates were estimated to be 23 percent below U.S. rates. This figure was computed from comparative national wage data for the electrical industrial equipment subsector for 1961. Comparable regional data for the subsector are not available. If wages for the whole electrical machinery and apparatus industry were compared for the regions where electrical industrial equipment production is concentrated (Middle Atlantic and Ontario), the Canadian advantage would be somewhat greater.

[19] Because plywood shipped from Washington State to the U.S. East Coast must be moved in U.S. vessels, the cost of transporting B.C. plywood to the U.S. East Coast has been less than that of shipping Washington State plywood. As it is unclear what would be done about shipping

situation similar to that of electrical industrial equipment in most respects. With access to the U.S. market and reorganization toward U.S. standards of efficiency, the electrical equipment producer would enjoy a free trade absolute advantage (X) of about 3 percent; in the other five subsectors, the absolute advantage for the reorganized Canadian producer would fall between 3 and 6 percent. Once again, the degree of reorganization necessary for these producers to approach U.S. standards of efficiency cannot be deduced directly from the unexplained residual in the diagrams; it depends partly on the present use of available tariff protection by Canadian producers.

Two products, men's clothing and trade books, differ in one important respect from the other four industries in this section. Both use large amounts of protected material inputs. Where these inputs are imported or where the domestic Canadian producer of these inputs charges as much as his tariff protection will allow,[20] the result is that costs of production will be raised more by expensive inputs than they will be lowered by Canadian advantages (mainly lower wages). Canadian protection on inputs may create a situation where, in spite of lower Canadian wages, Canadian producers are unable to sell at the U.S. price, even if their productive efficiency is up to U.S. standards. Thus, if free trade were to be established in either of these products but not across the board, the Canadian producer would have difficulty in surviving. He would be in a strong competitive position only if free trade were to be established across the board; then these inputs would no longer be protected and high priced, but his natural cost advantages would remain. These two examples illustrate the major problem in any partial approach to free trade: the producers of some goods may find that their natural advantage is wiped out by protection on inputs that have not been made part of the free trade arrangement.

---

regulations in the event of free trade between the U.S. and Canada, no Canadian transportation advantage has been shown in Figure 8; the item T has been entered as zero.

[20] The calculations behind these diagrams are based on the assumption that Canadian producers of protected inputs do, in fact, charge as high a price as Canadian protection will allow, that is, the U.S. price plus Canadian duty. Thus, item D_M should be considered a maximum estimate in each diagram.

Canadian Absolute Disadvantage under Free Trade:
Reorganization Not Sufficient to Allow Survival

Two of the Canadian industries studied — wrapping paper and
synthetic resins (Figure 10) — would seem to be in an unfavorable free trade position because in both instances the unexplained residual *U* lies entirely above the baseline. Hence, even
if they were to reorganize under free trade to U.S. levels of
efficiency, their costs would remain above the U.S. level; or, to

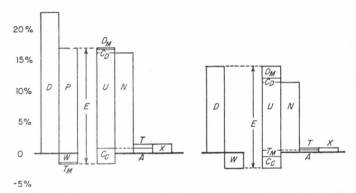

Figure 10. Cost analysis for 1961: (left) wrapping paper; (right) synthetic
resins (see Table 30). The baseline represents U.S. wholesale
price. Exchange rate: $1.00 Can. = $1.00 U.S.

restate, their basic disadvantages (especially higher Canadian
capital costs and higher transport costs on inputs) more than offset
their basic advantages (lower wages).[21]

The key reason these industries would be at a free trade disadvantage is that they are both capital intensive.[22] The wage ad-

[21] Note in Figure 10 that price information was available for wrapping
paper but not for synthetic resins. Hence *N* in this diagram represents net
protection used by wrapping paper producers, but net protection available
for synthetic resins.

[22] A free trade disadvantage is also likely to show up in industries in the
tobacco products group. This was the only sector where the evidence of
Part I pointed to an unambiguous disadvantage for Canadian locations.
Hence, except for subindustries that may have much more favorable cost
conditions than this sector as a whole, it may be concluded that the prospects for Canadian free trade growth in this sector are not good. For this

vantage of the Canadian location does not play as significant a role in reducing costs as it does for other industries; moreover, the higher cost of carrying capital in Canada does affect costs substantially because of heavy capital requirements. In the case of wrapping paper, higher capital costs more than offset Canadian labor cost advantages; in the case of synthetic resins, Canadian labor cost advantages are offset by a combination of these higher Canadian capital costs and higher costs due to greater distance from major sources of input supplies.

Because cost conditions in these industries suggest that firms located in Canada would have difficulty in competing in a free trade area, rationalization and reorganization would simply not be sufficient to allow either entry into U.S. markets or retention of Canadian markets. Industries falling in this category have received protection from the Canadian tariff in the classic sense. Protection has been a necessary condition for their survival; without the tariff, it is unlikely that they would exist in Canada. It must be stressed, however, that this conclusion does not necessarily apply to other products in the sectors from which these items were chosen.

Industries for Which Transport Charges on
Final Goods Are Apparently Critical

There is one additional possibility, illustrated by steel pipes and tubes in Figure 11. In this capital-intensive industry, higher capital costs almost offset the Canadian wage advantage. Hence, under free trade this industry would enjoy a small absolute advantage (A) — *but only provided* it could successfully rationalize its operations and eliminate higher costs due to restricted market size (U). (This proviso is critical, as will be seen below.) Moreover,

---

reason it was deemed unnecessary to examine this sector in greater detail. The subindustries actually studied in Part III were selected, one from each of the other fourteen sectors; all of these sectors appeared likely to provide some advantages to Canada — at least in some lines. The procedure of selecting sample industries in Part III only from favorably situated sectors will of course tend to bias our findings in a favorable direction. But this bias is of little practical consequence, since only one sector was excluded; note also that it is by far the least important sector.

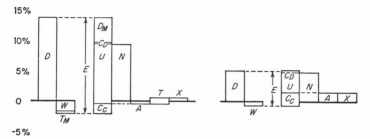

Figure 11. Cost analysis for 1961: (left) steel pipes and tubes; (right) gasoline (see Table 30). The baseline represents U.S. wholesale price. Exchange rate: $1.00 Can. = $1.00 U.S.

this advantage would apply *only* to its sales in Canada, not to its sales in the United States. This follows from the importance of transport costs on final products (T); for sales in the United States this disadvantage for the Canadian producer would more than offset his cost advantages (T straddles the baseline in Figure 11). (Of course, these same transport charges increase his advantage over his U.S. competition in the Canadian market.)

In brief, under free trade the Canadian producer will be unable to compete in the U.S. market; however, he will be in a strong competitive position in the Canadian market, provided he can achieve the present U.S. level of productive efficiency. The critical question is whether this level of efficiency is possible within the confines of the Canadian market.

The question is difficult to answer, especially since relative price information is not available. Hence, there is no way of knowing how much of its available protection the Canadian industry has been using. If it could be established that none of this net protection is now being used (that Canadian prices are within 4 percent of U.S. prices), it would imply that the Canadian industry had already achieved a U.S. level of efficiency within the Canadian market.[23] The Canadian industry would therefore be able to survive under free trade on the basis of its present techniques and the automatic 4 percent reduction in its costs from the abolition

[23] The reader will observe that the issue is somewhat more complicated than this. Present Canadian exports of this good and selling price in the U.S. market would also have to be examined.

of duties on its inputs. However, suppose one found that Canadian producers were now using some of their available net protection (that their prices exceeded those in the U.S. by more than 4 percent). This would suggest higher costs in the restricted Canadian market; and if these higher costs were due to technical diseconomies of scale in production, the free trade prospects of this industry would not be encouraging.[24] In this special case, distance to U.S. markets would become the critical disability of Canadian producers, and duty free access to U.S. markets would not offer a solution to the problem of Canadian scale inefficiency.[25]

[24] Technical scale effects in production cannot be overcome by duty free access to the U.S. market because transport costs (T) prevent this. However, Canadian prices and costs could be higher because of *other* inefficiencies of market size — that is, Canadian producers may have simply become less flexible and efficient in their less competitive milieu; this inefficiency could be eliminated as the Canadian tariff is removed. If present higher Canadian price is due only to this latter type of inefficiency, then it follows that no technical scale problems are involved in present production for the Canadian market only. And, even restricted to the Canadian market, the industry should be able to survive under free trade — provided, of course, it can successfully approach U.S. standards of managerial efficiency.

This is the only case in which "economies of market size" (U) must be divided for analytical purposes into technical scale effects in production and other inefficiencies of a small market. In other instances, the mix of these two effects is relatively unimportant because there will be pressures operating towards elimination of both in the event of free trade.

[25] Two other factors might make Canadian pipe production more attractive than this analysis suggests. First, it might be possible to concentrate on specialized types of pipe. The evaluation of this possibility would require extensive information about the internal structure of the industry. The second possibility is that technological changes might improve the position of the Canadian industry relative to the U.S. industry.

Since 1961, the year on which the data on the pipe industry are based, there has apparently been some improvement in the position of the Canadian steel industry vis-à-vis the U.S. steel industry, over and above the favorable effects of the decline in the international value of the Canadian dollar. However, in spite of this specific example, the possibilities of differential technological change between the two countries should be taken as a factor introducing an additional element of general inaccuracy and uncertainty into the estimates of the possible reactions to free trade, rather than as grounds for considering the results to be generally biased in one way or the other.

There are two conflicting general propositions regarding the probable effects of technological change on the competitive positions of countries at different levels of productivity. Both of these propositions have been made most frequently with respect to U.S. trade with Western Europe (including

Special Cases

For three of the products studied — gasoline, cotton gray, and wheat flour — government policies are sufficiently important to influence the outcome under a free trade arrangement.

Gasoline. In the United States, there is a system of import and domestic production quotas on oil. The domestic production quotas had a rationale independent of foreign complications; but once these were established, natural political pressures built up for import quotas as well. Since import quotas may be regarded as an extension of domestic quotas, the possibilities of a continuation of such quotas with free trade cannot be predicted. The issue is further complicated by restrictions imposed by the Canadian government: under the national energy policy, the market west of Ottawa is supposed to be reserved for Canadian oil.

The oil policies of the two countries raise problems which cannot be adequately dealt with here. Except for these complications, the situation in the gasoline industry is illustrated in Figure 11. This is a capital-intensive industry, in which higher Canadian capital costs more than offset the Canadian wage advantage. The Canadian industry appears, as a consequence, to be in a relatively weak competitive position under unrestricted free trade. But the major issue would continue to be the pattern of domestic and international oil quotas.

Britain) or with the underdeveloped countries, but they are logically general arguments, and presumably could be applied to Canadian-U.S. trade. According to one line of reasoning, technological change tends to cause a deterioration of the competitive position of the more advanced, high wage country, since the less advanced country is essentially copying the technology of the more advanced country. The less advanced country therefore finds technological improvement and increases in productivity less difficult than does the advanced country, whose further advance depends in large measure on new inventions. The other argument foresees a deterioration of the competitive position of the less advanced country on the grounds that the more advanced country already has an industry that is designed to develop and exploit new methods of production. Although either of these arguments might be applicable in a specific case, we see no a priori grounds for generally favoring one over the other, nor do we find evidence that one is more likely than the other to apply to the Canadian-U.S. situation in the foreseeable future. Hence, we do not believe that dynamic factors of this kind introduce a general bias into our results.

Cotton Gray. There is one important complication in cotton gray production that did not arise in any of the previous examples. In the year under consideration (1961), U.S. agricultural export subsidies resulted in U.S. cotton being priced approximately 26 percent cheaper to Canadian than to U.S. purchasers.[26] This price difference provided Canadian producers with a cost advantage of about 5 percent (item *FP* in Figure 12). This advantage is entered

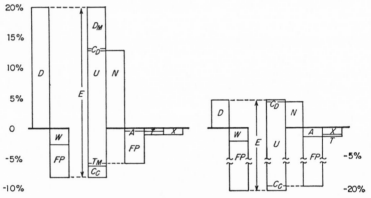

Figure 12. Cost analysis for industries with farm support, 1961: (left) cotton gray; (right) wheat flour (see Table 30). The baseline represents U.S. wholesale price. Exchange rate: $1.00 Can. = $1.00 U.S.

below the Canadian wage advantage; it results in a larger margin of Canadian advantages to be explained and in a larger unexplained residual (*U*).

No price comparison (*P*) is shown in this diagram. However, fragmentary information suggests a Canadian domestic price at least as high as the U.S. price plus the Canadian tariff. This high price, combined with the cotton subsidy to Canadian producers, results in a large unexplained residual (*U*) and strongly implies that either limited Canadian production runs now involve substantial loss of economies of scale, or that the lower Canadian

[26] The U.S. domestic price of cotton was about $0.33 per lb. as compared with an export price of about $0.245.

competitive pressures have allowed other inefficiencies to creep in.[27]

By 1964 the U.S. export subsidies were extended to cotton supplies destined for domestic use, thus eliminating the disadvantage of U.S. textile producers. Because of this legislative change, the item *FP* in Figure 12 will not occur in the future, whether there is free trade or not. Therefore, *FP* has been subtracted in the third last column, leaving a deduced Canadian absolute advantage in the event of free trade of less than one percent.

It should be stressed that cotton gray was not chosen as being typical of the textile industry; rather, it was chosen because quality differences in more representative products made comparisons extremely difficult. Thus, the results in the cotton gray case are not necessarily applicable to the textile area as a whole. For a more comprehensive view of the free trade position of the textile industry, reference should be made to the data in Part I.

Wheat Flour. There is a similar U.S. farm program for wheat; the U.S. price support for this important input also raised costs of U.S. domestic producers and thus gave Canadian flour millers an advantage of approximately 18 percent of total costs (item *FP* in Figure 12). In addition, lower Canadian wages provided an advantage of about 2 percent. Thus, if the farm program in the United States were to remain unchanged, Canadian millers would enjoy a basic cost advantage of approximately 20 percent in the event of free trade.

It is very unlikely that the U.S. farm program would remain unchanged, however. Certainly the 18 percent Canadian advantage due to the wheat price differential cannot be defended on the grounds of economic efficiency. One possible change would be to make the U.S. export subsidy available to domestic users, as was done in the case of cotton. This move would, however, raise a number of complications, not the least being the cost to the U.S. Treasury. If, in spite of such difficulties, a method were found of

---

[27] Economies of scale are relatively smaller in the textile industry than in heavy industry; therefore, the second of the two suggested explanations for *U* would seem to be more important. On the limited economies of scale in textiles, see E. B. Alderfer and H. E. Michl, *Economics of American Industry*, 3rd ed. (New York: McGraw Hill, 1957), pp. 342–343.

equalizing wheat prices to U.S. and Canadian mills, the Canadian millers would be left with a basic advantage of just over one percent.

Industry Studies: Conclusions

In this chapter and the one preceding, fourteen sample industries have been examined, one from each of the major industrial groups of Part I.[28] The three main objectives in breaking down the present costs of each industry were: first, to establish the net protection allowed by the entire Canadian tariff structure; second, to examine why and by how much costs in Canada are higher because of protection; and third, to determine which industries would have favorable prospects under free trade. In addition, it has been shown how the analytical framework of this section can easily be modified to take account of government subsidy programs that alter industry costs, such as the farm programs in cotton and wheat. And, in the auto chapter, the answers to two perplexing problems have been suggested. Why has there not been greater specialization of production in the limited Canadian market? And why have Canadian producers not specialized for export to the United States?

It must be confessed that our prime interest throughout has been the development and application of an analytical method, rather than the details of each industry studied. But even from the limited detail available, it has been possible to illustrate most of the major possible outcomes. However, because of our theoretical focus and because of the limited resources available for collecting data, it seems likely that one or more of our marginal industries (for example, steel pipes and tubes) in fact should be classified in another category. Clearly, policy prescriptions for any of these industries should be deferred until the questions raised have been examined in greater detail.

Despite this caveat, the overall picture provided by these studies seems reasonably clear and confirms our findings in Part I.[29]

---

[28] Excluding only the miscellaneous and tobacco groups.

[29] Each industry in Part III was analyzed for 1958 as well as 1961. The results were similar.

With free trade, most Canadian industries would enjoy an absolute cost advantage. (The exceptions to this rule are the highly capital-intensive industries; unless free trade has major effects on the Canadian capital market,[30] high interest rates in Canada will more than offset their favorable wage rates.) But most of the favorably situated Canadian industries must reorganize; unless present higher Canadian costs due to restricted Canadian market size can be overcome — and with free trade there seems to be no reason why they cannot[31] — these industries will be unable to achieve their potential cost advantage.

It should be emphasized again that this discussion is in terms of *absolute* advantage — that is, comparative costs at the present wage and exchange rate.[32] But, with the one exception noted below, the relevant indicator of an industry's prospects in the event of across-the-board free trade is *comparative* advantage — after the adjustment of wages and exchange to a new equilibrium level. The likely appreciation of both Canadian wages and the Canadian dollar deduced in Chapter 11 is confirmed here, since a majority of the sample industries studied would enjoy an absolute cost advantage under free trade. As Canadian costs rise with this wage and exchange appreciation,[33] the number of Canadian industries with an advantage would be reduced, and Canada would specialize in the reduced range of products.[34]

Hence, during the course of this adjustment process, it is likely that some of the favorably situated industries studied above would find their cost advantage slipping away. This possibility should

[30] See Chapter 11.

[31] Except, possibly, in cases similar to steel pipes and tubes, in which transport costs to U.S. markets may prevent increased Canadian scale.

[32] More precisely, at the exchange rate prevailing in the base year of this study. Except for the auto study (1963), 1961 data were used in all other comparisons, with a prevailing rate approximately of parity. To simplify both the calculations and interpretation, no adjustment has been made for the decrease in value of the Canadian dollar since that time. However, this has made the present relative position of Canadian producers better than the diagrams in this section imply. Or to put it another way, any expected free trade appreciation in the Canadian exchange rate toward parity (see Chapter 11) is already built into these diagrams.

[33] That is, as the U.S. baseline shifts down in these diagrams.

[34] Because of the relative size of the two economies, Canadian specialization need occur only in a minority of internationally traded goods.

be noted, for example, in a marginal industry like steel pipes and tubes. However, the unfavorable eventual prospect for steel pipes and tubes does not imply that the entire Canadian steel industry will be unable to compete, any more than the favorable prospect in upper shoe leather implies that Canadian producers will eventually dominate North American sales in all leather products. In both leather and steel, it is likely that Canadians will specialize in the small proportion of lines in which they enjoy the most favorable cost conditions. If Canadian specialization occurs in this way (as seems likely) in, say, one quarter or one tenth of the subindustries in each broad industrial grouping, any individual one of the sample subindustries we have selected is unlikely to exhibit an eventual Canadian comparative advantage, especially since the products in Part III were selected because they were representative of their industrial group. Thus, a product with atypical inputs,[35] which can be produced in Canada at particularly favorable costs, is even less likely to have been chosen. Yet such an item is the prime candidate for Canadian specialization.

Absolute advantage becomes the appropriate indicator of free trade prospects only in one instance: a single industry free trade scheme. But in this case, special account must be taken of higher costs in Canada because of protection that remains on inputs. This study identified two products (men's clothing and trade books) that may have favorable prospects under general free trade but unfavorable prospects because of higher input costs under a single industry scheme. The obvious advantage of such a scheme is opening the U.S. market; but because it would eliminate all the protection on the product involved and leave inputs protected, it forces a firm to operate under negative net protection.

For the Canadian producer, there are clearly pros and cons in comparing a single industry scheme with complete free trade. Under a single industry plan, he has to contend with negative protection;[36] but under complete free trade he may have to contend with a long-term unfavorable shift in the wage and exchange level quite un-

---

[35] For example, exceptionally heavy labor requirements.

[36] If the single industry selected is his own. It goes without saying that everyone is in favor of free trade in some (or any) other industry.

related to his own productivity and profit.[37] Both schemes provide the same benefit: that of opening the U.S. market to duty free entry of his product.

[37] Under a single industry scheme he may, of course, find pressure for a wage increase building up if his profits increase. But this is obviously a more manageable situation.

15

THE INCIDENCE OF TARIFFS
WHEN THERE ARE ECONOMIES
OF MARKET SIZE

If the advantages of a free trade arrangement are to be weighed against possible disadvantages, a study of the magnitudes involved will aid in the decision-making process. Although it is not possible, given the present state of the art, to measure the cost and incidence of protection with any high degree of precision, useful rough estimates may be derived.

The first sections of this chapter deal with theoretical difficulties. The discussion is built on recent studies, such as those on the cost of protection by Young and Johnson[1] and, more broadly, those on the cost of indirect taxation.[2] One major addition is made to this literature: detailed attention is given to tariff incidence when costs

[1] John H. Young, *Canadian Commercial Policy* (Ottawa: Royal Commission on Canada's Economic Prospects, 1957), Part III; Harry G. Johnson, "The Cost of Protection and the Scientific Tariff," *Journal of Political Economy*, 68:327–345 (August 1960). The recent literature on the cost of tariffs is summarized and discussed in A. J. Reitsma, "The 'Excess Costs' of a Tariff and Their Measurement," *Economic Record*, 37:442–455 (December 1961). For a discussion and criticism of earlier literature on measuring the cost of protection, see Jacob Viner, *Studies in the Theory of International Trade* (New York: Harper, 1937), pp. 589–593.

[2] For example, Arnold Harberger, "Taxation, Resource Allocation and Welfare," in *The Role of Direct and Indirect Taxes in the Federal Revenue System*, Conference Report of the National Bureau of Economic Research and the Brookings Institution (Princeton: Princeton University Press, 1964), pp. 25–70.

fall as the size of the market increases.[3] The studies of Part III of this book indicate that North American tariffs have limited the size of the market open to Canadian producers and have, as a consequence, raised costs; hence, any study based on the assumption of constant or increasing costs would be inadequate. The recent estimates of the cost of protection for a number of countries, which fall in the range from 0.05 percent to 4 percent of national income,[4] are all based on the assumption of constant or rising costs; thus regardless of how appropriate they may be for other cases, these methods would seriously underestimate the costs of North American protection. It is argued later in this chapter that the cost from limiting the scale of production has been more important for

[3] Recall that our "economies of market size" include not only technology-based economies of scale, but also the effects of larger markets on the competitive conditions within industries; this category therefore includes not only movements along cost curves which decline as output increases but also downward shifts of cost curves that result from the competitive pressures associated with large markets. See the discussion in Chapter 12 above.

[4] One twentieth of one percent was Verdoorn's estimate of the gains to be made by the EEC countries by the removal of internal tariff barriers. The basis for, and limitations of, this estimate may be found in Tibor Scitovsky, *Economic Theory and Western European Integration* (Stanford: Stanford University Press, 1958), p. 67. Although Scitovsky noted a number of limitations to Verdoorn's estimate, he concluded that the adjustments which might be made would lead to only "insignificant" changes in the estimate unless economies of scale were considered. However, Scitovsky did not adjust Verdoorn's estimate by including the possibility of decreasing costs; he preferred to keep this issue for separate treatment in his Part III, where he analyzed it largely in terms of the dynamic effects of the economies of scale. In particular, he considered larger markets and exposure to competition to be major incentives to adopt the newest methods. In the sections below on the cost of tariffs and on the consumption effects of protection, we attempt to integrate increasing returns into the discussion of the welfare implications of tariff reductions. This is done in terms of relative statics. In addition it should be recognized that Scitovsky's dynamic considerations may be important, but no attempt will be made here to quantify them.

Other estimates of the cost of protection may be found. Young's estimate of the cost of the Canadian tariff of about 4 percent of Gross National Expenditure will be used as a point of departure in our study below. In addition, the tariff cost to Chile has been estimated as "no more than 2½ percent of national income" by Arnold Harberger, "The Fundamentals of Economic Progress in Underdeveloped Countries: Using the Resources at Hand More Effectively," *American Economic Review*, 55:135 (May 1959).

Canada than the consumers' surplus cost, which has heretofore dominated the discussion. Since scale limitations are much more important to Canada than to the United States, the cost of the two tariffs to Canada will be taken as the central theme of this chapter, with the costs to the United States considered in one of the last sections.

It should be noted in passing that a low percentage estimate of the cost of protection does not imply that commercial policy is unimportant. Similar studies of major innovations indicate that their percentage effect on GNP was also rather small. Robert W. Fogel, for example, has estimated that the social saving attributable to the U.S. railroads in the transportation of agricultural products in the late nineteenth century was less than 2 percent of national income, and the savings in the transportation of all products was "well below" 5 percent of GNP;[5] yet the development of the railroads in the United States in the nineteenth century can scarcely be considered a matter of small importance.

Is the Burden Negative?

If the arguments for protection are valid, it is possible that the gains from the tariff may outweigh its cost. Therefore it is necessary to consider the case for protection in the Canadian context; this will indicate possible limitations of the discussion of tariff costs below.

The Political Question. Whether tariffs are necessary for national unity and independence is a difficult question, involving a number of major considerations on which the economist can claim no particular authority. However, it cannot be assumed that free trade between Canada and the United States would necessarily lead to political union. A greater degree of policy harmonization might occur, not as a result of any irresistible pressure, but rather because free trade would call attention to the gains that can be achieved in any case from harmonizing economic policies. Several

---

[5] Robert W. Fogel, *Railroads and American Economic Growth* (Baltimore: Johns Hopkins Press, 1964), pp. 211, 219, 223. Fogel's estimates are based on the difference between the costs of railroad transportation and the best alternatives.

questions with political implications are considered below in Chapter 17.

Although there is evidence that tariffs may contribute to national unity, contrary cases exist in which tariffs have been a major divisive influence within countries (for example, in dividing the U.S. North and South between 1830 and 1860). The broad political implications of the tariff are not clear.

The Level of Unemployment. Under certain circumstances, the most important being that foreign countries set their tariffs independently of the home country's tariff levels, protection may increase employment by shifting purchases from foreign to domestic goods. However, as tariffs tend to exacerbate other countries' unemployment problems, this independence condition cannot be taken as a foregone conclusion.

If unemployment is a problem, monetary and fiscal policies are much more effective weapons than tariffs for a number of reasons. They are more easily reversed if the problem of unemployment gives way to that of inflation. They are intrinsically less inflationary than tariffs[6] and therefore less likely to lead to conflict between the goals of full employment and stable prices. To some extent, the existence of tariffs makes domestic antitrust policies an ineffective means of protecting the consumer from high prices. If antitrust action splits up firms, it may result in higher costs; and tariffs provide the necessary protection for higher prices. A superior means of holding down consumer prices would be to open the domestic Canadian market to international competition.

Insofar as a reciprocal rather than a unilateral tariff reduction is being considered, the employment case for tariffs is even weaker; although the elimination of the Canadian tariff would result in some substitution of imported for domestic goods, the elimination of the U.S. tariff would increase the demand for Canadian goods. Hence both the magnitude *and* direction of change in the short-run level of aggregate demand would be uncertain. Thus, the argument against reciprocal tariff reductions on unemployment grounds

[6] Because tariffs directly raise prices. In contrast, the initial impact of expansionary monetary and fiscal policies is a reduction in interest and tax costs. It is, of course, true that, once full employment is approached, expansion policies will cause inflation.

rests on the degree to which disturbances themselves cause unemployment (the "structural" argument) rather than on the effect of tariffs on aggregate demand. Because reciprocal tariff reductions will lead to a fall in the demand for some products and an increase for others, some short-run unemployment may result from institutional barriers impeding the transfer of resources. Such unemployment may, however, be mitigated by a gradual rather than a sudden removal of tariffs and by policies that increase the mobility of factors.

The Terms of Trade. A classic argument for tariffs is that they tend to lower the world price of imports compared to the world price of exports. Thus, the country receives more in return for each unit of exports, and the level of real income may possibly be raised.[7]

In practice, the degree to which Canada can influence the world (or U.S.) prices of the goods in which she trades is limited, particularly when attention is turned from raw materials to the industrial sectors where the most important impacts of tariff reduction would be felt. The terms of trade argument for protection loses further significance if a reciprocal reduction of tariffs is considered; whatever small changes in the terms of trade occur as a result of such a reduction may be to Canada's advantage rather than to her disadvantage.[8] Thus, along with the unemployment issue, the terms of trade objection to tariff removal tend to disappear when reciprocal reductions are considered; the net effects of the reductions may be in either direction.

Growth. Even if tariffs result in a lower level of real national income at a given point in time because of the inefficiencies they cause, the long-run level of national income may nevertheless be

[7] For a statement of the terms of trade argument for protection, see Tibor Scitovsky, "A Reconsideration of the Theory of Tariffs," in American Economic Association, *Readings in the Theory of International Trade* (Philadelphia: Blakiston, 1950).

[8] This discussion has considered only the *net barter* terms of trade. The estimate in the section on the consumption effects of protection indicates that free trade would appreciably increase the real purchasing power of factor incomes in Canada; that is, the *single factoral* terms of trade would improve. This effect would be attributable largely to the improved efficiency of Canadian industry as a result of its access to a larger market.

increased if tariffs accelerate the rate of growth.[9] The validity of the growth argument for tariffs depends on affirmative answers to two key questions: Do tariffs accelerate growth, and if so, are the advantages of this growth sufficient to outweigh the costs?

It might be argued along any of three possible lines that protection will increase the rate of growth. First, under certain circumstances tariffs may reduce the rate of unemployment and therefore increase the rate of growth. However, this is not an argument in favor of tariffs as such, but rather in favor of full employment policies. As noted above, alternative and preferable policies may be adopted in the pursuit of this goal.

According to a second line of argument, tariffs may accelerate the rate of growth by increasing the rate of savings. This case is valid only if tariffs divert resources out of sectors with low savings rates and into sectors with high savings rates.[10] It is possible, for example, that tariffs will cause a transfer of production away from raw materials and toward manufacturing, a sector dominated by corporations whose financial organization may facilitate relatively high levels of savings.

We can see no logical problem with this argument; it does, however, raise a number of major empirical issues. In the Canadian

[9] Harry Johnson, "The Cost of Protection," p. 339 has illustrated this point: "If protection reduced national income by 5 percent below the free-trade level but raised the rate of growth from 2½ percent to 3 percent per annum, in about 10¾ years national income would be at the level it would have reached under free trade, and growing more rapidly than it would have under free trade; if the rate of growth rose only from 2½ percent to 2¾ percent, the free-trade level of national income would be reached in about 21 1/3 years."

[10] The savings-growth case for protection cannot be based on the effects of tariffs on the rate of savings through its influence on the level of aggregate income. Empirical studies of savings behavior point strongly toward the conclusion that the percentage rate of savings is not appreciably influenced in the long run by the aggregate level of income. (See, for example, James S. Duesenberry, *Income, Saving, and the Theory of Consumer Behavior* (Cambridge: Harvard University Press, 1949), and the extensive recent literature on the consumption function.) What contrary evidence exists, such as that based on budget studies and short-run time series, indicates that, if anything, the rate of savings is a positive function of income. Thus, if anything, growth will strengthen the comparative-static effects of a tariff, and growth may not be used as a means of escaping the static calculations of the cost of tariffs.

case, the most important is whether protection is in fact a major influence on the proportion of resources devoted to manufacturing. The evidence in this study suggests that the answer is no, and that the most important free-trade adjustments in each country would be within the manufacturing sector rather than between manufacturing and other sectors. Thus, this argument may apply in other cases, but it does not seem to hold for Canada.

The third argument for tariffs as a stimulus to growth applies (like the one above) only if tariffs shift resources into manufacturing. As manufacturing may, under certain circumstances, be the sector of greatest technological change, an increase in its relative size might contribute to technological improvement, and therefore to growth. Again, regardless of the merit of this argument in general, it has little validity in the Canadian-U.S. case because free-trade adjustment would be primarily *within* the manufacturing sector. But if the issue of innovation is pursued further, a strong case can be made for, rather than against, free trade. Because research is an overhead, it becomes less expensive as the volume of production is increased. In forcing Canadian manufacturing specialization, free trade would bring this increased volume and research capability.

Thus, none of the above growth arguments provides a basis for Canadian protection;[11] if tariffs are to be defended, then reasons other than growth must be given.

[11] The argument that the tariff has *not* accelerated Canadian growth seems to be a strong one. Growth is, however, a very complex phenomenon, and the factors which affect its rate are imperfectly understood; it is therefore possible that some important influence has been overlooked.

However, even if it were to be concluded that the tariff does promote growth, it does not necessarily follow that protection is advisable. Such a conclusion would depend on an affirmative answer to the second key question raised in the introduction to this growth discussion: are the advantages of growth sufficient to outweigh the costs?

Growth does not have a clear claim to precedence on our scale of values; the advantages of diverting resources into investment to increase future incomes must be weighed against the satisfactions forgone from reduced current consumption. To put the issue on a personal level: it is not clear to what degree an individual should scrimp at present in order that either he or his children may live in relative affluence in the future.

If full employment is assumed, the argument that growth should be given high priority implies that the savings decisions of individuals, businesses,

The Intrinsic Desirability of Manufacturing. Although some of the discussion of the intrinsic desirability of manufacturing may, like American nostalgia for the Jeffersonian pastoral existence, be dismissed as sentimentality, at least one logical argument[12] may be put forward for stimulating manufacturing by tariffs.

E. E. Hagen has demonstrated that if the returns to labor are greater in manufacturing than in other sectors, and if these differences cannot be explained either on the grounds of greater irksomeness of work in manufacturing or of nonmarket rewards in other sectors, and if protection increases manufacturing activity, then protection may lead to a higher level of real national income than does a system of laissez-faire.[13] The protection-induced shift to the high income sectors will lead to gains in monetary income that may more than offset the adverse effects of higher prices to consumers.

Because Hagen's precondition that protection increases manufacturing activity cannot be assumed, this argument has little relevance to the analysis of free-trade effects on Canada. And even in an instance in which Hagen's preconditions are fulfilled, a result that is more desirable than protection may be achieved by a combination of taxes and subsidies.[14]

---

and the government place too great an emphasis on current as compared to future consumption. This may be: under the pressures of advertising and easy credit, "impulse buying" may result in higher present levels of consumption than would be justified by a cooler and more rational consideration. On the other hand, the sociological pressures of our acquisitive society may result in accumulation of savings at a rate that is higher than might be considered optimum. If the case for protection is to be based on growth, the free-trade growth rate must be below the independently determined optimum growth rate and to a degree sufficient that the protection-stimulated increase in growth (if any) will more than compensate for the decrease in static efficiency (if any) resulting from protection. (For an algebraic formulation of this condition, see Johnson, "The Cost of Protection," p. 340, footnote 34.) The absence of guidelines for determining the optimum growth rate would make this second question much more difficult to answer than the first.

[12] In addition to the growth argument dealt with above.

[13] E. E. Hagen, "An Economic Justification of Protectionism," *Quarterly Journal of Economics,* 72:496–514 (November 1958).

[14] As Hagen himself notes, p. 512.

There is another objection to Hagen's argument for protection. His case depends on major imperfections inhibiting the movement of the labor

Infant Industry. Some aspects of this argument have already been dealt with in the two previous subsections. The infant industry argument has also been used to justify protection when there are economies of scale; thus, tariffs may allow a domestic industry time to scale up to an efficient level. However, we shall show later that in the case of reciprocal Canadian-U.S. tariff reductions, economies of scale are a major argument in *favor* of free trade.

The other important aspect of the infant industry case for protection is that it may allow a country time to develop talents and techniques it now lacks in an activity in which it otherwise enjoys a comparative advantage. Since Canadian protection dates back well into the last century, it can hardly be justified any longer as this sort of short-term subsidy measure.

Trade Diversion. The major protectionist arguments against a reduction in tariffs are presented in the previous subsections. There is also, paradoxically, a free trade argument that can be used to oppose North American tariff reduction. Bilateral Canadian-U.S. free trade may not lead toward, but rather away from, the multilateral free trade equilibrium.

A preferential free trade arrangement will have two opposing effects on efficiency. Because of the elimination of tariffs among the members, domestic producers will be exposed to competition from within the area, and efficiency will be encouraged. On the other hand, producers within the union will be given preference over those outside; therefore, purchasers within the union may switch from an external source of supply to a less efficient source within the union. In Jacob Viner's terms, a customs union or free trade area may be primarily "trade creating," leading to more efficiency, or it may be primarily "trade diverting," leading to less efficiency.[15]

---

force into the industrial sector. A direct attack on these imperfections, by such means as education, will not only work toward an elimination of the difficulty on which the case for protection is based, but will also tend to reduce inequalities in incomes. In contrast, either protection or a taxation-subsidy scheme would reduce the real incomes of low income groups and raise the incomes of high income groups. See Jacob Viner, *International Trade and Economic Development* (Glencoe, Ill.: The Free Press, 1952), pp. 69–71.

[15] Jacob Viner, *The Customs Union Issue* (New York: Carnegie Endowment for International Peace, 1950), Chapter IV.

The complications raised by "trade diversion" will be passed over in this chapter, for several reasons. The close natural ties between the United States and Canada in manufactured products means that trade-creating effects of a preferential arrangement are likely to outweigh trade-diverting effects. Furthermore, even where trade diversion occurs, it does not necessarily involve a decline in efficiency if economies of scale are sufficiently important. For example, after the establishment of a free trade area between the United States and Canada, an American firm might switch from a European to a Canadian source of supply. This change would nevertheless be desirable if the concentration of the Canadian producer on relatively fewer and longer production runs resulted in lowering per unit costs below those in Europe.[16] In Part III, evidence has been presented suggesting such large potential Canadian gains from increased scale. Furthermore, because British Commonwealth preference now results in Canadian use of Com-

---

[16] Although his argument was stated primarily in terms of "trade diverting" as contrasted to "trade creating" effects, Viner recognized that economies of scale might tip the free trader's evaluation in favor of a customs union. See *The Customs Union Issue,* p. 52, criterion #6. However, Viner did not believe that economies of scale resulting from a customs union were likely to be great (pp. 46–47).

In passing, it might be noted that major economies of scale would solve the apparent paradox which Viner noted: both free traders and protectionists usually favor customs unions. Viner concluded (p. 41) that, "If in the case of customs unions they agree in their conclusions, it must be because they see in customs unions different sets of facts, and not because an identical customs union can meet the requirements of both the free-trader and the protectionist." However, even if the commercial policies generally advocated by protectionists and free traders are contrary, their objectives are not. The free trader's basic objective is efficiency and minimum costs of production. The protectionist's objective is not the opposite: he certainly does not want to maximize costs. Rather, he wishes to increase production in the segments of the economy that he considers particularly important. Because their objectives are not necessarily in conflict, it is possible that policies might be discovered which both the protectionist and free trader could support. A Canadian-U.S. free trade area could be such a policy. If, as the evidence suggests, there are economies of large markets, a North American free trade area could result both in lower cost and a higher volume of manufacturing in Canada. This would satisfy the objectives of both protectionist and free trader, and resolve the paradox noted by Viner.

For a further discussion of the possibility that policies may reasonably gain the support of both "free traders" and "protectionists," see Appendices A and B.

monwealth rather than (more efficient?) U.S. sources of supply, formation of a free trade area may eliminate any trade diversion of this kind existing at present and allow substitution of lower cost for higher cost sources of supply.[17]

In this chapter a first approximation of the cost and incidence of North American protection will be derived without reference to trading complications with third countries; this method appears justified because any trade diversion is likely to be small compared to both trade creation and the reduction of trade diversion that now exists because of Commonwealth preference.

Conclusions. In the preceding sections, it has been concluded that the standard logical arguments for the tariff are of little relevance to the Canadian-U.S. case, for three major reasons: first, these arguments usually apply to unilateral tariff elimination, rather than the reciprocal elimination analyzed in this study; second, they depend on a free trade diversion of resources out of manufacturing — and the evidence indicates that this would not occur to any major degree in the Canadian case; and third, other (monetary and fiscal) policies can be shown to be preferable means for achieving economic objectives. The political case for protection provides the one possible exception: although the more extended

---

[17] In his *Theory of Customs Unions* (Amsterdam: North Holland Publishing Co., 1955), James Meade has provided an additional reason for modifying Viner's conclusion that trade diversion is unfortunate from the viewpoint of the free trader. Meade noted that Viner's discussion was exclusively in terms of the costs of production; yet tariffs are unfortunate not only because they encourage high-cost production, but also because they distort consumption patterns.

Meade's point may be illustrated with a hypothetical example, in which constant costs are assumed. Suppose that before the establishment of a common market, Canada had a tariff of fifty percent on cameras, but nevertheless imported them from Germany. A German camera costing $20 would, therefore, sell for the equivalent of $30 (plus transportation charges) in Canada. If, after the establishment of the union, the Canadians imported U.S. cameras of equivalent quality for $21, there would be a loss in the sense that the Canadians would be switching to a high-cost ($21) source of supply from a low-cost ($20) source. (The Canadian tariff of $10 on German cameras adds to government revenue; this $10 is therefore not a real cost.) However, cameras would now become cheaper in Canada, and therefore more would be purchased. The consumers' surplus on these additional sales might more than offset the increase in costs of $1 per unit on the original volume of sales; a net gain might therefore result.

discussion in Part IV suggests that one should be skeptical of political arguments, this issue involves too many complexities and imponderables to allow definite conclusions.

In brief, the assumptions on which the economic case for protection is based are highly restrictive and they generally do not apply to the Canadian-U.S. situation. It is therefore appropriate to turn to a consideration of the economic burdens of North American protection.

The Cost of Protection: Theoretical Issues When Costs Are Constant or Rising

The estimate of the cost of the Canadian tariff to Canada made by John H. Young in his study for the Royal Commission on Canada's Economic Prospects is taken as our point of departure. The clearest cost of the Canadian tariff is in the higher prices which Canadian consumers have to pay for goods. By calculating the higher payments of Canadian consumers for protected goods, and by subtracting the tariff revenues of the Canadian Government,[18] Young found this cash cost in 1954 to be between $0.6 billion and $0.75 billion, or about 3.5 percent to 4.5 percent of gross private expenditure net of indirect taxes.[19] Harry Johnson considered Young's estimate inaccurate because two effects of the tariff had been omitted, namely, the reduction in the quantity consumed of the protected items[20] and the increase in the incomes of the factors of production in the protected industry.[21]

These issues are clarified in Figure 13. The effects of a tariff GH are shown, on the assumption that the supply price of imports (GS_A) is not affected by purchases of the country under consideration. An abolition of the tariff GH would result in a fall in the domestic price from OH to OG; home production would fall from OU to OR; consumption would rise from OV to OW; and

---

[18] And, where important, transportation costs. See John H. Young, *Canadian Commercial Policy*, p. 166.

[19] *Ibid.*, pp. 68–73.

[20] Cf., Meade's criticism of Viner, mentioned above, footnote 17.

[21] Harry G. Johnson, "The Cost of Protection," p. 334. Young had discussed the possibility of tariffs affecting Canadian incomes in his seventh chapter; however, such effects were not included in his 3.5 to 4.5 percent estimate. See Young, p. 65.

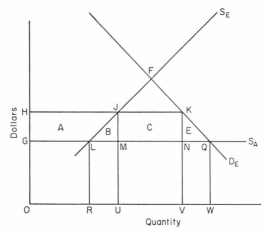

Figure 13. Estimation of the cost of tariffs: increasing cost industries.

imports would increase from *UV* to *RW*. Since the cost of the tariff on all products rather than on a single product is under consideration, the equilibrium supply and demand curves (S_E and D_E) are not Marshallian partial-equilibrium curves but represent equilibrium domestic responses as all tariffs are reduced.[22] That is, *OW* represents the demand and *OR* the domestic supply for this

[22] The demand curve shown in Figure 13 is different from the constant-utility curve used in Johnson, "The Cost of Protection." There are both major advantages and major disadvantages in using constant utility curves. They require an estimate not only of market responses, but also of the marginal utility of money; thus a major difficulty is added to an already complex problem of estimating demand curves. On practical grounds, it may reasonably be doubted that the added precision from a constant utility estimate will be significant compared to the probable error in estimating demand responses that will be involved in any case.

It is true that, if areas of utility changes are to be calculated, logic requires that there be homogeneity of the utilities to be added and this is the one major advantage of using constant utility curves. However, there is an equally compelling argument against their use. If an estimate of, say $1 billion is derived for the cost of the tariff, any qualification that this refers to dollars with utility equal to the current marginal utility of money is almost certain to be lost when this estimate is quoted. The interpretation of the figure is almost certain to be to the effect that an abolition of the tariff would lead to an increase in income equivalent to having $1 billion more in income at the present average price level. This is the concept used in defining D_E in Figure 13.

product on the assumption that the tariff on all other products as well as the tariff on this product are removed.[23] Because the price of protected goods is falling, the consumer will be better off; the gain in consumers' surplus will be measured by $GHKQ$, or areas $A + B + C + E$. However, there will be offsetting losses. Producers will also face lower prices; therefore their surplus (rents and quasi-rents on specialized factors of production) will fall by area A. Government revenue will fall by area C, resulting in a loss either in the form of curtailed government services or in the form of additional taxes elsewhere. The net gain from tariff elimination (the cost of the tariff) is therefore $B + E$.[24]

So much for the basic theoretical issues. The empirical problem is defining the shapes and sizes of the various areas in Figure 13. The most critical questions center around the supply curve. Young's tariff cost of 3.5 percent to 4.5 percent of gross private expenditure, it might be noted in passing, was based on the tacit assumption that domestic supply curves were infinitely elastic at the market price (that is, they had the shape HJS_E) and that domestic demand curves had an elasticity of zero (KV). Thus the areas A and E were assumed to be zero, and the cost of the tariff was taken as GH times OU, rather than $B + E$. Thus, as Johnson noted (p. 335), Young overstated the cost of protection by any change in economic rent (A) and understated it by any loss of consumers' surplus that might result from the decline in the quantity consumed (E).

How significant was Young's omission of areas A and E? Area A will be larger, the smaller the elasticity of the (general equilibrium) supply curve. Low elasticity of supply may be attributed to either of two basic causes: first, diseconomies of scale (that is,

[23] Because the *ceteris paribus* assumptions have been relaxed, the normally strong presumption that the demand curves for specific goods slope downward to the right is weakened. If an even higher tariff on a competing good is abolished, it is possible that the consumption of the good in question may fall, even though its price is declining. That is, OW may be less than OV. This would be a special case, however, and in the aggregate an increase in the consumption of protected goods may confidently be expected in the event of an abolition of tariffs.

[24] For a discussion and criticism of earlier literature in which changes in consumers' surplus minus changes in producers' surplus were interpreted as a measure of the cost of tariff, see Jacob Viner, *Studies,* pp. 589–593.

a less than proportional increase in output as a result of proportional increases in all inputs) and second, scarcity of specialized inputs, which will mean that additional units of inputs attracted into an expanding industry will be increasingly less suited to production.[25] The specialization of inputs is clearly a function of time. Capital, for example, may be highly specialized when invested in the form of, say, machinery to produce textiles and may be useless to produce anything else. However, when the time comes to replace the machine, the capital resources become mobile; they can be transferred without cost into other industries by taking the funds accumulated for replacing the (textile) machine and investing them in (e.g., auto) machinery, research, buildings, etc. Over a normal replacement cycle, then, inelasticity of supply due to specificity of capital will substantially disappear.

A similar, but perhaps less strong, argument may be made for labor. Workers develop skills that are, to varying degrees, specific to the product they are producing. Therefore, switching of labor into different pursuits may involve a cost in the sense that the value of acquired skills is lost. Over time, however, workers retire and the labor force turns over. When an industry begins to attract new entrants to the labor force (rather than workers from other industries), losses in acquired skills and training are no longer involved. Hence, the labor supply also becomes less specific and more elastic in the long run than in the short run.[26]

There are only two inputs which will remain specific even in the long run. First, some individuals may have inherent talents. For example, a musician requires specific native talents in addition to musical education, and these inherent talents may not be easily transferred into another occupation — even in the long run. Second, resources are often specific: nickel mines are useful in the production of stainless steel but not (directly) in the production of plastics. These two cases are, however, the exception rather

---

[25] Another reason for inelastic supply responses could be an appreciation of the general wage level (as opposed to the wage of specialized labor). This is not treated here, but is deferred for special consideration in the section below on the consumption effects of protection.

[26] Training may, of course, be considered as a special type of investment; thus, this labor argument may be considered as a subcategory of the capital argument above.

than the rule; hence it may be concluded that inelasticity of input supply tends to disappear with time.

Therefore, in the long run, area A may be dismissed as relatively unimportant, insofar as it is attributable to specific resources. As a consequence, in any long-term context, Young's omission of area A is unlikely to result in a substantial overstatement of the cost of the tariff to Canada. This is another way of stating the familiar proposition that gains from a tariff reduction are likely to be significantly greater in the long run, after turnover of the capital and labor supply, than they would be in the short run.

The only reason for upward sloping supply that we have discussed so far is the specific nature of inputs in the short run; there remains also the possibility of decreasing returns to scale. This, for example, might occur if there is congestion where production becomes highly concentrated.[27] But the possibilities of declining returns to scale are less important than those of increasing returns (or decreasing costs); in preceding chapters it has been established that there are major economies of scale in many of the industries that would be affected by free trade between the United States and Canada.

The Cost of Tariffs: Theoretical Issues When Costs Are Decreasing

"Economies of market size" were defined in Part III to include both economies of scale proper (that is, a movement along a downward-sloping average cost curve) and competitive pressures and incentives to adopt the most efficient methods of production (that is, downward shifts in cost curves). For the analysis of this section, the relative weight of these two cost-reducing factors is comparatively unimportant. Therefore, in order to prevent further complication of an already complex problem, the discussion will be confined to a movement along downward-sloping cost curves; however, shifts of the curves can be analyzed in a similar way.

Unfortunately, when increasing returns are considered, the

[27] If supply inelasticity were due to diseconomies of scale, area A would not represent quasi-rents. Rising costs would be a reflection of inefficiencies, rather than of higher prices of scarce factors. Thus, Young's (implicit) exclusion of area A from consideration would be correct.

marginal cost supply curves of Figure 13 are no longer relevant. When average costs are falling, marginal cost is below average cost, and any sales at marginal cost would involve losses and eventual bankruptcy. If a diagram is to be used to illustrate the cost of a tariff, then some alternative concept of supply must be found.

The substitute used will be the average cost curve. This is a valid procedure[28] if corporations follow a policy of average cost pricing (including "normal" profits); but even where they do not, the use of average cost may be justified on the grounds that unmanageable complications will be avoided.[29]

When a decreasing-cost industry is given protection, four cases must be distinguished.

No Production. In this case the tariff is insufficient to "protect" the domestic industry; that is, the foreign price plus the tariff is too low to provide a reasonable return to investment in the limited domestic market. Since this industry does not exist, it cannot be adversely affected by tariff elimination.

Domestic Production, but No Exports. In this case the tariff is sufficient to "protect" the domestic industry. A producer finds it is profitable to sell in the domestic market at a price less than or equal to the foreign price plus his tariff protection. However, either because of foreign tariffs or because his marginal costs are above foreign prices, he will not market in foreign countries.

Domestic Production and Exports with Double Pricing of Domestic and Export Sales. If his marginal production costs and foreign tariffs are sufficiently low and Canadian tariffs sufficiently high, a domestic producer may find it profitable to sell at a high price in the protected domestic market and at the (lower) world price in the export market. In this case, the tariff provides the domestic manufacturer with a high-price domestic base in which he can partially or completely cover his overhead costs.

[28] That is, valid for determining price and sales. For evaluating opportunity cost, the marginal curve is relevant.

[29] The rather difficult question of oligopolistic or monopolistic profits arising because of decreasing costs will be skipped over. However, where there is product differentiation, we may present theoretical illustrations of decreasing cost equilibria in which profits do not exceed the normal level. See Edward H. Chamberlin, *The Theory of Monopolistic Competition* (Cambridge: Harvard University Press, 1933).

Domestic Production with Both Domestic and Export Sales at World Prices. Costs to the domestic manufacturer may be sufficiently low, and either the possibilities of domestic competition or foreign anti-dumping duties so great, that he sells in both the domestic and foreign markets at the world price (or perhaps even lower). In this case his Canadian protection is of little consequence; its effect will be limited to restricting foreign penetration of his domestic base with differentiated products.

Cases two and three are the most critical for the evaluation of the costs of the tariff; as a preliminary, however, the first case may be quickly dealt with in Figure 14. Because demand facing the

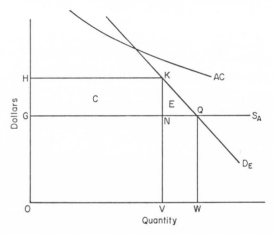

Figure 14. The tariff with decreasing costs and no domestic production.

producer (HKD_E) lies entirely below his costs (AC), there is no production, and the entire effect of the tariff is on the consumer. The net cost of the tariff will be confined to the loss of consumers' surplus (area E) on the reduction in consumption resulting from the tariff. The result is the same as it would be in an increasing cost case where the tariff was insufficient to make domestic production profitable.[30]

The second and third cases shown in Figure 15 are more complicated. As before, D_E is the general equilibrium demand curve,

[30] That is, if S_E in Figure 13 reached the vertical (dollar) axis above H.

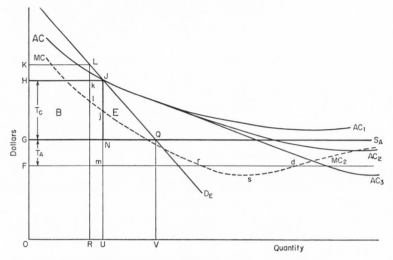

Figure 15. The cost of tariffs: decreasing cost industries.

S_A is the foreign supply price, and AC is the average domestic cost of production. AC_1, AC_2, and AC_3 represent three possible forms the average cost curve may take; each of these is drawn on the assumption that the exchange rate and the price level of domestic factors remain unchanged. (A methodological difficulty is introduced by the simultaneous use of general equilibrium demand curves and partial equilibrium cost curves on the same diagram; however, we wish to deal with the possibility of a change in the price of factors explicitly as a separate subject below.) The home (Canadian) tariff, T_C, is assumed to be just sufficient to induce domestic production of the good. Because foreign imports can enter at price OH, the demand curve facing domestic producers is HJD_E,[31] with an equilibrium at J. The cost of the tariff to the consumer is $GHJQ$, i.e., areas $B + E$.

In passing, it is interesting to note the effects of a tariff that is higher than that which barely induces home production. A tariff of

[31] Where there is product differentiation, the tariff's effect in excluding foreign competition will occur over a range rather than at a specific price. In this case, the demand curve will not be perfectly horizontal to the left of J.

GK will lead to an equilibrium price of *OK*.[32] Both production and consumption are lower (by *RU*) than in the previous case in which a tariff of *GH* was barely adequate to protect the domestic industry. The marginal utility of these *RU* units is represented by the area under section *LJ* of the demand curve; their marginal cost by the area under *lj;* thus, the net cost of the excess tariff, *HK,* is represented by area *LJjl*.[33]

Before we proceed, two major conceptual puzzles should be resolved. In this type of trade analysis, a country either exports *or* imports a good; it does not do both. How then can one explain why most categories of goods are simultaneously exported and imported? The answer is simply that any category in the trade statistics includes many subproducts, which may be distinguished both in terms of spatial and product differentiation. Thus, for example, a crosshauling of "fresh fruit" across the border might be explained either because Saskatchewan imports and British Columbia exports apples, or because British Columbia exports apples and imports oranges.

A similar, but more perplexing puzzle arises in the case of decreasing cost goods. Again trade theory seems to lead to unrealistic results: Canada should either not produce at all (Figure 14), in which case consumption will be entirely satisfied by imports, or alternatively produce to satisfy (at least) all of the domestic market — in which case there should be no imports whatsoever (Figure 15).

Again the problem is resolved by recognizing that any trade category includes many products — some of which may be subject

---

[32] The equilibrium price need not be *OK;* it might possibly be lower. However, because of the kink in the demand curve (*KLQ*) at *L,* there is a strong probability that the equilibrium price will be *OK*. This price is in line with English's conclusion that Canadian prices tend to be set at the U.S. price plus tariff. See the discussion above, Chapter 11. In order that the argument may be kept manageable, several important factors in the determination of Canadian prices are mentioned only peripherally. These are, specifically, oligopolistic interactions and the possibility of product differentiation and non-price competition.

[33] If the tariff is *GK* rather than *GH,* consumers' surplus will be *HKLJ* less; producers' surplus will be greater by *HKLk* minus *Jjlk*. The net cost of the excess tariff, *LJjl,* may alternatively be derived by summing these changes in consumers' and producers' surpluses.

to increasing, and others to decreasing, costs. Even if all sub-categories involve decreasing costs, there is no puzzle in explaining both Canadian production and Canadian imports; in some sub-categories Canadian consumption is completely satisfied by domestic production, whereas in other subcategories consumption is entirely satisfied by imports. This seems to be true, for example, in autos; General Motors entirely satisfies Canadian consumption of certain models of Chevrolet by domestic production, and of Cadillacs by imports.

Summary: Consumption Effects of Protection

Regardless of the combinations of increasing and decreasing cost products included in any trade category, we may conclude the following.

It is the Canadian, rather than the U.S. tariff that has the major impact on Canadian consumption. Canadians are worse off because of areas $E + B$. The consumer is also worse off because of areas A and C, but there is an offsetting gain in each case; duty receipts equal to C accrue to the Canadian taxpayer, and higher rents or quasi-rents equal to A accrue to Canadian income recipients.

In estimating the tariff cost, Young made no distinction between increasing and decreasing cost industries. Fortunately no distinction is necessary if the consumption effects alone are to be calculated.

However, several reservations about his technique remain. First, he underestimated the cost of the tariff to the consumer by triangle E. This applies to all protected goods — regardless of their cost conditions and (domestic or foreign) source. In addition, he overestimated the cost of the tariff by an area A; however, this area exists for increasing cost industries but not for decreasing cost industries. This is unlikely to be a serious omission for two reasons: first, our earlier evidence suggests that most manufacturing in Canada is in the decreasing cost category;[34] second, even in increasing cost industries A tends to disappear in the long run.

[34] The sample industries studied in the preceding two chapters consistently yielded positive values for U, compatible with the assumption of decreasing costs. If industries have increasing or constant costs, the estimates of U would be zero ± an error of estimate. The evidence in Part I is also consistent with the decreasing cost assumption.

The final, most serious limitation on Young's study was that he did not pursue the general equilibrium effects of protection on Canadian money incomes, to which we now turn. In Young's defense it should be pointed out that he studied the effects of the Canadian tariff only; and, as we shall see, this tariff has a much smaller effect on Canadian money income than the U.S. tariff.

The Effects of Protection on Canadian Money Income

In this discussion, the reader is requested to keep in mind two devices introduced to clarify a difficult argument. First, it has already been argued in Chapter 1 that the incidence of protection cannot fall on perfectly mobile factors of production. Instead the incidence will fall on labor and other immobile Canadian factors. It is the money return to these factors that is considered here; therefore, the term "money wage" should be understood to represent money returns to immobile factors in general.

Second, a movement in the exchange rate is an equivalent (though not identical) general equilibrium alternative to a wage change. Any shift in the wage rate discussed in this section, therefore, should be interpreted as a wage *or* exchange rate shift — or a combination of the two. Such movement is no problem in this analysis of costs of protection because both would have similar effects on Canadian real income; the ways in which their effects would differ are discussed in Chapter 11.

Factor incomes are more difficult to analyze in the decreasing cost case than in the rising supply curve case, shown in Figure 13. In that diagram, area *A* represents producers' surplus, that is, payments to scarce factors whose prices are bid up by expanding production of the good for which they are particularly suited. In contrast, the decline in the average cost curve in Figure 15 is not a reflection of declining factor prices, but rather of the more efficient use of factors in large-scale production.[35]

[35] In fact, where demand pressure is put on specific factors which are particularly suited to the production of this good, they may receive a rent or quasi-rent as production of the good is increased. Hence, where there are economies of scale, it is possible that the cost curve will be falling even though specific factor prices are rising. However, as was noted earlier, there seems to be little reason for expecting a major degree of factor specificity in the long run.

In fact, with free trade and the scaling up of industry, there may be a general equilibrium *rise* in wages. This rise would occur if increased labor demand after a tariff cut were sufficient to drive up wages in all sectors; this case is clearly quite different from the accumulation of quasi-rents by a small proportion of the labor force with specific talents who happen to find themselves in expanding industries. To illustrate: as a result of free trade, Canadian automobile wages may rise (or fall), not because of a shortage of workers specifically skilled for automobile production but because the demand for all labor in Canada has risen (or fallen). When a large proportion of industry faces decreasing costs, this general equilibrium change in wages becomes the critical consideration.

The Effect of Both the Canadian and U.S. Tariffs on Canadian Money Income. In analyzing the general equilibrium effects of bilateral tariff elimination on wages, a distinction must be made between the three possible average cost curves shown in Figure 15.

Canadian businesses with cost curves similar to AC_1 will be unable to compete with U.S. producers. If all, or practically all, Canadian manufacturers have costs of this kind, then in the event of free trade, either the Canadian exchange rate will have to fall, or relative wage rates and other factor prices in Canada will have to decline, or both. In such a circumstance, $B + E$ would be an overestimate of the free trade gain (cost of the tariff) to Canada; the free trade gain would be $B + E$ *minus* the decline in wages necessary to push a sufficient number[36] of AC_1 curves down to tangency with S_A.[37] (This quantity cannot be shown on Figure 15, but it may be estimated in other ways.)

Canadian cost curves need not be similar to AC_1, however; they might fall below S_A (that is, AC_2 or AC_3). With free trade in these circumstances, large-scale production would be cheaper in Canada than in the United States; thus, Canadian factor prices would tend to be drawn upward as Canadian industry rationalized. Consequently, $B + E$ would represent an *underestimate* of the

[36] That is, sufficient to generate full employment in Canada.

[37] Strictly speaking, not all this wage decline would need to be subtracted. For example, wages in the few industries which could previously export to the U.S. may also fall with a general equilibrium wage reduction. This would not involve a loss but rather an income redistribution from wage earners to owners of such an industry.

gain of free trade to Canada; it would be $B + E$ *plus* the rise in Canadian factor prices.[38]

In evaluating the effects of free trade, a critical question is obviously whether Canadian costs do or do not fall below S_A. What is the evidence? In fact, Parts I and III of this study have been devoted to answering this question. In Part I it was shown that, at U.S. scale and efficiency, Canadian costs in most, but not all aggregate sectors would fall *below* S_A.[39] The analysis of sample subindustries in Part III provides further support for this conclusion.

It is important to note that the probable course of factor payments in Canada following a free trade arrangement is not determined by the *average* position of present Canadian cost curves but by the position of the cost curves of the products in which Canada would specialize; these presumably would be industries with relatively low AC curves. For example, if Canadian production were concentrated in only half (or a third) as many items as are produced at present, the bottom half (or third) of the average cost curves would be the ones relevant in determining the effect of tariff removal on Canadian factor prices. And the smaller the necessary selection of favorable cost curves, the more favorable the implied adjustment in Canadian wages.[40] The analysis of parts I and III of this study indicates that this sort of selection process would yield a group of cost curves lying well below S_A in Figure 15. A free trade rise in Canadian money wages is implied; or, to restate, the cost to Canada of the two North American tariffs combined is substantially more than the loss of consumers' surplus $B + E$.

The Effect of the Canadian Tariff Only on Canadian Money Income. What would happen to Canadian money incomes if Canada

[38] Again, the issue is somewhat more complicated than this. For example, any increase in wages in industries which previously exported to the U.S. would reduce profits, and hence represent a Canadian income redistribution, rather than gain. However, this would be offset to a greater or lesser degree, by the gain such firms would enjoy from U.S. tariff elimination. It is evident that all the possible complications of this kind cannot be dealt with in a study of this scope.

[39] That is, below U.S. costs.

[40] This will be recognized as a restatement of the argument in Chapter 11, p. 201.

were unable to induce U.S. tariff cuts but unilaterally abolished her own tariff? For industries with increasing costs the answer is simple: the quasi-rents going to specific Canadian factors (area A in Figure 13) would fall as Canadian domestic product prices fall from OH to OG. This is the argument underlying the classical conclusion that tariffs increase money wages.

But for industries with decreasing costs, the problem is more difficult; here a distinction must be made between firms with cost curves AC_2 and AC_3 (Figure 15). Both lie below S_A, indicating Canadian industries with an advantage under reciprocal free trade. But only industries with costs AC_3 could, by expanding to efficient scale, compete in the U.S. market despite the U.S. tariff T_A.[41]

Do any Canadian firms have costs similar to AC_3? The ability of some Canadian manufacturers to export at present to the United States over American tariffs suggests that their costs are similar to AC_3. However, this is not an adequate proof, unless it can also be demonstrated that these firms sell in both the Canadian and U.S. markets at the same price. Double pricing allows a firm at present with costs AC_2 to export over the U.S. tariff. Suppose such a firm sells OU at price OH in the domestic market. It will also be profitable to sell volume md in the U.S. market at price OF (plus U.S. tariff) — provided area rsd is at least as large as area mjr. This illustrates the possible relevance of the "protected base" argument: as long as there is a U.S. tariff, a Canadian producer in this

[41] AC_3 falls below height OF, which is the U.S. supply price OG less the U.S. tariff FG. Would it not be possible for some Canadian firms with costs AC_2 to survive and export by selling at price S_A in both the U.S. and Canadian markets? It is true that, because they have to pay the U.S. tariff, they would not cover average costs on their U.S. sales. But because there would be no similar penalty in the Canadian market, these sales would more than cover their average costs. In other words, they might charge overhead to their Canadian sales while their sales in the U.S. at marginal cost or above would provide necessary economies of scale.

The difficulty is that such a firm would run the risk of U.S. antidumping measures. This would not be the (more offensive) dumping involved in selling at a lower price in the U.S. than Canada; but it still technically falls in this category, since the Canadian exporter would be absorbing the U.S. tariff. It is likely he would get away with it; but even a small risk that he would not is likely to deter the substantial investment expansion in Canada that such an operation would require.

special situation cannot survive, nor can he export, unless he is permitted by the Canadian tariff to charge his overheads to the Canadian consumer.[42] Such a firm would be vulnerable to unilateral Canadian tariff elimination.

If export performance does not allow us to differentiate between firms with costs AC_2 and AC_3, is there any other evidence? Of the fourteen sample industries studied in Part III, only two (leather and trade books) might have costs low enough to put them in the AC_3 category, (that is, with a net Canadian advantage X greater than the U.S. tariff). Even these two cases are, at best, ambiguous; an estimated Canadian free trade advantage of 8.9 percent on upper leather is unlikely to offset a U.S. tariff of 8.5 to 12.5 percent, and an estimated Canadian cost advantage of 5.5 percent in trade books might or might not allow a Canadian exporter to overcome a U.S. tariff ranging from 0 to 23 percent. The evidence seems to be that, although isolated Canadian industries can undoubtedly be found with potential costs in the AC_3 range, most do not have such costs.

In the light of this evidence, the effects of a *unilateral* elimination of the Canadian tariff (T_C) may be sketched out as follows: (1) Canadian manufacturing at inefficient scale that exists because of protection (shown at equilibrium point J in Figure 15) would, with certain exceptions,[43] be eliminated. (2) All Canadian cost curves would fall because the elimination of Canadian protection would decrease input costs; hence, some of the cost curves in category AC_2 (and even perhaps in AC_1) might be reduced to category AC_3. This increase in the industries in this efficient export category[44] would draw off unemployed resources created in (1). It is not clear whether this would be sufficient to generate full employment in Canada; however, the evidence in Parts I and III cited above suggest that it is likely (but not certain) that the

---

[42] The illustration that the tariff allows Canadian production of this good to survive does not, however, necessarily mean that the tariff is desirable.

[43] For example, an industry receiving negative net protection from the entire Canadian tariff structure (that is, an industry in which N in Figure 4 is negative).

[44] This would presumably include some Canadian industries driven out of small-scale operations; it may also include some industries that do not even exist in Canada at present.

employment generated in (2) will fall short of the unemployment created in (1). (3) Any remaining unemployment in Canada would create downward pressure on Canadian wages (or the exchange rate) toward a new equilibrium in which a sufficient number of firms find their costs have fallen into the AC_3 category to generate full employment. The resulting pattern of activity would involve increased trade between the two countries and greater scale and efficiency in Canada.[45]

In summary, the money income effects of a unilateral Canadian tariff cut are the following: Canadian money incomes in decreasing cost industries might rise but seem more likely to fall; this process would be augmented by falling money incomes of specific factors in increasing cost industries. This tentative conclusion that a unilateral tariff cut would lower Canadian money income cannot be accepted with any certainty[46] without a further (exceedingly difficult) investigation of Canadian cost curves; in fact, the result could be the opposite. Clearly this issue is more difficult to define than the effects of bilateral free trade examined in this study. Fortunately, it is also far less important, since a unilateral tariff reduction is unlikely to be considered in any serious policy negotiations. Therefore, we make no attempt at a definitive answer; but an informed guess is that the Canadian tariff has raised Canadian money (but not real)[47] income somewhat.

The Effect of the U.S. Tariff on Canadian Money Income. If the Canadian tariff has raised Canadian money wages by X percent and the two tariffs in combination have lowered Canadian money wages by Y percent, then the effect of the U.S. tariff has been to lower Canadian money incomes by the sum of these two effects,

[45] This conclusion is, in fact, not quite certain. It is conceivable that either the U.S. tariff, or the risk of U.S. tariff changes, would deter Canadian reorganization and scaling up to service U.S. markets. If this influence were strong enough, the result could be a depreciation in the Canadian dollar or wage level, sufficient to provide Canadian firms with as much protection as they now receive from the Canadian tariff. In such circumstances, Canadian scale and efficiency would not differ substantially from the present. The reader will note that this result depends on some very unlikely assumptions.

[46] As a further qualification, note that Canadian tariff elimination would automatically increase the profits (and hence factor returns) of export industries that enjoyed cost conditions AC_3 before the tariff cut.

[47] Because the Canadian tariff has also raised the Canadian price level.

that is, by $(X + Y)$ percent. No attempt has been made to estimate this effect, except by this sort of inference. But the reason the U.S. tariff has lowered Canadian money incomes is clear: by blocking many Canadian firms out of their natural North American markets it has forced them to produce at limited scale; and these firms have passed some of the resulting inefficiency back onto their factor payments. Even firms which export despite the U.S. tariff (and produce at efficient scale with cost curves AC_2 or AC_3) face the cost disadvantage of having to overcome the U.S. tariff; and this cost tends to be passed back onto immobile Canadian factors in the form of reduced money incomes.

The Cost of North American Tariffs to Canada: A Numerical Estimate

The Effects of Both Tariffs. The task remains of calculating the Canadian losses due to North American tariffs; following the argument of the previous section this involves estimating the effects on consumption (the sum of areas B and E) plus the effect on Canadian factor incomes.

The effect on factor incomes may be largely, but not completely, attributed to the U.S. tariff. It is estimated by comparing the present situation in which there are tariff barriers, with the probable level of factor incomes in the event of free trade.

It was shown in Chapter 2 that the manufacturing wage level (measured in domestic dollars) is 33 percent higher in the United States than in Canada; when adjustment is made for the difference in industrial structure, the wage differential is reduced to 30 percent[48] (plus a difference due to the discount on the Canadian dollar). However, northern U.S. manufacturing wages are 36 percent higher than in Canada.[49] Hence, it is possible that, with the upward pressures generated by free trade, Canadian wages could rise (by 30 percent) to the average U.S. level, and the Canadian dollar could rise to parity. Even in this case, wages in Canadian regions would still remain 6 percent below those in adjacent northern U.S. regions.

[48] Table 4.
[49] See Chapter 2, footnote 21.

In Chapter 11 the plausibility of a combined rise of the Canadian dollar to exchange parity and a rise of the average Canadian industrial wage to the U.S. level was considered. If these two changes were to occur, Ontario and Quebec would drop from their overall strong competitive positions to median positions. It was concluded that this level of adjustment might occur in the long run (although certainly not immediately upon the introduction of free trade). The possible error in this estimate was, however, recognized to be rather large: Canadian wages might not rise this far; but, on the other hand, they might rise somewhat farther if the intrinsic disadvantages of Canadian regions vis-à-vis *contiguous* U.S. regions were insufficient to justify the 6 percent wage differential at which average Canadian wages would be equal to average U.S. wages. Because of the very close proximity of the great majority of the Canadian people to the northern states, and because of the similarity of the two labor forces discussed in Chapter 2, the 6 percent wage differential would seem to be a reasonable estimate of the long-run divergence in the event of free trade. Overall wage parity may be taken as a first approximation to the long-run free trade equilibrium.

Noting the limitations of the estimate of exchange parity and equalization of average Canadian and U.S. wages, we calculate the depressing effects of the two North American tariffs on Canadian industrial wages at slightly more than 6 percent of Canadian GNP.[50] It must be stressed that this 6 percent calculation is based on long-run equilibrium assumptions; thus the full gain would not come to Canada immediately upon the adoption of free trade.

Tariffs affect not only factor incomes; they also create a burden on consumers in the form of higher prices. Young's estimate

[50] Specifically by $(30 + 130 \ (.08)) \ 15 = 6.06$ percent. The 30 percent is the appreciation in Canadian wages necessary to bring about equality of each wage level expressed in domestic dollars. The .08 is the exchange correction which must be applied to the entire Canadian wage level to bring it up to full equivalence with the U.S. level. Fifteen percent is the proportion of manufacturing wages and salaries in Canadian GNP. (Between 1958 and 1963 this proportion ranged between 15.2 and 14.6 percent.) Although wages in other areas, such as services, would also be pulled up by competitive forces in the event of free trade, these lower wages are not a net cost of protection, since most services cannot be traded internationally, and therefore higher free trade service wages would be offset by higher free trade costs of services

of the loss of consumers' surplus attributable to tariffs[51] is about 4 percent of Canadian GNP.[52] The evaluation of the other consumption cost E depends in part on the change in factor income estimated above because E is defined by a general equilibrium, rather than partial equilibrium demand curve and hence is influenced by changes in real income.

Therefore, a precise estimate of E would require information on the demand of each protected product in response to changes in both prices *and* incomes. This is clearly not feasible; therefore it is simply assumed that the income and price elasticities for manufactured goods taken as a group are each unity. That is, it is assumed that as the level of income rises, the proportion spent on manufactures remains stable; and, as the prices of manufactures fall, the amount spent on manufactures remains stable. These assumptions tend, if anything, to yield underestimates of cost.

Under these assumptions, area E is calculated as about four tenths of one percent of Canadian GNP from the formula derived in Appendix Q.

Thus, the total cost of both North American tariffs to Canada is estimated as approximately 10.5 percent of Canadian GNP. In this total, the consumption or price effects $(B + E)$ are slightly less important than the effect of lower wages. In addition, protection also probably lowers returns to other (immobile) factors in Canada, but these effects have not been included here.

It is important to emphasize that an estimated 10.5 percent

---

[51] Excluding the consumers' surplus triangle (E), and subtracting the Canadian government's revenue from tariffs. In terms of our diagrams, Young's estimate covered areas $A + B$ in Figure 13, nothing in Figure 14, and area B in Figure 15. Young estimated only the cost of *Canadian* tariffs, and did not evaluate the possible consequences of a bilateral reduction.

[52] Young's percentage of 3.5 to 4.5 of gross private expenditures is too high if GNP is taken as the base since gross private expenditures (net of indirect taxes) account for only about 70 percent of GNP; it is also too high because it includes area A in increasing cost industries (Figure 13). On the other hand, it is too low because Young omitted the effects of protection on government expenditures and retail distribution. Since we are considering only bilateral tariff reduction, Young's estimate may also be on the high side for our purposes, insofar as Young used prices in countries outside North America as a basis for comparison. Because of data difficulties, however, Young in general restricted price comparisons to Canada and the U.S. (p. 71). Therefore, the bias from this source cannot be very large.

lower Canadian GNP due to 100 years of North American protection cannot be recouped quickly. It is true that the consumption benefits would immediately follow free trade; but the effects on factor incomes would not, since wage adjustment is an extended process, complicated by numerous impediments and imperfections. If only half of this wage adjustment occurs in the planning time horizon, the benefits to Canada of free trade would still run between 7 and 7.5 percent of GNP; this would involve benefits of approximately 3 percent from wage appreciation, and the 4 to 4.5 percent from consumption effects induced by lower prices. Therefore the authors' estimated range of long-term benefits expected from free trade in manufacturing is 7 to 10.5 percent of Canadian GNP; and the longer the time horizon, the higher the percentage will be within this range.

The Effects of the Canadian Tariff. It is a difficult enough task to estimate the cost to Canada of both tariffs in combination, but it is even more difficult to break down this 10.5 percent cost into that attributable to the Canadian tariff and that due to the U.S. tariff. It is true that the 4 to 4.5 percent consumption effects $(B + E)$ can be identified with the Canadian tariff;[53] it is the income effects that are difficult to sort out. For example, it is not possible to determine, with any great measure of precision, either the direction or magnitude of the wage effects of the Canadian tariff if the U.S. tariff remains. However, it was tentatively concluded above that, in the face of U.S. protection, the Canadian tariff has probably raised Canadian money incomes; since its burden on the income side is, as a consequence, negative, the consumption costs of 4 to 4.5 percent provide a *maximum* estimate of the cost of the Canadian tariff.

The Effects of the U.S. Tariff. If the total cost to Canada of both tariffs is 10.5 percent, and the maximum cost of the Canadian tariff is 4 to 4.5 percent, the *minimum* cost of the U.S. tariff can be estimated at just over 6 percent of Canadian GNP.[54] It should

[53] With only one modification. Since only the Canadian tariff is considered, lower income in Canada due to the U.S. tariff (ΔY in Appendix Q, equation 10) is assumed equal to zero in the calculation of E. Hence E is reduced, but by only a fraction of one percent.

[54] No attempt is made in these estimates to take account of terms of trade effects. It is probably reasonable enough to assume that terms of trade

be emphasized again that this cost of 100 years of the U.S. tariff cannot be recouped quickly with a U.S. tariff elimination. It may take an extended time period, and even then there are no guarantees the losses will be completely recovered. On the other hand, the consumption gains from Canadian tariff elimination would be immediate.

The Cost of North American Tariffs to the U.S.

Because American GNP is roughly fourteen times as great as Canadian GNP, it is clear that the cost of North American tariffs to the U.S. as a fraction of their income is much smaller than the cost to Canada. But not only is the relative cost to the U.S. smaller, the absolute cost to the U.S. is also likely to be smaller for two major reasons. Because U.S. imports from Canada are much more heavily concentrated on raw and semifinished products on which U.S. tariffs are generally low (or zero), U.S. tariffs have a small impact on U.S. prices. Secondly, the gains from economies of market size following free trade would certainly be much less for the United States than for Canada because American plants are already closer to optimal scale of production. Indeed, the additional economies to be gained by U.S. firms from possible expansion into the Canadian market may be dismissed as a trivial fraction of GNP. Therefore, without having pursued the question in detail, the authors would be surprised if the gain to the United States from North American free trade would exceed a small part of one percent of U.S. GNP.

Unilateral Tariff Reduction

Trading relationships with the United States are of enormous importance to the Canadian economy, both because of the volume of trade with the United States and because of the economies of large-scale production. Although Canada is the most important trading partner of the United States, it can claim no such predominant significance for the U.S. economy. If the United States were

---

effects will roughly offset each other in the case of reciprocal tariff reductions; but this is a less valid assumption for a unilateral elimination of either tariff.

to consider a unilateral tariff cut, it would, in all likelihood, be applied to imports from all countries; and its most substantial effects would be on third country trade flows.

In fact, a good argument can be made for such a unilateral U.S. tariff cut, both on economic and political grounds. Although the gain in terms of U.S. GNP would be small, the potential disruption to the U.S. economy would likewise be relatively small. Furthermore, reducing tariffs (and other barriers) on imports from the less developed countries would be economically and politically preferable to the granting of aid (although a combination of lower duties and aid might be even better). This possibility is, however, dependent in part on a satisfactory outcome to the present move toward international monetary reform and clearly raises a whole host of issues beyond the scope of this study. But even if third country considerations were to induce a unilateral U.S. tariff cut, Canada would still receive tremendous windfall gains from the duty free entry into rich U.S. markets; this is likely to result in a minimum increase of 3 to 6 percent in Canadian GNP through a long term rise in the Canadian wage level.

If the Canadians were to consider a unilateral tariff reduction, they would also be likely to apply it to imports from all countries. However, in this case, the economic effects would be dominated by the resulting pattern of Canadian-U.S. trade. The evidence of the previous section suggests gains to Canada from such a move; however, a bilateral reduction is much preferred because the long-run gains from U.S. tariff elimination in all probability exceed gains from Canadian tariff elimination.

In the light of recent U.S. initiatives on trade liberalization, it is possible that Canada would find the United States receptive to the idea of reciprocal tariff reductions.[55] But there is no guarantee of it; and should the United States refuse to consider a reciprocal reduction, the only policy change open to Canada would be a unilateral reduction. The present work has not been sufficiently directed toward the unilateral question to form the basis for uni-

---

[55] There is a recent precedent that adds support to this conclusion: the Canadian-U.S. automobile agreement provides for limited free trade and also special employment and balance-of-payments provisions that are biased heavily in Canada's favor. Even its opponents in the U.S. have expressed a willingness to support free trade if it is not complicated by such provisions.

lateral policy recommendations; further study would be in order. In such a study additional problems should be kept in mind.

Any increased specialization occurring in Canada aimed at sales in the United States would result in increased customs receipts by the U.S. government. It may be concluded, therefore, that at least some of the windfall gains in efficiency resulting from this change in *Canadian* commercial policy would go to the *U.S.* public. In short, Canadians are likely to gain from increased specialization in Canada, but Americans are certain to gain.

Another problem is that although Canadian resource allocation might improve, it would remain nonoptimal because the U.S. tariff would continue to restrict the flow of goods. Moreover, Canadian specialization would be, at least in part, dependent on the U.S. tariff structure; thus U.S. tariff revisions could change the pattern of Canadian activity and impose irretrievable sunk costs on the Canadian economy. Any such losses could completely offset potential gains from specialization; in fact, the risk of these losses might even prevent specialization from occurring in the first place. Although the risk may be a minor consideration for other countries contemplating unilateral tariff reductions, it is especially serious for Canada because of the relative size of the Canadian and U.S. economies and because natural markets for many Canadian industries are more heavily concentrated in the United States than in Canada.[56]

Finally, there is a diplomatic complication. Although it may not be feasible to get U.S. tariffs down now, it may be possible in the future; and this possibility may be increased if Canadian tariffs

[56] If the United States is unwilling to cooperate in tariff reductions, there is no way the Canadian authorities alone can bring about an efficient allocation of Canadian resources — unless the Canadian government is prepared to stand ready to provide an export subsidy just equal to the U.S. tariff. By paying the U.S. duty, the Canadian government might ensure unobstructed entry of all goods into North American markets; but in the process the Canadian taxpayer would be subsidizing the U.S. taxpayer. Given present U.S. legislation, such export bounties could result in the imposition of increased U.S. tariffs; in such circumstances, the Canadian taxpayer could become involved in a series of escalating subsidies to the U.S. taxpayer. Moreover, the U.S. government would be in a position, through tariff manipulation, to tax the Canadian public — a situation the Canadian public would be unlikely to tolerate on either economic or political grounds.

exist and can be sacrificed at that date as a bargaining device. In weighing this argument estimates must be made of the possibility that U.S. attitudes will change in the future and of the (presumably limited) extent to which the Americans might view the Canadian tariff as an effective bargaining weapon.

It may be concluded that a unilateral Canadian tariff cut should not be considered unless bilateral cuts are shown to be clearly impossible.

Summary

Because of the importance of economies of market size, they must be taken into account in costs of the two North American tariffs. When this is done, costs of the two tariffs to Canada have been estimated at approximately 10.5 percent of GNP. Of this, no more, and possibly much less, than 4.5 percent can be attributed to the Canadian tariff. The balance can be attributed to the U.S. tariff; however, if this tariff is eliminated, it is likely that these losses would be recouped only after an extended time period — and even then perhaps not completely.

Although there is no detailed estimate of the cost of both tariffs to the United States, there are reasons for believing that it amounts to only a small fraction of one percent of U.S. GNP.

PART IV

Policy Issues and Conclusions

16

TIMING AND ADJUSTMENT ASSISTANCE

A number of policy issues have arisen in earlier chapters, such as the appropriate exchange rate arrangement in the event of free trade and the possible desirability of a unilateral tariff reduction on Canada's part in the event that the United States refuses to consider a bilateral agreement. There are, however, several policy questions which remain, most notably the optimum timing of tariff changes, the advisability and appropriate form of adjustment assistance, and the relative desirability of a free trade area (with independent tariffs on imports from third countries) as compared to a customs union (with common external tariffs). The last of these questions is considered in Chapter 17; timing and adjustment assistance are considered here.

There are two broad timing questions: one involving the most appropriate circumstances for the initiation of a free trade arrangement, and the other involving the speed and sequence of changes. Because a free trade arrangement is bound to create a number of specific problems (regardless of its overall desirability), it would best be undertaken when major disturbances, such as widespread unemployment or an international financial crisis, are absent. Full employment would not only free the policymaker to deal with the problems associated with free trade; it would also directly reduce these problems because adjustment tends to occur most smoothly when there is full employment.

Full employment and financial stability do not, however, provide the only important criteria for determining the best time to initiate tariff reductions. Equally important is the momentum of policy. From time to time, policies lead up to a point where the possibility of reciprocity is thrown into particularly sharp focus. One such time was the beginning of the second decade of this century. With the recent changes in automotive policy, with the accompanying public debate, and with the apparent loss of momentum of the postwar movement toward multilateral tariff reductions the time once more appears to be ripening for a hard look at the possibility of reciprocity.

A Sudden or Staged Reduction of Tariffs?

Tariffs might be completely abolished in one move. A second option, which is the orthodox approach used by the EEC and the EFTA, is a staging sequence. For example, cooperating countries might agree to reduce their tariffs by 20 percent per year, a scheme that would place them on a completely free trade footing after five years. (It is normally recommended that "nuisance" tariffs of less than about 3 percent be eliminated immediately.) The objective is to allow a firm time to adjust, in two respects, to its new competitive milieu.

Tariff reductions are phased so that increased import competition will not fall suddenly on the firm but will instead be introduced by a process of continuous pressure. Hence, the reorganization of existing capital facilities may be spread over an extended period. The nation does not appear to lose as heavily on sunk costs because the impact of obsolescence on investment is spread over time. However, appearances may deceive; it does not necessarily follow that the nation is better off as a result. Potential free trade benefits may be foregone because tariffs partially remain; these benefits might possibly be sufficient, in purely economic terms, to justify the more sudden obsolescence that would result from immediate tariff elimination. However, there may be political advantages in the "staging" option because it may appear to the public that tariff removal has been less damaging.

The other major adjustment for the firm would be the reappraisal of its new markets opened by the elimination of tariffs elsewhere. Access to new markets is the one completely unambiguous benefit of free trade; thus, it is generally in any nation's interest to seek immediate elimination of tariffs elsewhere,[1] regardless of the staging of its own tariff reductions. The asymmetrical nature of such an objective clearly limits its application: the United States and Canada cannot both simultaneously arrange for the partial retention of their own tariffs and the immediate elimination of the other's tariffs. However, variations on this theme are possible, and a recent proposal by the Canadian-American Committee allows for more rapid reduction of U.S. than Canadian tariffs.[2] Preferred treatment is recommended for Canada in order to ease a more severe adjustment problem. Because each country is likely to wish to maximize the speed at which the other country's tariffs are removed relative to its own, the timing aspects of this proposal are likely to be regarded as attractive by Canadians.

It is worth examining the assumption that adjustment will be more drastic in Canada than in the United States. For products in which Canada specializes, reorganization will be involved in Canadian scaling up; at the same time, adjustments will be necessary for those U.S. firms forced to contend with this new competition from Canada. Successful Canadian specialization implies either or both of two possible responses in the United States. First, if the

---

[1] One interesting possible exception to this general principle has been cited by the Canadian-American Committee in *A Possible Plan for a Canada-U.S. Free Trade Area* (Washington and Montreal: National Planning Association and Private Planning Association of Canada, February 1965), p. 49. Immediate U.S. tariff elimination would open new markets in the United States for all producers in Canada. However, subsidiaries of U.S. firms would be in a much stronger position than Canadian-owned firms to exploit these markets through the marketing facilities of their parents, and thus the Canadian-owned firms might lag seriously in the competitive race. Therefore the Committee recommends that U.S. tariff reduction be staged, partially as a means of allowing Canadian-owned firms to establish marketing facilities in the United States. This argument may have considerable merit, but it involves certain difficulties. It is true that temporary partial retention of U.S. tariffs does put the Canadian-owned company at less disadvantage in U.S. markets vis-à-vis the Canadian subsidiary of a U.S. firm; but it leaves *both* at a disadvantage in U.S. markets vis-à-vis U.S. domestic producers. It is clear that the net effect is to leave the Canadian subsidiary worse off; but it is not clear that the Canadian-owned company would be better off, since this depends upon a trade-off of two offsetting effects.

[2] *Ibid.*, p. 5.

Canadian expansion of output in the selected lines of specialization is not more than enough to satisfy the increase in U.S. demand, the U.S. response may be the relatively simple one of limiting expansion to other lines; no absolute U.S. contraction would be necessary in the lines of Canadian specialization. This appears to be a distinct possibility in at least some of the products in which Canada specializes. At a 4 percent rate of growth, the increase in demand in the United States would equal total Canadian demand in roughly two years. Thus, as a general proposition, for those items where Canadian production initially approximated the volume of Canadian consumption, Canadian production could double in about two years and treble in about four without there being any absolute contraction in the United States. For products whose demand grows more rapidly than average,[3] the periods involved would be even shorter. This possibility of obviating contraction of U.S. production of items of Canadian specialization provides support for gradual U.S. tariff reduction. In general, however, the period over which the U.S. tariff should be gradually reduced on these grounds is rather short.

It may be, of course, that the optimum scale of production is more than two or three times as great as current Canadian production, and Canadian specialization will require a more major U.S. adjustment in the form of absolute contraction of the production of the items in question. The degree of such contraction depends in part on the speed of Canadian expansion. Whereas the doubling of whole Canadian industrial sectors within two years would seem unlikely because of the supply stresses involved, the same cannot be said for specific products. That is, it would be very difficult for the Canadian automobile industry to double in size in two years' time; however, the doubling of Canadian production of, say, Buicks, would involve relatively minor supply problems if the Canadian production of other General Motors cars were simultaneously curtailed. In earlier chapters it has been argued that this type of specialization within industries would be more important than adjustments among industries. Therefore, very rapid rates of increase in the Canadian production of specific items may be expected, involving pressures for the corresponding U.S. production

---

[3] In Chapter 11, the possibility of Canadian specialization in rapid growth industries was considered.

to contract. However, precisely because this adjustment is being concentrated within industries, the contraction of specific lines in the United States will be much less painful than adjustment among industries would be. In the hypothetical example cited, the Canadian expansion of production of Buicks would involve U.S. contraction of Buick production, but this would scarcely create major strains on General Motors in the U.S. because they would be expanding the production of other cars to meet both the growth in U.S. demand and the Canadian demand following the curtailment of non-Buick production by General Motors of Canada.

This relatively painless type of adjustment, involving a large and diversified U.S. manufacturer and its Canadian subsidiary, is not, however, necessarily typical. In industries where there are independent and specialized U.S. firms and independent and diversified Canadian companies,[4] the problems of adjustment would be greater. Although the Canadian problem of production adjustment would be somewhat similar to the one for subsidiary companies (involving the dropping of some lines and the specialization on others), there would be greater marketing problems because the company would have no U.S. parent to handle its sales in the United States. The U.S. firm would also have special problems: having already been specialized in one or few products, it might find itself under pressure to shift production to another line in which it had no previous special experience. Even here, however, the problems of adjustment would generally be far fewer than in the orthodox intersectoral trade adjustment model: the prospective new line would at least be within the same product grouping.

The intraindustry nature of prospective adjustment supports the case for rapid tariff elimination; the greater relative degree of Canadian adjustment may be used to support more rapid U.S. than Canadian reduction. The Canadian adjustment is less likely to be hidden in the normal process of growth. Because Canadian machinery is less suited to long-run efficient production, Canadian equipment writeoffs would be greater.

---

[4] As noted in the footnote 23 of Chapter 11, the average size of Canadian firms is not greatly different from the average size of U.S. firms. Thus, shorter Canadian production runs are associated with greater diversification within the firm.

No matter what staging sequence may be selected, in one respect it is likely to be too fast, while in another respect it may be too slow. If the objective is to spread the shock of import competition, it may be too fast. The assumption cannot be made that staging will allow a slow, steady buildup of competitive pressure, allowing a relaxed and extended period of reorganization. Instead, the very first stage of tariff reduction may immediately confront a firm with the option of reorganization or bankruptcy and make a good deal of its machinery obsolete.[5] In another respect the same staging sequence may be too slow. As long as complete rationalization is not forced immediately, machinery appropriate only with protection may be reinstalled even after the process to free trade has begun. Clearly, any evaluation of the relative merits of various transitional measures requires a careful consideration of how each would affect existing capital and its replacement.

Timing and the Displacement of Capital Equipment. Consider the differential impact of free trade transition schemes on two major categories of capital equipment: (1) machinery that will be replaced now,[6] regardless whether free trade is introduced or protection continues. Once-and-for-all tariff elimination involves no capital loss for machinery in this category because its present productive value would not exceed its scrap value even if tariffs were retained. However, a staging sequence to free trade would involve an economic cost to the extent that there was reinstallation of machinery appropriate only with protection. For example, it would be perfectly rational for a firm to replace a machine that normally has a three year lifespan with a new machine of the same design, provided that tariff reductions do not make this machine obsolete until three years later. It may be in the firm's interest to reinstall such a machine even if it becomes obsolete two years later, provided the returns from this machine in the next two years cover the writeoff in the third. Therefore, decisions taken

[5] For the economy as a whole, however, the staging process is almost certain to spread reorganization over time, since many firms will not be in such a sensitive situation and will be able to defer at least part of their rationalization until a later stage.

[6] To simplify this discussion "now" is used to represent the time at which free trade is initiated — either by a once-and-for-all or staging process.

during the interim adjustment period can involve a cost extending into the period of full free trade.

The above illustrates the cost of staging in terms of inefficient equipment that may be reinstalled. Paradoxically, staging may also involve a cost even though *efficient* machinery is installed. Suppose a firm decides it is in its interest to replace a machine with a substitute whose anticipated life is twenty years and that this machine will be efficient under the free trade conditions to be fully realized only after a five year staging process. In this case, any tariffs that remain during the next five years will prevent the firm from fully exploiting the markets for which the machine was designed. Thus, the cost of the remaining U.S. tariffs that "get in the way" may exceed the value to a Canadian firm of the remaining Canadian tariffs; indeed, with this new rationalized equipment, Canadian tariffs may become superfluous. Since new investment is a lumpy process, rationalization is likely to either lead or lag. If it lags, the firm is temporarily in a noncompetitive position; if it leads, the firm may be faced with the choice of leaving some productive capacity idle or absorbing the remaining foreign tariffs in order to gain access to the markets that the machine was designed to serve.[7] In either case, the remaining tariffs will involve a burden, and pressures will grow for their elimination. The EEC experience provides an example of how the pressures induced by rationalization have accelerated the process of tariff reductions.[8]

It may be concluded that for all machinery that is due for replacement, a once-and-for-all tariff reduction is to be preferred on all counts. Staging is inadvisable because it may lead to reinstallation of inefficient machinery; alternatively, if efficient machinery is introduced, tariffs in other countries may prevent its optimum exploitation.

(2) Machinery with some present life left provided protection

---

[7] If foreign tariffs are absorbed, the cost is private and, from a *national* point of view, social; international social costs are, however, absent. If capacity is left idle, there are costs from all three viewpoints.

[8] Business psychology may also play an important role. Changes which may have been feared and resisted by the business community may not prove so injurious after all. Hence business confidence may also induce pressure for an accelerated program. It is desirable for any staging scheme to be made flexible enough to allow for such acceleration.

continues. Once-and-for-all free trade may make such machinery obsolete in either of two senses: the value of the machine to the firm may fall below its replacement cost, in which case it will not be replaced, although it may continue to be used until it wears out; or its value may fall below its scrap price, in which case it should be replaced immediately. Once-and-for-all tariff elimination would induce the most rapid rationalization of facilities. However, because of the imperfections in capital markets, it is by no means clear that tariffs should be eliminated suddenly. For the optimum allocation of capital, bygones should be considered bygones, and the future returns to rationalized facilities should control investment decisions. In an imperfect economy, however, past performance of a company will inevitably color expectations of its future performance. Thus, any sudden abolition of tariffs, which immediately makes equipment obsolete and reduces the equity value of companies, may make it very difficult for the companies to raise the funds necessary to acquire the new equipment appropriate to a free trade situation: their performance with the old capital equipment may adversely affect expectations regarding their ability to use new equipment profitably. This basic problem of capital market imperfection may be compounded by legal difficulties: if the writeoff of old equipment is sufficiently great, the equity of existing companies may be eliminated, and bankruptcies ensue. In contrast, if tariffs are reduced by stages, such potential financial crises may be avoided because the capital losses are spread over a longer period of time. Moreover, the total amount of capital losses will be reduced because there will be a greater possibility of synchronizing the introduction of new machinery and the normal replacement cycle for depreciated equipment.

The difficulty of synchronizing the introduction of new machinery with the replacement cycle is greater if the life of machinery is long. The strength of the case for a staging sequence varies directly with the remaining lifetime of existing capital equipment, and the time dimension of investment replacement is critical. If full free trade is to be deferred until all present equipment would normally be replaced, the time required would be the longest remaining life of any equipment — a concept that is of limited value because remaining lifetimes differ so widely. It is therefore more useful to consider the interval of time during which some sizable fraction — say, one half — of the present stock of machinery would normally be replaced. The U.S. tax guidelines provide an estimate of the lives of machinery by industry; from these guidelines, Table 35 has been derived, showing half-lives[9] typically running from five to eight years.

TABLE 35. *Estimated Half-Life of Machinery, 1964.*

Manufacturing sector[a]	Half-life (year)
Food	7.6
Tobacco	7.5
Textiles	6.2
Apparel	7.5
Wood products	5.0
Paper	7.7
Printing	5.5
Electrical equipment	4.7
Chemicals	5.5
Petroleum products	8.5
Rubber and plastics	7.0
Leather goods	5.5
Nonmetallic mineral products	8.1
Metallic products	8.3
Transportation equipment	5.4
Miscellaneous	6.0

Source: U.S. Treasury Department, Internal Revenue Service, *Depreciation Guidelines and Rules,* August 1964, pp. 6–10.
a See Table 1, note a.

Table 35 has been derived on the assumption that the North American economy is static. The existence of growth means that the five to eight year estimates shown in Table 35 tend to overstate the potential problem of adjustment in one sense and yet understate it in another. With a growing economy, more equipment was produced last year than was produced five years ago, and therefore there are relatively more young machines than might be expected simply on the basis of the depreciation rates. Hence, a longer period than that shown in Table 35 must pass before half of the present machinery would normally be replaced.

[9] That is, the period in which, in a static economy with a smooth past pattern of investment, half the installed machinery would become fully depreciated.

On the other hand, because the economy is growing, new capital formation exceeds replacement,[10] and therefore less than half the machinery must be replaced before a situation is reached in which newly produced equipment constitutes more than half the existing capital stock. Thus, the estimates of Table 35 overstate the adjustment problem in the following sense: the periods of time necessary for half the equipment to be newly produced are shorter than shown in the table.

In summary, if the adjustment problem is seen as one of capital losses associated with that proportion of present machinery that is not suited for use in a free trade situation, tariffs would have to be reduced gradually over periods somewhat longer than those shown in Table 35 for half the problem to be eliminated by the relatively painless means of replacing fully depreciated machinery. If, on the other hand, the problem is seen as one of providing efficient capital equipment for industry, the periods necessary to solve half of this problem through the normal flow of investment would be shorter than those shown in Table 35. There is, of course, no reason why one half rather than some other fraction (such as one third or two thirds) should be taken as the target in determining the most appropriate period for step-by-step tariff reductions. The data presented here do indicate that if the suggested [11] ten year period for Canadian tariff reductions is adopted, well over half the adjustment problem may be dealt with through normal replacement.

Human Capital. An issue of at least equal importance is the possible displacement of human resources. In limited respects, this would involve costs similar to those incurred with physical

[10] Evsey D. Domar, *Essays in the Theory of Growth* (New York: Oxford University Press, 1957), p. 161, presents the following formula:

$$\frac{R}{G} = \frac{1}{(1 + r)^m}$$

where:

R = replacement	r = rate of growth
G = gross investment	m = average life of capital

Thus, if the average life of capital is fourteen years and the rate of growth is 3 percent, replacement would constitute approximately two thirds of gross investment.

[11] Canadian-American Committee, *A Possible Plan,* p. 5.

capital and can be analyzed in a similar manner. For example, the cost involved in displacing an investment in education might conceivably be computed in a manner similar to that used in estimating the cost involved in displacing an investment in machinery. And parallel difficulties would be involved in any policy prescription. In one sense, an extended adjustment period would be desirable because this would allow any necessary displacement of the labor force to occur through the normal and relatively painless process of retirement. In another sense, a short period of adjustment would be desirable because it would minimize the risk of new entrants into a skill group which has limited free trade prospects. The ease of adjustment depends on a number of factors: the age pattern of the labor force; the percentage of the labor force displaced; the substitutability of skills and the ease with which they may be acquired;[12] and the physical mobility of labor.

Here the similarities of human and physical capital end because there are additional psychological and sociological effects that apply solely to the displacement of the human resource. Once a machine has been written off and replaced, no further costs are involved. This is simply not true for the labor force (except where the "writeoff" is a result of normal retirement or death); human capital must be successfully transferred to an alternative occupation, or there will be a continuing cost. Possible costs involve not only support from the public treasury but also severe social and psychological difficulties for those displaced.

Summary. If present human (and physical) capital is retiring (and wearing out) at the exact date on which tariffs are eliminated, a once-and-for-all tariff elimination is the appropriate policy on all counts. But these circumstances are so unlikely that the option of a staging sequence must also be considered. Since the desirability of staging depends on the remaining lifetime of existing capital, the policy choice is partially an empirical one.

The case for staging is that it tends to buffer and extend the incidence of obsolescence on human and physical capital. This reduces both economic and noneconomic dislocations of the la-

---

[12] The acquisition of skills is an investment; thus, the problem of imperfect allocation of capital also enters here. The "market" leaves much to be desired in the area of investment in humans.

bor force. It also reduces the chance that falling (machinery) asset values may result in bankruptcies and a financial crisis.

The case against staging is that potential free trade efficiencies may be lost in the interim period. This loss will occur insofar as natural markets may be left partially closed, inefficient machinery may be reinstalled, and new entrants induced into the labor force of industries with limited free trade prospects. Consequently adjustment problems may only be deferred, rather than eased. Furthermore, costs may be involved because equipment that would be scrapped under free trade may be left in operation and because labor that would be transferred may continue in the same employment.

The Industry-by-industry Approach as a Means of Limiting Disturbances[13]

The short-run disturbances associated with the introduction of free trade may be eased by cutting tariffs in stages; they may also be limited by adopting free trade in one or a few industries at a time and allowing these disturbances to work themselves out before free trade is extended to other industries. The European experience with the Coal and Steel Community preceded and laid the groundwork for the broader customs union. The recent (1965) automobile agreement between the United States and Canada[14] may prove to be North America's "coal and steel," leading on to other tariff reductions; on the other hand, there may be no sequel to the auto agreement: neither country has committed itself to more general reciprocal tariff reductions.

There are several advantages in the initial introduction of free trade in one industry. The industry concerned may find, perhaps contrary to its expectations, that free trade works in practice as well as in theory. With the advantage of this experience, the governments may be less inclined to look on a broader reduction of tariffs as a wild gamble. The industry whose tariffs have been eliminated may exert pressure for an extension of free trade to other industries from which it purchases expensive protected imports.

[13] See also Tibor Scitovsky, *Economic Theory and Western European Integration* (Stanford: Stanford University Press, 1958), pp. 145–151.

[14] This agreement is discussed in Appendix B.

But there are major problems associated with such an approach. First, an industry in isolated free trade might not prosper as it would if there were more general free trade (for example, because of remaining protection of inputs). There is no guarantee that the adjustment in this industry will even be in the direction required by more general free trade: it is possible, for example, that the chosen industry would expand very rapidly in the low wage country. After an extension of free trade to other industries, the general wage level might be bid up, with the result that pressures for contraction would be put on the industry of initial free trade. Thus, while an industry-by-industry approach might diminish the amount of adjustment that might be required in any given time period, it might greatly increase the total amount of adjustment over an extended period by causing adjustment first in one direction and then in the reverse direction. The possibility that single-industry free trade might lead in some respects away from rather than toward the general free trade situation might also cause political problems because each country might suspect the other of seeking quasi-protectionist advantage by limiting the agreement to products in which it enjoys an advantage.

In summary, then, there are major arguments both in favor of and against initiating a free trade arrangement in a single industry. No blanket approval or condemnation may be issued; the specific nature of any case in question must be closely considered.[15]

Adjustment Assistance

In view of the possible displacement of human and physical capital, a government undertaking tariff elimination may wish to buffer its impact with some sort of adjustment assistance. The arguments regarding adjustment aid are numerous and involved; an adequate treatment of the subject is therefore beyond the scope of this study. The major issues may, however, be noted.

The arguments in favor of assistance are both political and economic. By offering assistance, the government may soften the opposition to free trade of those who expect to be hurt. On equity

[15] For a study of the specifics of recent automotive changes, see Appendices A and B.

grounds, it may be argued that, if the country as a whole is to gain from free trade, the public should compensate those who lose. On economic grounds, adjustment assistance may be favored if it is designed to facilitate factor mobility into the more productive sectors of the economy. On the other hand, aid may be opposed on the ground that it sets an unfortunate precedent: the government should not be responsible for protecting all sectors of the economy from all possible losses, and it may be very difficult in practice to separate the injury caused to some industries by free trade from the misfortunes that normally occur from time to time even in the absence of commercial policy changes.

Our tentative conclusions are that, in general, the arguments in favor of assistance outweigh those against, although the specific nature of the adjustment assistance under consideration may be more important than the question of whether there will be assistance or not.

Labor Force Assistance. Probably the most common form of adjustment assistance is a subsidy going directly to the labor force. This may take the form of a payment of a percentage of past wages to any individuals thrown out of work, subsidized retraining in other skills, moving allowances, etc. The guidelines and objectives of such programs are twofold: in the interests of social justice, income payments are extended by the public, who gain from tariff elimination, to the displaced labor force on whom the costs of this change fall; second, in the interests of efficiency these payments should be made to increase the mobility of the labor force into a new occupational pattern. The resulting income level in a displaced employment sector should be sufficiently low to discourage new entrants (that is, below the labor supply price): subsidies or assistance (except possibly retraining) should not be extended to those who enter after the initiation of the program. At the same time, income of those remaining in the industry should not be so low as to create undue hardship. (Obviously this latter criterion is not a precise one and is heavily dependent on political judgments.) This could be achieved by a system of double pricing of labor, with an income subsidy paid to those employed in the industry at the time of tariff elimination but not to entrants after that time. Mobility might be increased by continuing the subsidy to those originally in the declining occupations even after they moved out. There are, however, major disadvantages to such an extension not only because of its possible costs but because some rather difficult questions of justice might arise. Even in the absence of this extension, however, exits from the industry would continue because of normal retirement, death, and quit rates.

An unemployed worker votes, but an unemployed machine does not.[16] Because of the vote and because of the social problems involved, adjustment assistance tends to be heavily directed toward the labor force. There are, however, means of assisting firms (that is, management and equity holders).

Special Credit Terms. By making loans available at attractive rates to firms over an adjustment period, costs would be reduced, and the industry would as a consequence be in a stronger competitive position. In spite of the secondary importance of credit costs as a determinant of competitiveness (Chapter 8), easy credit availability has a potentially important role to play: in the event of a once-and-for-all tariff elimination involving heavy capital losses, it might otherwise be difficult or impossible for firms with falling asset values to raise funds necessary for survival and expansion.

Duration

To the question: How rapidly should free trade be instituted? should be added another important timing question: How long should it last? Because of the adjustment costs associated with rationalization, it may be argued that any scheme should be made as permanent and as firm as possible. Arguing on these grounds, the Canadian-American Committee has recommended that no term be set for this agreement, with no provision for unilateral abrogation by either country.

If specific duration must be stated, it should be on the order of twenty-five years, with notice of termination required five years in advance. If such notice could only be given in the twentieth, forty-

---

[16] It is true that the machine's owner votes, but he may be in another country. In any case, there are few equity holders as intimately involved in the unemployment of machinery as workers are in their own loss of jobs.

fifth, and seventieth years (that is, five years before the termination of each twenty-five year period), a substantial review procedure might be involved, with the decision regarding continuation possibly having to be made at a time that was very inopportune. (For example, continuation decision might have to be made in the middle of an international political crisis.) In view of this, a case can be made for termination of the scheme with five years notice at any time after twenty-five years.

17

THE DEGREE

OF ECONOMIC INTEGRATION

Adjustment assistance and timing are not the only significant policy questions that must be raised if a free trade arrangement is to be considered. Also important are the technical aspects of a possible agreement. Is a customs union (with a common external tariff) to be preferred over a free trade association (with separate tariff schedules on imports from third countries)? Is the establishment of a common currency for the free trade area desirable, or should the present system of separate currencies and partially independent monetary policies be continued? Should an attempt be made to eliminate all restrictions on labor flows, or are the present low levels of restraint on labor movement between the United States and Canada satisfactory?

For each of these three questions, the first alternative involves the greater degree of integration; it also involves a greater loss of the essence of sovereignty. For all three questions, and particularly for the second involving a common currency, it is our opinion that the lesser degree of integration is desirable. The additional economic advantages that would flow from the higher degrees of integration would be small compared to those that arise from the abolition of tariffs; yet the loss of political independence associated with a common external tariff, a common currency, or a labor pool would be much greater than that coming from an elimination of tariffs.

Political independence is, of course, a matter of degree. No nation can live in isolation; nor would isolation be desirable even if it were possible. Just as economists have retreated from the concept of "perfect" competition toward that of "workable" competition in dealing with the practical problems of antitrust legislation, so it is necessary to consider commercial policy on the basis of "workable" independence rather than from some artificial concept of "perfect" independence. In entering a free trade arrangement, Canada and the United States would lose one element of freedom: they would commit themselves to allowing duty free imports from each other.[1] (Within free trade areas, temporary surcharges for balance-of-payments purposes are sometimes recognized as legitimate, although unfortunate.[2] Because the gains from a free trade arrangement are so dependent on industrial reorganization, and because such reorganization depends on the strength of assurances that tariff barriers will not have to be jumped, we believe that it would be unwise to permit even temporary surcharges on trade between the United States and Canada.)[3]

A Customs Union or a Free Trade Association?

With either a customs union or FTA, the United States and Canada would enjoy all the advantages of complete elimination of tariffs between the two countries. The difference between the two arrangements lies in the treatment afforded to other countries: in the case of a customs union, a common tariff is established on the products of third countries, whereas in the case of a free

---

[1] Even at present, under GATT, the two countries have voluntarily undertaken commitments which restrain their freedom. That is, they have undertaken not to raise their tariffs.

[2] For example the British have imposed surcharges, applying to EFTA members as well as outsiders, during their recent exchange difficulties.

[3] For a somewhat different position, see Canadian-American Committee, *A Possible Plan for Canada-U.S. Free Trade* (Washington and Montreal: National Planning Association and the Private Planning Association of Canada, 1965), pp. 11–12. Surcharges against the partner are not ruled out. However, it is recognized that preferable alternatives to surcharges may be found.

trade area each country is allowed to set its own external tariff against third countries.

If a customs union were undertaken, some explicit provisions would have to be made for the determination of the common external tariff.[4] In any such arrangement, Canada, with one tenth the population of the United States, could scarcely expect an equal voice. Thus, Canada's tariffs with third countries would, in effect, be made primarily in Washington. Because tariffs are a form of taxation, the determination of tariffs in another country's capital would probably raise the issue of "taxation without representation." The political stresses that it would involve are difficult to see with clarity ahead of time;[5] it may be predicted, however, that they would more than outweigh any economic gain that would flow from a customs union as contrasted to a free trade association.

Indeed, the economic balance would also appear to be in favor of the FTA rather than the customs union. It is true that differing external tariffs may raise some problems, notably, that of possible transshipment of imports, and, more broadly, the pressures to construct manufacturing facilities in the country with the lower external tariff on imported inputs. The question of transshipment may be met with the introduction of origin certificates for items that are shipped between the members and on which their external tariffs differ appreciably.[6] In order to prevent the evasion of origin

[4] See Canadian-American Committee, *A Canada-U.S. Free Trade Arrangement: A Survey of Possible Characteristics* (Washington and Montreal: National Planning Association and Private Planning Association of Canada, 1963), Ch. 4 and Appendix D; and Canadian-American Committee, *A Possible Plan,* pp. 21–22.

[5] An additional political advantage of the FTA is that it would allow the continuation of Commonwealth Preference by Canada. (The consistency of the Commonwealth Preference with a free trade association is illustrated by British participation in the EFTA.) The value of the preference to the Commonwealth would, however, be reduced by the establishment of a Canadian-U.S. FTA. Even where the Canadian Preferential rate is presently zero, the Commonwealth would be less well off in the Canadian market: their advantage vis-à-vis U.S. exports would be reduced to zero.

[6] Such certification would in practice be limited; those commodities which are not heavily traded internationally could be excluded. Even all of the remainder are not involved because goods could also be excluded on which the U.S. and Canadian tariffs are equal, or sufficiently close to cause no trade diversion. Moreover, even for the limited goods requiring such

rules by means of superficial fabrication, a certain percentage of domestic content may be required before tariff free passage of the common border is permitted. As this percentage can scarcely be set at 100 percent, however, the problem of readjustment of production within the free trade area because of differing external tariffs on inputs cannot be entirely eliminated. Nevertheless, economic distortions that will arise on this account will be counteracted by the associated pressures for a more rational international division of production. Specifically, the threat of loss of industry by the country with the higher external tariffs will create pressures for the reduction of such high tariffs. In contrast, there has been an observed tendency for the common external tariff of customs unions to reflect the duties of the more protectionist, rather than the less protectionist, participants.[7] Thus an FTA may be preferred to a customs union because it permits greater autonomy and because it tends to be less restrictive on imports from third countries.

A third advantage of an FTA is that it can more easily accommodate new members than can a customs union because there is no need to engage in the arduous process of establishing a common external tariff. For political reasons, ease of entry is a highly desirable characteristic. "Rich men's clubs" may cause resentment if they are closed. Although the entry of other countries (for example, of Latin American countries) into a North American FTA would involve difficulties that should not be underestimated, there are advantages in having the door open to such a possibility in the future. Of course, neither an FTA nor a customs union would preclude a simultaneous multilateral approach to freer trade through GATT.

---

certification, only trade flows in one direction (that is, from the low to the high tariff country) need be checked. Since only the more restrictive country need apply origin requirements, the other country would not be involved in their enforcement. As a consequence the application and administration of these content requirements would remain — like the present tariff — under the control of the country concerned.

[7] As for example, the Central American Common Market. See the *Report of the Fiscal Mission to Central America*, Joint Tax Program of the Organization of American States and Inter-American Development Bank (Baltimore: Johns Hopkins Press, forthcoming).

A Common Currency?

Members of a free trade group might replace their separate currencies with a common currency, which would become legal tender in each of the member countries. Clearly, a common currency would involve a distinct and substantial movement toward economic and political integration; it might conceivably be established without free trade, but it will be considered here as a possible free trade supplement.

One of the major effects of such a move would be to approach more closely a common capital pool. Already, there is a high degree of integration of the U.S. and Canadian capital markets. The greatest remaining barrier to capital flows is the exchange rate risk involved in international lending; one currency may be revalued in terms of the other before the complete repayment of principal and interest. Because the formation of a common currency area would (*permanently?*)[8] fix the exchange rate between the two countries, exchange risk on capital flows would be eliminated, and capital would become available in the capital-importing country (Canada) at lower cost. From the evidence on differences in capital costs given in Chapter 8, it may be inferred that a fixed exchange rate could conceivably reduce total costs in some Canadian industries by as much as one percent — depending on the extent to which flows of both equity and debt capital are currently subject to such a risk premium. It should be stressed that this one percent is an upper limit, and not the "best" estimate. In reality, the saving in the Canadian cost of capital would be less than this maximum. Exchange risk is not the only imperfection in the capital market; California interest rates are not identical at present with New York rates. Thus, some Toronto- or Montreal-New York interest rate differential might remain even if there were a common currency. Furthermore, even if the two separate currencies were retained, the interest rate differential between Canada and the United States might decline. For reasons outlined in Chapter 11, the free trade reorganization of Canadian industry might be expected to increase the Canadian supply of capital relative to de-

[8] Expectations regarding the permanence of the arrangement would depend in part on the accompanying degree of political integration.

mand. Thus, the size of the possible decrease in Canadian interest costs resulting from a common currency is further lessened.

Another result of a common currency would be the elimination of the exchange rate risk on the international trade in goods and services. It has already been argued in Chapter 11 that some Canadian free trade cost advantages would be offset by such a risk; for example, a firm considering production of a good in Canada for North American distribution might require a wage advantage in Canada to offset the risk that its Canadian-produced item may be suddenly revalued in the U.S. market by a change in the value of the Canadian dollar.[9] If this risk is eliminated, the Canadian location would be made more attractive in the long run, and the two major impediments (trading risk and higher Canadian capital costs) to the possible rise in Canadian wages to the level of adjacent U.S. regions would be reduced. It will be recalled from Chapter 2 that northern states in the United States have higher wages than southern states; as a consequence, were an equalization of wages in adjacent Canadian and U.S. areas to occur, the average Canadian wage would rise above the average U.S. level. However, complete equalization is to be regarded as extremely unlikely; at best it would be approached only after a long period of time.

Although the net economic gain from a common currency — probably much less than one percent of Canadian GNP[10] — would be much less than the economic gain from the elimination of Canadian-U.S. tariffs, the political consequences would be greater. The most important political consequence of a free trade area would be the loss of freedom in establishing the tariffs on goods from the North American partner. The political implications of a common currency would be much more extensive. A common currency implies a common central bank or, at the very least, close co-operation between the central banks regarding open market operations and other aspects of monetary control. Moreover, because of

[9] The exchange rate can move in either direction, resulting in either a gain or a loss. As a consequence the risk is not of an expected net loss; the risk relates simply to the uncertainty involved in a situation in which change may occur.

[10] The Canadian gain from lower capital costs would be further reduced to the extent that the capital payments are made to Canadian investors.

the relationships among monetary, fiscal, and debt management policies, this monetary integration would have major fiscal implications.

The case against a common currency may, perhaps, be stated most strongly in terms of the choice of alternatives that it involves. With an elimination of Canadian-U.S. tariffs, the "openness" of each economy would increase.[11] Thus, potential balance-of-payments surpluses and deficits would become greater and would call for an improved or increased set of instruments to govern balance-of-payments fluctuations; but, as a result of free trade, the instruments at hand would be reduced. Specifically, one potential means of adjustment — a change in Canadian-U.S. tariffs — would be eliminated. Since the major gains from industrial reorganization depend on assurances that free trade will continue, tariffs, temporary surcharges, import quotas,[12] and exchange controls would have to be ruled out as possible expedients for dealing with balance-of-payments crises. This implies either that provision must be made for financing larger cyclical balance-of-payments deficits[13] or increasing the effectiveness of other available instruments of adjustment. These include monetary, debt management, and fiscal policies, exchange rate flexibility, and perhaps measures to increase factor mobility and price flexibility. Unless major domestic institutional changes are to be considered, exchange rate flexibility has considerable claim to precedence among these alternatives. However, it would be automatically ruled out in a common currency area. Therefore, the authors would oppose the establishment of a common currency as part of a free trade agreement.[14]

A Common Labor Pool

The most important factor of production is labor. Since possible changes affecting the mobility of capital have been considered, it

---

[11] For a discussion of Canadian-U.S. openness, see Ronald J. Wonnacott, *Canadian-American Dependence: An Interindustry Analysis of Production and Prices* (Amsterdam: North Holland Press, 1961).

[12] Except, perhaps, quotas on items excluded from the agreement (for example, some agricultural products).

[13] And controlling political excitement when they occur.

[14] For additional objections to a binding of exchange rates in the adjustment period, see Chapter 11.

is also fitting to study the possibility of improving labor mobility in the event of a free trade arrangement.

There are a number of international barriers to labor mobility. Immigration policies may bar the movement of some individuals. Even if people are permitted to move, imperfections may be introduced into the labor market because of the nuisance and time involved in obtaining resident visas. Additional restraints to movement may be associated with government and private welfare programs. If an individual moves, can he transfer his retirement, health, and other benefits? A third international barrier to movement can be traced to the disinclination to move from one's homeland. This third "market imperfection" is based on political, social, and emotional factors that are not susceptible to straightforward analysis; it will therefore be excluded from the discussion below.[16]

There are three basic ways in which to handle the question of immigration laws. First, there is no reason why each country could not continue its present policies, retaining its regulations on nationals from the other country and from third countries. Present policies involve some barrier to migration between Canada and the United States particularly for foreign-born residents of North America. The historical level of migration would, however, suggest that the restraint on migration is not particularly great. Alternatively, as part of a free trade arrangement, immigration laws might be changed in either of two ways to allow free passage between the countries: as with tariffs, the elimination of internal barriers could occur while the two countries maintained separate immigration laws regarding third countries (the labor market equivalent of an FTA); or a common policy might be adopted regarding immigration from third countries (the labor market equivalent of a customs union). The movement of people is more important than the movement of things; therefore, it seems less likely that Canada would be willing to transfer control over immigration policy than she would control over tariff policy. Because common regulations on immigrants from third countries are apt to be re-

---

[15] Also excluded are such costs of moving as traveling expenses. These would exist regardless of the government policies followed; therefore, they need not be considered as a policy issue.

jected as a policy option, the key question is whether immigration restrictions between the two countries should be abolished.[16]

In recent decades, U.S. immigration laws have been based on national quotas, with native-born immigrants from Canada being exempt from quota limitations. Current legislation before the Congress will abolish the national quota system, and make training and skills the basis for immigrant eligibility. Apparently, U.S. immigration policy will therefore come closer to that of Canada, whose laws have not been based on national origin but rather on the skills of immigrants, and, more generally, on their expected ability to make a go of it in Canada. Because of the exercise of administrative judgment in determining eligibility, it is difficult to specify the effects of restrictions on immigration. Two points do, however, stand out: since the current U.S. legislative changes apparently reduce the disparity between U.S. and Canadian laws, difficulties associated with immigrants coming from third countries to the United States via Canada will probably decline; second, restrictions on immigration fall most heavily on the unskilled, and, in particular, those who are the most likely to become unemployed.

Therefore, if free trade is to be extended to free migration between the United States and Canada, the question of financial responsibility for unemployed migrants will arise. This leads into the general area of social welfare programs, including unemployment insurance and pension and medical benefits. In general, the more that varying programs in Canada and the United States can be "harmonized" (through such steps as making pensions portable), the more efficient the North American allocation of labor will become. However, attitudes toward welfare programs differ between the two countries: the allegation that programs are "socialistic" usually generates more political heat in the United States than in Canada. Because of the political strains that might arise if there were an attempt to integrate U.S. and Canadian welfare programs, it is questionable whether immigration laws should be modified as a supplement to North American free trade.

[16] Just as free trade in goods may be made provisional on meeting origin requirements, so free migration might be limited to those born in North America, or resident there for a specified period.

The implication is not that there would be no economic gains from the elimination of migration barriers. However, the extent of possible gains is not easy to calculate, even though a great deal of information on international migration is known. Between 1820 and 1964 approximately three and three quarters of a million people emigrated from Canada to the United States; the recent rate has been approximately fifty thousand per annum, or one fourth of one percent of the Canadian population. In spite of this migration from the lower to the higher income area, a significant difference in wages has remained, as may be seen from the data presented in Chapter 2. This differential may not, however, be attributed solely to restrictions on immigration imposed by governments; it is due to a number of other imperfections, including ignorance of opportunities elsewhere, the costs of moving, and the natural disinclination to leave one's native area.

The number of people willing to emigrate from Canada to the United States in any year is a positive function of the income differential between the two countries. Because free trade would increase the degree of specialization and the international interest of companies in both countries, it should stimulate the movement of people both ways across the Canadian-U.S. border; hence an increase in Canadian (gross) emigration as a function of the income differential might be expected. An elimination of immigration restrictions between the two countries would lead to a further increase in the gross emigration function.

It is not clear, however, that migration from Canada to the United States would increase as a result of a common labor pool *and* free trade; to the degree that free trade would reduce the Canadian-U.S. income differential, it would also cause a movement down the emigration function.

In summary, a common labor pool would increase net emigration, while free trade might increase or decrease it.

The relationships involved here are even more complex. We have thus far described only the direct dependence of emigration on income differences. In addition, it is likely that income differences are (inversely) dependent on emigration; that is, the more emigration takes place, the more incomes would be equalized.

In the process, average North American income would rise[17] because incomes for the individuals moving from Canada to the United States would be increased.[18] It is tempting to speculate on how this increase in income (following the elimination of U.S. immigration restrictions) might be calculated from Canadian labor supply and demand functions by applying a method analogous to the one employed in Chapter 15 to calculate the gains from the free movement of goods. (In this case, Canadian labor emigration would be the difference between domestic labor supply and demand *above* their intersection.) Such a calculation has not been made. There would, of course, be problems involved in specifying the functional relationships in this system. In addition, there is an even more serious difficulty: the reduction in Canadian wages cannot be as easily inferred from U.S. immigration restrictions as can the price increase on Canadian goods resulting from the Canadian tariff. And other complications, similar to those introduced in Chapter 15 would have to be recognized; for example, it is not even clear that the elimination of U.S. immigration restrictions would increase the average per capita income of Canadians.[19] Because some factors of production (for example, land) are scarce, it would seem that emigration should raise the per capita income level of those who remain. However, as economies of scale are partly dependent on local markets, this tendency might be partially or completely offset. Opening U.S. markets to Canadian producers with free trade would reduce the relative importance of this last point, but it cannot be ignored.

The conclusions of this chapter may be briefly stated. A customs

---

[17] One can think of circumstances in which this conclusion would not follow, but they are very unlikely.

[18] As long as all migration is voluntary, problems of psychic (non-monetary) income do not affect this conclusion.

[19] That is, per capita income of those who remain in Canada. The possibility of migration raises a nice question regarding the basic responsibility of the Canadian government: is it only to those who will remain in the country, or is it to all Canadians, regardless of where they live? Specifically, does the government have a responsibility to facilitate or discourage emigration if the movement will raise the income of the emigrants and raise the income of Canadians taken as a whole — but reduce the average income of Canadians who remain at home?

union involves political commitments which neither country wishes to make, whereas the economic advantages lie with the FTA; a free trade association is therefore preferred. Although there are economic advantages in a common currency area, there are also economic disadvantages. Until balance-of-payments difficulties can be more efficiently dealt with, and the two domestic economies develop greater internal flexibility, the disadvantages seem to outweigh the advantages. Because there are also political difficulties, such an arrangement is judged undesirable at this time. An elimination of migration barriers between the United States and Canada is a more debatable question. On economic grounds, gains might be expected from such a move, especially for those whose mobility is increased. Because these gains are so difficult to estimate and appear to be relatively small, it may be unwise to jeopardize the much larger gains from free trade by injecting controversial policies of this kind.

18

CONCLUSIONS

With free trade between the United States and Canada, there would be significant changes in the North American economy. In particular, free trade would increase the possibility of specialization and would lead to a greater exploitation of economies of scale. Because of the preponderant size of the U.S. economy, the advantage of free trade access to larger markets would be much more significant for Canadian than for American producers; therefore, the primary focus of this study has been on the changes that free trade would bring to the Canadian partner. This is not to argue that the effects on the United States would be trivial, particularly if subsectors of the economy are considered. However, the major changes would occur in Canada, with the benefits and risks being heavily concentrated there.

The evidence presented in this work indicates strongly that free trade in manufactured goods would yield substantial economic gains. The cost of North American tariffs to Canada was estimated at roughly 10.5 percent of Canadian GNP. The cost to the United States is relatively and absolutely much smaller, amounting to a fraction of one percent of GNP. All of this cost would not be eliminated immediately upon the adoption of free trade; there would be costs and strains of reorganization, with some firms facing acute problems. The pattern emerging from a period of rationalization cannot be precisely predicted, but the general outlines can be drawn.

Canadians would not become hewers of wood and drawers of

water. Indeed, it seems unlikely that there would be any substantial shift in the Canadian employment mix between services,
resources, and manufacturing, regardless whether or not resources
were included with manufactured goods in the agreement. (To the
limited extent that they enter international exchange, services are
already freely traded; hence, tariff elimination would not affect this
sector directly, and indirectly only insofar as changes in other
sectors influenced the relative demands for services.)

The prospects for Canadian resource sectors are good. Since
Canadian resources now receive less protection than U.S. resources, this Canadian sector might be expected to gain from
free trade. An expansion in demand for Canadian resources is,
however, unlikely to change the pattern of Canadian employment
markedly, partly because the supply of resources tends to be inelastic, that is, dependent on the availability of rich ore bodies,
etc. Furthermore, even limited tendencies toward the expansion of
employment in resource materials would be counteracted by the
rising supply price of labor resulting from the reorganization of
Canadian manufacturing. It seems likely, therefore, that increased
demand for resources will result more in rising wages than in
increased employment.

Agricultural products raise special problems of analysis, both
because of the widespread use of quotas and because the greatest
natural markets of the United States and Canada are not one
another (as they are for manufactured goods) but rather third
countries. Therefore, this area has generally been excluded from
the analysis.

Most of the specialization in Canada resulting from free trade
would occur *within* manufacturing industries rather than *between*
them. Because the competitive positions of Canadian industrial
sectors do not vary widely it seems unlikely that any of the broad
industrial groups examined in this study would disappear from
Canada. Instead it is to be expected that specialization would
occur in subindustries within each broad industrial group, with
Canadian concentration drifting toward labor-intensive activities.
However, major gains from free trade do not depend on this type
of specialization; they depend primarily on the exploitation of
economies of scale, defined broadly to include not only engineering

economies but also managerial and organizational efficiencies associated with specialization and competition in a larger market.

It has often been contended in Canada that, with free trade, U.S. manufacturing would simply increase its output by 10 percent, while Canadian industry would have to close down. This contention has been established as generally implausible, and it is particularly unlikely in growth industries. In these industries, new facilities are constantly being built. The question is: Where should these facilities be located? Canadian locations have major advantages. In particular Canadian labor costs are lower (and will continue to be in the foreseeable future, even though they can be expected to drift upward toward the U.S. level with free trade). Furthermore, contrary to common belief, transport and capital costs do not substantially offset this labor advantage because most Canadian industry lies either within or close to the North American industrial heartland. This potential strength of the Canadian competitive position would ease the major problems of production rationalization and marketing in the United States that Canadian firms would, with few exceptions, face. These same favorable cost conditions may induce U.S. producers who presently have no Canadian subsidiaries to expand in Canada rather than in the United States. It is even more likely that U.S. firms with existing Canadian subsidiaries would rationalize these facilities rather than write them off in favor of building new ones in the United States. Obviously every industry would not rush to Canada; any widespread movement would cause offsetting pressures in the form of rising Canadian costs as factor supplies became strained. There would, however, be a tendency for growth industries to expand in Canada.

In declining industries, the Canadian outcome would be less favorable. An American firm is unlikely to increase its facilities in Canada if it would involve closing down some of its U.S. facilities. Furthermore, the industry may be contracting not just relatively but also absolutely. In this case the obvious plants to eliminate will be those in Canada because the production aimed at a small market there would generally be inefficient in the new North American context. For rationalization to take place in Canada, wage (or other) operating cost advantages must be at least sufficient to cover costs of rationalization. By definition, declining industries face difficulties anywhere; but these difficulties would be even more severe in Canada.

Because Canada would become the area in North America where the greatest adjustments were taking place, it would be the area on which the pressures of both growth and decline would focus. There is a parallel conclusion: free trade would provide an additional impetus for particularly efficient (and fast growing) firms in any industry, but it would speed the demise of the inefficient. The relative sizes of the Canadian and U.S. economies imply that short-term reorganization problems would fall most heavily on Canada. However, these adjustment difficulties should not be exaggerated. In particular, Canada's small size means that it is not necessary for Canadians to compete with Americans all along the line; it is necessary only that they compete successfully in the production of a relatively limited number of products. The smaller the economic size of a country, the fewer are the lines of specialization required to balance trade and employ resources fully; hence, the easier it becomes to find subindustries in which competition may be successfully undertaken.

In order for Canada to take full advantage of the generally strong competitive position associated with its lower wage costs, several important conditions must be met in the period immediately following the establishment of free trade. One major requirement is sufficient flexibility and imagination by management to recognize and grasp the new opportunities for specialization opened up by freer access to the U.S. market. In short, it is essential that, in the face of a new set of circumstances, Canadian management not "die of shock" in exaggerated fear of possible injury from U.S. competition.

A similar onus would fall on the Canadian labor force. The lower wage is an advantage to Canadian locations only if Canadian workers are approximately as vigorous and diligent as their U.S. counterparts. We see no reason to doubt the high quality of the Canadian labor force. However, the free trade adjustment process would also require something extra of the labor force, namely, recognition of the need for, and vigorous cooperation in, major short-run changes. It is here that government adjustment assistance can be helpful. It is also important that the labor force cooperate in the period of adjustment by a degree of discipline and restraint in labor bargaining. It would, for example, be disastrous for the process of adjustment if Canadian unions were to take the long-run advantages of free trade as the basis for immediate insistence on wage parity with the United States. The long-run tendency for Canadian wages to rise toward U.S. levels under free trade requires vigorous expansion of industrial output. This expansion can be facilitated by short-run wage restraint.

Several limitations apply to any such study of free trade location pressures. Growth in selected U.S. areas (for example, Houston) has recently been heavily dependent on defense and space expenditures by the U.S. government. Canadian regions — and indeed many U.S. regions as well — can hardly expect an equal stimulus, although there is considerable scope for intercountry defense procurement. Amenities such as climate may also influence location decisions. Thus, Canada — like the industrial heartland in the U.S. North — may be at some disadvantage in the competition with California to attract and hold industry. In addition, there are certain market imperfections that can cause difficulty even for firms whose costs are competitive. Advertising and associated consumer loyalty make things difficult for the newcomer; although advertising is partly associated with the issue of economies of scale, it also involves something more. There seems, however, to be some general tendency to overestimate the significance of advertising in inducing "habit buying" because it is most important in the highly conspicuous sectors of the economy (consumer durables). Similarly, national preferences in purchases may provide some market imperfection. However, here, too, there would seem to be some tendency to overstate the difficulty. In part, past U.S. resistance to purchases from Canada has been associated with the problem of potential interruption of supply. This potential difficulty has, in turn, arisen from the possibility of tariff changes or reclassification, something which would be eliminated by free trade. In general, however, it cannot be maintained that economic forces will work out precisely as foreseen in any economic analysis. The forces considered in this study are powerful influences on location decisions, but there is no assurance that they will be controlling factors in every case.

The political significance of a bilateral free trade agreement cannot be foreseen with precision. There clearly would be some political implications: most obviously, each country would lose some degree of control over its commercial policy because it would commit itself by treaty not to impose tariffs on imports from the partner. Because it would cause an increase in trade across the common border, a free trade arrangement would tighten the already close economic ties between the two countries.

Yet paradoxically, Canada may become more dependent, yet less vulnerable. Specifically, Canada would be ensuring through such a treaty that U.S. tariffs would not be raised against Canadian exports, and this possibility is one of the major present sources of Canadian vulnerability. Moreover, freeing trade will have fewer critical implications for monetary and fiscal independence than does a fixed exchange rate. If a high degree of autonomy over these policies is judged a major objective in Canada, no commitment should be made to keep exchange rates frozen, for example, via a common currency arrangement. For similar reasons of autonomy, a free trade association is to be preferred over a customs union. The political case against fixed exchanges and a customs union draws support from economic considerations: a fixed exchange rate may not provide the authorities with sufficient scope to deal with balance-of-payments adjustments, whereas a customs union may not allow each partner to keep tariffs on third countries at as low a level as it would wish.

Because possible U.S. domination is a matter of concern in Canada, the initiative for any movement for free trade must come from Canada rather than the United States. In the final analysis, it must be the Canadian public who weigh the respective gains and losses from free trade. And public weighing of gains and losses is the purpose of the democratic process.

APPENDIX A. *Canadian Automotive Protection, 1961–1964: Content Provisions, The Bladen Plan, and Export Incentives*

In recent years, a number of major changes have taken place in the tariffs on automobiles and parts traded between the United States and Canada. Most conspicuous, perhaps, has been the 1965 agreement for conditional elimination of all tariffs on new cars and original equipment parts. The path to this modified free trade agreement was not a direct or smooth one, however; the negotiations that led to its signing were a result of the unpleasant prospect of U.S. retaliation against Canadian automotive export incentives. Consideration of the 1965 agreement itself will be deferred until Appendix B; the present appendix will deal with the earlier changes in Canadian automotive protection in 1962 and 1963. For simplicity, the present tense is used throughout this appendix to refer to 1964.

The Canadian export incentive programs of 1962 and 1963 differed in detail from the recommendations of Dean Bladen in his Royal Commission report.[1] Nevertheless, the programs introduced in an alternative form the major innovation recommended by the

---

[1] *Report of the Royal Commission on the Automobile Industry* (Ottawa, April 1961), hereafter referred to as the *Bladen Report*. The tariff changes are specified in PC 1962–1/1536 of October 26, 1962, and PC 1963–1/1544 of October 22, 1963.

For further discussion, see Harry G. Johnson, "The Bladen Plan for Increased Protection of the Canadian Automotive Industry," *Canadian Journal of Economics and Political Science,* 29: 212–238 (May 1963), reprinted in Johnson, *The Canadian Quandary* (Toronto: McGraw-Hill, 1963), pp. 133–166. See also Neil B. MacDonald, "A Comment: The Bladen Plan for Increased Protection for the Canadian Automotive Industry," *Canadian Journal of Economics and Political Science,* 29: 505–515 (November 1963); Johnson, "Reply," *ibid.,* 515–518; Johnson, "The New Tariff Policy for the Automotive Industry," *Business Quarterly* (University of Western Ontario), 29: 43–57 (Spring 1964).

report, namely, export incentives. By encouraging exports, and particularly exports of parts, the government hoped to stimulate Canadian employment, improve the current account balance, and contribute to the efficiency of the Canadian industry by making possible longer production runs.

Issues of great complexity were introduced by both the Bladen recommendations and the recent (1962–63) changes. Evaluation of their probable effects is made doubly difficult because of the previously existing system of import duties compounded with Canadian content requirements. Two broad questions arise when the recent (1962–63) tariff revisions are considered; they will form the central framework of this appendix: Do the revisions reduce the total excess of Canadian costs above world costs? Do the revisions increase the quantity of automotive production in Canada?

The first question is the key to the free trade position;[2] an affirmative answer means that the changes may be approved by the free trader, even though they lead to a result which is definitely "second best," that is, inferior to a position where all tariffs are removed. An affirmative answer to the second question is the most important hurdle in gaining the approval of the protectionist. His objective is not the direct opposite of the free trader — he certainly does not want to maximize costs as such, but rather wishes to increase output and employment in the protected industry. Thus, it is logically possible that some changes may be considered desirable (although not "optimum") by both free traders and protectionists, provided that a small amount of production at a high level of excess costs is replaced by a larger quantity of production at costs only slightly above world levels. The protectionist and freer trade positions are not mutually exclusive; it is important to recognize this when considering recent tariff changes.

Unfortunately, the original tariff schedule, the Bladen recom-

---

[2] Strictly speaking, the costs of protection are not simply the excess production costs attributable to tariffs. The loss of consumers' surplus should be added to the costs, and the increase in producers' surplus (quasi-rents) should be subtracted. See, for example, Harry G. Johnson, "The Cost of Protection and the Scientific Tariff," *Journal of Political Economy*, 68: 327–45 (August 1960), and the discussion above, Chapter 15. The excess costs may, however, be treated as a first approximation to the costs of protection; they will be so considered in this appendix.

mendations, and the changes of 1962 and 1963 all involve such a large number of important details that the analysis below becomes messy; as far as we can determine, inevitably so. Indeed, the degree of complexity has become so great as to be in itself a major obstacle to the development of wise policies.

The Protection Offered by the Canadian Automobile Tariff Prior to 1962

Completed automobiles and essentially all parts have been tariff-free if British in origin since the 1930's. It is to the most-favored-nation tariff applying to the United States, continental European countries, and Japan, that attention must be turned in order to find the protective significance of the Canadian automotive tariff schedule.

The MFN tariff on completed automobiles (tariff item 438a) is 17.5 percent. Products generally used in the manufacture of automotive parts (438b) are also subject to a MFN tariff of 17.5 percent if they are of a class or kind made in Canada, but are otherwise duty free. The 17.5 percent MFN tariff on a long list of automobile parts (item 438c) is suspended if both of two conditions are fulfilled: the part must be of a class or kind not made in Canada, and a Commonwealth (in effect, Canadian) content requirement must be met: 40 percent of the factory cost of automobiles if per annum Canadian production by the company in question is less than 10,000 units; 50 percent between 10,000 and 20,000 units; and 60 percent over 20,000 units. With only Volvo and Studebaker currently producing less than 20,000 units, only the 60 percent content requirement is of primary importance. Brake linings and clutch facings (item 438g) and piston casings (item 438j) are subject to a MFN tariff of 25 percent regardless of fulfillment of content requirements, as are parts not otherwise provided for (item 438f), including engines. (The collection of the 25 percent duty on automatic transmissions was suspended prior to the order-in-council of October 1962.)[3]

---

[3] Items 438d, 438e, 438h, and 438i give the tariffs on trucks, ambulances, motorcycles, etc., and are not dealt with in this paper. Items 438k to 438w specify temporary duties on a number of parts, ranging from free to 7.5 percent for most favored nations.

The multiplicity of tariff regulations makes any analysis of the degree of protection on specific parts very difficult. In order to make the problem manageable, therefore, the complications of the schedule will be dealt with by stages. In example A, it will be assumed that all automobile parts bear a 17.5 percent tariff but are duty free if the 60 percent content requirement is met. (This initial example closely parallels a section on p. 142 of Johnson's review of the Bladen Plan; those familiar with that review may wish to skip example A.) In example B, complications are introduced by the inclusion of duties collectable even if content requirements are fulfilled. As long as content requirements are met, tariff exemptions on specific imported parts (items 438k to 438w) are unimportant, and they will be ignored in the discussions below.

Because of the complexities, simple numerical examples are used in which round numbers are chosen wherever possible (e.g., $1000 for the factory cost of a U.S. automobile). The simple examples are, however, accompanied by general algebraic formulations, in which the following symbols are used:

c = Canadian content requirement = 60 percent unless otherwise specified;

t = tariff on completed automobiles = 17.5 percent of Canadian factory price;

u = tariff on specific part;

v = fraction of U.S. price of completed U.S. automobile represented by dutiable import;

x = average protection to Canadian content.

Throughout, transportation costs are assumed to be zero, and nonprice national preferences are similarly ignored.

Example A. All Parts Duty Exempt If 60 Percent Canadian Content

Numerical example	In symbols
Assumed U.S. factory price = $1000	1
Maximum Canadian factory price = $1175	$1 + t$
60 percent Canadian content = $705	$c(1 + t)$
Imported content = $1175 − $705 = $470 = 47 percent of automobile, at world prices	$(1 + t)(1 − c)$

World (U.S.) price of Canadian content $1000 − $470 = $530 $\qquad c(1 + t) − t$
Average protection of Canadian
Content = (705/530) − 1 = 33.02
percent $\qquad\qquad x = t/[c(1 + t) − t]$ (1)

Hence, if all imported parts were exempted from duty on the fulfillment of the content requirement, the 60 percent content requirement would give average protection of 33 percent to the "sixty percent" of the vehicle made in Canada; the incentive to produce in Canada would far exceed the 17.5 percent tariff. The protection afforded to Canadian parts may be considered as the sum of two components, the first consisting of the 17.5 percent duty on final automobiles, and the second consisting of the protection which may be transferred from the duty free imports to the Canadian content. In the above example, this second element of protection to the Canadian content amounts to approximately 15.5 (i.e., 33 − 17.5) percent. The smaller the Canadian content requirement, the larger is the quantity of duty free imports, and the larger this second component consequently becomes. In the limit, if content requirements were to approach zero, this second component of protection to Canadian content would approach infinity. Conversely, as Canadian content requirement increases, this second component decreases, so that as the content requirement approaches 100 percent, this second element tends to disappear, and the effective protection approaches the 17.5 percent level at which duties are imposed on final automobiles. The lower the content requirement, the greater is the level of protection; hence the Canadian system of a variable content requirement discriminates in favor of the smaller firms. This discrimination is not, however, very important, as all firms except Studebaker (and since its recent entry, Volvo)[4] must meet the same 60 percent requirement.

---

[4] The Volvo entry into Canada is attributable to the smaller content requirement for small-scale producers, and to the five-year graduated duty moratorium on imported parts that was granted to Volvo. Similar concessions are expected to result in the establishment of Canadian assembly lines for Renault and Peugeot automobiles. Since the graduated content requirement and the duty moratorium increase the attractiveness of the Canadian market to new entrants, they tend to fragment the Canadian

A complication arises because all parts are not exempted from duty when content requirements are met (e.g., those in tariff item 438f). Insofar as such parts are imported in spite of the "specific" duties, the second element of protection noted above will be eroded. This complication will now be considered.

Example B. Some Parts Dutiable; Others Duty Free If 60 Percent Canadian Content

Numerical example	In symbols
Assume that a \$200 engine is imported, subject to a 25 percent duty.	v u
Assumed U.S. price = \$1000.	1
Maximum Canadian price = \$1175.	$1 + t$
Duty = \$50.	uv
Maximum price to Canadian factory, excluding duty paid = \$1175 − \$50 = \$1125.	$1 + t - uv$
60 percent Canadian content = .6 × \$1125 = \$675.	$c(1 + t - uv)$
Total imported content = \$1125 − \$675 = \$450, or 45 percent of the world price of the vehicle (including the engine).	$(1 - c)(1 + t - uv)$
Canadian content, at world prices = \$1000 − \$450 = \$550.	$c(1 + t - uv) - (t - uv)$
Protection on Canadian content = (675/550) − 1 = 22.73.	$x = \dfrac{t - uv}{c(1 + t - uv) - (t - uv)}$ (2)

Thus, if some parts are imported over "specific" tariffs, the effect is to reduce the protection given by the 60 percent content requirement to the parts made in Canada. The effect on the protection of

market, thus increasing the barriers to efficient production. Doubts may therefore be entertained regarding the priority granted to the efficiency objective in the determination of automobile tariff policy.

Canadian content is equivalent to a decrease in the tariff on final automobiles by an amount equal to the specific tariff times the proportion of the automobile involved; this may be seen by inspecting equation (2), in which $t - uv$ replaces the t of equation (1).

Because the importation of parts in schedule 438f over the 25 percent tariff will erode the level of protection to Canadian content, automobile manufacturers have a particular incentive to make up the Canadian content with parts in item 438f rather than those for which tariffs are waived upon fulfillment of 60 percent content (item 438c). Thus, the special tariffs provided by item 438f have two opposite effects on the level of protection: those parts under 438f are provided with protection over and above the average level of 33 percent which they would otherwise receive; where these parts are nevertheless imported over the tariff (or where they are produced at costs of more than 33 percent above U.S. levels), then the protection on the remaining Canadian content is eroded below the 33 percent level.

These are three possible outcomes. First, and simplest, it is possible that item 438f parts are among those which can be produced in Canada at the lowest excess of costs over world levels. In this case, they would be included in the 60 percent produced in Canada even if they were not given special protection. After their inclusion in item 438f, they will continue to be produced in Canada, and the special 25 percent duty will make no difference. The second possibility is that the excess Canadian cost of engines is sufficiently high that they would be imported in the absence of the special 25 percent duty, but the excess cost is sufficiently low that the 25 percent duty will lead to their production in Canada. In this case — the only one in which the 25 percent special duty actually "protects" engine production — automobile producers will find that, as a result of the engine production, they can abandon production of some other parts and still fulfill their content requirement. As the 60 percent content requirement must be met whether engines are produced in Canada or not, the production of engines will not lead to any sizable[5] change in total automobile

---

[5] Because of the regulations regarding the calculation of the content base, the inclusion of engines would tend to lead to a small increase in the

parts: engines will merely supplant other parts. Furthermore, Canadian automobile producers will be worse off, since they will be forced by the 25 percent tariff to choose a 60 percent Canadian content which does not represent the least-cost combination. The third possible outcome of the 25 percent duty on engines is that these parts will be imported over the duty because their excess costs of production in Canada are very high. In this case, the tariff will be to the disadvantage of the companies concerned; duties will have to be paid.

Thus, where item 438f is effective in protecting Canadian production of engines (and other specified parts), the Canadian automotive industry is distracted away from relatively efficient to relatively less efficient parts production; as long as content requirements are met but not significantly exceeded, there will be no sizable net change in Canadian production. In short, unless parts subject to specific duties were produced by independent manufacturers whom it was desired to protect at the expense of other automobile producers, or unless there was some intrinsic merit in engine production as contrasted to the production of other automobile parts, then the special duties provided by item 438f were a ridiculous addition to the system of protection based on a content requirement.[6]

Canadian dollar value of Canadian parts production per automobile. This follows from the increase in the "factory cost of production" of Canadian automobiles that would result from domestic engine production. This small increase in the (Canadian dollar) production of parts in Canada would be directly attributable to relative Canadian inefficiency; any extra employment might as well be provided by raking leaves.

Insofar as higher Canadian costs lead to higher automobile prices and hence to lower sales in Canada, the increase in Canadian parts per automobile might be offset, or more than offset, by a decline in sales. Thus, total parts production (in Canadian dollars) might be either increased or decreased by these specific duties. Canadian parts production in real terms (that is, measured at world prices) would decline.

[6] Other difficulties introduced by the specific duties may be illustrated by reference to the procedure followed by one of the producers in the past when dealing with an automobile component on which such duties were imposed. Although the component itself was subject to specific duties, the parts from which it was made were not. As a result, the automated American production line for this component was periodically stopped so that a number of the unassembled parts could be removed and shipped to Canada for assembly there. Since the automated U.S. line then continued with empty spaces, nothing (except the payment of duty) was saved by

Protection Prior to 1962: Summary and Conclusions. If consideration is given only to the basic structure of automobile tariffs, consisting of the 17.5 percent duty on completed cars and the predominant 60 percent content requirement, then assembly and parts production up to this 60 percent level were provided with average protection of approximately 33 percent.

Special duties on some parts provided by tariff item 438f regardless of the meeting of Canadian content may be condemned. They tend to distort Canadian production toward a less efficient pattern of parts production and are therefore objectionable on free trade grounds. Furthermore, they give little or no incentive to increase total production, and there is therefore little or no reason for the protectionist to favor them.

The Bladen Report: The Extended Content Suggestion

In his *Report of the Royal Commission on the Automotive Industry,* Dean Bladen made seven major recommendations, emphasizing (p. 57) that "these are not discrete items from which a selection is invited; they constitute a unitary plan." However, this exhortation will be ignored, and little attention will be paid to a number of Bladen's suggestions, such as those to revise the content requirements and to impose tariffs on British automobiles. This section will rather concentrate on Bladen's two most notable innovations, that is, his proposal that all motor vehicles and parts be admitted free of duty provided that content requirements are met, and that exports of vehicles and parts be included in the calculation of Canadian content.

Under these suggestions, the special protection afforded to engines and other parts by tariff item 438f would be eliminated; these parts could be imported free of duty if the content requirements were met. As noted in the previous section, the proposed abolition of the special duties may be applauded by free traders and possibly also by protectionists. The suggestion that exports of parts be

---

not having the assembly of the component completed in the United States. There were, however, considerable costs in the procedure followed. First, there were the costs of interrupting the automated U.S. line; second, there were the costs of assembling the parts in Canada.

counted in calculating Canadian content can also be applauded by free traders, and possibly by protectionists. It would not have much effect on the total quantity of Canadian automotive production, but it would cause a reorganization of the Canadian industry; production would tend to be narrowed to those parts on which the excess of Canadian costs over world costs is smallest, while the scale on which these parts are produced would be increased.

This may be illustrated by an example. (The complications introduced by the inclusion of exports of completed automobiles in Bladen's extended content plan will be ignored.)

Example C. All Parts Duty Free If 60 Percent Content Requirement Is Met; Exports of Parts Included in Content; U.S. Parts Tariff of 8.5 Percent; Canadian Tariff of 17.5 Percent on Completed Automobiles. Unfortunately, the complications of this problem are so great that it is not possible to reduce it to a simple algebraic solution similar to those of examples A and B. The most probable direction of a number of changes which would flow from such a policy can, however, be identified.

The effects of an extended content provision will be evaluated with the aid of Figure 16, in which the behavior of a single automobile producer is considered. To the right from the origin O, the fraction of the Canadian car (measured at world prices) necessary to meet the 60 percent content requirement is marked off as OU. The precise value of OU depends on the degree to which Canadian costs exceed American costs; it reaches its minimum value of .53 when full advantage is taken of the tariff on final autos, that is, when Canadian costs of completed automobiles are 17.5 percent above U.S. costs. (The figure .53 is derived in example A above.) To the left from U, the fraction of the automobile which the assembly process represents is marked off as TU.

On the vertical axis, parts costs as a fraction of world (i.e., U.S.) parts costs are shown, with ON representing the world level. Canadian costs of assembly are shown as TK, that is, KQ more than the American level. From E to F, H, and J, the costs of Canadian parts are graphed, starting from those parts with the relatively lowest excess over world costs, and working successively to the highest cost parts at J. Given the 17.5 percent final tariff and the 60 percent content requirement, then $EFHJKL$ is subject to

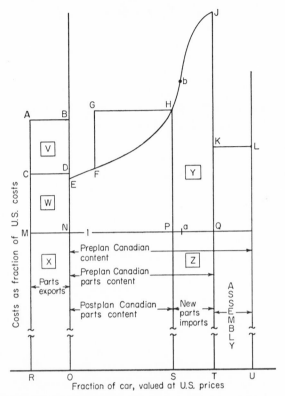

Figure 16. Extended content plan for parts: single automobile manufacturer.

the restraint that its average height cannot be more than 33.02 percent more than the height of *NPQ*; it is possible for *E* to lie below *N*.

If the vertical distance between *E* and *J* exceeds (approximately)[7] 8.5 percent, then the manufacturer under consideration will find it to his advantage to export parts over the U.S. tariff and expand imports under the extended content scheme. The manufac-

[7] Since exports and imports of parts influence the Canadian cost of production of automobiles, they also influence the net volume of imports permissible under the 60 percent Canadian content requirement. Hence, the U.S. tariff of 8.5 percent is not a precise measure of the difference in excess Canadian parts costs necessary to make exports and imports advantageous under the extended content plan.

turer will start exporting the parts whose Canadian costs are lowest and importing those whose Canadian costs are highest. In graphical terms, he will start exporting the parts at E, and move to the right toward F. He will import parts whose Canadian costs are highest, starting at J and working to the left toward H, stopping when FG is only sufficient to compensate for the U.S. duties which must be paid. The range of Canadian parts exported, EF, will depend, among other things, on the dispersion of Canadian parts costs and the absorptive capacity for these parts in his U.S. operations. Parts between E and F will now be produced both for export and for use in domestic automobiles; those between F and H will be produced in Canada for home use but not for export; and those between H and J will now be imported and not produced in Canada.

In order that additional imports of parts ST may take place duty free, the quantity of exports must be at least OR. The average Canadian cost of production of parts exports is OD; the total cost of those goods to the American parent will therefore be $RCDO$ (areas $X + W$) plus the 8.5 percent U.S. tariff (area V). The increase in costs to the American parent, which previously was able to make parts OR at an average cost of ON, will therefore be represented by areas $W + V$, where W may be either positive or negative. The Canadian subsidiary will gain. Since it can now import ST of parts duty free at an average price of SP, its costs will be lowered by Y. Since FG is sufficient to compensate for the U.S. tariff, there is a net gain to the combined operations of the Canadian manufacturer and the U.S. parent, i.e., $Y > V + W$.

Something remains to be said about the relative size of parts exports and additional parts imports, i.e., $W + X$ and Z. The restraint on $W + X$ is that it must be sufficiently great that the content requirement is met. The shifting of Canadian production from parts ST to parts OR will mean that Canadian content, that is, the numerator for the content requirement, will have changed by $[W + X - (Y + Z)]$. The factory cost of vehicles produced in Canada, that is, the denominator for the Canadian content requirement, will have changed by $[-Y]$. If content requirements are to be met, then:

$$W + X - (Y + Z) = -0.6Y,$$
$$\text{i.e., } W + X = 0.4Y + Z,$$
$$\therefore W + X > Z.$$

That is, the value of parts exports measured at Canadian prices will be greater than the increase in parts imports measured at import (world) prices. Also, $W + X < Y + Z$; that is, the Canadian cost of parts exports needed to fulfil content requirements will be less than the previous Canadian cost of production of parts which will now be imported.

The results of the extended content plan, when applied to parts exports and additional original equipment parts imports, may now be considered:

1. Measured at world prices, there may be either an increase or a decrease in the total quantity of parts produced in Canada per Canadian automobile. The condition $W + X = 0.4Y + Z$ does not allow the relative sizes of OR and ST to be determined.

2. There will be a decline in total parts production *per automobile* in Canada, valued at Canadian prices; this follows from $W + X < Y + Z$. It is not possible to tell whether total parts production (at Canadian prices) will fall, rise, or stay the same. The fall in Canadian automobile costs may be partly passed along to the consumer; if so, the increase in automobile sales may more than offset the decline in the Canadian value of parts per automobile. As the direction of change in automotive production is uncertain, it is not clear whether the extended content arrangement would be desirable when judged by the protectionist criterion.

3. There will be a net gain from a free trade viewpoint. The company in question will take advantage of the extended content plan by increasing both exports and imports of parts only if its overall profits are thereby increased. Its U.S. costs will rise by $W + V$; its Canadian costs will fall by Y; hence $Y > W + V$. *A fortiori,* $Y > W$; that is, the excess costs attributable to the Canadian tariff will decline.

It is true that there may be a rise in the quantity of parts (at world prices) produced in Canada, the high cost area. However, the relevant question is not the quantities of exports and imports, but rather the total excess costs attributable to commercial policy.

This falls, since $Y > W$. To the extent that Canada can produce some part at costs below world levels ($OE < ON$), the free trade conclusion is strengthened. It is also strengthened insofar as concentration of Canadian parts production leads to a fall in per unit costs.

4. The Canadian balance on merchandise account will improve; $W + X > Z$.

5. The Canadian balance on current account may either improve or decline. There will be a tendency for the merchandise account balance improvement to be offset by an increase of remittable profits to U.S. parents.

This facet of the extended content plan, applying to exports of parts in return for additional imports of parts, is the most straightforward segment of Bladen's extended content plan. The plan was also to be applied to two other areas — repair parts and completed automobiles. Problems arise in analyzing these proposals because Bladen's definitions of the Canadian content base, while explicit and unambiguous, lead to anomalous results. Specifically, in defining the content base (that is, the denominator in calculating content), Bladen excluded Canadian-made repair parts sold in the Canadian market[8] and included Canadian manufactured automobiles sold abroad.[9]

A 60 percent content requirement might seem to preempt 60 percent of the market for Canadian producers. Because of the anomalies in the content base, however, this is not the case in the repair parts market. Suppose that a Canadian automobile producer manufactured and sold $60 of repair parts in Canada. Because these parts are excluded from the content base under the Bladen Plan, there could be a duty free importation of either original equipment or replacement parts up to the limit of a full $100 rather than $40. With the Canadian content rising by the $60 in repair parts,[10] and the content base rising by only the $100 in imports, the content requirement would still be met. Insofar as replacement parts were being produced in Canada, the market share reserved for Canadian production would be 37.5 (i.e., 60/160) percent rather than 60

[8] *Bladen Report,* pp. 59, 70–71.
[9] *Ibid.*
[10] *Ibid.,* recommendation 7b, p. 58.

percent. This exclusion of replacement parts from content denominator means that more duty free imports could accompany the production for the Canadian market of replacement parts than of original equipment parts (which are included in the "factory cost of motor vehicles produced in Canada," and hence in the content base). Thus, there would be a special incentive to produce for the replacement parts market.

This incentive might be expected to have two results. The major automobile manufacturers would find it attractive to absorb independent parts producers in order to gain credit for their replacement parts sales, even where no savings in costs would result from such takeovers. Secondly, there would be an incentive to push sales of domestically produced parts in the Canadian replacement market, even at prices below cost. In other words, the Bladen proposals would encourage Canadian manufacturers to "dump" in the Canadian replacement parts market. A probable outcome would be a Canadian replacement parts market dominated by the major Canadian automobile producers, with much of the content credit being used to gain duty free entry for original equipment parts.

An anomaly of a different sort would have resulted from Bladen's content definitions for completed automobiles which were exported; the anomaly would have blocked fulfilment of Bladen's apparent hope of providing an incentive to export not only parts, but also completed automobiles. Under his definitions, the total value of the foreign and Canadian content of the completed automobiles would be added to the content denominator, yet only the Canadian content itself would be added to the numerator. Insofar as the extended content provision led to a decrease in direct Canadian content of completed automobiles below 60 percent (that is, insofar as additional imports of parts ST in Figure 1 were imported to be used in Canadian automobiles), exports of automobiles would hinder rather than aid in the fulfilment of Canadian content. Exports of completed automobiles might, therefore, decrease, although insofar as there was a fall in the price of Canadian automobiles there would be an offsetting encouragement.

Bladen's Extended Content Plan: Conclusions. The Bladen proposals for extended content provisions would lead to a number of anomalies, but on balance they might be expected to operate to reduce excess costs of protection. That is, free traders could approve of them, even though there might possibly be an increase in parts production in Canada, the high-cost country. Specifically, the following aspects of the Plan would operate to lower the excess costs of protection:

Insofar as some exports of parts took place prior to the adoption of the plan, they could be included in Canadian content, and thus duty free imports could be expanded. (In contrast, no credit of any sort was to be allowed for such exports under the 1962 and 1963 arrangements; base-period exports were explicitly excluded from credit.)

Insofar as there was a significant dispersion of excess costs of various Canadian-made parts before the plan was adopted, there would be an importation of the most costly and an expansion of production of those with the least excess cost. (This is illustrated in Figure 1). One of the contributing features in lowering excess costs would be the removal of special protection of parts in tariff item 438f.[11]

[11] The abolition of the "class or kind" provision of item 438c, as suggested by Bladen, would also clear the way for Canadian companies to choose the lowest cost combination to meet content requirements; such an abolition might therefore be approved. (However, the situation becomes less clear if account is taken not only of the extended content plan but also of the other proposals by Bladen, including the suggestion to modify the content schedule to make it more progressive.)

For a different conclusion, see Johnson, "The Bladen Plan," pp. 161–165, where Bladen's proposal to remove the "class or kind" provision is attacked. Johnson argues that such a removal would be discriminatory against the large producers *even if the present content schedule were retained*. (See the last complete sentence on p. 163 and its context.) This, it would seem to me, either attaches undue significance to the 2 or 3 percent of the market occupied by Studebaker and Volvo or uses the term "discriminate" in a rather strange sense. Insofar as manufacturers other than Studebaker and Volvo are concerned, the present content schedule is nondiscriminatory, that is, it is 60 percent for each. The "class or kind" provision discriminates against the smaller producers in the sense that they are penalized if they do not make as broad a product mix as the largest company. Thus, the removal of the "class or kind" provision would remove a discrimination against the smaller producers rather than create discrimination in their favor. Excluding the Studebaker and Volvo cases, the proposition that the abolition of the "class or kind" provision would be discriminatory may be accepted only if it is assumed that large producers should be given an advantage compared to small producers, over and above any advantage they gain from their greater efficiency.

Throughout this paper, the economies of scale have been dealt with peripherally. However, there are grounds for believing them to be substantial in the automobile industry. Insofar as this is the case, the concentration of production would lead to further cost savings.

There would be a number of undesirable consequences of the extended content plan, although these would not be sufficient to offset the favorable effects on excess costs:

Either present imports of automobiles from the U.S. would have to be curtailed, or parts imports would have to be decreased sufficiently to compensate for the inclusion of completed auto imports in the content base.

There would be a number of distortions introduced into Canadian production because of the anomalies rising out of the definitions used in content calculations.

It must be emphasized that the above conclusions apply only to Bladen's extended content scheme, whereby content credit would be granted for exports. Thus they are not necessarily valid for the Bladen Plan as a whole, which includes such suggestions as a modification of the percentages in the content schedule and an imposition of a 10 percent duty on British automobiles. There is, however, justification for our having taken this partial view of the Bladen Report: it was Bladen's suggestion to provide incentives for exports which, *in a very modified form,* became the basis for the policies of 1962 and 1963.

Recent Changes in Automobile Tariffs

October 1962. Prior to October 31, 1962, the 25 percent MFN tariff on automatic transmissions had been suspended. In October (PC 1962–1/1536), it was announced that henceforth this tariff would be enforced, but that remission of the 25 percent duties on transmissions and engine blocks (up to a limit of 10,000 per motor vehicle manufacturer) could be earned. For every dollar of Canadian content of exports of motor vehicle parts in excess of the Canadian content of exports of parts during the base period from November 1, 1961, to October 31, 1962, duties would be remitted on a dollar of transmission or engine imports.

There are a number of reasons why this proposal would be less desirable than the Bladen proposals from the point of view of minimizing excess costs. Automatic transmissions were not produced in Canada prior to the order. The 1962 changes, on the one hand, created pressures to produce such transmissions in Canada; on the other, they created pressures to increase exports of parts to earn duty remissions. Insofar as manufacture of automatic transmissions was the outcome,[12] there is a priori reason for believing that there was a transfer of Canadian production from parts manufactured at relatively low excess cost to automatic transmissions, which, because they were not previously manufactured, presumably are produced in Canada only at relatively high excess cost. No significant net increase in Canadian parts production could be expected, since the unchanged content requirements would still be enforced. In contrast to the Bladen Plan, which would have abolished specific duties on parts and hence encouraged the choice for Canadian production of those parts with the lowest excess cost, the 1962 change introduced an additional specific duty, and therefore encouraged an irrationalization of the Canadian industry.

Not all companies undertook the production of automatic transmissions; imports continued in spite of the tariff.[13] Thus, there was an incentive to increase exports in order to earn remission of these duties. As each dollar of additional exports would lead to remission of duty on one dollar of transmission imports, the export incentive would be equivalent to the duty, i.e., 25 percent. As the U.S. duty on parts averages about 8 percent, it is possible that the new parts exports would be produced at an excess cost, i.e., Canadian costs of production would be greater than U.S. costs of production; and that, therefore, from an international point of view there would be

[12] General Motors announced that it would set up a transmission plant; this decision was presumably a result of the changes of October 1962. The plant did not actually begin operation during the October 1962–October 1963 period.

[13] Canadian imports of automatic transmissions (item 5649, in millions of Canadian dollars):

1960	1961	1962	1963
27.7	32.6	45.6	44.1

an increase in excess costs. As the relatively most advantageous Canadian parts would tend to be chosen for export first, the opposite outcome is also possible; the Canadian costs of production might be less than the U.S. cost, and the export incentive would simply offset the effects of the U.S. tariff. In this case, there would be a decline in excess costs from an international viewpoint — the American tariff collections are not a net cost because they add to U.S. government revenue. From the Canadian viewpoint, however, there would be an increase in excess costs — the U.S. tariffs are in essence a tax on Canadian exports, with the revenues being lost to Canada.

In summary, the 1962 changes regarding transmissions probably led to an increase in total excess costs from the international viewpoint; they increased excess costs from the Canadian viewpoint. They provided an incentive to distort production toward less economically produced lines; encouragement was offered to Canadian parts exports at excess Canadian costs, and possibly at excess world costs.

The conclusions for the engine tariff modifications announced in the same 1962 order-in-council are similar, although not so unfavorable. Canadian exports were encouraged at excess Canadian costs, and perhaps at excess international costs. However, because a 25 percent tariff on engines existed before the 1962 changes, the worst feature of the transmission change was avoided; there was no distortion of Canadian production beyond that existing previously. It might even be thought that, since the 1962 modification provided an escape from engine duties, there might be a rationalization of Canadian production; engine production at high excess costs might be supplanted in favor of the production of other Canadian parts. However, such an outcome was intentionally[14] dis-

---

[14] In explaining the engine regulation, the Department of Finance press release of October 29, 1962, stated (p. 3):

"Automobile engines also carry a statutory Most-Favoured-Nation rate of 25 per cent. There has been no temporary free entry provision. The large companies produce most of the engines required for their own use, but import some for particular purposes. They do not produce any for sale to other automobile companies. The smaller companies have had no choice but to import all their engines.

"The Government has concluded that a provision similar to that for

couraged by the 1962 order-in-council: there was a 10,000 limit on the number of engines (per company) on which duty would be remitted as a reward for increasing exports.

Thus, except for the advantage of simplicity, the 1962 changes must be adjudged inferior to the Bladen extended content proposal. The latter was aimed at, and would have resulted in, a rationalization of Canadian production. The 1962 changes were primarily a program for pushing exports; any resulting modification of parts production for Canadian automobiles was perverse in the sense that it increased excess costs; in the case (engines) where a rationalization of Canadian parts production might possibly have occurred, such a rationalization was intentionally discouraged by the 10,000 unit limit.

October 1963. The policy initiated by the order-in-council of October 22, 1963 (PC 1963–1/1544) superseded and broadened the engine and transmission experiment of the previous October. Tariffs on all imports of motor vehicles and original equipment parts were to be remitted to the extent that the Canadian content of exports of motor vehicles and parts of the company in question exceeded that of the base period, November 1, 1961, to October 31, 1962. This remission of duties was to apply only to companies with major Canadian assembly operations: a company could qualify only if 40 percent of the total number of motor vehicles that it sold were produced in Canada.

Although they might be considered a logical extension of the changes of October 1962, these modifications were considerably less objectionable from the point of view of efficiency; that is, they were less likely to lead to a rise in excess costs in the automobile industry. Indeed, while the 1962 changes might have been expected to operate toward an increase in excess costs because of

---

automatic transmissions should be made for engines, but there should be a limit on the number which can be imported by each company under these arrangements for refund of duties. Such a provision should be of particular benefit to the small companies, in that it will make possible a considerable easement of the duties which they now have to pay. It will also enable the larger companies to secure duty free entry of those types of engines which it is not economical for them to make in Canada, providing, of course, they export an equivalent value of Canadian automobile parts."

the new duty on transmissions, it is difficult to tell whether the 1963 changes will raise or lower excess costs. There are several possible outcomes:

1. There will be an increase in parts exports to gain duty remissions on parts previously imported over specific duties. This will happen where the excess costs of exports (*ND* in Figure 1) plus the U.S. tariff on parts (*DB*) are less than the 25 percent (or 17.5 percent) Canadian duty to be remitted. Insofar as such an increase in Canadian exports occurs, there will be an increase in Canadian excess costs (which include U.S. tariffs on Canadian parts), although this increase may be small. From an international viewpoint, there may be either a rise or a fall in excess costs.

2. There may be a change in the composition of Canadian parts production for use in Canadian automobiles. That is, some parts subject to specific duties (e.g., engines) may now be imported rather than produced in Canada. Such imports would require *two* compensating moves: in order to maintain Canadian content, the production of other parts for use in Canadian automobiles (e.g., stampings) would have to be increased; in order to earn rebate of the duties on engines, exports would have to be increased.[15] This response to the 1963 regulations would be profitable if the excess cost of engines were greater than the sum of the excess cost of stampings, the excess cost of parts exportable to the United States, and the U.S. tariffs on these items. If such were the case, there would be a decrease in excess costs from both the international and from the Canadian viewpoint; there would also be an increase in Canadian production.

Both (1) and (2) may result to some degree; the first can happen insofar as engines and other parts subject to specific duties were imported over these duties prior to 1963; the second can occur insofar as such parts were produced in Canada because of these specific duties prior to 1963. After exports rise to the point where

---

[15] The double compensation for new imports is required only in the case of parts imports. Since imported automobiles are not included in the content base, additional imports can take place duty free with only one compensating move, namely, an equivalent increase in the Canadian content of exports.

remission has been gained on most or all [16] parts duties previously collectable, a third possibility will appear:

3. The auto maker may ignore the 60 percent content requirement and pay duty on any excess of imports over and above the credit allowed under the 1963 order. If he does so, his imports will be at least the sum of the original 40 percent foreign content allowed plus all parts whose excess costs are greater than 17.5 percent, i.e., parts to the right of U plus those between a and Q in Figure 1. He will disregard the content requirement if his costs of doing so are less than his gains. The costs will be the 17 percent duty on parts aQ, plus the 17 percent duty on the parts to the right of U previously duty free because of content fulfilment, less any duty credit gained by further exports, plus the excess costs (if any) of the additional parts exports, plus the U.S. tariff on these exports. The gain will be the saving of excess costs on parts aQ, i.e., $abJQ$. Having once committed himself to nonfulfilment of the content requirement, the manufacturer will continue to increase exports as long as he can develop lines whose excess costs, including the U.S. tariff, are less than 17.5 percent, and as long as there are any duties collectable at the 17.5 percent rate.

Once it has been decided to disregard the content requirement, and when (and if) remission of all resulting duties has been earned by additional exports, then the fourth possibility will be opened:

4. Insofar as additional exports can be found whose excess costs (including the U.S. tariff) are less than the excess costs of additional parts that could be imported, parts imports will grow, with tariff remissions being gained through additional exports. There will be a movement in imports from b toward H while exports of parts increase; over this range (but this range only), the 1963 program will operate in a manner similar to the Bladen Plan.

It should be noted that the above four possible reactions will not all occur at the same time. The first and second can, and probably will, occur simultaneously, but the third presupposes the operation of the first and/or second, and the fourth presupposes the completion of the third. The clearest conclusion is that the precise over-

---

[16] Strictly speaking, all duties at rates of 17.5 percent and higher. Tariff items 438k to 438w, mentioned in footnote 3 above, raise complications; these are, however, unimportant and will be ignored.

all effects are decidedly unclear; from a conceptual (and from an administrative) viewpoint one may wonder if the situation has not got out of hand. Nevertheless, some general implications of the 1963 order may be noted.

In the primary stages of the plan, while (1) and (2) are operating, the overall effect on excess costs is uncertain; therefore, from the point of view of the free trader, it is not clear whether the effects are desirable or undesirable. On the basis of the protectionist criterion of the quantity of production, (1) and (2) are clearly advantageous. The first leads to a rise in exports with no change in imports. The second leads to increases in imports, but for every such increase there must be *both* an increase in exports and a substitution of domestic production for other imports. In the initial stages, therefore, the major effect of the 1963 program will be on the quantity rather than on the efficiency of Canadian production; in this respect, it may be contrasted to Bladen's extended content proposal. When possibility (3) becomes relevant, there will be a gain from a free trade viewpoint; the savings in excess costs ($abJQ$) exceed any excess costs of additional Canadian exports. There will also be a gain from a protectionist viewpoint; there will be an incentive to increase exports not only by the amount of the rise in imports, but also sufficiently to gain remission of the duties on parts previously waived under the content provision (438c). After remission of duties on these parts has been achieved and (4) becomes applicable, any further increase in exports will be matched by increases in imports; the gains in this stage will be from a free trade rather than from a protectionist viewpoint. While (2), and (3), and (4) are occurring, there will be a further gain in reducing excess costs; the concentration of Canadian production on relatively fewer lines will allow the manufacturers to reap the advantages of large-scale production.

There is no guarantee that the fourth possibility would have become relevant, even if the 1963 scheme had been continued, that is, if there had been no threat of retaliation from the United States. Nevertheless, it is of some interest to compare the final possible outcome of the 1963 program with a situation of free trade in automobiles and parts in North America. If the fourth possibility were to become relevant, there would be two major differences be-

tween the 1963 arrangements and the situation that would exist
under free trade. In the first place, there would be restraint on the
balance of trade arising from automobile transactions, with Canada having a favorable overall [17] automobile balance of at least
the amount of Canadian exports in the 1961–62 base period. This
restraint would insulate the Canadian market from import competition; thus, Canadian automobile prices might remain considerably higher than those in the United States. Secondly, Canadian exports would be subject to U.S. duties averaging between 6.5
and 8.5 percent. It is unlikely that any large proportion of this
tariff would have been shifted to U.S. consumers or producers;
thus it would fall primarily on Canadians, either in the form of
higher automobile prices, or in the form of lower wages in the
automobile industry.

In the short run, during the period when only possibilities (1)
and (2) are relevant, the refusal to permit content credit for exports under the 1963 regulations creates problems quite apart from
the possible effect on excess costs. One of the most pernicious implications of the content requirement is that it can offer incentives
for inefficiency. Under certain circumstances, it is possible that
these incentives, in combination with the 1963 incentives to adopt
longer and more efficient production runs, will create uncomfort-
able dilemmas for automobile producers. Reconsider for a moment
Example A, the simplest illustration of the content requirement.
Since the 60 percent content requirement applies to Canadian
rather than world costs, it may be met with the production of only
53 percent of the automobile in Canada (measured at world costs),
provided that this 53 percent is produced *inefficiently* enough that
Canadian costs are 33 percent higher than world costs. Any reduction of Canadian costs per part will mean that more of the automobile must be produced in Canada to meet the content requirements and thus qualify for the suspension of duties on imported
parts under item 438c.

This feature of the content requirement may be expected to create problems for a Canadian manufacturer who was just nicely

---

[17] Excluding imports from European producers not directly affected by
the program.

meeting his content requirement prior to 1963 and who decides to expand parts production for export under the recent incentive arrangement. As his production and exports rise, the Canadian cost of the parts in question may fall. Since these parts are used in Canadian automobiles as well as being exported, any such fall in the Canadian cost of parts will jeopardize his fulfilment of the content regulations and, since fulfilment is an all-or-nothing proposition, the manufacturer will face the possibility of a very stiff penalty for taking advantage of the export incentives; namely, he will face a 17 percent tariff on all parts under item 438c. (In the event, the severity of the penalty would almost certainly be mitigated by cabinet action.) He may respond to the threat of non-fulfilment of content in either of two ways: by initiating Canadian production of some part or parts previously imported from the United States or, alternatively, by slackening cost control on parts (or assembly) intended exclusively for the Canadian market. Both of these responses would defeat a purpose of the 1963 regulations, the second obviously so, because it would involve inefficiency pure and simple; the first also, because it would involve a further diversification of Canadian automotive production, whereas the 1963 regulations were aimed at the concentration of Canadian production in relatively narrow areas in order to reap the advantages of large scale production.

APPENDIX B. *The Automotive Agreement of 1965*

In the previous appendix, it was noted that a change in automotive policy might possibly meet the approval of both protectionists and free traders: the change might lead both to an increase in the volume of domestic production of the item in question and to a decrease in the total excess costs of production. The purpose of this Appendix will be to evaluate the probable effects of the Canadian-U.S. automotive agreement of 1965 on the basis of these two criteria.[1] In addition, the distribution of efficiency gains from this agreement will be addressed. Equity is an obvious consideration here, and there is also some question as to whether the division of gains may jeopardize the competitive position of the Canadian industry after 1968.

The Efficiency Issue

Duty free exchange of autos can be expected to reduce costs, especially in Canada. The issue is to what degree the restrictions built into this scheme may offset these efficiency gains. The probable overall effects of the agreement on Canadian excess costs in the automotive industry[2] will be considered here.

---

[1] Other analyses of the 1965 agreement may be found in H. E. English, "Automobility — Predicament or Precedent?" *Canadian Banker* 72: 23–35 (Summer 1965); and U.S. Senate, *Hearings before the Committee on Finance on H. R. 9042,* September 14–21, 1965, pp. 58–80 and 397–443.

[2] Defined as the amount by which the cost of producing autos in Canada exceeds the cost at which they could be imported duty free. Although excess costs are not the only penalty of protection, the trend in these costs is the most important issue from the free trade viewpoint. Protection also results in a distortion of consumption, that is, a loss in consumers' surplus over and above the total of excess costs of production. The possibility of reducing this consumption cost is closely dependent on what happens to excess costs of production.

Although the agreement provided for generally duty free passage of automobiles and parts between the two countries, there were a number of important exceptions to the free trade principle. Several automotive categories, such as tires[3] and replacement parts, were excluded from duty free treatment. More significantly, the privilege of duty free automotive imports was confined on the Canadian side to the manufacturers of motor vehicles, who were required:[4] (1) to maintain the ratio of the net value of their production of motor vehicles in Canada to the net value of their sales in Canada at not less than the ratio in the model year 1964. Thus, as their sales in Canada grow, their production of finished vehicles must grow at least proportionately.[5] In the fulfillment of this condition, Canadian-produced vehicles are counted regardless whether they are sold in Canada or exported: (2) to maintain, in the production of vehicles *in Canada* a level of Canadian value added *in absolute dollar terms* that is at least as great as that achieved in model year 1964.[6] As Canadian production of vehicles expands,

[3] Tires could, however, pass duty free when mounted on new automobiles.

[4] The first two of these conditions were laid down in the definition of manufacturer in the Canadian Motor Vehicle Tariff Order 1965, a definition included in Annex A to the Canadian-U.S. agreement. The text of this agreement may be found in a news release of the Canadian Department of Industry, January 15, 1965, or in U.S. Senate, *Hearings,* pp. 17–21. Commitments (3a) and (3b) were included in the letters of undertaking by the four major Canadian automotive producers to the Canadian government, sent just prior to the signing of the intergovernmental agreement. These letters are reproduced in a news release of the Department of Industry, April 26, 1965, and in U.S. Senate, *Hearings,* pp. 45–55.

[5] Where imports of completed vehicles exceed the limit set by this condition, the manufacturer can maintain his generally duty free status by paying the tariff on those vehicles over the limit. Because the popular Mustang was not produced in Canada, Ford exceeded the limit of imports under condition (1) in 1965, and paid duty on the overquota Mustangs. See U.S. Senate, *Hearings,* p. 217.

[6] The italicized phrases are essential to an understanding of this commitment. Previous content requirements had been a *percentage* of the value of cars manufactured in Canada.

Ford anticipated some initial difficulty with this condition. Ford was in the process of concentrating its Canadian production of engines, greatly expanding the volume of a limited range and terminating the production of other engines. Although the concentration was associated with an increase in Canadian production of engines, it created difficulty in meeting

the relative importance of this requirement obviously will decline;[7] (3a) to increase the total Canadian value added in vehicles and in original equipment parts by an amount equal to 60 percent[8] of the growth in the value of their automobile sales in Canada (and by 50 percent of their commercial vehicle sales). In the achievement of this condition, in contrast to condition (2), value added in Canadian parts counts whether these parts are used in the manufacture of Canadian cars or are exported; (3b) to increase Canadian value added in vehicles and original parts by a total amount of $260 million (Can.) over and above that achieved in model year 1964 and that required to fulfil (3a). This increase, which is to be accomplished by the 1968 model year, will, like that in (3a), include not only Canadian value added in Canadian-built cars but also Canadian content in exported original equipment parts. Imports by the foreign parent (or associated) companies,

---

the level of Canadian value added in Canadian-built cars, since both exports and imports of engines were increasing. In addition, economies of scale were resulting in lower costs per engine, decreasing the contribution of each Canadian engine in meeting the Canadian value added requirement. The combined result was that Ford expected a shortfall of $22 million in its Canadian value added in model year 1966. Ford therefore declined to be bound firmly by condition (2), offering to make compensatory purchases of components from Canadian vendors.

Ford pointed out another problem involved in meeting content provisions. Because cars must be imported by Ford at *dealer* price (a Canadian antitrust provision), an imported vehicle costs Ford of Canada more than an identical, domestically produced vehicle. Hence, as the proportion of the Canadian market satisfied by imports increases, the valuation of Canadian sales increases (even though no more vehicles are sold). Hence, Ford's content provision becomes more difficult to meet. See U.S. Senate, *Hearings,* pp. 50–52.

The potential difficulties in maintaining Canadian content in the event of an increase in the efficiency of Canadian operations are discussed in Appendix A.

[7] Although the absolute level was not to increase with a growth in the market, a downward revision in the absolute level of Canadian value added is to be made in the event of a decline in sales below the level established in the base year. See U.S. Senate, *Hearings,* p. 46.

[8] The 60 percent applies to the "big four" automobile manufacturers, whose letters of undertaking have been published. We understand that Volvo, whose letter has not been made public, undertook a commitment of only 40 percent. As Volvo production is much less than 10,000 units per annum, this 40 percent is in line with previous content requirements. See Appendix A.

whether directly from the Canadian subsidiary or from independent Canadian parts producers, will be counted toward the fulfilment of conditions (3a) and (3b).

The larger commitments included in the $260 million are: General Motors, $121 million; Ford, $74.2 million; Chrysler, $33 million; and American Motors, $11.2 million.

The above commitments restrict the freedom of action of the automobile companies in a number of ways: assembly in Canada must be maintained in Canada above a floor of well over 90 percent of their Canadian new car[9] market (that is, above the floor set by the ratio of vehicles assembled in Canada to vehicles sold in Canada in 1964). Canadian content in these Canadian-built cars must not fall below the *absolute* level established in 1964.[10] And within four years, total Canadian automotive production must rise by $260 million plus 60 percent of the rise in the Canadian market.

Of the conditions, the third is overriding in the sense that it

---

[9] For simplicity, the analysis of this first condition is being confined to automobiles. Similar conclusions follow for trucks and buses, which are also included in the agreement.

[10] Unlike this Canadian content requirement, the U.S. origin restraint in Annex B, Section 3a of the agreement did not limit competition within the integrated North American market. Rather, this U.S. origin provision was included to limit the import of autos from outside countries through Canada into the United States. Specifically, Annex B provided for duty free entry of automotive products into the United States from Canada only if they contained at least 50 percent North American content (40 percent prior to January, 1968).

The possibility of Japanese or European companies establishing assembly plants in Canada as a way in which to achieve duty free penetration of the U.S. market was one of the grounds for opposition to the agreement in the United States. See, for example, U.S. Senate, *Hearings,* pp. 272, 291. Because the Canadians technically maintained most-favored-nation treatment by providing duty free automotive imports *from all countries* by companies meeting the specified conditions, this duty free Japanese-European entry into the United States via Canada is possible under the agreement, provided that 50 percent value is added in Canada. This indirect leakage through the U.S. tariff wall may be desirable from a free trade standpoint, although it may involve an indirect support of the Canadian industry at the expense of a decline in the duty revenue of the U.S. government. A broader reciprocal arrangement with these countries would be a preferable and less capricious way of reducing U.S. auto tariffs on third countries.

places an overall floor on Canadian automotive production; in meeting this floor, Canadian producers are likely to find that they have exceeded the floors on assembly (condition 1) and on Canadian content in Canadian assembly (condition 2) along the way. But because this is not guaranteed, conditions (1) and (2) may be binding and should be examined. Moreover, conditions (1) and (2) are in the treaty and presumably are as permanent as the treaty itself. On the other hand, condition (3a and b) is a side commitment by the auto companies, with an unclear legal status. Apparently, the 60 percent commitment is to be continued after 1968, on the base reached in that year. (The $260 million is a single commitment. Once the increase is achieved, it must be maintained, but there is no provision for additional increases other than the 60 percent condition 3a.) Although the government could "retaliate" against the auto companies if they all failed to meet the commitments specified in their letters, it is unclear what steps could be taken if a single company reneged either before or after the 1968 date.

Assembly: The First Condition. This will ensure about the same sort of growth of auto assembly in Canada as would have occurred under preexisting protection.[11] Indeed, as imports of automobiles from the United States have constituted a small and fairly stable percentage of the Canadian automobile market in the past, and as Canadian assembly is now tied to past performance, it might seem that changes in the volume of Canadian assembly under this first condition will be trivial. However, this conclusion must be subjected to two reservations. Insofar as increased efficiency allows a fall in Canadian automotive prices relative to European prices, the share of North American cars in the Canadian market will tend to rise, and thus Canadian assembly will rise under condition (1). As the total European share in the Canadian market has been less than 10 percent, this effect will not be particularly great.

[11] That is, prior to the Export Incentive Program of 1962. The situation prior to 1962 is used as the basis for comparison for two reasons: the 1962–1964 period may be considered unstable in the sense that U.S. countermoves were a distinct possibility; and the net effects of the export incentive program on total Canadian excess costs in the automotive industry were unclear.

The second reservation is more difficult to evaluate. The relative contribution of specific lines to a manufacturer's overall sales is both difficult to predict and subject to considerable year-to-year variation. In the recent experience of the Ford Motor Company, for example, it is clear that the Edsel was a major disappointment; the public acceptance of the Mustang exceeded expectations; and the Falcon's share of the market has varied considerably since its introduction. If, as seems likely, the automotive agreement results in a major reduction in the number of models produced in Canada, the manufacturers will have to plan on overshooting condition (1) by a safety margin in order to ensure its fulfilment.[12]

This first condition permits specialization based on tariff free exchange; hence it allows a reduction in excess costs per unit produced in Canada. Specifically, it permits Canadian concentration on relatively few models, the extension of the production runs of these models for the export market and imports of other models whose Canadian production is terminated.[13] This may be expected to contribute to efficiency for two reasons: there are substantial economies of scale in automotive assembly, and the comparative costs of various models may differ between the United States and Canada because of such factors as different relative prices of capital and labor. Although the second of these points has dominated economics literature on the subject of gains from trade, there is strong reason to believe that the first is by far the more important in the operation of the automotive agreement. (See Chapter 13.)

The Second Condition: Protection to Parts. The second condition, which places a floor on the absolute level of Canadian value

[12] The companies are not absolutely bound by this condition. However, tariffs must be paid on overquota imports. See footnote 5, above.

[13] Under this first condition, efficiency in automobile assembly is promoted in approximately the same way as efficiency in parts production would have been promoted under Bladen's extended content plan. There is, however, one obvious and major advantage of the present arrangement over the export incentive program it replaced: U.S. automotive tariffs are eliminated, and therefore the scope for rationalization and specialization in the Canadian industry is greatly enhanced.

On the potential contribution of the Bladen Plan to efficiency in the production of parts, see Appendix A. For a more critical interpretation, see Harry G. Johnson, "The Bladen Plan for Increased Protection of the Canadian Automotive Industry," *Canadian Journal Economics and Political Science,* 29: 212–238 (May 1963).

added, provides some protection for Canadian parts manufacture. (The term "protection" is used to cover not only tariffs but all regulations that tend to isolate domestic production from import competition.) This protection for parts is, however, different in two important respects from that provided to assembly under the first condition. Although growth of the Canadian assembly process in step with the growth of the Canadian market is provided by the first condition, the second assures only that the *absolute* Canadian value content in Canadian-built automobiles will not decline. Since content includes assembly work as well as parts, the absolute total of Canadian parts is permitted to decline as assembly increases. Thus, not only does this second condition not guarantee the growth of the Canadian parts input into Canadian-built cars, it allows a gradual decrease.

But if the protection to parts under condition (2) is in one sense less than that provided to assembly under condition (1), it is in another sense greater. Since Canadian-built cars count in the fulfilment of the first condition regardless of their destination, there is no limit on the speed with which specialization in assembly may take place. For example, there is no restraint on the immediate elimination of the Canadian assembly of all cars with the exception of one model per manufacturer, provided that the increase in the production of these single models is sufficient to maintain total production. On the other hand, condition (2) prevents the same sort of rapid specialization in parts. It is true, of course, that if General Motors, for example, produced only one model, there would need to be only one size of wheel produced in Canada for G.M. cars, and in this sense parts specialization would take place. However, specialization of a second type is restrained. Because under condition (2) only Canadian parts (and assembly) *going into Canadian-produced cars* are counted, and because there is an obvious limit to the input of specific parts per auto (five wheels, one battery, etc.), it is not possible for Canadian production of parts to be concentrated on, say, wheels at the expense of batteries (except insofar as an overall increase in Canadian automobile production allows a decrease in Canadian parts content per car).

The difference in the speed of adjustment allowed in parts under condition (2) as compared to assembly under condition (1) is quite ingenious. Immediate elimination of most models assembled in Canada would cause no particular adjustment problem, since provision is made for expanded production by the same company in other models by an equivalent amount. There would be no particular adjustment problem in the United States either: production of the model of Canadian specialization could be curtailed (or possibly even eliminated) by the U.S. parent, with compensatory increases in the other models for export to Canada. As the adjustment takes place within the same company, it may be timed at the optimum speed as seen by that company; there is no problem of major injury.

Moreover, this specialization in assembly will result in relatively painless specialization *within* parts. Although the Canadian battery manufacturer will find his original equipment orders confined to fewer sizes (because there are fewer models assembled in Canada), he will find his volume increasing in these sizes. Thus he will also be in a position to see the obvious sense in the change.

At the same time, the battery maker is unlikely to produce a broad range of parts; he is unlikely to produce wheels, for example. Thus, if there were Canadian specialization in the production of wheels and elimination of battery production, the battery maker would be hard hit. (In addition, the independent U.S. wheel producer might also be hard hit[14] and would hardly be consoled by the increase in U.S. battery production.) But this sort of specialization *between* parts is restrained. The permitted rate of adjustment is, moreover, a variable dependent on the rate of growth of overall Canadian automotive production;[15] most rapid adjustment is permitted when it is easiest to accommodate, that is, when total automobile production is booming.

All three types of adjustment, that is, specialization among assembled vehicles, specialization within single parts, and specialization among parts, may be expected to bring lower costs. As condi-

[14] But not necessarily. For example, his production might not decrease because the imports from Canada were less than the increase in the U.S. market.

[15] The more rapid the growth in Canadian auto assembly, the greater the reduction in the number of different parts needed to fulfill condition (2) and, hence, the greater the potential specialization of parts.

tions (1) and (2) permit all three types of adjustment, and as the quantity restraints are no more — and in some cases are less binding than under the pre-1962 protective system, conditions (1) and (2) may be considered acceptable from the free trade viewpoint. If objection to these two points is to be made by a free trader, it must be on one of two grounds. First, while the overall effects are in the right direction, an even better result might have occurred if there were no such conditions. This argument comes close to being incontrovertible:[16] to a free trader, there is nothing like unconditional free trade. The question then becomes one of the political feasibility of a better agreement. Secondly, objection may be made on the ground that the permitted rate of adjustment is too slow, and its outcome too uncertain. The detailed implication of the first two conditions are, however, reassuring: the speed of only one of the three adjustment processes (specialization among parts) is subjected to restraint. But this adjustment is the most likely to cause transitional difficulties; and it may be speeded up in rapid growth periods when these problems are least grave.

The Third Condition: The Letters of Intent Regarding the Overall Volume of Canadian Auto Production. As noted above, it is not entirely clear precisely how binding these commitments are from a legal point of view. However, it seems reasonable to assume that they will be met *in toto* by the auto manufacturers. In these circumstances, they will provide the overall floor on Canadian auto and parts production[17] with the first two conditions discussed above ensuring only a floor on auto assembly in Canada, plus some restraint on the speed of interpart specialization.

---

[16] However, it should be noted that the literature in favor of free trade is replete with the argument that tariffs should be eliminated in stages as a means of smoothing adjustment. The Canadian conditions may be considered an alternative (and preferable?) means of smoothing the adjustment process — provided, of course, this scheme does lead toward free trade.

[17] The first two conditions ensure only that total Canadian value added in autos and parts production remains at its absolute level in 1964 (condition 2). Conceivably the assembly provision (condition 1) might ensure some growth in total value added but only if Canadian automobile sales increase at an extraordinary rate. This third condition, however, ensures a very rapid growth of Canadian auto and parts production by about 60 percent of any increase in Canadian sales, plus $260 million.

Under the preexisting tariff arrangements,[18] 60 percent Canadian content was ensured; consequently, the only additional content provision of the agreement is the $260 million commitment to increase Canadian value added. This protective measure may increase aggregate excess costs; however, costs are at the same time decreased by the duty free exchange and specialization allowed by the scheme. How are these likely to trade off?

Increased Efficiency Induced by Duty Free Exchange. Since the agreement allows much greater latitude for Canadian specialization, it will clearly operate toward reduction of the excess of Canadian over U.S. costs per unit of output; the greater the economies of scale (and the greater the relative cost differences based on differences in factor prices, etc.), the more pronounced this reduction will be. A number of parts are already produced in Canada as cheaply as in the United States;[19] these are precisely the parts in which Canadian production may be expected to increase, replacing production of parts involving excess cost. Furthermore, as Canadian production lines lengthen, the number of parts that are produced in Canada as cheaply as in the United States may be expected to increase.

A similar decline in the Canadian excess costs may be anticipated in assembly. Indeed, for the largest companies, a substantial elimination of excess costs of Canadian assembly may be anticipated after the interim period of adjustment. General Motors of Canada is already producing in the 300,000–600,000 unit range in which Bain estimates that substantially all the economies of scale on a single line may be achieved.[20] Since the automotive

[18] That is, prior to the Export Incentive Program of 1962.

[19] Although most of the congressional objections to the agreement were based on the U.S. abandonment of the most-favored-nation principle and on the failure of the agreement to provide really free trade, there were a number of objections on the protectionist ground that U.S. producers could not compete with less expensive Canadian products. This protectionist objection was made on behalf of bearing manufacturers and the makers of extruded rubber products. See U.S. Senate, *Hearings,* pp. 290–302, 305–308.

Other parts in which Canadian producers are competitive might also be mentioned, for example, springs.

[20] Joe S. Bain, *Barriers to New Competition* (Cambridge: Harvard University Press, 1956), p. 245. See also Chapter 13 above.

agreement permits the concentration of production of each Canadian company on one or a few models, General Motors should be able to gain substantially all the economies of scale in its Canadian assembly operations after an interim period of adjustment. Not only should General Motors be able to produce cars as cheaply in Canada as in the United States, it should, at the same time, be able to pay wages which are closer to U.S. levels (but not necessarily equal; there are undoubtedly some Canadian disadvantages in automotive production, such as higher priced inputs[21] from other industries).

Ford is also producing a sufficient quantity of automobiles in Canada to permit the substantial elimination of excess costs with specialization; its production in recent years has been about 150,-000 units, at which there are only "moderately" higher costs for single-model production lines.[22] Chrysler is currently at the volume where single-model production costs would be "substantially" higher than at the optimum volume; American Motors Canadian production is below the 60,000 unit level and hence is at insufficient scale to make production of even a single model "economical."

Excess Costs Induced by the Commitment to Increase Canadian Value Added by $260 Million. If the specialization allowed by the scheme discussed in (1) above leads to production in Canada at U.S. cost levels, then it is reasonable to expect that the Canadian industry could produce additional vehicles and parts at or near this same cost.[23] In this case, little or no excess cost would be involved in the additional $260 million value added commitment. It may, of course, be argued that the Canadian industry cannot achieve these U.S. cost levels, and that excess costs would consequently be incurred on this $260 million commitment; however, an equally plausible case can be made for expecting that this additional Canadian production will be at lower-than-U.S. cost

---

[21] Both because of inherent disadvantages discussed in Chapters 13 and 14 and because the "free trade" agreement does not cover products which are inputs into the auto industry.

[22] Bain, *Barriers*, p. 245.

[23] Either through an increase in scale of existing lines or through an increase in the number of lines produced in Canada. Large increases in Canadian production might lead to a general rise in automotive wages and higher Canadian costs.

levels,[24] which would result in negative excess costs. Hence, there is no guarantee that any excess costs would result from (2). But in any event, the favorable effects of (1) may be expected to dominate any excess costs of (2); the effects of (1) and (2) together will be to reduce excess costs in the industry. This implies substantial efficiency gains in North American auto production as a result of the scheme.[25]

Before we leave the efficiency implications of this scheme, there are two structural effects worth examining.[26]

Is Canadian Assembly Favored over Parts Production? The content requirements of this scheme, conditions (2) and (3), do not distinguish between parts and assembly. However, a floor is placed on assembly (condition 1), with no similar floor provided for parts production. Hence the scheme seems to encourage assembly, since firms simultaneously satisfy two restrictions (that is, on both assembly and value added). In the early stages, it seems likely that the auto companies will favor vehicle production.[27] However, even after their assembly requirement is completely met an additional value added commitment will remain. Since this can be met via either vehicle or parts specialization, it cannot be predicted with any assurance that assembly will be favored over parts in the final mix of Canadian production.

[24] Primarily because of lower Canadian wages.

[25] It is exceedingly difficult to compare the efficiency of this scheme with unrestricted free trade. If the Canadian production induced by the 60 percent content requirement and the $260 value added commitment is at higher-than-U.S. cost, then unrestricted free trade would be judged preferable from the point of view of efficiency alone. But if this Canadian production occurs at U.S. cost levels or below, the value added restrictions of this scheme do not limit its efficiency; hence, complete free trade would not be preferred on efficiency grounds.

[26] There are, in addition, a couple of other minor structural effects which are only noted here in passing. First, the scheme discriminates in favor of the use of Canadian machinery by the Canadian auto industry because the auto companies can count depreciation on this as value added; but they cannot so count depreciation on imported machinery. General Motors pointed out that this discrimination would tend to raise Canadian auto costs and make reorganization more difficult. (See U.S. Senate, *Hearings*, p. 47.) Second, replacement parts remain protected; however, their production in Canada is no longer subsidized in the sense that it was under the prior export incentive scheme

[27] See, for example, Chrysler's projections in U.S. Senate, *Hearings*, p. 233.

Difficulties for Smaller Companies. It has already been pointed out that increased specialization allowed by the scheme will permit each of the auto manufacturers to reduce per unit excess costs. The possibilities of substantially complete elimination of these costs are not, however, the same for each of the companies: the prospects are very good for General Motors; for American Motors they are much poorer, at least in the foreseeable future. This may lead to intergovernmental difficulties when the Canadian-U.S. agreement is subjected to a critical evaluation in 1968.

The problem may be confined to American Motors, as Chrysler's volume is growing rapidly. The overall increase in the Canadian market and the improving fortunes of Chrysler in both countries may make it possible for Chrysler assembly in Canada to pass the 150,000 unit level (where there are only "moderate" disadvantages of scale) without great disturbance to its U.S. operations. Indeed, Chrysler is already moving rapidly in this direction. In the current (1966) model year, Chrysler plans to manufacture 70,000 Valiants (in the U.S., Dodge Darts) in Canada for shipment to the United States. With an anticipated Canadian market of about 30,000 units,[28] total Canadian production of this single model will be about 100,000 units in model 1966.

For American Motors, the situation is much more difficult. Not only are they the smallest of the "Big Four" but both their relative and absolute sales have been declining in the United States and in Canada during the recent years of generally booming automobile sales. At the time of this writing (June 1966) American Motors is producing at an annual rate of about 30,000 units, or well below the 60,000 figure where assembly becomes "uneconomic." Thus, if other Canadian automobile companies reduce their prices to U.S. levels and raise their wages toward U.S. rates (assumptions which will be considered in the section on auto prices and wages, below), American Motors will find itself in a tight competitive bind.

One conceivable way out of this bind would be to raise Canadian production to the more efficient 60,000 to 100,000 unit level and ship more autos to the United States than are imported from that country. Whether this would be in the overall interests of

[28] In model 1965, over 31,000 Valiants were sold in Canada.

American Motors would depend on whether the marginal costs of the extra units in Canada were lower or higher than the marginal costs in the United States (and on American Motors alternatives for fulfilling their commitment under condition 3).

The probability of American Motors making such a decision cannot be predicted, of course, without a great deal of factual information which is not publicly available. One thing is, however, quite clear: a decision along this line, involving a net import of automobiles from Canada and, possibly, an *absolute* contraction of the U.S. operations of the most vulnerable of the U.S. producers might put the U.S. government under pressure to reconsider the automotive agreement.

Such pressures would be likely to be concentrated on a removal of remaining restrictions on automotive trade and, in particular, on an elimination of the Canadian condition for tariff free automotive imports. It should be noted, however, that whereas the chances of net American Motors shipments of cars to the United States are increased by the Canadian conditions (and, in particular, condition 3b), the basic dilemma of American Motors would exist even if there were completely free trade. That is, with unrestricted free trade, there would be pressures on American Motors to acquire the advantages of scale by lengthening its production runs. This could be done by lengthening the Canadian line and eliminating the production of one model in the United States; it could alternatively do so by eliminating its Canadian production altogether and importing all its cars to be sold in Canada. Even if the former might be the outcome with unrestrained free trade, the U.S. government will be under pressure to block it unless the latter option is also opened up by an elimination of the Canadian conditions.

The problem, in brief, is this: if American Motors does not expand their Canadian production run much beyond the size of the Canadian market, they may be put in an untenable position in the Canadian market if and when Canadian prices fall to U.S. levels; if they do expand Canadian production greatly, net exports may be reflected in an absolute reduction in their U.S. production. (During the negotiation of the original agreement, it appeared that all of the resulting increases in Canadian automotive assembly could be absorbed by each of the big four within the growth of their North American markets.)[29] The U.S. government may be expected to object to such an absolute fall unless the alternative option of a rise in U.S. production by American Motors at Canadian expense is opened up.

The strength of this problem depends on the tendency for car prices to be equalized and for wage differentials to decline, outcomes that may be highly desirable on other grounds. These will be discussed below under auto prices and wages.

Balance-of-Payments Effects

In this section, the balance-of-payments implications of only the third condition will be examined;[30] since this condition provides the effective overall floor on total Canadian production, it is the overriding one in determining balance of payments effects.

Production and balance-of-payments effects may be expressed algebraically. Let:

v = value of North American vehicles sold in Canada in (model year) 1964

g = growth in v between (model) 1964 and 1968 (as a fraction)

B_c = automotive component[31] of Canada's bilateral merchandise account balance with the United States

X_c = exports[31] of participating Canadian automotive manufacturers to countries other than the United States

M_c = imports[31] of participating Canadian automotive manufacturers from countries other than the United States. (This does *not* include Canadian imports from nonparticipants in the program, e.g., B.M.C.).

[29] The possibility that there might be some absolute decline in U.S. production of some specific parts was, however, to be anticipated as a result of the agreement. There was a presumption that such displacement would be concentrated in the areas where Canadian costs were already lower than U.S. costs.

[30] We choose not to discuss the well established objections to dealing with a (real or imagined) balance-of-payments problem by restrictions on the exchange of a single good with a single trading partner. These objections are by now so well known that they scarcely require repetition. But they should be kept in mind in the discussion of this section.

[31] Excluding replacement parts, which were not included in the agreement.

The subscript 1 stands for automobiles, 2 represents commercial vehicles included in the program. All figures in the expressions below are in Canadian dollars.

If Canadian condition (3) is just barely fulfilled, automotive production in Canada will increase between (model) 1964 and 1968:

$$\Delta P_C = .6g_1v_1 + .5g_2v_2 + \$260 \text{ million.} \tag{1}$$

The net effect of the operations of Canadian car and associated parts manufacturers on the Canadian merchandise account balance will change by the amount of the change in their Canadian production, shown in expression (1), less the change in their Canadian sales, $(g_1v_1 + g_2v_2)$.[32] Since their transactions with third countries are included in their production and sales, the bilateral balance with the United States will change as follows:

$$\Delta B_C = \$260 \text{ million} - 0.4g_1v_1 - 0.5g_2v_2 - (\Delta X_C - \Delta M_C). \tag{2}$$

If the simplifying assumption is made that the relative sizes of the Canadian markets for automobiles and for specified commercial vehicles remain the same as in 1964,[33] expression (2) becomes:

$$\Delta B_C = \$260 \text{ million} - 0.42(\$1{,}513 \text{ million})g - (\Delta X_C - \Delta M_C).[34] \tag{3}$$

If the complications of Canadian transactions with third countries are for the moment ignored, it may be seen that expression (3) will be positive (that is, the Canadian deficit with the United States will decline) unless the Canadian automotive market grows by more than 40 percent in the four year period, or at a compound rate of about 9 percent per annum. Is this a realistic growth rate?

The rate of growth of the Canadian auto market is difficult to predict; it has been extraordinarily high in recent years (12 per-

[32] And, strictly speaking, less the change in inventory.

[33] The Canadian market for automobiles is about four times as large as the Canadian market for specified commercial vehicles; see U.S. Senate, *Hearings,* pp. 126–133.

[34] The figure $1,513 million for the 1964 Canadian market for North American vehicles was derived by subtracting Canadian auto exports to the United States from Canadian domestic production, and by adding imports from the United States. (D.B.S., *Trade of Canada,* and D.B.S., 42,001 and 42,209.)

cent per annum between model year 1960 and 1964), but this was
a period of economic recovery to a high level of capacity utiliza-
tion. In the U.S. hearings, expert witnesses assumed annual growth
rates in the range of −3 percent to +8 percent.[35] A rate of 4 to 5
percent per annum might be regarded as a reasonable expectation
of growth in 1964–1968 in the absence of a price cut. How much
more could the Canadian market grow as a result of a price cut?

There is an upper limit of approximately 10 percent on the
amount by which Canadian new car prices (ex tax) may fall.
With such a fall, they would approximate U.S. prices;[36] they could
not go lower because U.S. residents can, under the new agreement,
buy cars in Canada duty free. If a price elasticity estimate of
− 1.333 for the U.S. auto market[37] is taken as valid for Canada,
then the additional increase in the Canadian market which could
come from a price decrease would be, in value terms, 3 percent.
(This 3 percent applies to the whole 1965–1968 period; since the
10 percent price decrease does not occur each year, the 3 percent
increase likewise does not occur each year.) Hence, it may be concluded that the Canadian auto deficit with the United States will
be reduced even with this sort of price cut and a normal market
growth rate of 4 to 5 percent. For the deficit to remain at its
present level, the growth of the Canadian market will have to be
at the upper end of the −3 to +8 percent range, and the additional
gain of about 3 percent in market size will have to result from a
price cut.

But the U.S. balance with Canada is obviously a mirror image of
the Canadian balance with the United States; hence, these assumptions (of a high Canadian market growth and a Canadian price

[35] Specifically, Ford presented estimates of its Canadian automotive
market and its merchandise balance over the four year term of the commitments. The upper and lower market growth rates considered were 7.7
percent and −3 percent; 2.6 percent was taken as a median estimate.
With these rates, the negative merchandise balance of Canadian Ford in
(model year) 1968 was estimated to lie between −$106 million (U.S.)
and −$160 million (U.S.) compared to −$183 million in model 1964 and
−$125 million in model 1963. See U.S. Senate, *Hearings,* pp. 211–212.

[36] See Chapter 13.

[37] The U.S. Senate Subcommittee on Antitrust and Monopoly uses the
elasticity estimate of −1.2 to −1.5.

cut)[38] are necessary to prevent a deterioration in the U.S. balance of payments.

The form of equation (3) raises some rather interesting political problems, as the U.S. merchandise account is tied directly to a number of factors which are normally considered to be outside the area in which the United States can properly express official interest. These are, specifically, the change in exports to and imports from third countries by Canadian automobile producers and the rate of growth of the Canadian market for North American automobiles, which depends in turn on the overall growth of the Canadian automobile market and the share of this market held by third countries. On each of these points, Canadian pricing is an important issue. Therefore, it is not surprising that, in the congressional hearings, explicit concern was voiced over the apparent unwillingness of Canadian automobile manufacturers to cut prices.[39]

One of the puzzles of this scheme is that both countries have concluded that it will have favorable balance-of-payments effects. This paradox is resolved as follows. The Canadians view their resulting balance of payments as involving less deficit than would

[38] Or, in the absence of a price cut, the more optimistic assumption of about 9 percent per annum growth in the Canadian market.

[39] Senator Douglas, in particular, stressed that if Canadian prices were not cut, the growth in the Canadian market would suffer, and the required increase in Canadian production would be reflected in a decrease in the United States. See U.S. Senate, *Hearings,* pp. 200, 228.

Nat Weinberg, representing the U.A.W. at the Senate Hearings, suggested that the agreement be amended to increase pressures on the Canadian companies to cut prices. This could be done by providing for duties on Canadian cars in the event that the difference in price (excluding tax) between Canadian cars sold in Canada and Canadian cars sold in the United States exceeded the difference in costs of production between Canada and the United States. The U.A.W. firmly stressed, however, that they did not want dumping duties applied because a rationalization of production required Canadian cars to be sold more cheaply in the United States than in Canada during the adjustment period when Canadian costs exceeded U.S. costs. U.S. Senate, *Hearings,* pp. 246–258.

The effects on the U.S. balance of payments of price stickiness in Canada are not entirely adverse. Higher profits of U.S.-owned automobile manufacturers are reflected in higher dividends. On the balance-of-payments implication of profits, see the testimony of Assistant Secretary of the Treasury Merlyn Trued, *Hearings,* p. 368.

have occurred under preexisting protection;[40] under previous protection the growth in North American auto markets and production would have been reflected in a (roughly) proportional growth in the Canadian auto deficit with the United States. Hence the Canadians viewed this scheme with favor by comparing it with the past. On the other hand, Americans view it with favor by comparing it with what "might have been." The United States viewed the Canadian alternative to this arrangement as a high tariff policy. In the process of reducing auto trade,[41] this would also have greatly reduced or eliminated the existing U.S. surplus. Hence the United States viewed this limited free trade scheme with favor as a means of maintaining a strong U.S. surplus position.

One may speculate that the U.S. negotiators may have recognized that Canadian bargaining advantages would tend to disappear with the rationalization of the Canadian industry. By 1968 the strongly protectionist option will involve an additional staggering cost for Canada, in the form of sunk capital installed during the interim period of reorganizing for international markets.[42] Hence, by 1968 the United States may be less inclined to accede to Canadian balance-of-payments restrictions.

Auto Prices and Wages

At the time of this writing, auto prices in Canada remain substantially above those in the United States.[43] This is a critical issue for at least four reasons:

Unless prices fall and Canadian sales expand more rapidly as a consequence, Americans may be justified in the fear that the ex-

[40] That is, Canadian protection prior to the export incentive scheme of 1962.

[41] This would also have raised Canadian auto costs and prices and reduced Canadian auto sales. The costs of such a policy to Canada are obvious. Yet the Canadian negotiators seemed to have impressed the Americans with their willingness to exercise this option.

[42] Much of this sunk cost might appear to fall on the auto companies; but in fact their capital expenditures during 1964–1968 will have been heavily underwritten by the Canadian consumer and taxpayer.

[43] Because individual Canadians are not allowed duty free import, Canadian domestic prices can thus still be set by the auto companies above the U.S. level.

pansion of canadian auto employment ensured by the agreement will be at U.S. expense.

Canadian producers will be producing identical vehicles on a high volume basis for sale in both the United States (at the U.S. price) and in Canada (at the higher Canadian price). This raises a number of complications, including the possibility of U.S. antidumping measures.[44]

To the degree that higher Canadian costs reflect inefficiency (as well as scale effects), a price reduction may be necessary to force elimination of this element of higher costs.

The scheme raises an equity issue, which has become a matter of public controversy. This is worth examining in some detail.

Initially the auto companies benefited by the remission of tariffs on their Canadian imports; as long as their Canadian prices remained unchanged this came at the expense of the Canadian consumer-taxpayer. According to the auto companies, this gain is now being passed on (beginning in the 1966 model year) to the consumer in the form of a reduced price in Canada relative to the U.S. price. Some issues are raised by the way in which this relative price reduction was effected.[45] But taking these claims at their full face value, the Canadian consumer-taxpayer may now be about as well off as he would have been without the agreement.

During this controversy, the major saving of the scheme to the auto companies was largely overlooked. It is not the saving in tariff remission but the cost reductions that are made possible through increased scale.[46] This is a windfall gain which is going to the auto companies exclusively. This has been justified as a contribution to cover their organization costs. The difficulty here is that two sets of costs are involved, and they are extremely

[44] However, as U.S. antidumping provisions require proof of injury, it is not likely that they will be invoked. (In contrast, the countervailing duties in response to a direct or indirect government subsidy, which appeared possible following the introduction of the export incentive program, do not require proof of injury.)

[45] By and large, this took the form more of a U.S. price increase than a Canadian price decrease. For example, in the 1966 model year certain extras were included as standard equipment in both countries, but U.S. consumers were assessed higher prices on these items than Canadians.

[46] Estimated in Chapter 13 as 7 to 8 percent of total factory costs.

difficult to sort out: turnaround costs[47] and the cost of investment that a growing auto industry would have incurred in any case.

Little case can be made for "subsidizing" the normal capital expansion of the auto companies, especially in view of their easy access to investment funds. A stronger case can be made for subsidizing turnaround costs of the industry; but these are transitory, once-and-for-all costs. As this turnaround period passes, the issue becomes whether the windfall gains of the scheme will go to the consumer in the form of a price reduction to U.S. levels[48] or continue to accrue as profits to the auto companies — in which case they are likely to be partially expropriated by the unions in the form of higher wages.

On several grounds it may be argued that the reduction of Canadian prices to U.S. levels should be given precedence over a rise in Canadian automotive wages relative to U.S. wages. The sale of identical Canadian-built automobiles at prices lower in the United States than in Canada inevitably leads to difficulties on both sides of the border, and the sooner this price discrepancy is eliminated, the more smoothly the integration of the markets may take place. The possibilities of increased efficiency, particularly in Canada, have been held out as a major advantage of the automotive agreement, and the gains can be made most evident if the Canadian consumer finds the relative price of his car declining.

There is, however, one counterargument to be made in favor of an early emphasis on (relative) wage increases rather than price reductions in Canada. The labor market is less perfect than the new car market, that is, new car purchasers find it much easier to switch to the least expensive car than workers find it to switch to the highest-wage employer. Thus, the potential problem regarding American Motors will be exacerbated by emphasis on price reductions rather than wage increases in Canada: American Motors cannot hope to survive in the Canadian market if its prices there are significantly higher than those of its competitors, but it might survive while paying wages less than those of its competitors.

[47] Associated with the rationalization of the industry. Thus, these should be defined to exclude model changeover costs, which occur in any case.

[48] Even though factory prices were to be equalized, costs to consumers would not become identical. Differing transport charges might leave a differential of about one percent, and sales and excise taxes differ.

Although the potential problem of American Motors is a difficult one, it is our judgment that the difficulties that may be expected from a continuing Canadian-U.S. automobile price differential are even greater, indeed, possibly great enough to jeopardize a future move to unrestricted free trade. As long as other Canadian industries are protected, and costs of inputs to Canadian auto producers are higher as a consequence, it seems unlikely that the Canadian industry can afford both a parity price of autos and a near-parity wage. As a consequence, if the unions do achieve full or near parity, there might be some question of the industry's ability to survive under unrestricted free trade. This, in turn, might lead the Canadian authorities to oppose complete tariff elimination. But if auto price parity is achieved first, the Canadian industry will be in a position to compete effectively under unrestrained free trade. And the auto unions could then bargain for a Canadian wage as close to parity as an internationally competitive industry could afford.[49] Hence, initial emphasis should be on price rather than wage equalization.

[49] If and when free trade is initiated in other (supplying) industries, auto wages could rise even closer to the U.S. level.

APPENDIX C. *Derivation of Wage Costs*

U.S. wage rates were derived by comparing wage payments to production workers with hours worked as reported in the 1958 United States Census of Manufactures. As a consequence, they represent average hourly earnings rather than base wage rates. But the difference is not substantial when relative wage rates rather than absolute wage levels are being examined. The largest single source of difference is that average hourly earnings include premium paid for overtime, but base wage rates do not.[1]

Canadian wage rates were more difficult to estimate. The best interindustry breakdown appears in the D.B.S., *Review of Man-Hours and Hourly Earnings,* 1945–1961; however, wage rates are available in this source for each province rather than for each region. As a consequence the computation of a wage rate for a region (for example, the Maritimes), required employment weights for each province in the region. D.B.S., *The Manufacturing Industries of Canada,* Sections B to F, 1958, provided the source for this information in the form of total wages paid in each industry and province. (For example, in the food and beverage sector in Newfoundland, total wages paid were about $5,333,000. This was divided by the provincial wage rate ($1.03) referred to above. The resulting computed employment of about 5,180,000 man-hours in Newfoundland, along with similar figures derived for each of the other provinces within the Maritimes, were used to derive an average wage rate for the region.)

[1] For a further discussion of this point and detail on how these U.S. figures were derived, see R. J. Wonnacott, *Manufacturing Costs and the Comparative Advantage of United States Regions* (Minneapolis: Upper Midwest Economic Study, University of Minnesota, Study Paper 9, April 1963).

APPENDIX D. Estimated Percentage That Average Wage Levels in Comparison Areas Are Higher or Lower (−) Than in Ontario, 1958 (in percent, $1.00 U.S. = $1.00 Can.).

Manufacturing sector[a]	Maritimes	Quebec	Ontario	Prairies	British Columbia	Upper Midwest	West Lake	East Lake	Lower Midwest	Middle Atlantic	New England	South	Capital	Florida	Southwest	Mountain	Pacific Southwest	Pacific Northwest
Food	−31.5	−4.1	0	17.1	22.6	51.4	45.2	44.5	49.3	43.8	24.0	4.1	13.7	−0.7	8.9	28.1	52.7	40.4
Tobacco	b	−5.2	0	b	b	b	−21.8	−10.3	b	−16.7	−24.6	4.6	b	−23.0	b	b	−30.4	b
Textiles	12.4	−1.6	0	28.7	56.6	27.9	34.9	42.6	7.8	35.7	27.9	11.6	24.0	11.6	3.9	2.3	40.3	38.8
Apparel	30.7	−6.1	0	−3.5	77.2	33.3	35.1	50.9	21.1	43.9	30.7	7.0	27.2	19.3	7.9	22.8	43.0	38.6
Wood products	−25.4	−17.9	0	25.4	42.5	51.5	37.3	54.5	30.6	41.8	20.1	−8.2	19.4	4.5	−0.7	61.2	72.4	80.6
Paper	5.3	−1.6	0	−10.0	25.8	14.7	14.7	21.6	2.1	11.1	7.9	12.6	6.3	19.5	20.5	3.2	23.7	34.7
Printing	−29.2	−4.0	0	−17.8	b	28.2	34.7	30.7	16.3	33.7	16.3	8.9	26.2	24.3	11.9	26.7	46.5	47.0
Electrical equipment	b	−5.7	0	−10.2	14.8	22.2	27.3	37.5	14.2	26.1	10.8	10.2	39.8	9.1	13.6	10.2	32.4	41.5
Chemicals	−21.7	−9.5	0	−9.5	b	15.9	27.0	37.6	27.5	29.1	23.3	25.9	18.5	4.2	48.7	42.3	32.8	67.7
Petroleum products[c]	b	b	0	−5.6	b	22.6	31.2	25.2	19.2	27.4	6.8	−1.3	7.3	18.0	31.6	31.2	23.9	22.2
Rubber and plastics	b	−23.5	0	−12.6	9.8	10.4	22.4	44.3	8.7	16.9	8.7	21.3	8.7	−16.4	15.8	b	29.0	b
Leather goods	17.7	−14.5	0	27.4	62.9	b	41.9	41.9	18.5	28.2	34.7	12.1	35.5	16.9	7.3	b	44.4	b
Nonmetallic mineral products	−15.5	10.3	0	−5.7	16.1	23.0	31.6	34.5	27.0	31.0	26.4	8.0	23.6	−3.4	8.6	28.7	40.8	47.1
Metallic products	−3.6	−9.7	0	−12.2	12.2	18.4	32.1	38.8	19.9	30.6	14.3	19.9	35.2	−4.1	14.8	36.7	32.7	40.8
Transportation equipment	−16.1	−10.6	0	−12.6	13.6	22.1	32.7	40.7	25.1	33.2	30.2	20.1	35.2	4.5	33.2	13.1	34.7	23.6
Miscellaneous	−16.1	−13.8	0	−1.7	16.1	21.3	21.3	25.9	21.3	25.9	2.3	−4.0	17.8	24.7	1.7	54.6	56.3	28.7

a See Table 1, note a.
b Wage data inadequate.
c Estimates in this row are less reliable than in the rest of this table.

APPENDIX E. *Derivation of Model*
of Competitive Location

A new firm is considering location k for the production of a good already being produced by n_j competitors at j locations. There are m spatially located markets, each involving (projected or actual) total sales of this good represented by S^m. In addition the ratio of expected sales penetration of any market m by a producer at j and a producer at location k is determinate and is designated as:

$$\frac{R_{jm}}{R_{km}}. \tag{1}$$

The definition of this ratio will be the prime practical difficulty in applying this analysis. It is discussed in greater detail later. However, it will be argued that this ratio may be reasonably approximated by some inverse function of the relative distance of the two producers from the market, e.g.,

$$\frac{R_{jm}}{R_{km}} = \left(\frac{{}^k d^m}{{}^j d^m}\right)^q, \tag{2}$$

with ${}^k d^m$ representing distance from k to m. As an illustration, suppose $q = 1$, ${}^k d^m = 1000$ and ${}^j d^m = 500$. In this case the ratio of sales penetration is equal to 2; i.e., since he is twice as close to market m, a producer at j can expect to capture twice the sales of a producer at k. Moreover, the ratio of sales penetration by any two producers is assumed independent of the pattern and number of other competitors, although, of course, their absolute sales are not. Hence the proportions of any market supplied by two producers will reflect this ratio of sales penetration. Formally, if $P(j, m)$ represents the proportion of market m supplied by a producer at j, then

$$P(j, m) = \left(\frac{R_{jm}}{R_{km}}\right) P(k, m) \tag{3}$$

or

$$P(j, m) = \left(\frac{_k d^m}{_i d^m}\right)^q P(k, m). \tag{4}$$

Since all suppliers service the total market,

$$P(k, m) + \sum_j n_j P(j, m) = 1. \tag{5}$$

Substituting (4) into (5),

$$P(k, m) + \sum_j n_j \left(\frac{_k d^m}{_i d^m}\right)^q P(k, m) = 1 \tag{6}$$

$$P(k, m) \left[1 + \sum_j n_j \left(\frac{_k d^m}{_i d^m}\right)^q\right] = 1 \tag{7}$$

$$P(k, m) = \left[1 + \sum_j n_j \left(\frac{_k d^m}{_i d^m}\right)^q\right]^{-1}. \tag{8}$$

Expression (8) indicates the expected *proportion* of the total sales in market m that a new firm located at k can hope to service. This proportion multiplied by the total sales in this market (S^m) provides an estimate of total sales in this particular market:

$$_k S^m = S^m \left[1 + \sum_j n_j \left(\frac{_k d^m}{_i d^m}\right)^q\right]^{-1}. \tag{9}$$

And this firm's total sales in all markets are

$$_k S = \sum_m S^m \left[1 + \sum_j n_j \left(\frac{_k d^m}{_i d^m}\right)^q\right]^{-1}. \tag{10}$$

If k is allowed to represent in turn all alternative locations, sales potential from each may be estimated and, if the firm's motivation may be described by this type of behavior, the site may be selected at which $_k s$ is maximized. If warranted, area population or income may be substituted for total sales, and transport costs for distance.

For purposes of illustration, consider the following spatial pattern in which S_1 and S_2 represent markets, and n_1, n_2, and n_3 represent established competitors. (Mileage distance is shown in brackets.)

Assuming $q = 1$ the sales potential at k is given by

$$^k s = \$10,000,000 \left[1 + 2 \left(\frac{500}{100} \right) + 1 \left(\frac{500}{700} \right) \right]^{-1}$$

$$+ \$1,000,000 \left[1 + 2 \left(\frac{1000}{1500} \right) + 1 \left(\frac{1000}{1500} \right) \right]^{-1},$$

which is equal to $\frac{7}{82}$ of the \$10,000,000 market plus one third of the \$1,000,000 market. As this illustration indicates, it is a very simple mechanical task to sort out the resulting market shares of all competitors as well. A comparison of these shares with present shares gives an estimate of the incidence of this move on the firms already established in this industry.

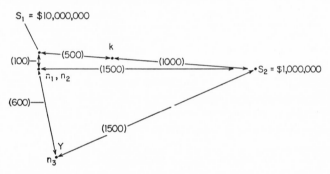

Figure 17. The location of industry: proximity to markets and to competitors.

It is evident that the crux of this theory is the set of ratios of market penetration. The fact that these ratios are relatively few in number is one of its operationally attractive aspects and adds to the flexibility of the model since these ratios can be defined in whatever way seems most appropriate. In this model the ratios are defined as homogeneous functions of distance. The value of the exponent q is critical since this is a reflection of the importance of distance in influencing market patterns. However, a priori the range of values of q may be reduced. Its lower bound is surely zero. At this point competitive distance to market becomes irrelevant, and all markets are equally divided among competitors. Its upper bound may tentatively be regarded as 1, since intuitively this bound seems to throw about as much importance on competitive location as would be warranted in any case.

This model may be put to use in several ways. If the behavioral assumptions of the model apply and it is feasible statistically to estimate q in a specific industry, the best location to maximize sales by a new firm may be estimated. Alternatively, since only a discrete number of locations is being considered, q might be set equal to 1, and optimal location determined on this basis. Then the model might be used to determine whether optimal location is independent of q. If it is, or if optimal location switches only when q is driven to unrealistically high values, then optimal location may be assumed independent of this type of distance orientation, and no statistical estimation of behavioral patterns is necessary.

In summary the model is highly flexible because it throws the whole burden of proof on a set of ratios which are limited in number; consequently, tests of sensitivity are easily carried out. Moreover, these ratios are easily modified whenever additional information is available. For example, a limit of $R_{jm}/R_{km} \geq 1/100$ may be imposed if evidence suggests that market penetration will be of this order regardless of location. Alternatively, foreign supplies could be imposed as an exogenous element in the definition of these ratios.

APPENDIX F. *Breakdown of Estimated Market for Each Good in Each North American Region*

For each good this breakdown involved four sets of computations.

U.S. Markets for the U.S.-produced Good

The total U.S. market in all regions for a domestically produced good was computed by reducing total U.S. production in all regions (r^u) by the proportion of this output exported (e^u):

$$r^u(1 - e^u). \tag{1}$$

U.S. production (or value of shipments) in all regions was estimated from the *1958 U.S. Census of Manufactures*. Only value added, rather than value shipped figures were available; hence value of shipments estimates for these sectors were derived by applying the average value shipped to value added ratio within each of the available subindustries. In turn these estimates were checked out against control totals provided by the census. The proportion of domestic U.S. output that was exported (e^u) was estimated from the 1947 U.S. Input-Output table.[1]

The total U.S. market was then allocated to regions in the following way. 1947 interindustry value flows[2] (x_{ij}) were allocated to each area according to the 1958 spatial location of user industries.[3] Letting z_j^m represent the proportion of industry j that is located in area m, the interindustry market demand for good i in area m is estimated as:

[1] Computed by reaggregating the U.S. 1947 interindustry matrix that appears in W. D. Evans and Marvin Hoffenberg, "The Inter-Industry Relations Study for 1947," *Review of Economics and Statistics*, 34: 97–142 (May 1952).

[2] *Ibid.*

[3] Computed from the 1958 *Census of Manufactures*.

$$\sum_j x_{ij}z_j^m \qquad \begin{aligned} i &= 1, \ldots, n \text{ goods} \\ m &= 1, \ldots, t \text{ areas.} \end{aligned}$$

The regional consumption of good i is computed by breaking up its total consumption (c_i) into areas according to the proportion of national income originating in each region (y^m):

$$c_i y^m \qquad \begin{aligned} i &= 1, \ldots, n \\ m &= 1, \ldots, t. \end{aligned}$$

The total demand for each good i in each market area (S_i^m) is the sum of demands on interindustry and consumption accounts:

$$S_i^m = \left(\sum_j x_{ij}z_j^m + c_i y^m \right) \qquad \begin{aligned} i &= 1, \ldots, n \\ m &= 1, \ldots, t. \end{aligned}$$

For each good in turn, the market demand in each area was expressed as a percentage of the total U.S. demand.[4] This provided the necessary allocation of the U.S. market among regions.

U.S. Markets for the Canadian-produced Good

Total Canadian production of each good in all regions (r^c) was derived by summing value shipped figures appearing in D.B.S., *Manufacturing Industries of Canada, 1958*, Sections B to F. The proportion of total production that was exported (e^c) was derived from the Canadian Input-Output Table;[5] in turn the proportion of Canadian exports going to the United States (e_u^c) was derived from *U.N. Commodity Trade Statistics, 1958*. This yielded an estimate of total Canadian exports to the United States of:

$$r^c(e^c)(e_u^c). \tag{2}$$

This total was allocated to U.S. consuming regions in the same way that domestic U.S. production was distributed above.

[4] Each of these percentages may be found in R. J. Wonnacott, *Manufacturing Costs and the Comparative Advantage of U.S. Regions* (Minneapolis: Upper Midwest Economic Study, University of Minnesota, Study Paper 9, April 1963), p. 26.

[5] D.B.S., *Supplement to the Interindustry Flow of Goods and Services, Canada*, 1949, Table 1.

Canadian Markets for the Canadian-produced Good

Total Canadian production of each good in all regions, r^c, derived directly above, was reduced by the proportion of the good exported (e^c, derived from the Canadian Input-Output Table). This yielded a total of the Canadian produced good going to domestic consumption:

$$r^c(1 - e^c). \tag{3}$$

This total was allocated to Canadian markets by a technique almost identical to that used to distribute U.S. production to U.S. markets. Each 1949 Canadian interindustry value flow[6] (the use of good i by industry j, represented by x_{ij}) was allocated to each area according to the 1958 spatial location of user industries.[7] Letting z_j^m represent the proportion of industry j that is located in area m, the interindustry market demand for good i in area m is estimated as:

$$\sum_{j=1}^{n+f} x_{ij}z_j^m \qquad \begin{array}{l} i = 1, \ldots, n \text{ goods} \\ m = 1, \ldots, t \text{ areas.} \end{array}$$

Note that user industries are defined to include f nonmanufacturing sectors. The consumption of good i in region m is computed by breaking up its total consumption (c_i)[8] into areas according to the proportion of national income originating in each region (y^m):[9]

---

[6] Computed by reaggregating the Canadian 1949 interindustry matrix that appears in D.B.S., *Supplement to the Interindustry Flow of Goods and Services, Canada,* 1949, Table 1.

[7] The location of n manufacturing industries was taken from area value of shipments figures in D.B.S. 31–204. The location of f nonmanufacturing industries was taken from value of production figures in various publications: agriculture, and fishing and trapping from D.B.S., *Survey of Production,* 1959; metal mining, smelting and refining and coal mining, crude petroleum and natural gas, and nonmetal mining, quarrying, and prospecting from D.B.S., *General Review of the Mining Industry,* 1958; forestry from D.B.S., *Operation in the Woods,* 1958; and construction from D.B.S., *Construction in Canada,* 1958.

[8] This included the consumption figures in the Canadian interindustry table as well as expenditures on transportation, storage, trade, communications, electric power, gas, water utilities, finance, insurance, real estate, services, and government; each of these expenditures was assumed to be geographically distributed with income.

[9] Derived from D.B.S., *Income and Expenditures,* 1949.

$$c_i y^m \qquad \begin{matrix} i = 1, \ldots, n \\ m = 1, \ldots, t. \end{matrix} \quad (4)$$

The total demand for each good i in each market area (S_i^m) is the sum of demands on interindustry and consumption accounts:

$$S_i^m = \sum_{j=1}^{n+t} x_{ij} z_j^m + c_i y^m \qquad \begin{matrix} i = 1, \ldots, n \\ m = 1, \ldots, t. \end{matrix}$$

For each good in turn, the market demand in each area was expressed as a percentage of the total Canadian demand. Thus, the proportion of the total market demand for good i in area k is $S_i^k / \sum_m S_i^m$.

Canadian Markets for the U.S.-produced Good

Total U.S. production of each good in all U.S. regions (r^u) was derived above. Only a portion of this was exported, e^u, also derived above; and only a proportion of this U.S. export went to Canada, e_c^u, derived from *U.N. Commodity Trade Statistics*, 1958. This yielded a value of U.S. exports to Canada as follows:

$$r^u (e^u)(e_c^u). \qquad (5)$$

This total was allocated to Canadian regions according to the domestic distribution of Canadian production derived above.

APPENDIX G. *Breakdown of Estimated Market for Each Good in Each Region, 1958 (in millions of dollars).*[a]

Manufacturing sector[b]	Maritimes	Quebec	Ontario	Prairies	British Columbia	Upper Midwest	West Lake	East Lake	Lower Midwest	Middle Atlantic	New England	South	Capital	Florida	Southwest	Mountain	Pacific Southwest	Pacific Northwest
Food	265.0 / 17.4	969.2 / 63.8	1,592.5 / 104.8	766.0 / 50.4	394.3 / 25.9	2,203.1 / 7.8	6,798.1 / 24.1	5,979.8 / 21.2	4,720.9 / 16.7	14,225.7 / 50.4	2,895.5 / 10.2	7,490.5 / 26.5	1,573.6 / 5.6	1,384.8 / 4.9	5,602.1 / 19.8	2,266.0 / 8.0	6,168.6 / 21.8	1,636.6 / 5.8
Tobacco	14.7 / 2.4	97.5 / 16.0	119.3 / 19.5	36.3 / 5.9	25.9 / 3.7	106.0 / 0.1	300.2 / 0.3	284.9 / 0.2	242.5 / 0.2	688.2 / 4.3	124.3 / 0.1	348.5 / 0.3	72.7 / 0.1	66.7 / 0.1	254.6 / 0.2	163.6 / 0.1	300.2 / 0.3	78.9 / 0.1
Textiles	2.4 / 16.0	422.4 / 109.7	319.0 / 82.8	76.9 / 20.0	43.0 / 11.2	154.8 / 0.2	874.0 / 0.9	840.8 / 0.9	420.4 / 0.4	4,016.1 / 4.3	697.0 / 0.7	2,091.0 / 0.2	254.3 / 0.3	121.7 / 0.1	564.3 / 0.2	99.6 / 0.1	763.4 / 0.8	165.9 / 0.3
Apparel	23.9 / 6.2	190.2 / 7.0	301.1 / 124.7	124.7 / 4.6	76.8 / 11.2	337.4 / 0.2	1,417.0 / 0.5	1,133.6 / 0.4	755.7 / 0.3	3,886.6 / 0.6	634.2 / 0.7	1,578.9 / 0.4	377.8 / 0.1	269.9 / 0.1	1,093.1 / 0.4	269.9 / 0.1	1,281.9 / 0.4	337.4 / 0.8
Wood products	50.6 / 1.9	240.1 / 19.1	398.6 / 174.4	174.4 / 13.9	134.0 / 10.7	321.4 / 0.1	1,399.0 / 0.5	1,190.3 / 0.4	662.9 / 0.3	2,599.4 / 57.9	552.1 / 0.3	1,547.3 / 0.1	284.7 / 0.1	254.5 / 0.1	997.1 / 0.1	252.7 / 0.1	1,216.8 / 0.4	631.7 / 0.4
Paper	62.4 / 5.0	241.5 / 15.8	338.6 / 85.7	85.7 / 5.6	74.9 / 4.9	324.6 / 21.4	1,905.7 / 31.2	1,439.9 / 26.5	691.8 / 14.8	3,486.8 / 57.9	832.8 / 12.3	1,877.5 / 34.5	296.4 / 6.3	352.9 / 19.1	1,157.5 / 22.2	268.2 / 5.6	1,072.9 / 27.1	409.4 / 14.1
Printing	51.0 / 3.3	191.9 / 14.8	315.7 / 122.3	122.3 / 9.4	76.6 / 5.9	338.2 / 0.2	1,515.6 / 0.7	1,277.6 / 0.7	726.5 / 0.2	3,281.6 / 1.6	588.7 / 0.3	1,340.2 / 0.6	350.7 / 0.2	275.5 / 0.5	1,039.6 / 0.5	250.5 / 0.6	1,227.4 / 0.6	313.1 / 0.2
Electrical equipment	49.1 / 3.8	241.3 / 40.3	447.7 / 145.2	145.2 / 24.3	91.7 / 15.3	421.8 / 0.2	2,751.4 / 0.2	2,457.9 / 0.5	1,155.6 / 0.2	4,402.2 / 0.3	788.8 / 0.3	1,797.6 / 0.1	440.3 / 0.3	311.9 / 0.1	1,284.0 / 0.1	293.4 / 1,779.3	1,779.3 / 0.6	440.3 / 0.3
Chemicals	55.7 / 9.3	270.7 / 55.2	468.5 / 185.6	185.6 / 37.9	99.4 / 20.3	627.8 / 2.8	2,424.6 / 0.6	2,273.0 / 10.0	1,320.5 / 5.8	5,979.0 / 21.9	1,039.1 / 4.6	3,398.7 / 14.9	497.9 / 2.2	389.7 / 1.7	1,861.7 / 8.2	606.2 / 2.7	1,796.8 / 7.9	433.0 / 1.9
Petroleum products	77.4 / 324.5	324.5 / 37.3	544.2 / 278.1	278.1 / 32.0	130.4 / 15.0	405.2 / 0.3	1,932.5 / 1.3	1,449.4 / 1.0	794.8 / 0.5	3,303.9 / 2.2	436.3 / 0.3	1,231.2 / 0.8	327.2 / 0.2	218.2 / 0.1	3,054.6 / 2.1	342.9 / 0.2	1,745.5 / 1.2	342.9 / 0.2
Rubber and plastics	8.9 / 19.5	83.3 / 13.3	159.8 / 83.3	62.6 / 10.0	29.5 / 4.7	158.8 / 0.3	870.5 / 1.3	889.6 / 1.6	489.3 / 0.9	1,347.1 / 2.5	292.3 / 0.5	648.6 / 1.2	152.5 / 0.3	108.0 / 0.2	457.5 / 0.8	108.0 / 0.2	660.9 / 1.2	180.0 / 0.3
Leather goods	3.1 / 13.7	70.2 / 4.3	102.1 / 33.1	33.1 / 6.0	20.7 / 1.3	80.3 / 0.3	418.0 / 1.6	333.7 / 0.3	253.2 / 0.2	1,065.2 / 1.0	506.5 / 0.5	474.3 / 0.4	96.4 / 0.3	68.4 / 0.2	265.3 / 0.3	60.3 / 0.1	317.6 / 0.3	80.3 / 0.1
Nonmetallic mineral products	13.7 / 0.8	140.7 / 34.5	243.9 / 106.4	106.4 / 26.1	59.8 / 14.6	245.8 / 0.7	1,287.7 / 3.8	1,169.7 / 3.5	608.9 / 1.8	2,329.7 / 6.9	403.0 / 1.2	1,101.0 / 3.3	245.8 / 0.7	196.6 / 0.6	815.9 / 2.4	235.9 / 0.7	943.7 / 2.8	235.9 / 0.7
Metallic products	176.0 / 51.7	907.1 / 266.6	1,793.1 / 527.1	496.8 / 146.0	323.6 / 95.1	1,349.9 / 7.0	11,082.3 / 57.5	9,708.1 / 50.4	3,793.4 / 19.7	16,456.9 / 85.4	2,529.7 / 13.1	6,030.7 / 31.3	1,499.6 / 7.8	1,015.2 / 5.3	4,277.7 / 22.2	1,103.6 / 5.7	5,817.0 / 30.2	1,449.6 / 7.5
Transportation equipment	113.4 / 22.3	427.9 / 84.2	792.2 / 155.9	281.4 / 55.4	171.7 / 33.8	777.0 / 1.2	4,594.7 / 7.1	5,067.7 / 7.8	2,702.8 / 4.2	6,824.5 / 10.6	1,250.0 / 1.9	3,277.1 / 5.1	878.4 / 1.4	608.1 / 0.9	2,466.3 / 3.8	540.6 / 0.8	3,783.9 / 5.9	1,047.3 / 1.6
Miscellaneous	31.0 / 6.1	107.9 / 21.2	175.2 / 34.5	67.9 / 13.4	43.7 / 8.6	346.1 / 0.4	1,602.9 / 1.9	1,391.4 / 1.7	750.4 / 0.9	3,474.0 / 4.1	635.9 / 0.8	1,411.1 / 1.7	346.4 / 0.4	271.9 / 0.3	1,039.4 / 1.2	245.6 / 0.3	1,333.4 / 1.6	315.8 / 0.4

[a] Two estimates appear for each industry and area. The first is derived by distributing the total Canadian (U.S.) output (less exports) to Canadian (U.S.) consuming regions. The second figure is derived by distributing U.S. exports to Canadian markets, and Canadian exports to U.S. markets.

[b] See Table I, note a.

° More than zero, but less than 0.05.

APPENDIX H. *Maximum Transport Costs:*
Markets Independent of Distance

Total demand by each area m for each good i (S_i^m) was expressed in physical terms (tons) by applying the 1958 ton-value ratio (v_i) for each good.[1] Total ton miles required to service all markets for good i from potential supply location k is:

$$^k r_i = \sum_m v_i S_i^m \, {}^k d^m. \tag{1}$$

For convenience, supply locations are defined to coincide with demand locations; but in general this is not required by the model.

Transport costs are computed by applying the cost per ton mile for each good (b_i). These costs are expressed as a proportion of total sales by dividing by the total value of sales of good i [2] as follows:

$$^k \sigma_i = \frac{b_i \cdot {}^k r_i}{\left(\sum_j x_{ij} + c_i \right)}, \tag{2}$$

with $^k \sigma_i$ representing the proportion of the cost per sales dollar of good i that will be required to cover transportation charges to service the North American market, assuming the industry is located in k.

---

[1] The only ton-value ratio available was that observed for rail shipments through the United States; this was computed by using Interstate Commerce Commission, *Freight Revenue and Wholesale Value at Destination of Commodities Transported by Class 1 Line Haul Railroads, 1956,* Table Appendix A. The commodities were regrouped according to SIC categories. Since the ton-value ratio at starting point was preferred, value figures were derived by subtracting aggregate freight revenue from aggregate value at destination. These adjusted value figures were then appropriately divided into the tonnage figures taken from the same table.

[2] It may be recalled that the total sale of good i is the sum of its sale on interindustry account (Σx_{ij}) plus its sale on consumption account (c_i).

The percentage that total cost in any comparison area k is higher or lower than in Ontario (designated here as area 1) is simply

$$100({}^{k}\sigma_i - {}^{1}\sigma_i) \qquad (k = 2, 3 \ldots 18). \quad (3)$$

Each of these estimates is shown as the *second* of each pair of cost figures in Table 11.

APPENDIX I. *Minimum Transport Costs:*
Markets Dependent on Distance

Potential sales of good i in market m by a firm located in k is estimated by equation (9) in Appendix E, setting q equal to 1:

$$^k s_i^m = S_i^m \left[1 + \sum_j n_j \left[\frac{^k d^m}{^i d^m} \right] \right]^{-1}, \qquad (1)$$

and the firm's potential sale in all markets is

$$^k s_i = \sum_m {}^k s_i^m. \qquad (2)$$

From each potential location point k, the physical ton-mile transport required to serve all markets in each good i ($^k f_i$) is computed by applying appropriate ton-value ratios (v_i) and interarea distance figures:

$$^k f_i = \sum_m v_i {}^k s_i^m \cdot {}^k d^m. \qquad (3)$$

These physical transportation requirements are converted into dollar costs by applying the ton-mile cost (b_i) involved in shipping each good; total transport costs are expressed as a proportion of sales by dividing by the total sales captured in all markets by this firm:

$$^k \beta_i = \frac{b_i \cdot {}^k f_i}{^k s_i}. \qquad (4)$$

The percentage that total cost in any comparison area k is higher ($+$) or lower ($-$) than in Ontario is simply:

$$100(^k \beta_i - {}^1 \beta_i) \qquad (k = 2, 3 \ldots 18). \qquad (5)$$

Each of these estimates is shown as the *first* of each pair of cost figures in Table 11.

APPENDIX J. *Techniques Used to Estimate Bounding Limits on the Percentage by Which Total Costs May Be Higher in Comparison Areas than Regions of Greatest Resource Concentration, Because of Difference in Resource Costs, 1958 (Tables 14 and 15 in text).*

The total costs that potentially may be devoted to transporting a specific resource for an industry were computed as follows. Cost per ton mile of shipping the resource[1] was divided by the value of a ton of the resource in shipment[2] to derive the cost of shipping a dollar's worth of this resource one mile. The latter in turn was multiplied by the distance involved in shipping each resource from the relevant resource extraction point to the potential processing location;[3] this provided an estimate of the cost incurred by the firm in moving a dollar's worth of the resource. The impact of this cost on the total costs of the user industry was derived by multiplying it by the proportion of the total costs of that industry devoted to the purchase of this resource.

Primary Iron and Steel Industry

This industry in Canada had a total output in 1958 valued at $590 million. Its iron ore requirement of $62 million and its coal

---

[1] Interstate Commerce Commission, *Carload Waybill Statistics*, 1959. Unless specified otherwise, shipment by rail was assumed.

[2] Derived from Interstate Commerce Commission, *Freight Revenue and Wholesale Value at Destination of Commodities Transported by Class 1 Line Haul Railroads*, 1959.

[3] If a firm is considering locating in a region which has a relevant domestic source of resource supplies, it is assumed that the transit distance is zero on the assumption that the processing firm locates right at the resource site.

requirement of $39 million represented 11 percent and 7 percent of its total costs, respectively.[4]

The minimum estimate of differential iron ore costs was based on the assumption that a firm in any location would draw upon supplies from whichever of the following sources was closest: Maritimes, Quebec, Ontario, British Columbia, Upper Midwest, West Lake, East Lake, Lower Midwest, Middle Atlantic, South, Southwest Mountain, Pacific Southwest, or Pacific Northwest.[5] The maximum estimate was based on the assumption that Labrador becomes the major export source.

Because transporting ore by ship is substantially less expensive than rail transport, all costs were computed by assuming that the ore is transported by ship on the Great Lakes or down the Atlantic seaboard[6] and by rail wherever necessary. (Ore shipments from Labrador to Southern California were assumed to go by sea through the Panama Canal because this represented the apparently least expensive route.)

The minimum estimate of coal costs was based on the assumption that a firm located in any area would draw its supply of coal from the closest of the following coal producing areas: the Maritimes, West Lake, East Lake, Middle Atlantic, South, or Mountain.[7] For the maximum estimate it was assumed that the major supply concentration was located on the border of the U.S. South and the Middle Atlantic area.

Nonferrous Metal Products

In 1958 this Canadian industry had a total output of $1,531 million;[8] its input of copper, lead, and zinc ore was $263 million, representing 17 percent of total output of the industry.

[4] D.B.S., 41–203, *The Primary Iron and Steel Industry,* 1958. This Canadian source provided much better input detail than any available U.S. source.

[5] D.B.S., *Canada Yearbook,* 1959, p. 526.

[6] Shipping rate used was the Duluth-Cleveland rate from U.S. Bureau of Mines, *Minerals Yearbook,* VI, 1957, p. 607.

[7] D.B.S., *Canada Yearbook,* 1959, p. 536. Commodity Research Bureau, Inc., Harry Jiler, ed., *Commodity Yearbook,* 1959 (New York: C.R.B., 1959).

[8] D.B.S., 41–202, *Non-ferrous Metal Products; General Review,* 1958.

The minimum estimate was based on the assumption that a firm located in any area would draw its supply from the closest of the ore-producing areas. In all but four of the eighteen areas there was production of ore.[9] These four areas were New England, Capital, Florida, and Pacific Southwest. For calculation of the maximum estimate it was assumed that the major supply concentration was located in the Southwest.

Petroleum Products

The total output of this industry for Canada in 1958 was $1,383 million and the input of crude petroleum was $734 million, or 53 percent of total output.[10]

To calculate the minimum estimate it was assumed that a firm located in any area would draw its supply of crude petroleum from the closest of the following producing areas: Prairie, Upper Midwest, West Lake, East Lake, Lower Midwest, South, Southwest, Mountain, or Pacific Southwest.[11] For the maximum estimate it was assumed that the Southwest was the major export source.

It was assumed that all shipments of crude petroleum were by pipeline. It was only possible to get shipping rates for Canadian pipelines,[12] and these rates were used throughout.

Coal Products

In 1958 this industry in Canada had a total output of $83 million; the input of coal was $51 million which represented 61 percent of total output.[13]

---

[9] D.B.S., *Canada Yearbook*, 1958. Commodity Research Bureau, Inc., *Commodity Yearbook*, 1959.

[10] D.B.S., 45–201, *Products of Petroleum and Coal*, 1958.

[11] D.B.S., *Canada Yearbook*, 1958. Commodity Research Bureau, Inc., *Commodity Yearbook*, 1958.

[12] D.B.S., *Canada Yearbook*, 1962, p. 833.

[13] D.B.S., 45–201, *Products of Petroleum and Coal*, 1958.

The calculations were similar to those for coal in the primary iron and steel industry.

Flour Milling Industry

In 1958 this Canadian industry had a total output of $218 million; the input of wheat was $147 million which represented 67 percent of total output.[14]

Since wheat is produced in all eighteen areas all minimum estimates are zero. The Prairies, Upper Midwest, Lower Midwest, Southwest, and Mountain were assumed major export areas for calculations of the maximum estimates.

Slaughtering and Meat Packing Industry

The total output of this industry in Canada in 1958 was $1,050 million; the input of livestock and meat was $752 million representing 72 percent of total output.[15]

The minimum estimate was zero for all areas since livestock and meat are produced in all areas. For the maximum estimate it was assumed that the major export areas are the West Lake and Lower Midwest.

Tobacco Products

In 1958 this industry had a total output in Canada of $305 million and an input of tobacco of $174 million, representing 57 percent of total output.[16]

The minimum estimate was based on the assumption that a firm located in any area would draw its supply of tobacco from the closest of the following areas where tobacco is grown: Quebec, Ontario, West Lake, East Lake, Middle Atlantic, New England,

[14] D.B.S., 32–215, *Flour Milling Industry*, 1958.
[15] D.B.S., 32–221, *The Slaughtering and Meat Packing Industries*, 1959.
[16] D.B.S., 32–225, *The Tobacco and Tobacco Products Industries*, 1958.

South, Capital, or Florida.[17] The maximum estimate was based on the assumption that the South is the major area of supply concentration.

Textiles

The total output of this industry in Canada in 1958 was $739 million; the input of cotton was $43 million, or approximately 6 percent of total output.[18]

To calculate the minimum estimate it was assumed that a firm located in any area would draw its supply of cotton from the closest of the areas in which cotton is grown: Lower Midwest, South, Southwest, or Pacific Southwest.[19] The maximum estimate was based on the assumption that all firms in any area would be supplied from the Southwest.

Lumber

Lumber was an input for the following three industries:

(1) Furniture. The total 1958 output of this industry in Canada was $309 million; the input of lumber was $195 million, representing 6 percent of the total output.[20]

(2) Wood products (except furniture). In 1958 the total output of this industry in Canada was $488 million; its input of lumber was $191 million, which was 39 percent of total output.[21]

(3) Pulp and paper. The total 1958 output of this industry in Canada was $1,395 million; the input of lumber was $361 million, representing 20 percent of total output.[22]

Since the minimum estimate of differential lumber costs was based on the assumption that a firm would draw its supplies from the nearest producing area, and since lumber if produced in all

[17] D.B.S., *Canada Yearbook*, 1960. Commodity Research Bureau, Inc., *Commodity Yearbook*, 1958.

[18] D.B.S., 34–201, *General Review of Textile Mills*, 1958; 34–205, *Cotton Textile Industries*, 1958; 34–209, *Wool Textile Industries*, 1958.

[19] Commodity Research Bureau, Inc., *Commodity Yearbook*, 1959.

[20] D.B.S., 35–202, *Furniture Industry*, 1958.

[21] D.B.S., 35–201, *General Review of the Wood-using Industries*, 1958.

[22] D.B.S., 36–204, *Paper and Pulp Industry*, 1958.

eighteen areas, the minimum estimates are all zero. For the maximum estimate it was assumed that for the furniture and wood product industries British Columbia or the Pacific Northwest are the major sources of lumber supply; for pulp and paper, it was assumed that Quebec is the major wood supplier.

APPENDIX K. Supplementary Ranking of Regions by Proximity to Intermediate Manufactured Supplies, 1958.[a]

Manufacturing sector[b]	Pacific Northwest	Pacific Southwest	Mountain	Southwest	Florida	Capital	South	New England	Middle Atlantic	Lower Midwest	East Lake	West Lake	Upper Midwest	British Columbia	Prairies	Ontario	Quebec	Maritimes
Food	16	15	13	11	12	2	9	6	4	8	3	1	10	14	17	5	7	18
	16	13	15	12	11	2	9	5	3	8	4	1	10	14	1	6	7	17
	15	11	17	13	14	3	9	5	2	8	4	1	12	10	18	7	6	16
Tobacco	15	18	14	12	11	2	8	7	4	9	5	1	10	13	17	6	3	16
	14	17	15	13	11	3	8	6	4	9	5	1	12	10	18	7	2	16
	12	15	17	14	11	4	5	6	3	10	7	1	13	8	18	9	2	16
Textiles	17	16	13	12	11	2	8	6	3	9	4	1	10	14	18	5	7	15
	17	14	15	12	11	3	8	5	3	9	4	1	10	13	18	7	6	16
	15	13	17	12	11	3	7	4	2	9	6	1	14	10	18	8	5	16
Apparel	18	17	14	12	11	1	8	2	3	9	7	5	10	15	16	6	4	13
	18	15	14	12	10	2	6	1	3	9	7	4	11	17	16	8	5	13
	18	14	15	11	10	3	5	2	1	9	7	4	12	16	17	8	6	13
Wood products	12	16	15	13	14	2	10	6	4	8	3	1	11	9	17	5	7	18
	9	12	16	14	15	3	10	6	4	11	5	1	13	2	17	8	7	18
	3	11	16	13	14	5	9	8	4	12	6	1	15	2	18	10	7	17
Paper	14	17	15	13	12	2	9	6	4	8	3	1	10	11	18	7	5	16
	12	15	16	14	13	2	9	4	5	10	6	1	11	8	18	7	3	17
	10	12	17	14	13	5	9	3	4	11	7	1	15	6	18	8	2	16
Printing	15	18	14	13	11	2	9	5	3	8	4	1	10	12	17	7	6	16
	14	16	17	13	12	2	8	3	4	9	6	1	11	10	18	7	5	15
	11	14	17	15	12	4	9	3	2	10	6	1	13	8	18	7	5	16
Electrical equipment	16	15	13	12	11	2	9	6	4	8	3	1	10	14	18	5	7	17
	16	14	15	13	12	2	9	5	3	8	4	1	10	11	18	6	7	17
	11	13	17	15	14	3	9	5	2	10	4	1	12	8	18	7	6	16

Category																	
Chemicals																	
18	6	5	17	14	10	1	3	8	4	7	9	2	12	11	13	15	16
16	5	7	18	14	10	1	4	8	3	6	9	2	12	11	15	13	17
17	6	7	18	12	13	1	4	9	2	5	8	3	14	11	16	10	15
Petroleum products																	
18	5	4	17	12	10	1	3	7	6	8	9	2	15	11	13	14	16
18	3	6	17	13	12	1	5	7	4	9	11	2	15	8	14	10	16
18	2	9	17	11	13	1	7	8	3	10	12	4	15	5	14	6	16
Rubber and plastics																	
15	7	5	17	14	10	1	4	8	3	6	9	2	11	12	13	16	18
15	6	7	17	16	10	1	4	9	3	5	8	2	11	12	14	13	18
14	6	8	17	15	12	1	5	9	2	4	7	3	10	11	16	13	18
Leather goods																	
15	7	6	18	14	10	1	4	8	3	5	9	2	11	12	13	16	17
17	6	7	18	13	10	1	5	8	4	3	9	2	11	12	15	14	16
16	5	7	18	10	12	1	6	9	3	2	8	4	14	15	17	11	13
Nonmetallic mineral products																	
18	7	5	17	14	10	1	3	8	4	6	9	2	11	12	13	16	16
16	7	6	18	15	10	1	4	8	3	5	9	2	11	12	14	13	17
16	6	7	18	11	13	1	4	9	2	5	8	3	14	12	17	10	15
Metallic products																	
16	7	5	17	14	10	1	3	8	4	6	9	2	12	11	13	15	18
16	7	6	18	14	10	1	3	8	4	5	9	2	12	11	15	13	17
15	6	7	18	13	11	1	4	8	2	5	9	3	14	12	16	10	17
Transportation equipment																	
17	7	5	18	14	10	1	3	8	4	6	9	2	12	11	13	15	16
16	7	5	18	14	10	1	3	8	4	6	9	2	13	11	15	12	17
16	7	6	18	11	12	1	2	8	3	5	9	4	15	14	17	10	13
Miscellaneous																	
17	7	5	18	14	10	1	3	8	4	6	9	2	11	12	13	15	16
17	7	6	18	11	10	1	4	9	3	5	8	2	12	13	16	14	15
16	6	7	18	8	13	1	4	10	2	5	9	3	14	15	17	12	11

ᵃ For explanation of these rankings, see footnotes 2 and 4, Chapter 7.
ᵇ See Table 1, note a.

APPENDIX L. *Higher Capital Costs in Canada Due to Protection*

In the main body of Chapter 8, the higher capital costs that would remain in Canada in a period of free trade were analyzed. This appendix is devoted to an analysis of the extent to which capital costs are higher in Canada because of protection. Both sets of cost differences explain current high Canadian costs of capital. However, those cost differences resulting from protection (analyzed in this appendix) would tend to disappear with free trade, leaving only the cost differences that are independent of protection (analyzed in the main body of Chapter 8) to determine changing North American industry patterns.

There are two major reasons why Canadian protection raises capital costs in Canada: first, machinery and equipment is more expensive in Canada due to protection on these items; and second, investment in plant is more expensive because of the Canadian protection on building materials.

Machinery and Equipment

The extent to which total costs in each manufacturing industry could be higher because of higher machinery prices allowed by protection is shown in the first column of Table L-1. This estimate involved applying the average Canadian tariff on the machinery and equipment used by each sector[1] to the estimated depreciation

---

[1] The average tariff paid on machinery imported from the United States was computed by dividing total duties collected on all items by the total value of imports by each Canadian user industry. In many instances it was not difficult to associate the machinery imports (e.g., shoe manufacturing machinery) with the Canadian user sector (leather products); other machinery imports (e.g., metal working machinery) were distributed to user industries on the basis of institutional information about the industry taken from Royal Commission studies and other sources. The admittedly somewhat arbitrary nature of the latter distribution may affect the specific esti-

TABLE L-1. *Estimated Percentage that Total Costs in Each Industry Are Higher in Canada because of Canadian Tariff Protection on Machinery and Equipment, and Construction Materials (maximum estimates, 1958).*

Manufacturing sector[a]	Machinery and equipment	Construction materials
Food	0.17	0.019
Tobacco	0.10	0.016
Textiles	0.16	0.008
Apparel	0.07	0.002
Wood products	0.17	0.018
Paper	0.93	0.037
Printing	0.05	0.030
Electrical equipment	0.18	0.018
Chemicals	0.57	0.077
Petroleum products	0.03	0.145
Rubber and plastics	0.20	0.014
Leather goods	0.06	0.004
Nonmetallic mineral products	0.39	0.056
Metallic products	0.33	0.038
Transportation equipment	0.19	0.020
Miscellaneous	0.23	0.016

Sources: See references in text, Chapter 8.
[a] See Table 1, note a.

of machinery and equipment in that sector.[2] The resulting estimated higher cost incurred by each investing Canadian sector was in turn expressed as a proportion of total costs by dividing by total costs (value shipped). It should be emphasized that this is a maximum estimate of the effect on Canadian costs because it is based on the assumption that Canadian domestic producers of

---

mates for each industry in Table L-1; however, it should not affect the general conclusions for all manufacturing sectors taken together. The average tariffs computed in this way for each sector are shown in Table L-2.

[2] Figures on machinery and equipment depreciation were not available; however, annual figures on gross expenditure on these items were available by industry for Canada in Department of Trade and Commerce, *Private and Public Investment in Canada.* Each of these gross investment figures was reduced to an estimate of depreciation by applying the ratio of depreciation to gross investment in each sector on machinery, equipment *and* plant available in Department of National Revenue, *Taxation Statistics.* (To the degree that machinery is more rapidly depreciated than plant, this estimating procedure may result in a downward bias in the cost estimates in column (1) of Table L-1.)

TABLE L-2.   *Average Weighted Tariff Protection on Machinery and Equipment*
Used by Each Canadian Industry.

Manufacturing sector[a]	Percent
Food	13.3
Tobacco	10.8
Textiles	07.8
Apparel	07.8
Wood products	12.0
Paper	19.7
Printing	03.7
Electrical equipment	10.4
Chemicals	13.5
Petroleum products	11.8
Rubber and plastics	13.5
Leather goods	12.0
Nonmetallic mineral products	12.3
Metallic products	15.3
Transportation equipment	13.5
Miscellaneous	13.5

[a] See Table 1, note a.

machinery and equipment take full advantage of all the protection they are afforded and sell their machinery at the maximum price allowed by the Canadian tariff (that is, the U.S. domestic price plus the Canadian duty). Cost effects cannot be greater than this but they may be less to the extent that Canadian produced machinery and equipment is sold to Canadian users at a price less than the maximum allowed.

It is evident from the figures in Table L-1 that there is a wide variation between sectors in terms of the higher costs they face because of protection on machinery and equipment. At one extreme, costs in the pulp and paper sector could be up to almost one percent higher in Canada — because of the heavy reliance of this sector on machinery and equipment and because the equipment this sector purchases is generally more heavily protected than machinery purchased by other sectors. On the other hand, costs of some sectors are left almost unaffected by Canadian machinery duties. For example, costs in printing and publishing are not substantially altered because the machinery used by this sector is almost unprotected; the same is true to a somewhat smaller degree of costs in the apparel sector. It may also be noted that cost effects are also low in leather, and petroleum and coal products — because of the fact that machinery expenditures in these sectors represent an unusually low proportion of total costs.

Construction Materials

The effects of Canadian protection of these items on total manufacturing costs are shown in column (2) of Table L-1. No attempt was made to distinguish between the construction materials used in plant investment by various Canadian industries; as a consequence, an average tariff of 7.8 percent on construction materials was used in all computations.[3]

Protection on construction materials must necessarily be treated differently from protection on machinery and equipment. The Canadian tariff on machinery and equipment provides protection to Canadian domestic producers that allows a maximum increase in Canadian prices of machinery and equipment by the full amount of the tariff. However, plant costs in Canada cannot become more expensive by the full amount of the Canadian tariff on construction materials. This follows because construction materials make up only a proportion (about one third) of the costs of constructing a plant in Canada; Canadian labor costs, etc., explain the balance. As a consequence, the 7.8 percent tariff on construction materials can explain, at most, only about 2.33 percent[4] higher cost level of plant construction in Canada.

This maximum estimate of higher plant costs was applied to depreciation of plant in each manufacturing sector[5] and in turn

[3] This average was computed by dividing duties collected on imports of construction materials from the United States by the value of these imports, taken from D.B.S., *Trade of Canada*. (Again, the difficulties involved in computing a weighted average of tariffs in this way should be noted; a full discussion of this issue appears in Part III.)

[4] About one third of 7.8 percent. This rough estimate of one third was derived by analyzing the input requirements of the construction industry in the 1949 interindustry table for Canada.

[5] Figures on plant depreciation were not available; however, figures on gross expenditure were available by industry for Canada in *Private and Public Investment in Canada*. Each of these gross investment figures was reduced to an estimate of depreciation by applying the ratio of deprecia-

divided by total costs of each sector, to generate the estimates shown in column (2) of Table L-1. It should be noted that these estimates are also maxima and depend on the assumption that all Canadian-produced construction materials are sold at the maximum price allowed by the Canadian tariff (that is, the U.S. domestic price plus the Canadian duty). If Canadian producers of these items do not take full advantage of their protection, the impact on total costs will be less.[6]

The impact of protection of construction materials on total costs again varies widely between sectors; however, it is evident from Table L-1 that in all cases the impact must be regarded as negligible, especially in view of the fact that, as maximum estimates, these figures almost certainly overstate.

Conclusions

There are a number of reasons that protection on machinery and equipment has a much greater impact on Canadian costs than protection on construction materials:

First, tariffs on machinery and equipment, which average 10 to 12 percent, are higher than tariffs of about 7 to 8 percent on construction materials.

Second, Canadian protection of 10 to 12 percent on machinery and equipment makes it possible (but of course does not ensure) that Canadian domestic prices of machinery and equipment could be higher by that percentage. Canadian protection of 7 to 8 percent on construction materials does *not* allow Canadian plant costs to be that much higher because of labor and other (unpro-

---

tion to gross investment expenditure in each sector on machinery, equipment and plant available in *Taxation Statistics*. (To the degree that plant is less rapidly depreciated than machinery and equipment, this estimating procedure may result in a slight upward bias in the cost estimates in column (2) of Table L-1.)

[6] In the extreme, if Canadian producers do not take advantage of their protection by raising their price at all, the impact of the tariff on construction materials would be only about one tenth the figure shown in column (2) of Table L-1. In this case only construction materials actually imported from the United States would be more expensive, and these have recently accounted for only about one tenth of Canadian domestic consumption. (See the 1949 Canadian Interindustry Table.)

tected) input requirements involved in plant construction in Canada. Whereas the tariff on machinery and equipment fully protects Canadian production of machinery and equipment, the tariff on construction materials protects only a portion of Canadian domestic plant creation.

Third, in general, depreciation on machinery and equipment exceeds that on plant for most industries.[7] This can be owing either to greater machinery requirements or to a more rapid depreciation of machinery over time.[8]

Compared with the effects of the tariff on machinery and equipment, the tariff on construction materials may be effectively disregarded. It is of interest, however, to consider how the effects of the tariff on machinery and equipment compare with the other higher costs of capital in Canada. The machinery and equipment tariff has about the same impact on manufacturing costs as either the higher interest rates on debt in Canada, or the higher costs in Canada caused by the 11 percent tax on machinery and equipment (analyzed in Chapter 9). All of these affect costs by less than one percent, but in almost all cases the effect is less than 0.5 percent. While these influences may have marginal significance in the cost picture of firms, none compares with the possible higher costs of equity used for investment in Canada.

[7] The one exception is the petroleum and coal products sector, in which construction materials are more critical than machinery and equipment. This atypical result is due to very heavy plant investment requirements in this sector, along with light machinery and equipment requirements. (This somewhat strange investment pattern was even more pronounced in 1958, the year of this study, than in preceding periods.)

[8] To the degree that the estimating techniques of this study have not fully accounted for this faster depreciation, machinery and equipment tariffs may be even more important relative to construction material tariffs than these figures suggest.

APPENDIX M. Capital Structure of U.S. Corporations, 1958 (*in millions of U.S. dollars*).

Manufacturing sector[a]	Debt					Equity				Total debt and equity
	Short term (less than 1 year)		Long term		Total debt	Reserves not reflected elsewhere	Capital stock (capital surplus and minority)	Earned surplus and surplus reserves	Total equity	
	Loans from banks	Long-term debt coming due	Loans from banks	Other long-term debt						
Food	1,371	741	309	2,217	4,683	188	4,646	8,059	12,893	17,531
Tobacco	287	32	6	528	853	2	866	1,032	1,900	2,753
Textiles	344	46	124	872	1,386	37	2,370	3,468	5,875	7,261
Apparel	256	12	27	171	466	4	862	1,011	1,877	2,343
Wood products	268	49	238	493	1,048	20	1,616	2,317	3,953	5,001
Paper	99	65	190	1,282	1,636	89	2,567	3,433	6,089	7,725
Printing	115	35	81	300	531	49	930	1,560	2,539	3,070
Electrical equipment	401	32	172	1,488	2,093	229	3,483	4,381	8,093	10,186
Chemicals	325	82	451	2,500	3,358	240	6,483	7,770	14,493	17,851
Petroleum products	234	86	1,138	3,698	5,156	311	12,815	13,002	26,128	31,284
Rubber and plastics	105	15	41	682	843	148	875	1,645	2,668	3,511
Leather goods	95	6	21	148	270	25	415	593	1,033	1,303
Nonmetallic mineral products	104	29	164	632	929	79	2,129	3,200	5,408	6,337
Metallic products	1,259	268	1,022	6,833	9,382	1,001	15,136	22,342	38,479	47,861
Transportation equipment	937	32	102	1,854	2,925	292	4,600	9,444	14,336	17,261
Miscellaneous	282	30	91	500	903	24	1,812	2,217	4,053	4,956

Source: Federal Trade Commission, *Quarterly Financial Report for Manufacturing Corporations,* Fourth Quarter, 1958.
[a] See Table 1, note a.

APPENDIX N. *Ratios for Translating Gross into Net Investment in Tables 22 and 23 (depreciation machinery, equipment and plant divided by gross expenditures, machinery, equipment and plant).*

Manufacturing sector[a]	1958	1961
Food	0.69	0.66
Tobacco	0.38	0.30
Textiles	0.90	0.94
Apparel	0.84	0.83
Wood products	0.86	0.62
Paper	0.88	0.91
Printing	0.54	0.74
Electrical equipment	0.79	0.83
Chemicals	0.74	0.78
Petroleum products	0.50	0.46
Rubber and plastics	0.88	0.92
Leather goods	0.61	0.77
Nonmetallic mineral products	0.79	1.03[b]
Metallic products	0.64	0.54
Transportation equipment	0.78	0.86
Miscellaneous	0.66	0.48

Source: Calculated from data in Department of National Revenue, *Taxation Statistics*, 1960 and 1963.

[a] See Table 1, note a.

[b] See footnote 9, Chapter 9.

APPENDIX O. *Estimated Percentage That Total Costs in Comparison Areas Are Lower (−) or Higher Than in Ontario, by Industry, 1958 ($1.00 U.S. = $1.00 Can.).*[a]

Comparison areas	Food	Tobacco	Textiles	Apparel	Wood products	Paper	Printing	Electrical equipment	Chemicals	Petroleum products	Rubber and plastics	Leather goods	Nonmetallic mineral products	Metallic products	Transportation equipment	Miscellaneous
								Manufacturing sector[b]								
Maritimes I	−2.16	−1.04	2.47	6.17	−5.52	0.75	−6.02	−2.10	−2.11	−0.55	−2.12	4.00	−2.94	−0.66	−2.63	−3.01
II	7.18	1.12	1.59	0.68	23.55	11.27	3.40	2.55	11.57	50.88	2.08	1.27	61.19	16.18	4.28	1.68
III	0.75	0.91	0.21	0	2.15	0.86	0	0	0	2.16	0	0	0	0.39	0	0
IV	0	0	0	0	0	0	0	0	0	0	0	0	0	0	0	0
V	5.77	0.99	4.27	6.85	20.18	12.88	−2.62	0.45	9.46	52.49	−0.04	5.27	58.25	15.91	1.65	−1.33
Quebec I	−0.28	−0.47	−0.31	−1.24	−3.89	−0.22	−0.82	−1.03	−0.93	−0.33	−4.28	−3.27	1.96	−1.80	−1.73	−2.58
II	0.21	0.16	−0.14	0.08	0.84	0.89	0.05	0.09	0.54	0.49	0.13	0.12	0.62	0.24	0.12	0.12
III	0.19	0.17	0.09	0	0.60	−0.72	0	0	0	1.00	0	0	0	0.11	0	0
IV	0	0	0	0	0	0	0	0	0	0	0	0	0	0	0	0
V	0.12	−0.14	−0.36	−1.16	−2.45	−0.05	−0.77	−0.94	−0.39	1.16	−4.15	−3.15	2.58	−1.45	−1.61	−2.46
Prairies I	1.17	−0.32	5.70	−0.71	5.52	−1.43	−3.67	−1.86	−0.93	−0.26	−2.29	6.18	−1.09	−2.27	−2.06	−0.32
II	5.54	0.55	1.35	0.40	20.20	8.73	2.43	1.74	8.30	39.73	1.20	0.80	43.30	11.91	3.46	1.16
III	−0.27	1.32	0.09	0	−2.36	2.97	0	0	0	−1.50	0	0	0	1.50	0	0
IV	0	0	0	0	0	0	0	0	0	0	0	0	0	0	0	0
V	6.44	1.55	7.14	−0.31	23.45	10.27	−1.24	−0.12	7.37	37.97	−1.09	6.98	42.21	11.14	1.40	0.84
British Columbia I	1.55	1.93	11.23	15.53	9.25	3.65	4.39	2.68	2.10	1.01	1.79	14.17	3.04	2.27	2.22	3.01
II	1.18	−0.22	−0.04	−0.14	9.42	1.91	−0.16	−0.45	0.09	4.70	−0.44	−0.26	−6.11	−0.84	0.29	−0.13
III	0.32	2.19	0.13	0	−4.76	5.00	0	0	0	2.24	0	0	0	3.34	0	0
IV	0	0	0	0	0	0	0	0	0	0	0	0	0	0	0	0
V	3.05	3.90	11.32	15.39	13.91	10.56	4.23	2.23	2.19	7.95	1.35	13.91	−3.07	4.77	2.51	2.88

Region		1	2	3	4	5	6	7	8	9	10	11	12	13	14	15	16
Upper Midwest	I	3.52	2.39	5.55	6.70	11.19	2.09	5.82	4.03	1.55	1.06	1.89	6.01	4.35	3.40	3.62	3.98
	II	1.33	0.11	0.56	0.08	6.90	2.18	0.65	0.50	2.01	14.37	0.26	0.20	13.21	4.01	0.93	0.20
	III	-0.31	0.43	-0.06	0	-1.84	-1.54	0	0	0	-2.11	0	0	0	0.23	0	0
	IV	-0.52	-3.35	-1.26	-0.35	-0.79	-1.07	-0.48	-1.07	-1.58	-4.11	-1.11	-0.76	-1.27	-1.38	-1.00	-0.73
	V	4.02	-0.42	4.79	6.43	15.46	1.66	5.99	3.46	1.98	9.21	1.04	5.45	16.29	6.26	3.55	3.45
West Lake	I	3.10	-1.98	6.94	7.06	8.11	2.09	7.14	4.96	2.63	1.46	4.08	9.45	5.98	5.96	5.34	3.98
	II	-1.45	-0.32	-0.32	-0.21	-4.19	-3.08	-0.73	-0.51	-2.79	-7.79	-0.52	-0.38	-13.35	-3.27	-1.07	-0.49
	III	-0.14	-0.13	-0.07	0	-0.95	0.93	0	0	0	-2.45	0	0	0	0.81	0	0
	IV	-0.52	-3.35	-1.26	-0.35	-0.79	-1.07	-0.48	-1.07	-1.58	-4.11	-1.11	-0.76	-1.27	-1.38	-1.00	-0.73
	V	0.99	-5.78	5.29	6.50	2.18	-1.13	5.93	3.38	-1.74	-12.89	2.45	8.31	-8.64	2.12	3.27	2.76
East Lake	I	3.05	-0.94	8.48	10.23	11.84	3.06	6.33	6.82	3.66	1.18	8.07	9.45	6.53	7.19	6.66	4.84
	II	-0.71	-0.09	-0.07	-0.09	-1.41	-1.45	-0.34	-0.29	-1.21	-2.32	-0.23	-0.16	-5.44	-1.38	-0.46	-0.27
	III	-0.03	-0.13	-0.04	0	-0.54	-0.50	0	0	0	-2.31	0	0	0	0.17	0	0
	IV	-0.52	-3.35	-1.26	-0.35	-0.79	-1.07	-0.48	-1.07	-1.58	-4.11	-1.11	-0.76	-1.27	-1.38	-1.00	-0.73
	V	1.79	-4.51	7.11	9.79	9.10	0.04	5.51	5.46	0.87	-7.56	6.73	8.53	-0.18	4.60	5.20	3.84
Lower Midwest	I	3.38	2.01	1.54	4.23	6.65	0.30	3.37	2.58	2.68	0.90	1.59	4.18	5.11	3.69	4.11	3.98
	II	0.02	0.24	0.24	-0.03	2.44	-0.12	0.02	0	0.03	4.80	-0.15	-0.05	1.72	-0.78	-0.02	-0.12
	III	-0.34	-0.13	-0.15	0	-1.25	1.61	0	0	0	-2.81	0	0	0	0.77	0	0
	IV	-0.52	-3.35	-1.26	-0.35	-0.79	-1.07	-0.48	-1.07	-1.58	-4.11	-1.11	-0.76	-1.27	-1.38	-1.00	-0.73
	V	2.54	-1.23	0.37	3.85	7.05	0.72	2.91	1.51	1.13	-1.22	0.33	3.37	5.56	2.30	3.09	3.13
Middle Atlantic	I	3.00	-1.51	7.09	8.82	9.08	1.57	6.94	4.75	2.83	1.28	3.09	6.36	5.87	5.67	5.43	4.84
	II	-1.16	-0.03	-0.24	-0.07	-2.99	-1.86	-0.49	-0.29	-1.79	-5.29	-0.19	-0.14	-7.45	-1.66	-0.56	-0.23
	III	0.20	-0.04	0.02	0	0.34	0.06	0	0	0	-1.98	0	0	0	0.31	0	0
	IV	-0.52	-3.35	-1.26	-0.35	-0.79	-1.07	-0.48	-1.07	-1.58	-4.11	-1.11	-0.76	-1.27	-1.38	-1.00	-0.73
	V	1.52	-4.93	5.61	8.40	5.64	-1.30	5.97	3.39	-0.54	-10.10	1.79	5.46	-2.85	2.94	3.87	3.88
New England	I	1.64	-2.24	5.55	6.17	4.38	1.12	3.37	1.96	2.27	0.32	1.59	7.81	5.00	2.65	4.93	0.43
	II	-0.83	0.01	0.09	-0.02	-1.51	-1.07	-0.26	-0.08	-1.31	-1.23	0.01	-0.09	-4.06	-0.40	-0.39	-0.07
	III	0.35	0.06	0.07	0	0.58	-0.09	0	0	0	-0.36	0	0	0	0.31	0	0
	IV	-0.52	-3.35	-1.26	-0.35	-0.79	-1.07	-0.48	-1.07	-1.58	-4.11	-1.11	-0.76	-1.27	-1.38	-1.00	-0.73
	V	0.64	-5.52	4.45	5.80	2.66	-1.11	2.63	0.81	-0.62	-5.38	0.49	6.96	-0.33	1.18	3.54	-0.37
South	I	0.28	0.42	2.31	1.41	-1.78	1.79	1.84	1.86	2.52	-0.06	3.88	2.73	1.52	3.69	3.29	-0.75
	II	0.43	0.19	0.27	0.03	3.60	0.13	0.20	0.19	0.54	8.01	0.10	0.03	6.03	1.93	0.33	-0.02
	III	0.03	-0.44	-0.12	0	-0.04	1.40	0	0	0	-2.53	0	0	0	0.19	0	0
	IV	-0.52	-3.35	-1.26	-0.35	-0.79	-1.07	-0.48	-1.07	-1.58	-4.11	-1.11	-0.76	-1.27	-1.38	-1.00	-0.73
	V	0.22	-3.18	1.20	1.09	0.99	2.25	1.56	0.98	1.48	1.31	2.87	2.00	6.28	4.43	2.62	-1.50

(continued on next page)

APPENDIX O *Continued*

Manufacturing sector[b]

Comparison areas		Food	Tobacco	Textiles	Apparel	Wood products	Paper	Printing	Electrical equipment	Chemicals	Petroleum products	Rubber and plastics	Leather goods	Nonmetallic mineral products	Metallic products	Transportation equipment	Miscellaneous
Capital	I	0.94	2.34	4.78	5.47	4.22	0.89	5.41	7.23	1.80	0.34	1.59	7.99	4.46	6.53	5.75	3.34
	II	-1.60	-0.11	-0.29	-0.12	-4.39	-2.51	-0.72	-0.47	-2.30	-8.40	-0.33	-0.23	-11.28	-2.51	-0.85	-0.37
	III	0.20	-0.14	-0.01	0	0.07	0.41	0		0	-1.18			0	0.19		0
	IV	-0.52	-3.35	-1.26	-0.35	-0.79	-1.07	-0.48	-1.07	-1.58	-4.11	-1.11	-0.76	-1.27	-1.38	-1.00	-0.73
	V	-0.98	-1.26	3.22	5.00	-0.89	-2.28	4.21	5.69	-2.08	-13.35	0.15	7.00	-8.09	2.83	3.90	2.24
Florida	I	-0.05	-2.09	2.31	3.88	0.97	2.76	5.00	1.65	0.41	-0.84	-2.99	3.81	-0.65	-0.76	0.74	4.63
	II	2.17	0.55	0.87	0.19	10.10	2.53	0.90	0.76	4.05	22.00	0.57	0.35	21.39	5.90	1.35	0.32
	III	0.30	-0.11	0.04	0	0.96	2.26	0	0	0	0.10	0	0	0	0.88	0	0
	IV	-0.52	-3.35	-1.26	-0.35	-0.79	-1.07	-0.48	-1.07	-1.58	-4.11	-1.11	-0.76	-1.27	-1.38	-1.00	-0.73
	V	1.90	-5.00	1.88	3.72	11.24	6.48	5.42	1.34	2.88	17.15	-3.53	3.40	19.47	4.64	1.09	4.22
Southwest	I	0.61	1.46	0.77	1.59	-0.16	2.91	2.45	2.48	4.74	1.48	2.89	1.64	1.63	2.74	5.43	0.32
	II	1.83	0.22	0.70	0.11	9.15	2.30	0.75	0.59	2.84	13.30	0.34	0.24	16.47	4.74	1.23	0.25
	III	-0.31	0.62	-0.22	0	-0.73	2.81	0	0	0	-4.69	0	0	0	-0.06	0	0
	IV	-0.52	-3.35	-1.26	-0.35	-0.79	-1.07	-0.48	-1.07	-1.58	-4.11	-1.11	-0.76	-1.27	-1.38	-1.00	-0.73
	V	1.60	-1.05	-0.01	1.35	7.47	6.95	2.72	2.00	6.00	5.98	2.12	1.12	16.83	6.04	5.66	-0.16
Mountain	I	1.92	2.45	0.46	4.59	13.30	0.45	5.51	1.86	4.12	1.46	4.98	6.15	5.44	6.81	2.14	10.22
	II	2.34	0.13	0.81	0.17	12.39	3.87	1.15	0.86	3.62	23.90	0.54	0.35	21.77	6.26	1.95	0.51
	III	-0.29	1.18	-0.03	0	-2.35	3.23	0	0	0	-2.23	0	0	0	1.02	0	0
	IV	-0.52	-3.35	-1.26	-0.35	-0.79	-1.07	-0.48	-1.07	-1.58	-4.11	-1.11	-0.76	-1.27	-1.38	-1.00	-0.73
	V	3.45	0.41	-0.02	4.41	22.55	6.48	6.18	1.65	6.16	19.02	4.41	5.74	25.94	12.71	3.09	10.00
Pacific Southwest	I	3.61	-2.77	8.02	8.64	15.73	3.35	9.59	5.89	3.19	1.12	5.28	9.99	7.72	6.05	5.67	10.55
	II	0.19	-0.24	0.12	-0.11	3.67	-0.70	-0.26	-0.20	-0.58	7.79	-0.28	-0.24	-1.10	-0.58	0.50	-0.02
	III	0.22	2.49	-0.07	0	-2.63	5.22	0	0	0	-1.36	0	0	0	3.13	0	0
	IV	-0.52	-3.35	-1.26	-0.35	-0.79	-1.07	-0.48	-1.07	-1.58	-4.11	-1.11	-0.76	-1.27	-1.38	-1.00	-0.73
	V	3.50	-3.87	6.57	8.18	15.98	6.80	8.85	4.62	1.03	3.44	3.89	8.99	5.35	7.12	5.17	9.80

Pacific Northwest																
I	2.77	3.74	7.71	7.76	17.52	4.92	9.69	7.54	6.59	1.04	7.61	9.40	8.92	7.57	3.86	5.38
II	1.91	−0.01	0.41	−0.01	10.52	2.27	0.41	0.08	2.64	17.96	−0.15	0.01	9.45	2.47	1.16	0.09
III	0.16	2.29	0.10	0	−4.76	4.51	0	0	0	1.68	0	0	0	4.70	0	0
IV	−0.52	−3.35	−1.26	−0.35	−0.79	−1.07	−0.48	−1.07	−1.58	−4.11	−1.11	−0.76	−1.27	−1.38	−1.00	−0.73
V	4.32	2.67	6.96	7.40	22.49	10.63	9.62	6.55	7.65	16.57	6.35	8.65	17.10	13.36	4.02	4.74

a The following costs are included: I labor costs (Table 2); II transportation costs (first set of figures in Table 11); III resource costs (an average of the pair of figures for each area and industry shown in Tables 14 and 15); IV capital costs (taken from column 10 in Table 17); V totals.

b See Table 1, note a.

APPENDIX P. *Estimated Percentage that Total Costs in Comparison Areas Would Be Lower (−) or Higher than in Ontario (assuming that the average Canadian wage rises to the average U.S. level), by Industry (1958 base).*

Comparison areas		Food	Tobacco	Textiles	Apparel	Wood products	Paper	Printing	Electrical equipment	Chemicals	Petroleum products	Rubber and plastics	Leather goods	Nonmetallic mineral products	Metallic products	Transportation equipment	Miscellaneous
Maritimes	I[b]	−2.16	−1.04	2.47	6.17	−5.52	0.75	−6.02	−2.10	−2.11	−0.55	−2.12	4.00	−2.94	−0.66	−2.63	−3.01
	II[c]	5.77	0.99	4.27	6.85	20.18	12.88	−2.62	0.45	9.46	52.49	−0.04	5.27	58.25	15.91	1.65	−1.33
Quebec	I	−0.28	−0.47	−0.31	−1.24	−3.89	−0.22	−0.82	−1.03	−0.93	−0.33	−4.28	−3.27	1.96	−1.80	−1.73	−2.58
	II	0.12	−0.14	−0.36	−1.16	−2.45	−0.05	−0.77	−0.94	−0.39	1.16	−4.15	−3.15	2.58	−1.45	−1.61	−2.46
Prairies	I	1.17	−0.32	5.70	−0.71	5.52	−1.43	−3.67	−1.86	−0.93	−0.26	−2.29	6.18	−1.09	−2.27	−2.06	−0.32
	II	6.44	1.55	7.14	−0.31	23.45	10.27	−1.24	−0.12	7.37	37.97	−1.09	6.98	42.21	11.14	1.40	0.84
British Columbia	I	1.55	1.93	11.23	15.53	9.25	3.65	4.39	2.68	2.10	1.01	1.79	14.17	3.04	2.27	2.22	3.01
	II	3.05	3.90	11.32	15.39	13.91	10.56	4.23	2.23	2.19	7.95	1.35	13.91	−3.07	4.77	2.51	2.88
Upper Midwest	I	1.27	2.53	1.54	−0.71	6.65	0.30	−1.02	−0.93	−1.91	−0.32	−3.77	−2.19	−0.22	2.65	−2.46	−1.62
	II	1.77	−0.28	0.78	−0.98	10.92	−0.13	−0.85	−1.50	−1.48	7.83	−4.62	−2.75	11.72	5.51	−2.53	−2.15
West Lake	I	0.80	−1.88	2.91	−0.35	3.57	0.30	0	0	−0.83	0.08	−1.71	1.32	1.43	−0.10	−0.75	−2.23
	II	−1.31	−5.68	1.26	−0.91	−2.36	−2.92	−0.90	−1.58	−5.20	−14.27	−3.34	0.18	−13.19	−3.94	−2.82	−3.45
East Lake	I	0.75	−0.86	4.48	2.87	7.29	1.28	−0.52	1.84	0.21	−0.32	2.26	1.32	1.96	1.15	0.57	−0.78
	II	−0.51	−4.43	3.11	2.43	4.55	−1.74	−1.34	0.46	−2.58	−9.06	0.92	0.40	−4.75	−1.44	−0.89	−1.78
Lower Midwest	I	1.08	2.47	−2.46	−3.18	2.11	−1.50	−3.47	−2.37	−0.77	−0.48	−4.18	−4.01	0.61	−1.03	−1.97	−1.64
	II	0.24	−0.77	−3.63	−3.56	2.51	−1.08	−3.93	−3.44	−2.32	−2.60	−5.44	−4.82	1.06	−2.42	−2.99	−2.49
Middle Atlantic	I	0.70	−1.42	3.12	1.41	4.54	−0.22	0.10	0.67	−0.62	−0.10	−2.69	−1.84	1.99	−0.38	−0.65	−0.78
	II	−0.78	−4.84	1.64	0.99	1.10	−3.09	−0.87	−0.69	−3.99	−11.48	−3.99	−2.74	−6.73	−3.11	−2.21	−1.74
New England	I	−0.66	−2.15	−1.55	−1.24	−0.16	−0.67	−3.47	−3.00	−1.19	−1.06	−4.18	−0.39	0.45	−3.42	−1.13	−5.16
	II	−1.66	−5.43	−2.65	−1.61	−1.88	−2.90	−4.21	−4.15	−4.08	−6.76	−5.28	−1.24	−4.88	−4.89	−2.52	−5.96
South	I	−2.01	0.59	−1.69	−5.99	−6.32	0	−5.01	−3.10	−0.93	−1.44	−1.90	−5.44	−3.04	−2.36	−2.80	−6.32
	II	−2.07	−3.01	−2.80	−6.31	−3.55	0.46	−5.29	−3.98	−1.97	−0.07	−2.91	−6.17	1.72	−1.62	−3.47	−7.07

Manufacturing sector[a]

Capital	I	−1.36	2.50	0.76	−1.97	−0.33	−0.89	−1.43	2.24	−1.64	−1.04	−4.18	−0.18	−0.11	0.46	−0.35	−2.27
	II	−3.28	−1.10	−0.80	−2.44	−5.44	−4.06	−2.63	0.70	−5.52	−14.73	−5.62	−1.17	−12.66	−3.24	−2.20	−3.37
Florida	I	−2.50	−1.99	−1.69	−3.53	−3.56	0.97	−1.84	−3.30	−3.03	−2.22	−8.77	−4.34	−5.20	−6.84	−5.34	−0.97
	II	−0.55	−4.90	−2.12	−3.69	6.71	4.69	−1.42	−3.61	−0.56	15.77	−9.31	−4.75	14.92	−1.44	−4.99	−1.38
Southwest	I	−1.69	1.88	−3.23	−5.84	−4.64	1.11	−4.39	−2.48	1.29	0.10	−2.89	−6.52	−2.93	−3.32	−0.65	−5.23
	II	−0.70	−0.63	−4.01	−6.08	2.99	5.15	−4.12	−2.96	2.55	4.60	−3.66	−7.04	12.27	−0.02	−0.42	−5.71
Mountain	I	−0.37	2.62	−3.53	−2.85	8.77	−1.35	−1.32	−3.11	0.67	0.07	−0.80	−1.97	0.87	0.76	−3.96	4.60
	II	1.16	0.58	−4.01	−3.03	18.02	4.68	−0.65	−3.32	2.71	17.63	−1.37	−2.38	21.37	6.66	−3.01	4.38
Pacific Southwest	I	0.94	−2.66	4.00	1.24	11.18	1.58	2.75	0.94	−0.26	−0.26	−0.48	1.80	3.16	0	−0.40	4.96
	II	0.83	−3.76	2.55	0.78	11.43	5.03	2.01	−0.33	−2.42	2.06	−1.87	0.80	0.79	1.17	−0.90	4.21
Pacific Northwest	I	0.47	3.86	3.69	0.35	12.97	3.15	2.86	2.56	3.14	−0.34	1.83	1.22	4.36	1.51	−2.20	−0.22
	II	2.02	2.79	2.94	−0.01	17.94	8.86	2.79	1.57	4.20	15.19	0.57	0.47	12.54	7.30	−2.04	−0.86

ᵃ See Table 1, note a.

ᵇ I Estimated percentage that total costs in comparison areas would be lower (−) or higher than in Ontario because of interregional wage differences *only*, assuming that the average Canadian wage rises to the average U.S. level.

ᶜ II Estimated percentage that total costs in comparison areas would be lower (−) or higher than in Ontario, assuming that the average Canadian wage rises to the average U.S. level.

APPENDIX Q. *Technique for Estimating Consumers' Surplus Item E.*

In Figure 18, E is the sum of areas 4 and 5, and is calculated by a simple geometrical evaluation of areas and dimensions under a demand curve.

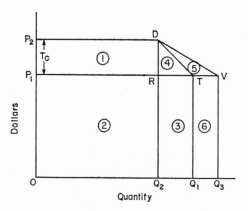

Figure 18. Calculation of consumers' surplus.

Let:

b = higher price on Canadian goods due to tariffs, less duties collected, as percent of GNP

c = duties collected, as percent of GNP

Δy = change in money income due to change in factor prices, as percent of GNP

m = percent of GNP spent on manufactures

x = higher Canadian price due to the tariff. (The terms in which this is measured may be set arbitrarily, since this item will eventually disappear from the calculations.)

Since area $1 = b + c$ (1)

and $P_1P_2 = DR = x$,   (2)

therefore $P_1R = (b + c)/x$.   (3)

Moreover, noting (1), and that area 1 plus area 2 equals m, it follows that

area $2 = m - (b + c)$.   (4)

From (4) and (3)

$Q_2R = x[m - (b + c)]/(b + c)$.   (5)

Since a price elasticity of 1 is assumed for the partial equilibrium demand curve DT (ignoring income effects),

area 1 + area 2 = area 2 + area 3
    or area 1 = area 3.

Therefore, from (1),

area $3 = b + c$.

And noting (5), it follows that

$RT = (b + c)^2/x[m - (b + c)]$ (6)

It is now only necessary to account for the general equilibrium income effects which shift demand from DT to DV. A proportion $(m/100)$ of any increase in Canadian money income (in this case Δy, following U.S. tariff removal) will be spent on manufactured goods; i.e.,

$$\text{area } 6 = \left(\frac{m}{100}\right)\Delta y. \qquad (7)$$

Noting (5), it follows that

$$TV = \frac{(b + c)\left(\frac{m\,\Delta y}{100}\right)}{x[m - (b + c)]} \qquad (8)$$

and from (6) and (8)

$$RV = \frac{(b + c)\left[b + c + \frac{m\,\Delta y}{100}\right]}{x[m - (b + c)]}. \qquad (9)$$

Finally, noting (2) and (9), and that area E is equal to areas 4 plus 5, it follows that

$$\text{area } E = \frac{1}{2}\left[\frac{(b+c)\left[b+c+\dfrac{m\,\Delta y}{100}\right]}{m-(b+c)}\right]. \qquad (10)$$

All areas are expressed as a percent of Canadian GNP.

In these calculations, b is set equal to 4, c equal to 1.4,[1] m equal to 34.3,[2] and Δy equal to 6.

Strictly speaking, this formula is correct only if the prices of all manufactures are raised the same percentage by protection; for all other cases, it involves an underestimate of E. (Note, however, that E is small compared to other components of the cost of tariffs; hence this sort of error is unlikely to be significant.)

[1] Department of Finance: *Public Accounts of Canada.*

[2] Derived from D.B.S. *National Accounts, Income and Expenditure,* 1963; D.B.S., *Inventories, Shipments and Orders in Manufacturing Industries,* December, 1964; and United Nations, *Commodity Trade Statistics.*

Index

INDEX